FEDERAL WAY PSYCHOLOGY CLINIC

Date 2008 10 07

Application for Services

New Client: Tonn Lynch for Dimitris Lynch Birthdate 6/11/62

Address 2004 Bakery Sq #107 City St Thomas VI

Zip 00802 SSN 480904512 Phone 512 775 9245

Person who has insurance: _____ Relationship father

Birthdate _____ SSN _____ Phone _____

What prompted you to seek assistance at this time? _____
_____

Has anyone in your family had counseling or psychotherapy before?   Yes   No
Has drinking or using drugs ever been a problem?   Yes   No

    Marital Status: Single   Married   Widowed   Divorced   Sep.d
    Date of Marriage _____ Name of Spouse _____
    Spouse's occupation _____ How many times have you been married?

Children name(s) and birthdates: Last saw 7/5/08. EOWE   4/07 - $85,000

Corroborate the matl.   reduce visits by 4 hrs.

Brother/sister(s) name(s) and age(s): _____ Sander 8 yr Korea.
_____
_____

Father _____ Mother _____

Medical History of Person seeking Therapy

__Accident prone
__Allergies
__Alcoholism
__Anxiety
__Arthritis
__Asthma
__Bad headaches
__Bowel trouble
__Cancer/Tumors
__Convulsions
__Depression
__Diabetes
__Eating disorder
__Epilepsy
__Eczema/skin prob.

__Eye/Sight problem
__Fainting spells
__Fatigue
__Head injuries
__Heart trouble
__Hi/low blood pressure
__Indigestion
__Injury
__Insomnia
__Irritability
__Joint trouble
__Kidney trouble
__Memory lapses/gaps
__Mood swings
__Muscle trouble

__Nervous breakdown
__Numbness
__Pain
__Panic attacks
__PMS
__Shaking
__Short of breath
__Smoke cigarettes
__Surgery
__Swelling
__Thyroid trouble
__Ulcers
__Unconsciousness
__Vomiting/nausea
__Weakness

Other:_____
Prescription medications _____
Physician _____

SERVICES CONTRACT

This agreement sets forth the terms of payment and agreements for services that I have requested in the Application for Services.

Client Name _____

Payment of client portion of fees is due in full, each session. The client (or person financially responsible for the client) agrees to pay either 1) on date of service or 2) within ten (10) days after receipt of explanation of benefits from the insurance company for services provided. If collection efforts become necessary, the client agrees to pay all collection costs, including court costs and reasonable attorney fees. The venue would be King County.

Health Insurance Company: _____
Name of person on insurance policy: _____
I authorize FEDERAL WAY PSYCHOLOGY CLINIC to bill my insurance: Yes   No

- CLIENTS HAVE ACCESS TO THEIR FILES UPON REQUEST

___I authorize my Dr. Ruddell to keep a client file.
___I request that a client file not be kept.

- SIGNATURE ON FILE

__I authorize use of this form on all my insurance submissions.
__I authorize release of information to all my insurance companies.
__I understand that I am responsible for my bill and timely payment of fees.
__I authorize insurance payment directly to Federal Way Psychology Clinic.
__I permit a copy of this authorization to be used in place of the original.
__I accept the terms of this Service Contract as stated above.

- DISCLOSURE STATEMENT

I have received a copy of Dr. Ruddell's Disclosure Statement. My signature indicates that we reviewed 1) the license status of Dr. Ruddell, 2) consumer rights, including confidentiality, 3) Dr. Ruddell's education and training, 4) therapeutic orientation and 5) fees and payment arrangements have been agreed upon.

- RELEASE OF INFORMATION

I authorize an exchange of information between: _____

_____
and Dr. Ruddell, Federal Way Psychology Clinic, for the purpose of treatment planning and therapy, or _____.
This release is valid for 90 days, or until _____.

- Dated this __8__ day of __October__ _____, 2008.

_____   _____
Client   Witness

_____   _____
Signature of financially responsible party   Relationship to the client
Signature on this form indicates that the financially responsible party has a copy of Dr. Ruddell's disclosure statement, release of information was discussed and fees arrangements have been agree to.

ITIO a Child

by Tom Lynch

Copyright and License Agreement

Preface

This book is distributed under standard copyright with an additional license as shown on the back of the title page. Before proceeding please be sure you agree to the copyright and license.

Texas law stipulates that divorce professionals should act in the best interest of the child, so case documents and correspondence involving a child are titled as, *In the Interest of the Child*, or more simply *ITIO a* Child. I made that moniker the title of the book both because of its irony, and because this book is written ITIO a child.

Recently the state of Texas demonstrated it had sufficient staff and initiative to separate over 400 children from FLDS parents in just a matter of days based on a prank call from a woman in Colorado. Many people who watched these events on television did not support the FLDS, but they were still caused to wondered how Texas had the power to remove so many child from their parents so quickly without hard evidence and without due process. Was this an anomalous occurrence, or one that is indicative of an endemic problem? This book explains there is an endemic problem by telling the story of a child of a regular family in a typical divorce who has been exploited for profit. The divorce described is my own, and the child is my son. This afforded me direct access to the professionals involved and access to a number of documents that are not usually seen by the public. Even if the reader is not especially interested in Texas or divorce per se, he or she should find this rare viewing of the correspondence between the attorneys to be enlightening.

This is a non-fiction work and it is backed by many documents and tape transcripts. All documents and transcripts reproduced here are as they appeared in attorney records and court files or other appropriate sources unless otherwise noted. No poetic licenses or edits were applied. There are no made up characters or stories.

In this edition I dropped the somewhat academic introduction in favor of an epilogue that brings the reader up to date to the summer of 2008. There are no other changes. I began this edition directly with the chapter "Marriage Without Child" and kept the same starting page number so indexing and citing will remain consistent. This manuscript starts in March 1994 and extends to July of 2008.

The author or his staff may be contacted at ITIOaChild@gmail.com.

Marriage Without Child, 1994 to 1998

The Honeymoon Period

We settled as a married couple in the Clarksville neighborhood in Austin. We lived in a condo leased from Marion Winik, so we inherited the bathtub that Marion had written about in her book, *Telling*. According to the book she had washered her child's diapers in that tub. She also explained that her husband had AIDS, and she had helped euthanize him.

At this time I was working on D & M's K5 microprocessor project at AMD. I was proud of the position. AMD competed with Intel, Intel was compared with superman, and we were on the 5th generation of the architecture, so this project was called Kryptonite 5, or just K5. My group was doing the floating-point microcode. It was a fantastic opportunity for all us. The first to market always makes the most money, so every day that passed meant the processor would be less profitable and that we would be losing in the competition. Consequently we worked long hours. Most of the time H* was in Massachusetts finishing up her degree, she came back periodically.

H* announced that it was nice that she didn't have to finish school. She had been having some difficulties. Her advisor had dropped her. Her ex boyfriend, Ravi, was running the computer lab. No doubt his presence made things awkward.

The situation reminded me of the story of my mom and father's romance causing mom's grades to suffer at school. Mom became a housewife in the late 50s, so there were no repercussions. However, H* was in graduate school, not high school, and times have changed. I did not want H* to fall short due to swooning over our relationship. I wanted, rather I had dreamed, that our relationship to be a springboard to success. I imagined working on projects together with her.

We argued to no avail, so I ended by dictating that she go back to Massachusetts and work something out. Later when H* was back from Massachusetts we had a quiet evening drinking wine and talking. She was in a good mood. The subject drifted to the new advisor. She said, "He isn't as smart as the other professors, but he is smart for an American. Americans are not as smart as foreigners." She paused, and then excused me from the generalization.

"Thanks," I said. "How charming," I thought. Perhaps this explained why my opinions only invoked ire. I said nothing more.

She continued, "My adviser isn't as smart as the other professors, but he is pretty nice. Americans are so easily manipulated." H* explained that Americans were naïve as they always took people at face value. All she had to do was be a bit coquettish, and her new adviser responded. She was to write a distributed search program in C++ and then graduate.

H* continued to tell a story about the *Smith Brigade*. I had never heard of them. "They were Americans. They were stupid. They were all wiped out. All of them, to the last man was killed and they deserved it as they were so stupid." It was another story of naïve Americans. It represented something profound to H*, but I didn't get it. The Smith Brigade conversation moved into strategy. "Attack is the best defense," she explained in earnest.

At the time, based on the way she was talking, I thought that the Smith Brigade must have been made of dozens of people. Later H* explained that it was 6 people who were in a fight under a bridge. She didn't say how many of the enemy they took out before succumbing.

Wrong Skin Color - Honeymoon Period Over

At this time we also dined out on occasion. Casa Acapulco became our favorite restaurant. It was the place where we had our first conversation and then subsequently visited many times for lunch with Mohamed, CC, and other members of the team. It was a place of safety and comfort. It reset our point of view about the relationship.

One night while we were there she went off and started screaming again, like at Sweetish Hill. I was embarrassed. I didn't want to suffer another moment of it. We had been drinking so she couldn't drive the car home. I called for a taxi. Because we were so close to downtown, it arrived almost immediately. She refused to take the cab. Instead, while I was holding the back door of the taxi open for her, she dramatically took off into a bad east Austin neighborhood. I yelled that it was not a good place for a pretty young woman to walk late at night. The speed of her gate increased. She had thrown down the gauntlet. If I cared for her well being at all, I was to chase after her. I gave the cabby five dollars and sent him off. I followed her with the car. I apologized profusely through the open window, for I do not know what, while coasting slowly down the street. I begged for her to get in. It took about two blocks, then all was right again.

But the incident was not over, indeed it was never to end. She held a grudge for what she called 'you abandoning me.' It was added to the list of perceived torts I had committed against her, along with 'taking' the $5000 dollars (the money she brought into the marriage), having spoken down to her, not having read her thesis, and not having called her soon enough on her first return trip to Massachusetts. She often repeated the list when nagging. At these times she did her best to attack my sense of worth as a person. I discovered early on that it was dangerous to tell her anything personal. I tried to appease her complaints by making excuses.

I recall a Saturday when we were at the apartment and she was nagging, but it was not having any affect. I had become jaded. She needed something more to get under my skin, and she found it. She said, "Not only should I have married Ravi, but I love him!" She explained that she did not love me. "I couldn't marry him only because my father would not have put up with a dark skinned man!" When H* flipped out she always tried to say the most vicious things within the grasp of her imagination. I surmised it was just for the affect, so I didn't take her that seriously. I asked if she wanted out. She replied that she definitely did not want out. It all made no sense.

The Exorcist Fit

After finishing up in Massachusetts H* just moped around our place all the time. It wasn't until writing this, that I realized it was about the time Ravi was married. One evening I came home from AMD and she was in the bedroom sitting on the floor next the wall. She was rolled up in a ball with her head face down on her knees. She was not crying, rather she was just not responsive.

I said to her, "You are going to be miserable if you keep on like this." Then suddenly she popped her head up with a contorted nasty looking face, and she did a combination scream and snarl, "I may be *miserable*, but you, *you*, are going to go *insane*!" She said it with such passion that she began foaming at the mouth. I was stunned. I reeled out of the house. It was a scene right out of *The Exorcist*. I ran it over in my head, and could not figure the meaning of it. It was true enough that I couldn't keep living like that. Was that all she meant? Was it a threat?

Later I suggested that we make some changes to get her out of the house more. Besides being unhealthy staying at home so much, I didn't care to come home to another exorcist act. We decided to make a high tech startup, and searched for office space. Eventually we decided upon some executive suites in the Omni building downtown. The Omni building was beautiful. It had an atrium open to 15 floors. One side of the building was all glass windows. At the bottom of the atrium there was a bar and cafe, which had no walls except for potted plants sitting on the floor. H*'s office window had a view of downtown, and that floor of the building was filled with people active in small businesses. All in all the surroundings were busy and pleasant. If cabin fever was the problem, then this was the ultimate solution.

H* complained that her career was suffering because she worked for a no-name company while I was aggrandizing my career while working at AMD. I can only begin to describe how frustrating and disappointing it is to love someone and to work so hard for their success, just to be nagged and berated at every step. Nothing I said, or thought, for that matter was correct, and she let me know it. My stomach was in a knot each time we spoke. All I could do is give her whatever she wanted.

H* made no friends at the Omni building or in Austin in general. No one called the house for her. I didn't see her dial the phone, or answer it. Apparently the venture was failing to providing a good environment for H*. A peculiar thing was that she would sit and work quietly all day. It was only when communication was required that problems arose. There was no lack of diligence. She had printed stacks of marketing research. Though her technical prowess remained cloaked. It was telling that she had been happy at AMD, which is a more controlled environment.

Sheep Shit and Cancan

H* and I had not yet gone on a honeymoon. In part this was because she had been going to school, and in part because it was not obvious it would be much fun to be harangued in pretty settings. I thought perhaps it was a vicious circle issue. Perhaps she was always in a bad mood and nagging so much because she felt I hadn't planned a big honeymoon. When our first anniversary approached, by a sort of coincidence, I had a paper accepted at a conference in St Etienne. This meant that part of a trip to France could be expensed. We would be in Paris in the spring.

It was thrilling to be in St. Etienne at a conference as an erudite couple. We fantasized that we were sort of like Marie and Pierre Curie. I was proud to be able to deliver the paper with H* sitting in the audience. We toured the hexagon, ending in Paris. The beginning of the trip went well, and it was as romantic as we planned. H* was amazing and prepared. She jumped out of bed at 7 every morning, including the day after the flight. I could not shake jet lag. I was half asleep for much of the trip.

We stumbled around Bourgogne drunk. I played the buffoon in the village of Volnay. We were walking on a path through picturesque vineyards. I was sleepy and suggested laying down on the grass and taking a nap. "Hmmm," I thought, "Perhaps this might lead to more." H* was concerned about cleanliness and tidiness, and could not be persuaded to even sit on the grass.

We walked further down the path that led between Pomar and Volnay. We happened upon a small grass covered hill with a tree in the middle of it. It was inviting. I did not question why it had not been planted with vines. I played to the Iowa stereotype, and decided to show her how a country boy could lie down on the bare ground and take a nap with no fear of a little dirt, and no repercussion from it. With my straw hat tipped back, I laid down with my head against the tree and started to nap. I left H* to contemplate the scenery. I slept about five minutes, when the smell got strong. It was the place the farmers were keeping their manure for fertilizer. It was a veritable pile of sheep shit. The surface had hardened, and grass grew on top, but it still smelled when indented.

I didn't actually have anything on me when I got up, but I smelled like a whole flock of sheep. You might say I had *terroir*. In Volnay we stopped at a winery and inn. The owner laughed and talked to us like it was no big deal. I hadn't told her, but the story was in the wind. She poured three big glasses of wine and talked about her winery. It was wonderful. No one had made me feel that good since before I had met H*.

We went south. We drove through the Alps on some D grade roads. There were breathtaking views. H* was on the edge of her seat most of the drive. We stopped to camp at a beautiful place near a large rail bridge that crossed a gorge. H* was afraid and refused to get out of the car. That night while I camped, she slept in the car with the doors locked. Though strangely in the middle of the night she got out and started walking directly towards the cliff's edge. I intercepted her. She offered no explanation, but went back to the car. The next day we drove along the Mediterranean coast, and got a place in Monte Carlo that was up on a precipice overlooking a beach. Then we drove back to Paris through the Loire Valley. Our schedule was getting tight so we cut out Bordeaux and Brittany to make more time for Paris.

In Paris we had tickets to the Opera. We saw Tony Randall walking in the atrium during intermission. H* wanted to see the cabaret show at the Moulin Rouge, so we got a couple of tickets.

We had a small table by the wall. H* sat facing the stage. We ordered a bottle of champagne, and when it was finished, another. I commented that times had changed. What was racy Burlesque in the 20s, was barely arousing in the 90s. I suggested that the Moulin Rouge had become a sort of museum. H* became angry. She said that it was unfair treatment towards women. I could see that the bottle was teetering, and I was filled with dread. I reminded her that it was her idea to come to the show, and that I wasn't the person to get angry at about the feminine condition at the Moulin Rouge.

When the show ended, and the lights came up, H* stood up like a soldier at attention, pointed at me, and yelled at the top of her lungs, in English: "He is an American and he did not like your show!" She then took the remaining travel cash and threw it up in the air. There were many people there, all nicely dressed in fashionable clothing and expensive jewelry. Some looked politely away and ignored her, or smiled and made comments to their dates. Others gaped in disbelief.

I thought about the loss of dignity at having to crawl around on the floor, and weighed it against the value of the travel money. Then I realized, the humiliation was already complete, it could not go lower. I crawled around on all fours in my best suit, and picked the money off of the sticky floor of the Moulin Rouge, while H* and the exiting crowd watched my butt wave around. Then I went outside and pitched my wedding ring. I threw it low, and as hard as I could. It flew down the pavement going ting, ting, ting. H* was calling after me, and I got in a cab alone and went back to the hotel. I was furious, and I was done with H*. H* then came back to the hotel - and took my picture while I complained about her behavior. Why, when everything was going so well, why had she set things up like that? She started crying, and told me how much the wedding ring meant to her. She implored me to go look for it the next day. I did not find it, nor did I replace it. In fact, my intention was to divorce. I had had enough. H* pleaded not to.

Tom Has a Nasal Operation

I was having difficulty breathing at night. I saw a doctor who said I had a deviated septum. Dr. Peter Scholl straightened it. He said he saw some scar tissue that had been left by a previous straightening of the septum done by Dr. Brad Winegar, and that he would remove it as a favor. It was done as out patient surgery. H* waited and took me home afterwards. I was not happy with the outcome. It appeared that the front of my nose was weak afterwards. I would wake up not being able to breath because it was compressed shut. Dr. Scholl said he hadn't touched that part of the anatomy.

"It Is Korean Tradition to Buy the Newlyweds a New House"

H* surprised me by explaining that Mr. Choi said that it was Korean tradition for the wife's parents to buy the newlyweds a house. I suspected that Mr. Choi's charity was partly related to the thing he must have known when he extracted the promise I not consider divorce after I asked permission to marry his daughter - his daughter was hell to live with. I had been told that Mr. Choi was a rich man, that he owned a building in downtown Seoul, which the family lived at the top of, and that he owned a company doing security. I figured he could pay some tribute. I imagined a budget for a starter house in South Korea was a couple thousand. However, I was in awe when he said he was sending $300,000. Though this feeling was fleeting as H* made it clear that only she would be handling the money, and that it was to be hers only and we were not to spend it. "I hired an attorney to make sure you don't get it," she explained. It would be hard to buy a house without spending money. H* had hired Mr. David Canion Esq. to advise on how to bring the stocks into the U.S. and to prevent me from claiming any ownership. I ignored it. The peek of my anger had passed, so independent of the money, I decided to give the relationship some more time. After all, I had promised God to stick it out. The talk of money seemed to settle H* down. Perhaps it made her feel safer. Perhaps finally she would stop screaming and nagging.

H* Doesn't Seem to Like Her Cooking

Occasionally H* made dinner. She followed the recipe books by the letter, and created some very tasty meals. Rather than bringing pots of food to the dining area, H* would place the food on the plates in the kitchen, and carry them to the table. Then we would sit down. She made it clear where each of us sat at the table. One evening after setting the plates down she walked back into the kitchen. This was not uncommon for either of us to do, as invariably something would get left off the table. While she was in the kitchen I quietly switched the plates. After we ate I explained what I had done. In her high pitched fast rate nagging voice, she said that my insinuation made her sick. She went into the bathroom, and I could hear her throwing up.

H* set to work on our startup, but it was impossible for me to participate. Any time I inquired, she would become angry. And even worse, whenever we tried to do books or discuss what was happening she would start screaming. I never knew what to write checks for. Sometimes I became so frustrated that I tried to get through to her by yelling over her screaming, but this did not help. It only served to bother those in neighboring offices. I told the corporate attorney to register the business as "Tempered Hardware and Software." If anything came out of the ordeal, it would surely be *tempered*.

While driving to the office one morning H* blew up, kicked, and cracked, the windshield in the car. It was a gymnastic maneuver. She slid down in the chair placing her back on the bottom, lifted her legs up over the dash, and then she started kicking, shaking, jogging her elbows back and fourth, and screaming. We hadn't even started our day yet. Later she apologized, not for having the fit, but for having kicked the window so hard. She said she didn't realize she was that strong. It was not small crack, rather it looked to have been hit by a large baseball. Volvo replaced the windshield on 1997 02 21. It was just a normal day when heading to *Tempered* Hardware and Software.

Figure 5: Invoice for Fixing Broken Windshield

40

H* Nags and Screams On An Entire Vacation to Big Bend

Gopi and Rahde, some long time friends, suggested that we relax and get out of Austin for a while. My memory of the sheep shit trip was still strong, but our friends appeared to have a calming influence. At this point H* had never acted out in front of people we knew. It might be a pleasant getaway after all. We all piled into their car and drove up to Big Bend park for a weekend.

On the first night I had difficulty getting to sleep in the park lodge because of the big mechanical clicking clock and the smelly bed. Finally around 4 am I put the clock outside, and fell asleep sprawled over the desk. In the morning I woke up late. Alas, these were new items for her list.

In the packed car, for eight hours on the return trip, H* prodded screamed and nagged. She complained about my behavior, about my putting the clock out, about my waking up late, and of course the rest of the list too, including my having abandoned her, her $5000 dollars, having spoken down to her, not having read her thesis, and not having called her soon enough on her first return trip to Massachusetts. I replied, "I read you Goddamn thesis," then realized the irony, it made it sound like the other points were valid because I had not addressed them specifically. All of her nagging was delivered repeatedly in a high pitch loud rushing voice working up to a screech, emanating from a squashed and stressed evil looking face - for eight hours with precious few pauses. The fact my friends didn't drop us at the side of the road is a testament to the strength of our bond, though there were limits, we never went out with them as a couple again.

IN DISTRICT COURT 98 OF THE STATE OF TEXAS

IN AND FOR THE COUNTY OF TRAVIS

IN THE MATTER OF THE MARRIAGE OF:)
)
PETITIONER: THOMAS WALKER LYNCH)
)
and)
)
RESPONDENT: H)
)
and)   CAUSE NO.
)
IN THE INTEREST OF:)   FM1-02879
)
D)   CERTIFIED COPY
)

DEPOSITION OF RADHE GOPINATH

BE IT REMEMBERED: That pursuant to

Stipulation re Notice of Taking Deposition, and on

Monday, the 11th day of June 2001, commencing at the

hour of 3:35 p.m. of said day, before me, Josie Amant,

C.S.R., License Number CSR-3390, a Certified Shorthand

Reporter, personally appeared RADHE GOPINATH, called

as a witness herein, at The Inn at Morgan Hill, 16115

Condit Road, Morgan Hill, California, and being by me

first duly sworn, was examined as a witness in said

cause.

1 A P P E A R A N C E S   2

2

3 For the PETITIONER:
  (VIA TELEPHONE)   LAW OFFICE OF EDWIN J. TERRY
4   805 West 10th Street
                                    Suite 300
5   Austin, TX 78701
                              BY: KARL HAYS, ESQ.
6

7 For the RESPONDENT: GARY A. CALABRESE, ESQ.
  (VIA TELEPHONE)   808 Nueces Street
8   Austin, TX 78701

9
  VIDEOTAPE OPERATOR   TALTY LEGAL VIDEO SERVICES
10   2131 The Alameda
                                    Suite D
11   San Jose, CA 95126
                              BY: MATT CHROUST
12

13

14

15   INDEX OF EXAMINATION

16 Examination by: Page

17   Mr. Hays   4

18   Mr. Calabrese   23

19

20

21

22

23

24

25

TALTY COURT REPORTERS, INC.

1   THE VIDEOTAPE OPERATOR: This is the

2 videotape deposition of Radhe Gopinath taken by

3 petitioners in the matter of Lynch versus Lynch in the

4 Travis County, Texas District Court 98, Cause Number

5 FM1-02879, held in the offices of The Inn of Morgan

6 Hill, 16115 Condit Road, Morgan Hill, California, in

7 Board Room 3 on June 11th, 2001 at approximately 3:35

8 in the p.m. California time.

9   The court reporter's name is Josephine

10 Pagliaro-Amant, CSR Number 3390. The court reporter

11 is representing the firm of Talty Court Reporters,

12 located at 2131 The Alameda, Suite D, San Jose,

13 California. My name is Matt Chroust. I'm the

14 videotape operator representing the firm of Talty

15 Legal Video Services, located at 2131 The Alameda,

16 Suite D, San Jose, California.

17   Counsel will now please state your appearance

18 for the record.

19   MR. HAYS: This is Karl Hays, K-a-r-l,

20 H-a-y-s, for Tom Lynch. Also, here with me is Jodie

21 Wellburn, who is a legal assistant with my law firm.

22   MR. CALABRESE: And my name is Gary

23 Calabrese, that's G-a-r-y, middle initial A., last

24 name C-a-l-a-b-r-e-s-e. I represent the respondent in

25 this case, H

1   . My address, for the record, is 808   4

2   Nueces Street, N-u-e-c-e-s, Austin, Texas, 78701,

3   phone number 512-472-9394, fax number 512-472-9550.

4   RADHE GOPINATH,

5   being first duly affirmed by the Certified Shorthand

6   Reporter to tell the truth, testified as follows:

7   EXAMINATION BY MR. HAYS

8   Q   Will you please state your full name for the

9   court reporter.

10   A   Radhe Gopinath, R-a-d-h-e, G-o-p-i-n-a-t-h.

11   Q   Where do you currently reside?

12   A   In Gilroy. 1282 Wagon, W-a-g-o-n, Way, W-a-y,

13   Gilroy, G-i-l-r-o-y, California, 95020.

14   Q   And how long have you lived in Gilroy,

15   California?

16   A   A year and a half.

17   Q   Prior to living in Gilroy, California, where

18   did you live?

19   A   In Los Gatos, California.

20   Q   And how long did you live there?

21   A   I lived there for -- since '96, so about three

22   years.

23   Q   And before that, where did you reside?

24   A   Austin, Texas.

25   Q   How long did you live in Austin, Texas?

1   A   I personally lived in Austin for just over a   5

2   year, but my husband had been there longer.

3   Q   During the time that you lived in Austin,

4   Texas, did you have occasion to meet Tom Lynch?

5   A   Yes.

6   Q   How did you meet him?

7   A   He and my husband were very close friends, so

8   when I married my husband and moved to Austin, the

9   four of us, Tom, my husband and I and H   hung out

10   together a lot.

11   Q   You, also, know H   ?

12   A   Yes, I do.

13   Q   And did you meet her through your connections

14   with -- with Tom?

15   A   Yes.

16   Q   How long would you say that you have known both

17   Tom and H   ?

18   A   Six years now. Since '95.

19   Q   Did you keep in contact with Tom and H

20   after you moved from Austin?

21   A   I did keep in touch with Tom, but not with

22   H   .

23   Q   What sort of contact have you had with Tom

24   since moving from Austin?

25   A   I'm sorry. Can you repeat that question.

1   Q   What sort of contact have you had with Tom   6

2 since moving from Austin?

3   A   We used to talk on the phone every now and

4 then, but then the last two years, I've had just

5 minimal contact with him, maybe a phone call every few

6 months.

7   Q   Have you had occasion to personally visit with

8 Tom since your move from Austin?

9   A   No, I haven't been able to do that.

10   Q   During the time that you lived in -- in Austin,

11 how frequently would you see Tom and H   ?

12   A   We would -- on certain weeks, we would meet as

13 often as four or five times a week and then there were

14 some weeks when we would meet maybe a couple of times,

15 but it was very frequent.

16   Q   What sort of things would you do when the two

17 of you -- when the four of you got together?

18   A   Just going out together to the movies, eating

19 out. Just short trips here and there and maybe

20 cooking dinner at home. But we were out a lot of the

21 time.

22   Q   What sort of work does your husband do?

23   A   He used to work at AMD. He was an engineer

24 there.

25   Q   And what was -- what particular job did he do

1 at AMD?   7

2   A   He was like a manager at AMD. His background

3 is in computer engineering and he and Tom were

4 colleagues there.

5   Q   Did you ever have occasion to meet Tom and

6 H   's child D.   ?

7   A   No, I haven't been able to do that because I

8 myself have a -- I have a child who has autism and I

9 do a home-based program with her, which is one of the

10 reasons I haven't been able to be in touch with Tom as

11 much as I would have liked to.

12   Q   You yourself, you're, also, married; is that

13 correct?

14   A   Yes.

15   Q   Did you ever have the opportunity to go on

16 vacations anywhere with Tom and H   ?

17   A   Yes.

18   Q   How many times did you and your husband go on a

19 vacation with them?

20   A   One big trip. That was to Big Bend.

21   Q   Do you remember when that was, what time of

22 year?

23   A   I'm not exactly sure of the month, but I know I

24 was pregnant at the time, so it was probably sometime

25 in -- must have been in '96, early '96 or late '95.

			8
1	Q	How did all of you get to Big Bend?	
2	A	We drove together in our car.	
3	Q	Did you take your vehicle or Tom and H_____'s?	
4	A	No. My vehicle.	
5	Q	How long was the trip?	
6	A	Several hours. I mean from Austin to Big Bend,	

7 several, several hours, I think, must have taken at

8 least eight hours or so.

9   Q   How long was the vacation, the entire vacation?

10   A   I'm sorry? How long was the --

11   Q   How long was the entire vacation?

12   A   The entire vacation. I think it was supposed

13 to last a couple of days.

14   Q   Do you remember if you went for part of a week

15 or if you went for like a weekend or what?

16   A   It was more like a weekend. The reason I'm

17 very confused now is because that was just -- you

18 know, H_____ threw such a fit when we were there and

19 she wanted to cut short the trip, so at this point,

20 I'm not sure if we intended the vacation to be longer

21 than it actually did last.

22   MR. CALABRESE: Court Reporter, I'm

23 objecting to the responsiveness of the answer.

24   THE WITNESS: I'm sorry. I didn't hear

25 that.

1   MR. CALABRESE: For the record, the court   9

2   reporter is supposed to note that I'm objecting to the

3   responsiveness of the answer.

4   THE WITNESS: Oh.

5   MR. CALABRESE: Did you get that, Miss Court

6   Reporter?

7   THE COURT REPORTER: Yes.

8   MR. CALABRESE: Hello?

9   THE COURT REPORTER: Yes.

10   MR. CALABRESE: Thank you.

11   Q   (By Mr. Hays) Did anything unusual happen on

12   that trip?

13   A   Yeah. I mean one of the things that happened

14   was H   was upset during the trip. It looked like

15   she and Tom had had a big fight when we were there and

16   what happened was unusual because it was away from

17   Austin and it happened, you know, while we were

18   supposed to be on vacation, but the behavior itself

19   was not unusual when she was with us, which is that

20   she was constantly -- you know, she was fighting with

21   Tom, she was shouting in public and -- and then, of

22   course, the clincher was that she wanted to cut short

23   the trip and Tom actually had to go off and try to

24   find her a ride back home from Big Bend and, you know,

25   Gopi, my husband, and I, we were upset that the

50

1 vacation was not going very well and so I spoke to   10

2 H   and tried to convince her that she should just

3 stay and we should all drive back together.

4   MR. CALABRESE: Court Reporter, this is Gary

5 Calabrese again objecting to the responsiveness of the

6 answer.

7 Q   (By Mr. Hays)   Would H   ever get upset

8 when you guys would go out here in Austin?

9   MR. CALABRESE: Objection, form.

10   THE WITNESS: Should I answer that?

11 Q   (By Mr. Hays)   Did she ever get upset when you

12 guys would go out here in Austin?

13   MR. CALABRESE: Same objection.

14   THE WITNESS: Yes, she would.

15 Q   (By Mr. Hays)   Did you notice any changes in

16 her demeanor when you guys went out?

17   MR. CALABRESE: Objection, form.

18   THE WITNESS: Yeah. I mean she -- it was --

19 she didn't -- she would often shout in public or have

20 little temper tantrums in public and say and do

21 embarrassing things, things that were embarrassing to

22 all of us.

23 Q   (By Mr. Hays)   Did you ever --

24   THE WITNESS: And really cut down Tom. I'm

25 sorry.

1   Q   (By Mr. Hays) Did you ever see Tom and H   11

2   ever have any fights?

3   A   Yeah.   They would argue constantly.

4   Q   And where would these fights occur?

5   A   And where would what?

6   Q   Where would the fights usually occur?

7   A   Everywhere. It didn't -- I don't think, you

8   know, they were very choosy about where. It happened

9   everywhere, whether we were at home or in somebody

10 else's place or in a restaurant.

11 Q   How often would these fights occur?

12 A   Regularly. It would be rare if they were not

13 fighting anytime we went out.

14 Q   How would H   act when these fights would

15 occur?

16 A   She would get very irritated with Tom for one

17 reason or the other and then just keep on about the

18 point, whatever the point was.

19 Q   What tone of voice would H   use?

20 A   Very shrill, very high-pitched.

21 Q   How would Tom react in those situations?

22 A   Tom would be very embarrassed when her voice

23 went up and, usually, he would sometimes reply, but it

24 would be very soft, his voice would be very soft and

25 then he would just sort of try to ignore her from that

1   point on.   12

2   Q   What, if anything, seemed to upset H   on

3   the Big Bend trip?

4   A   I'm not exactly sure at this point, but I know

5   that it had something to do with -- we had separate

6   rooms, adjoining rooms and it seems like Tom slept on

7   a table or on the floor or something like that and his

8   back was paining and she wouldn't let him sleep on the

9   bed with her, something like that, that night.

10 Q   On the --

11 A   I'm sorry?

12 Q   Were there any fights that occurred on the trip

13 down to Big Bend?

14 A   I'm not sure at this point because -- I'm not

15 sure, no.

16 Q   Were there any fights that occurred while you

17 were down actually at Big Bend after you had arrived?

18 A   Yeah. Actually, this -- I think there had been

19 something, an argument brewing by the time we reached

20 Big Bend. I'm not sure about that, but I know --

21 because it was several years ago, but I know that once

22 we were there, it blew up into something big between

23 them and she wanted to leave and the next day -- maybe

24 it was for breakfast, I'm not sure, but we were eating

25 in the cafeteria there and she was very upset and she

1   was yelling at him. I remember that.   13

2   Q   You'd mentioned something earlier about -- did

3   -- well, let me ask you this. Did she express any

4   desire about what she wanted to do at that time?

5   A   She wanted to go back to Austin.

6   Q   What was Tom's reaction to that?

7   A   Tom was like this is the middle of Big Bend, I

8   mean give me a break. I mean how are you going to get

9   back? I mean that was what his initial response was,

10 but I think later he tried to find her a ride back.

11 Q   Do you know if he actually found her a ride

12 back?

13 A   I think he did. It was either a bus or some --

14 something like that. I'm not sure, but he did find

15 her something back.

16 Q   Did H   go back or did she stay?

17 A   No. She stayed.

18 Q   Do you know why she stayed?

19 A   Yeah, because I actually spoke to her and --

20 I'm not -- I can't remember if my husband, also, spoke

21 to her, but our intention was, basically, to try to

22 convince her that, you know, we should just all have

23 -- you know, try to salvage the rest of the trip, have

24 a good time and go back together. And we didn't

25 really want her, you know, going off all by herself.

1 Q   After that, how was the rest of your trip?   14

2 A   It wasn't great, because she was, obviously,

3 very upset with Tom and she would keep complaining

4 about him and she would keep -- sometimes she would

5 yell at him and then there would be these periods of

6 total silence, so there was a lot of tension between

7 them.

8 Q   On those occasions during that trip when she

9 would yell at Tom, what would -- what, if anything,

10 would Tom do?

11 A   Tom might say something, but just maybe a one

12 line or something and just leave it at that. I know

13 some -- I know a couple of times, he might have, you

14 know, made a remark to either my husband or me, but

15 nothing beyond that.

16 Q   Did you during the time that you had occasion

17 -- during the times that you had occasion to go out

18 with you and your husband and Tom and H   , did you

19 ever see any incidents of physical violence between

20 the two of them?

21 A   No, I did not, but there was one time when I

22 saw some scratches on Tom and I asked him about it.

23 Q   What did he say had happened?

24 A   I think he said something like H   gave

25 them to him.

15

1   Q   Where were the scratches?

2   A   I think they were on his face.

3   Q   What did they look like to you?

4   A   Just scratches. Nail marks maybe. I'm not

5 sure. They just looked like scratches.

6   Q   I'm sorry. Can you repeat that. I didn't

7 hear.

8   A   Scratches. They looked like scratches.

9   Q   Was there any indication from the scratches

10 what might have caused them?

11   MR. CALABRESE: Objection, form.

12   THE WITNESS: Because it wasn't a single

13 scratch. They were -- it was -- they were multiple

14 scratches, so that's the reason I asked Tom what

15 happened, because I thought H   might have caused

16 it.

17   MR. CALABRESE: Objection, responsiveness.

18   Q   (By Mr. Hays) Where on his face were the

19 scratches located?

20   A   Close to his cheek.

21   Q   On both of his cheeks?

22   A   I can remember only one cheek.

23   Q   How many scratches do you recall seeing?

24   A   I don't remember exactly. I know there was

25 more than one. This was a long time ago. I can't

56

1 remember the details to that extent.   16

2 Q   Did you ever have occasion to see any sort of

3 verbal attacks that may have been brought against

4 Mr. Lynch?

5 A   What do you mean by that? Do you mean did

6 H   scold him or yell at him?

7 Q   Well, I believe you've said there have been

8 occasions where H   would yell at him.

9 A   Yes.

10 Q   On any of the occasions that you observed

11 fights between Tom and H   , did Tom instigate any

12 of those fights?

13   MR. CALABRESE: Objection, form.

14   THE WITNESS: Well, I mean I'm not sure if

15 you could call them instigation, because it could be

16 any remark that Tom -- you know, a casual remark that

17 Tom made could set her off. It could even be, you

18 know, discussion we might be having on, you know,

19 anything, maybe jobs or anything like that and so we

20 could never tell what would set her off.

21 Q   (By Mr. Hays) Did you ever have occasion to

22 talk to H   about these altercations that she

23 would have with Tom?

24 A   Yes. Actually, I had one opportunity only.

25 There was only one time when H   and I went out

1   together by ourselves alone without our husbands and   17

2   we actually went shopping to the mall and, afterwards,

3   we were sitting in the food court and -- and then we

4   were talking and she was complaining about Tom and she

5   was, basically, very unhappy and she said that she

6   couldn't stand him, she couldn't stand his habits, he

7   was very dirty, he wouldn't pick up his clothes and he

8   was not responsible and things like that and, you

9   know, that he was not -- he was spending all the money

10   and things like that and so at that time, I,

11   basically, told her -- I was, also, newly married at

12   that time, but I told her that, hey, you know, guys --

13   I'm sorry, but guys tend to sometimes be very messy

14   and have such habits and that's okay and it's all the

15   small stuff, you know, why sweat the small stuff. Tom

16   seems to be a great guy, he seems to be a lot of fun,

17   very honest and the two of you could have a very good

18   life together if you could look past all these small

19   petty things.

20   Q   What was H   's reaction to your advice?

21   A   She actually said that it may not be -- it may

22   be small stuff to me, but not to her and, you know,

23   something like, it may not be important to you, but

24   it's very important to me, that kind of thing and she

25   said that, you know, looking past it and putting up

1 with all these things, these are compromises that may   18

2 work for you, but not for me, that is, for her.

3   Q   Did you ever have occasion to get into any sort

4 of disagreement with H   ?

5   A   In the sense that -- if you mean did she say

6 anything to me -- you know, to me personally against

7 me, yeah. There were times when she made remarks that

8 were rude and pretty hurtful to me, but we never got

9 into an argument about it because I didn't argue back.

10   Q   What sort of things would she say that you

11 considered rude?

12   A   One of the things that I remember very clearly

13 was it was right after -- she had just graduated, she

14 had just completed her Ph.D. and we were having a

15 party for her and we'd all had dinner at a restaurant

16 and then we went back to their place to continue the

17 party and there were several of us, maybe nine, ten of

18 us, sitting on the steps outside her apartment and it

19 was, in fact -- it was only the first or the second

20 time that I was meeting H   and she told me in

21 front of all these people, she said that, you know, I

22 had to watch my weight, I had a weight problem and if

23 I did not, then I would lose my man, I would not be

24 able to keep my man and I was outraged by that.

25   Q   Were there any other occasions that she would

1 talk to you about your weight?   19

2 A   About my weight, yeah. She used to mention

3 that off and on, yes. I remember a time when -- you

4 know, she was always a very slim person and I -- but

5 she was very conscious of her weight and I told her

6 once, "Well, you don't have anything to worry about.

7 You're quite fine. In fact, if anything, you know,

8 you're quite on the small side." And she said, "Well,

9 you know, you have to stay like me and you have to

10 watch it; otherwise, look at you, you know, you could

11 just lose your man" and similar remarks.

12   MR. CALABRESE: Objection, responsiveness.

13 Q   (By Mr. Hays) Did H   ever talk to you

14 about her opinion of Americans?

15   MR. CALABRESE: Objection, form.

16   THE WITNESS: It would just come up in the

17 kind of things she would say. She --

18 Q   (By Mr. Hays) What was your impression of

19 H   's opinion of Americans?

20   MR. CALABRESE: Objection, form.

21   THE WITNESS: I think she thought always

22 that somehow Asians were superior to Americans as far

23 as intelligence was concerned, that Americans were

24 dumb, comparatively, anyways.

25   MR. CALABRESE: Objection, responsiveness.

60

1   Q   (By Mr. Hays) Did she ever say anything about   20

2   whether or not she felt Americans were stupid?

3   MR. CALABRESE: Form.

4   THE WITNESS: I think she has used that word

5   actually, that, you know, in spite of being an

6   American, he's managed to do something like this, some

7   kind of remark like that, yeah.

8   Q   (By Mr. Hays) Did she ever say anything about

9   what she thought about Tom's level of intelligence?

10   A   She -- she certainly thought that she was more

11   intelligent than he was and she often would say things

12   like, you know, "stupid American."

13   MR. CALABRESE: Objection, responsiveness.

14   Q   (By Mr. Hays) What kind of a housekeeper was

15   H   ?

16   MR. CALABRESE: Objection, form.

17   THE WITNESS: She was -- as far as

18   cleanliness went, I think she was almost fanatical

19   about it. It was something I think that almost

20   tortured her. She would -- you know, at one point,

21   for instance, she used to love to cook, I think,

22   because she had lots of cookbooks and, you know, she

23   has cooked sometimes and enjoyed it, but I think often

24   it was very hard for her because of the cleanliness

25   factor because to cook meant to clean and cook meant

1 things would get dirty and that was hard for her to   21

2 deal with.

3   MR. CALABRESE: Objection, responsiveness.

4 Q   (By Mr. Hays) Did you have any conversations

5 with her about cleanliness?

6 A   Yeah, because it was a very big issue for her,

7 especially the fact that Tom would not pick up things

8 and help her with the housecleaning. I -- I actually

9 had a very good cleaning lady help me at home -- you

10 know, help me in my house, so I actually suggested

11 that H   might want to use her, also, and she.

12 She actually said that, you know, she couldn't let

13 anybody else -- she couldn't trust anybody else to do

14 the work right and when I said that this lady Aida was

15 actually very, very good, then H   said, "Well,

16 maybe good enough for you, but not good enough for

17 me."

18 Q   Did you have any occasion to have -- to have

19 issues with her about cleanliness?

20 A   Did I have what with her?

21 Q   Did you have occasion to have an issue with her

22 about cleanliness?

23 A   This was it, about -- oh. Okay. Okay. Yeah.

24 I know. There was one instance which was -- actually,

25 we were in the house and we were all getting ready to

1   go out and I wanted to have a drink of water and I   22

2   went into the kitchen and I was about to use a cup off

3   her draining board and she came and said that -- to

4   put it down, because she said she had just cleaned it

5   and that we could just -- and, you know, we could just

6   go out and get a drink, because we were leaving

7   anyway.

8   Q   When you lived in Austin, did you have a job?

9   A   No, I did not.

10   Q   Did H   ever talk to you about that?

11   A   About getting a job? Actually, soon after --

12   soon after I met H   , I became pregnant and -- but

13   there was always talk about H   getting a job,

14   because Tom wanted her to get a job and she had just

15   finished her Ph.D. and the idea I always thought was

16   that H   would get a job, but somehow nothing much

17   happened there.

18   Q   Did you ever have any discussions with H

19   about her getting a job?

20   A   No, not any personal discussions, no, but I

21   know that my husband and I, we were always surprised

22   that, you know, here was this couple who had no plans

23   to have a child, they had, you know -- H   had no

24   plans to get a job, she was hardly cooking at home, so

25   what was happening to their lives.

Figure 6: Radhe Deposition

Taking a Break to Do Something Constructive, Oscar 8

An old colleague called with a proposal. We had somewhat of a special relationship because I had given him a ride to San Antonio one time when his car broke down. No one else would do it. It was only an hour drive each way. In modern American society where men seldom confide in each other, this kind of thing is often enough to establish a friendship. Brian was also a fellow ham operator. He had a mental block and couldn't do Morse code, so he had been concentrating on higher frequency radio equipment where code wasn't used. For example, he had a satellite receiver. Brian called to propose that we go work on OSCAR 8, the new ham satellite. It was a wonderful proposal, and it was just the sort of break I needed. I flew out to Orlando with Brian. We helped the folks working on the antenna array. We also watched a launch at Cape Canaveral.

I got to know Brian a little bit better. Brain is ultra analytical, but one can see the pain when he talks about his parent's divorce. It became apparent that he was a fundamentalist Christian. Jesus music played in the background when I called the house. Brian's father is a psychologist who works with divorcing spouses, among others. Brian married a woman who worked for the attorney general's office, Sandy. Sandy attends the Unitarian Church and fancies herself to be a feminist activist.

After we got back from Orlando, Brian invited us to a barbecue party. H* met Sandy, and Sandy suggested that H* call her some time and they would go to lunch. To my knowledge H* did not see Sandy again until showing up at her place some years later. In part this was because H* had an issue with using the phone. I only saw her use the phone on a couple of occasions. She had me dial if someone was to be called, and she ignored the phone when it rang. It was a running joke, the woman with a PhD who did not know how to use a phone. Though apparently she had been communicating with her father who was in Korea. Perhaps it was during the night or while I was at work, or even possibly it was by email or surface mail.

The Money Promised for the Newlyweds House Arrives from Korea

Apparently a Korean stock certificate worth about $300,000 had arrived. It was a curse. Every night H* was crying. If I tried to talk to her, she just screamed at me that it was none of my business, or that she didn't know. Apparently she had been told to sell the certificate at the right time, but she had no idea when that would be. She couldn't take her mind off of it, so she cried. It was absolutely brutal. And not only was she driving herself nuts over it, she was driving the stock broker nuts. He was calling me on the side and asking what was going on, even though my name was not on the account. I repeatedly reminded him that the account was owned solely by H*. I called Mr. Choi and he explained he wanted his daughter to take responsibility. I emphasized that she wasn't handling it well, but he gave no reply. I tried to call him again to explain how out of control the situation was, but he refused to even take the call. The stock broker kept calling me directly, wanting me to explain what was going on. He said that H* was making no sense. I told him I knew nothing, and had nothing to do with it; though I wished it out of my life so that H* would stop crying. The broker sold it. A week later Mr. Choi called and said to sell it. H* told me it had gone up another 20%. She also said that Mr. Choi had a friend who was going to tell him the right time to sell it. Apparently the fact it was sold was my fault. In her opinion I now owed her more money due to my bad advice of getting rid of it.

So here was a new item for H*'s get even list, the difference in the actual selling price, and the one that would have occurred at this later date. After the sale, there was about $285,000 dollars sitting in an AG Edwards account under H*'s name. Though she spent $10,000 on a new server for the startup.

A.G. Edwards & Sons, Inc.
INVESTMENTS SINCE 1887

One North Jefferson, St. Louis, MO 63103

Member SIPC — For Acct of: TAE YUNG CHOI — Page 1 of 2

Account Number — Taxpayer ID — Statement Period 06/12/96 to 06/28/96

H

Activity Summary

	Amounts Added	Amounts Subtracted	Balance
Beginning Cash and Money Fund Balance			.00
Sales	101,503.25		
Checks/Withdrawals		-101,503.25	
Ending Cash and Money Fund Balance			$.00

Your Investment Broker

FRANK M. NETHERTON
A. G. EDWARDS & SONS, INC. (512) 472-6852
301 CONGRESS AVE
SUITE 100
AUSTIN TX 78701

Total Account Value $282,870.75

Account Positions

Note	Quantity	Description	Price	Valuation	Est Annual Income	Est Annual % Yield	Type
		Equities		$282,870.75			
	16,518	ULTRAK INC # COMMON NO PAR	17 1/8	282,870.75			1
		Total Account Value		$282,870.75			

SEE REVERSE FOR EXPLANATION OF CODES AND POSITION PRICING METHOD.
If this statement does not agree with your records, please contact us at the above address in St. Louis promptly. Please include your full account number.
Certain cash items, receipt and delivery of securities entries, and trades settling after the statement period will appear on your next statement.

Figure 7: AG Edward's Statement Showing Stocks From Korea In H's Name*

H*: "You are a Parasite"

Our company won a contract to do part of a chip design for Chromatic. We had a secrecy agreement as Chromatic was planing to use the resulting chip to compete with my prior employer, AMD, and they didn't want an issue made of it. The contract was worth only a few hundred thousand dollars and I had hired two employees to assist, but the contract established the legitimacy of the company, Tempered Hardware and Software.

H* changed the nagging list. Shortly after we switched places I cam home and she now screamed that it was my responsibility as a husband to bring in the money, and not her responsibility. She also had expectations of owning a house and having a savings account like other employees who had two working spouses. I came home from the office. She was in the living room and she let me have it. She stood up and craned her head forward as though having it incrementally closer to my ear would add further emphasis. To the front of her list of screaming nags she repeated, "You just a parasite taking money from family", "you owe me $10,000 for the computer," "you take $5000 from me," "you abandoning me," "you don't care about my thesis," "I should have married Ravi," "you not call," etc. and this was intermixed with the threats, "I divorce you", "I should kill you," "I will kill you." She screamed so hard an long that there was foam on the corner of her mouth.

I was better off when I couldn't understand what she said when she nagged, but after hearing it so many times, like a foreign language lesson, I could make most of it out. It was horrible vicious material, and it depressed me. As I loved her, I believed there must be an element of truth to it. This made it hurt more.

H*: Have to Wash the Dishes .. again and again

One day Ram and Deepa came by and asked us out. H* said she couldn't go because she had to wash dishes. We had a dish washer, but I normally did my dishes by hand and put them in the drying rack. H* went into the kitchen took the dishes out of the drying rack and started washing them. What she hadn't noticed was that Ram had followed her into the kitchen. He commented that she didn't need to wash the clean ones. H* was mad, but she did not let down her polite public face grow ugly, especially in front of Ram. Instead she knocked them out of the picture the next time she was out with Deepa. At that time she politely told Deepa that she was too fat, and said something insulting about her husband, the specifics of which Deepa did not relay back to me.

H* was back to nagging almost daily and having a major fit about once a week, though one could not predict exactly when the major fit would occur, Saturday morning was as good of a time as any.

It wasn't only the dishes she would obsessed over. H* would vacuum the same spot repeatedly, often while nagging. It was an affective display that conveyed the message that she was Cinderella figure.

When We Had Dinner Guests Over

While H* drove the new Volvo, I got by on my motorcycle. Rather than do another winter on the motorcycle I bought an old Porsche 914. I rationalized that I could auto cross the Porsche as a stress outlet. I felt a stress outlet. I bought it from an old college roommate very cheap, as it did not run. H* instantly didn't like him, so after the transaction, we didn't see him again. I took the the car to Bruce Lipshy's Porsche dealership to have it repaired. They charged, but delivered a car that did not run. I hired Wayne Bush Esq. to settle the matter. In the end, I received what I had spent on the repair bill, plus the amount of the lawyer fees. In other words, after all the time and trouble over months, I broke about even, monetarily. Of course that was better than losing money. The thing of most value turned out to be meeting the attorney, Wayne. Wayne was curious about the world, and had pet theories. He once made a point by saying something was "as square as the color yellow." After the law suit was settled we invited Wayne and his girlfriend over for dinner.

I gave Wayne a copy of Kafka's *The Trial*. It was a sort of play on how each step had to be discussed with Wayne, while we were on the clock. Can you imagine being left in a legal limbo for years while having to constantly pay an attorney? A few months had been bad enough. Kafka made short work of that thesis. Few people appreciate the value of a good attorney. A good attorney is what stands between having one's day in court, and hell. I don't think Wayne understood the complement.

I had broken my rule about not saying anything personal to H* when I relayed a comical story about an acquaintance, Wilbur. He was a traditional Pakistani man who prided himself on being both machismo and hippie at the same time. He had a trippy girlfriend, Mary, who once blew his cover by explaining in public that Wilbur sat while peeing. Wilbur nearly died of embarrassment. Wilbur was never going to see the end of the ribbing from the guys. When Mary continued, it was clear that she had an agenda, that Wilbur was to be sacrificed to the cause of social rectification. Though this was probably just a convenient cover for communicating to Wilbur that she was displeased about something else - and that she could punish him at will. Her attack was highly affective. The bubbly and talkative Wilbur was reduced to a blubbering heap. He then sincerely explained that when he stood to pee while wearing shorts that he splattered his legs, and he sat to avoid that. Their seven year old relationship ended shortly afterwards. H* was quiet during my retelling of the incident, but the story was duly registered.

At dinner with the Bush's H* built up to it, and then retold the story, but with a slight variation. She said that I was the one who sat while peeing. If it had been familiar company perhaps it might have been funny, but we did not know the Bushs. The Bushs just looked at each other. It is strange how such an insult can leave so little room for reply. I couldn't think of anything to say to repair the social damage, if indeed there was any. If I said, "Who cares," I would have verified the statement. If I looked embarrassed, I looked guilty. If I denied it, it made it seem like a valid point worthy of debate. I remember Wilbur's answer - but that didn't seem like a very good response either. If I had come out and been honest about her motives, it would have set her off and made our guests uneasy. Also, since the Bush's were not familiar with the context, it would have appeared I had purposely provoked her. Certainly there was humor in the topic, so I attempted to bring it out. I said I did whatever I found to be the most convenient in the bathroom, and smiled. They might have laughed at the joke, but the Bush's said nothing.

This one wasn't quite the magnitude as the setup at the Moulin Rouge, though at least at the Moulin Rouge we were anonymous. Chances are that we will never see any of those people again.

After our dinner guests left, I confronted H* directly for the first time since knowing her. She screamed and nagged. I threw some crystal wine glasses against the wall and yelled that she should stop screaming and insulting, and listen to me for a change. After having ignored her hundreds of times, I had finally taken the bait. I was not going to get what I wanted, my say, but she was going to get what she wanted - under my skin. She egged me on. I picked her up and held her over my head. I told her, "Shut up or I will take you out back and throw you off the balcony!" She chanted down from above, "Do it! Do it! Do it! Throw me off!

Throw me off!" This little five foot two woman was so much in control that I was now a marionette doll literally strung below her. The accuracy of the image almost made me laugh, though I wasn't happy, She had made an art form out of mental abuse and that art was a kind of puppetry. The marriage was an undeclared war. I set her down, she had won the battle. I went upstairs and went to bed.

Sailing On Lake Travis

Gene, a long time friend from Iowa, came and visited Austin. We drove out to lake Travis. We took 2222 out to four points where it meets up with 620. 620 runs along a ridge and periodically one can see the lake through the hills and the scrub. It has a beautiful blue green color that reminds me some of the views of the Mediterranean in southern Europe. The ridge winds down a hill, where 620 crosses the dam. On the dam, the lake extends from just below the road on one side, off into the distance. On the other side, far down below, a creek runs away over the rocks.

We turned off the highway and went down a winding road to get to the marina where I had rented a sail boat. Once at the marina we descends the white stair cases cut into the face of the limestone escarpment, where we arrived at the dock, went to the boat house, finalized the arrangements, threw our stuff in the boat. We motored out of the cove, took off the sail covers, and hoisted the main and jib.

It is typically slow sailing on Travis. After a couple of times back and forth, we went back to the cove. We were back at the cove and wouldn't you know, the engine wouldn't start. I used the cell phone to call the marina to have us towed back in. I wasn't going to sail a boat I didn't own back into the marina as I was afraid to hit the dock hard or worse.

There was a large bang in the distance. I didn't pay much attention to it. Then there was a whish sound, and a potato grazed H*'s cheek and slammed into the deck. I sailed over to a nearby dock, and ran up the hill. There were some very nice houses at the top of the hill. A neighbor told me some boys had been firing a potato cannon. Later the marina made a report to the sheriffs office.

H*'s Korean Cure for Snoring

On the fourth of July 1997 H* and I had unprotected sex. Once. H* was absolutely confident that nothing could happen on one occasion. She explained that for her to get pregnant we would have to try for a long time.

I awoke one night to find that someone had broken into the house and was squarely sitting on top of me trying to suffocate me in bed. The shadow was hunched over me, one hand had my nose pinched shut, the other clamped over my mouth. I could not scream and I could not move well because of the sheets. I tried to move my legs up to launch the person across the room, but the sheets were in the way. I managed to free my arms before passing out, and grabbed the attacker's wrists and ripped them from my face. They were not a man's wrists. I had managed to get some purchase with my legs when I realized it wasn't an intruder. It was H*. My heart was racing, and I gulped down air. I was very confused.

I demanded an explanation from her. She joked it was a Korean method for stopping snoring. She persisted in giving just that explanation for a couple of days, and then started denying that anything had ever happened.

H* told me I could leave. She said she was having the child, but wouldn't require child support or any money. She said I should simply leave everything and go. I could walk free.

The nasal valve in my nose had completely collapsed. It was an awful thing for a person to squeeze the nose of someone who had an operation, but apparently she wasn't concerned that a dead person would complain. I started inserting spreaders. The spreaders easily got lost and were difficult to replace, so I learned to make them by cutting ink pen tops with a knife.

Three years later I was at the Mayo Clinic for the digestive problems, fasciculations, and a collapsed nasal valve. Dr. Grisolano put me out and took a biopsy from my stomach. He discovered tissue damage.   I told him about H*'s death threats. He asked if she had a "mental history." I told him she had no history at all, as she had immigrated from Korea. He then demurred. The threats would not be taken seriously. Dr. Grisolano was stumped as to the source of the scar tissue. Another doctor diagnosed the nasal valve collapse, and later Dr. Moore used a tissue graft of cartilage from my ear to fix it.

Having had a great deal of time to think about this incident, I now find it is more likely that H* was gating my breathing so that my heart would be injured. The result would be an apparently natural heart attack rather than a very hard to explain husband dead from suffocation. How would H* know to do this? Perhaps it was like Grandma Finns knowhow for inducing miscarriages being passed on. Indeed once a woman has decided that life and death is her decision, at what age is the cut off for the victim? Although doctors and philosophers who have studied this question have provided a seemingly reasonable answer, these are not the people who execute the decision. For example, it was discovered that the SIDS disease is often maternal infanticide after the original research subjects confessed, see "The Death of Innocents: A True Story of Murder, Medicine and High-Stakes Science" by Richard Firstman and Jamie Talan. It turns out that Kohlberg died young from digestive issues, given the controversy surrounding him it makes one wonder. And what about Grandma Finns first husband and her son? H*'s actions begged questions that I had never thought of before.

Vacation to Korea

In late October H* said she needed to visit Korea to sign some papers to sell her house. I had no idea she had a house in Korea. She had told me she had never been married before, so I assumed she had lived at home. She explained that it wasn't really her house, but it was just in her name so that her father could avoid taxes. I thought it was an excellent idea to meet up with her family and find out what was going on with her. I couldn't wait to have a conversation with the 'family' about H*'s behavior. I assumed that her family would be a lot like my family.

We flew into Seoul in mid December of 1998 and stayed almost two weeks. H*'s father indeed owned a building. It was a six story building. There was a car dealer at the bottom, a restaurant in the middle, a number of offices, and an apartment at the top. The Chois had three daughters and one son. H* was the oldest, followed by her sister who married a stock broker and lived in Seoul. The third sister was living with her husband in Italy and was studying architecture. The Chois youngest child lived with them in the apartment. He worked as a news cameraman.

The Chois had an elevator key that allowed entrance to the top apartment. It was unusual to ride in an elevator and then to see the doors open to a living area. Just outside the elevator there was a mat where everyone put their shoes. The apartment spanned two floors, with a cross walk going from the son's bedroom over open dining area to the parents bedroom. Stairs met the cross walk by the parents bedroom. On the side of the dining area there was a living room with a large television that was never turned off. Three channels on the television gave instructions on how to play the game Go.

One evening the Chois invited some family over. It wasn't clear how they were related. I do not understand Korean, so the conversation went right past me. There was a big fight. Mr. Choi was red and yelling. The guest managed to tell me in English that Mr. Choi's nick name in the family was *The General*.

H*'s sister and family were very nice to us. H* explained that they had converted to being Catholic. We picnicked in the park with them. The Chois drove me through downtown. It was truly imposing and huge, with tall buildings on both sides of the street as far as one could see. We visited a mountain with H*'s brother-in-law and climbed to the monastery on top. We also went to a country festival. The festival had dancing and lots of homemade alcoholic drinks akin to cider, but made from rice.

After the papers for the house had been signed (apparently, I never saw them) Mr. Choi suggested we visit a resort island before leaving. On this island it was possible to travel from a beach, to an orange grove, to snow at high altitude in one afternoon. On the sides of the trails there were fresh orange peels left in the snow by snacking hikers. At the beach, there were women who were famous world over for diving for abalone. There was a demonstration village set up.

H* took me to a ranch to ride horses, and we stopped by a dive shop and arranged a dive trip to a nearby rock. I dove off the rock with a guide. The guide ran into some other divers harvesting abalone. As abalone are now protected, the guide and the other divers wrestled underwater. They surfaced and dropped their gear, and started sparing with each other on our rock. H* and I just watched in disbelief. The dive itself was interesting, and the side show made it somewhat exciting.

I can honestly say we had a great time during the trip. H* did not have a single fit. This left me with the impression that she was much better when around her family.

H* Citizenship Interview

In January of 1998 H* received a summons in the mail to come to San Antonio for a citizenship interview. She had filled out all the papers, and now the INS wanted to know if the marriage was valid. I was to go with her. After a little bit of difficulty finding the building and the correct office, we checked in and sat down. The place looked a lot like a doctor's lobby, with a waiting room and someone at the front counter. There was a door people entered to go to the back after they were called.

If this had been a doctor's office, then everyone would have been waiting to find out if the ailment was terminal, as the room was very quiet. Everyone was nervous and spoke in hushed tones. We had to sit in the waiting room for some time before the interview. During this time H* started to become angry. I don't recall what it was about. We went back and fourth in whispered voices that were creeping up in volume. I cautioned her to relax for a while. Then boom, right there in the INS waiting room, she started screaming and nagging. It was unintelligible, but loud and obnoxious. She went on seemingly forever when, no doubt out of mercy for me, the lady at the counter called our names.

We went into the back and were led to a desk where a young Hispanic woman was going to interview us. She asked a couple of basic questions. Then I asked if she heard the ruckus out front. She had. I said, "You know, if she is confident enough to do that in the INS lobby, and I put up with it, then the marriage must be real." The interviewer agreed, and dismissed us. It may have been shortest citizenship interview in INS history.

Afterwards H* stopped sex all together. She would fend off any passes curtly. She elbowed me in the neck when I tried to kiss her. I asked her to promise not to that again, because it really hurt. She didn't even hesitate, she promised. It was classic H*, she kept her promise, the next time she kneed me in the groin. Another time she just reached over and grabbed my face leaving scratches. I was sleeping and working at night behind a locked door. It drove H* nuts. On one occasion she tried to shoulder the upstairs door. She shook the down stairs bedroom door until the lock mechanism fell apart.

Married with Child 1998 to 2000

D* is Born, and Already there are Conflicts

On the tenth of April 1998 at Saint David's hospital, H* had a difficult time delivering D*. She told the doctors that she wanted to have a natural birth. H*'s sister believed that natural birth gave a mother a stronger bond to the child, and H* wanted to give that every opportunity. Several hours of agony went by before she sought the sanctuary of the epidural.

Her parents had arrived the prior week to help with the baby. After a few hours there was some noise at the door to H*'s delivery room. Mr. Choi was trying to enter and the nurse was not allowing him to, H* raised her head and cried out, "Apaa", which is Korean for father. She wanted her frather. The nurse didn't let him in.

After a night of labor, Dr. Cowboy John Baker used a pair of forceps and pulled 10 and ½ pound D* out of his mother and plopped him down on a pan, and said with cheerfully with a Texas draw, "Another banana head." Indeed his head was elongated.

The nurse put a little blue hat on him, wrapped his blood covered body in a blanket, and then placed him in a little glass room that served as a human incubator. To my great surprise, sitting next to D* was a baby born to someone from my home town in Iowa, and there peering through the glass was Allen. We talked while watching the babies. I thought how lucky my son would be to have a father like me. I would teach him fundamentals of mathematics, like from my thesis, as he grew up. We would have hobbies like sailing, and building projects together. It would be grand adventure, and he would get all of the good that I had, without any of the bad. He would benefit from what I learned. Later I enrolled him to play hockey with my friend's son, but H* took him out of the program. I find it ironic that a woman who is so close to her father denied her own child his father.

H* had a fourth degree tear. She spent a couple of days in recovery. On her second night she got up to use the restroom. I had just fallen asleep on the couch in the room. I heard a thud. H* had passed out in the restroom and had hit her head on the tile curb for the shower. A doctor came and explained that women don't hurt themselves when they faint due to the way they fall. He even demonstrated by dipping and turning his waist, but he left out part where she hit her head. H* appeared to be ok. What a rough few days she endured.

She stayed in the hospital the next day. Everything had calmed down. I went and saw a movie to clear my head, while H* napped. I had just watched my son being pulled out of his mother. I returned to find my friends Dan and Samantha were visiting. H* was upset that I had not remained while she napped. It became another item for the nag list. "You didn't even stay with me at the hospital when I had D*." She had her energy back, she had recovered.

I thought we were entering a new era in our marriage, where H*'s motherly instincts would shine, and we would have a new joint interest in raising a child that would take the focus off or our marital problems. I had heard many people say, "don't you two have anything better to do?" and now we did. I had considered that boredom was a component of H*'s behavior. Now she had something new to focus her attention on, so she would not be nagging at me all the time.

Mr. Choi: "I'm Taking the Baby to Korea"

The next day we came home with the baby. The in-laws were waiting anxiously. Unfortunately we had to go back to St. David's as H* was bleeding badly. We left baby D* with grandma and grandpa Choi, and went back to the emergency room. The emergency room doctor grimaced when he examined H*. He gave her more stitches. The emergency room itself was filthy. While we were waiting I used Windex and paper towels to clean oily layers of dust off of H*'s gurney, and off of the cabinets in the room where she was to get stitches.

We picked up pain pills and went back to the apartment. H*'s mother started nagging at H*. Her father told her that he was taking the baby to Korea. H* balled and screamed hysterically. I told her not to worry, as there was no way that was going to happen. Mr. Choi was upright like a big red erection. He ejaculated orders. I took baby D* and tried to find a safe place for him. I didn't want to place him on top of the bed or the large desk, as the cradle could be knocked down from those places. I didn't want to put him on the floor in the room less he be trampled if the hoard came upstairs. I placed him on the floor inside to the left of the closet opening. I figured I could protect the narrow entry way if needed. This caution turned out to be fortuitous. The Chois were having a mutual conniption downstairs. Then H* came running up the stairs. She was on enough pain pills to numb a horse, and had 145 stitches. I threatened to push Mr. Choi down the stairs if he attempted to follow. I begged H* to lay down and rest, but she remained standing in a confrontational stance. I told her I would remove her parents from the apartment. Then she started screaming at me. She didn't want them to leave, and she continued saying "Who are you to threaten to push *my* father down the stairs?" H* then picked up a suitcase and threw it at the opening of the closet where the baby was laying. I deflected it. She later claimed she was throwing the suitcase at me but had a bad aim.

H* laid down and went to sleep. I called a good friend, and we asked the in-laws to leave the apartment. They initially refused to leave, but I made it clear that they would leave, nicely or per force, at their option. Then they chose to leave voluntarily, so I got them a hotel room, and my friend drove them over. None of their possessions were left at the apartment.

"Who are you to threaten to push my father down the stairs," became an addition to the nag list, and when she really wanted to drive it home she started adding a direct death threat to the list, "I am going to kill you," she would say.

The Chois never apologized, but they did offer an explanation. Apparently Mrs. Choi felt that H* was a bad mother for having left the baby while she was in the emergency room, so she was going to let H* know about this. As foreigners they may have felt helpless while we were gone. Hence, they threatened to take the baby because H* was not a good mother. All this explanation did was convince me that they were all insane. What sane person, let alone a mother, would decide to punish a new mother on the day she arrived home with her new born? No matter how it was cut, the conclusion was that it was inhuman.

I took up the habit of walking away from H* when she had a fit. She would follow me. I took to locking doors behind me when walking away. She broke the patio door when I walked that direction. She threw her weight against the downstairs bedroom door. I could hear the door cracking, it flexed and came out of the door jam. However, the upstairs bedroom had a solid fire door. When she threw her weight upon it, she bounced off. Then she started screaming in a higher pitch voice.

73

I didn't have the energy but I resolved to watch out for D*'s well being because I had to. I didn't do this out of some Fatherhood Initiative type "your son needs a basketball coach," or "you can have it all" type argument. I closed my office downtown and set up in the upstairs bedroom behind the locking fire door. We made a deal that I would watch the baby during the day, and that in the evenings I would work upstairs while H* watched the baby downstairs. I was never far from D* for the next three years.

The Chois did not leave Austin, but instead got an apartment down the street. For a short while H* either breast fed the baby, or fed the baby milk that had been pumped by a machine. However, she didn't like the machine and she found it inconvenient to leave the office to feed the baby, so we started using formula.

My mother and Grandmother came to help after the Chois left. We picked them up on Tuesday afternoon, and by evening they were sterilizing the kitchen. They complained the mop boards and the bathrooms were dirty, and cleaned them. This could not have set well with H*. It was symptomatic. H* had never been accepted as part of the aunt network, in part because we lived over a thousand miles away from my home town, but also in part because of the information about her going home. I was upset with my mother over it, but couldn't blame her. H*'s own family was on the other side of the world. Exacerbating her isolation was the fact that she shunned the people she had met in Austin. She had even pushed me away. I still wonder if our marriage would have gone differently had I still lived in my home town where H* could have run with the pack of cousins.

Mom commented that while they were cleaning the other rooms, H* was taking clean dishes out of the cabinets and re-washing them. "Yeah, we know all about that mom, don't worry," I told her.

The Chois Have Baby D* Wrapped in Blankets in Summer

I had looked forward to H*'s folks visiting because H* had acted like the person I thought I had married when we were in Korea. In hindsight I should have known that at best I was trading problems, because I had seen the Generalissimo in action in Korea, but my attention was focused on H*. I now suspect that the Generalissimo to be at the heart of many of the problems; though I do not believe this makes H* innocent. After the incident on the day we brought baby D* home, the in laws were apologetic and our relations with them slowly began to improve.

After my parents left we had to work out a baby watching schedule. H* had her job at Motorola, and I was working on THS. H* emphasized that she had to work on her career, and that she wasn't going to become a house wife. I had neven even suggested that she be a housewife. She explained that her father had also advised her to cultivate her career. We worked out an arrangement where H* spent the day at her job, and then would watch D* in the evenings so I could get some work done. In order to give some flexibility to this schedule, I hired a nanny. Once in a while I would have a meeting and couldn't schedule the nanny, so I would take D* along.

A good part about this arrangement, was that D* would never be far from me. To some extent I could hear what was going on downstairs while I worked. H*'s usual mode of babysitting was to fix herself something to eat, and then sit in front of the TV all evening while the baby did whatever it wanted. She typically didn't even put him in bed. He played until he dropped.

74

H* only breast fed for a couple of weeks. She tried to use a machine so that she could leave bottles when she went to work. We bought the one with the best reviews, but H* did not like it. She told me that she could not make milk for the baby without her parents help, and she started to take the baby to the apartment down the street where the in laws had moved. By summer she started taking the baby to the in laws on the weekends. She would tell me that she was going to make some time for me to work, and then head off with the baby.

One day H* told me that I should not give baby D* any salt. This was a peculiar request as the baby was on formula, and was not eating anything solid. No one had control over his salt intake. Because the request was so strange I gave him a little bit of salt. He took it greedily. It was mid summer here in Texas and very hot outside.

That weekend after H* left with the baby I decided to make an afternoon visit on the in laws to check on D*. H* was not there. Mr. Choi told me I had to have permission to see him. I entered the apartment anyway. It was sweltering - the air conditioning was off. I found D* on the floor in an empty bedroom, *the door had been shut and the windows were closed. He was wrapped in blankets.*

I had changed doctors to Dr. Coldwater at the Austin Regional Clinic. After the incident with the blankets, I took advantage of the in-laws request to watch D* again by suggesting that Mr. Choi accompany me to see Dr. Coldwater. We met in Dr. Coldwater's office, and I brought up the incident with the blankets. Mr. Choi was surprised. He stuttered and he said that he had been heating the baby in order to prevent colds. He made out as though he was an uneducated foreigner who didn't know better. What a big fat liar my father in-law is, the concepts of cold temperature and having a disease that causes one's nose to run are completely unrelated in Korean language and Korean culture. The word for cold temperature, "choowo" -- is not alike in any way to the word "kangki" - a type of cold disease.

Later I asked Dr. Coldwater to be a witness, but she refused to even speak with me. Her staff said it was policy not to speak with people getting divorced. I wonder how quickly she would have responded if a woman asked her to repeat an abuse related statement about a father. Chances are, history shows, it would have been milliseconds.

Attorney Karen Kretchman's Advice: Divorce When the Baby is Older

H* was asking for a divorce, and with all that had happened I considered that it was a good idea. We talked about it. She wanted a divorce, but she would keep D*, and I wouldn't see him. She nagged and accused me of trying to steal her baby.

I spoke with an attorney in Austin by the name of Karen Kretchman. She told me flat out that there was no way to divorce and win custody until the baby was three, independent of what had happened. In addition I was advised to avoid Child Protective Services, as there were a number of horror stories related to them. Once they entered a situation, they took over. They had placed one child in a home where he had been raped. The vast majority of the CPS workers were women who had bad experiences with men. It was explained to me that neither one of us would have a say, but I, as a man, would be viewed suspiciously. Indeed there was little hard evidence of our problems, especially as Dr. Coldwater refused to speak about what she heard. Clearly, as a cute, ostensibly soft spoken, vulnerable as a recent immigrant, new mother, H* had a great deal of leverage for garnering sympathy. Also should

I strike out with allegations, it would no longer be my word against hers, as now Mr. Choi and Mrs. Choi could contribute. When I eventually did take action, my lawyer informed me that my parents could not be used as witnesses, 'because they were too close.' Yet, he expected H*'s parents to speak.

More H*-isms:

Corporal Punishment of Baby D*

On Thursday evening Mom was coming out of the bathroom downstairs when she heard H* angrily telling someone off in one of her nagging spells. My mother couldn't figure who H* was yelling at because I was upstairs and Grandma was in the kitchen. Mom looked in the guest room and was surprised to see H* changing the baby. She was nagging at the six month old baby in English while saying that it was bad for having pooped its diaper. Before she pulled the new diaper up she whacked him and told him not to do it again. We had not yet started potty training. Mom and Grandma tried to talk to H* about it. H* said she was "just teasing."

Late on Monday evening, after H* came home from work she was bottle feeding D*. D* fell asleep, Mom watched aghast as H* shook him to wake him up and hit him. Grandma came to see what was going on. H* was mad that baby D* had fallen asleep during feeding. My very mild mannered Grandmother told H* simply, "That is not the way to do it." Again H* replied, "I was just teasing," and she became angry with my parents. The air grew so thick you could cut it. My parent's baby shower gifts disappeared. Mom was very upset. She suspected that they had been thrown away. She was particularly upset over a Waterford clock and my baby clothes. Mom was in tears when we put her back on the airplane to return to Iowa.

At that point I had not seen H* hitting D*. I didn't know where the mother-in-law phenomena and Korean custom stopped, and abuse of the baby started. It was clear enough that mom was mad at H*, but it was beyond my imagination that an intelligent adult could scream and spank a six month old baby for pooping its diaper. Of course there were cultural issues, and what do I know about raising babies? Doctors slap a baby to make it breath after it is born. Where is the boundary between a reasonable slap, and abuse?

It is interesting, especially in the light of Steve Freitag's later conclusions (see section on that subject) that H* never stopped talking to D* about bowel movements. When he got older she kept repeating the lesson that he always had to poop before eating in order to make room for new food. She seems infatuated with the subject.

H* started taking the baby to her parents place in the afternoons. I was told I had to have permission to visit my son. In addition H* stayed with the baby at her parents some evenings. All other times I watched him. Later I hired a part time nanny to help.

H* had picked the pediatrician. She was a female doctor with an all female staff. The doctor did not like me coming with the baby and openly scoffed. The nurse had set an appointment for shots on a day the doctor was out. The office really played it up by letting D*, I, and Mr. Choi sit in the waiting room for 45 minutes before informing us the doctor was not in that day, and that the nurse could not administer the shots without a doctor present.

1. When D   was born, my mother and I went down to see our new grandchild who was a six months old new born. H   , my daughter in-law, was feeding D   and he fell a sleep while she nursed. I was reading in the chair not far from her. I looked up and saw her spank and jerk the new born because he had fallen a sleep. I told H   she should not do that. She then pretended she was playing with him. That was not the case.

Then few days later D   had messed his diaper, I had walked by the bedroom and she scolded the new born told him he was a bad boy, and hit him on the butt. Again I asked why and she again said she was kidding.

I have worked in a day care and my mother worked for a abuse center for small children. We know when someone is kidding or not.

My mother retried at 70 and they still wanted her to come back. She is now 91.

I base this information on working at a day care, raising my own, and experience with nieces and nephews

Now when I see him after he has been with H   : he is out of control and very hyper for a few days. It is very hard to handle him for the first few days.

Sandra Lynch

Sandra J Lynch

Dec 9, 2002

Figure 8: Sandra Lynch Letter Witness to H* Spanking Newborn D*

D* started cruising when he was about a year old. One day I happened to be descending the stairs when D* knocked something off of the coffee table. H* was watching TV and did not see me. She jumped up and laid into him. I could not believe my eyes. Mom had not exaggerated at all. H* clobbered him on the side of the head knocking him down, and before I could stop her, she had flipped him over, torn off his diaper, and was spanking him hard. The whole time she was nagging at the baby. H* was completely out of control, and she was wearing the bright red scowling exorcist face.

I demanded that in the future I would be in charge of punishment if there was to be any. H* relented, but that made me fearful, as it wasn't in her character to give in like that.

"D* Fell Backwards from a Chair"

June 06 1999 I was working up stairs, it was late, nearly 11:00. heard a blood curdling scream from D* downstairs. It certainly wasn't the usual boo-boo scream. H* was watching TV and D* was just balling. She replied, "he fell backwards off of a chair." That was all she said. I drove him to the emergency room at Brakenridge hospital. A doctor diagnosed a contusion on the back of the head.

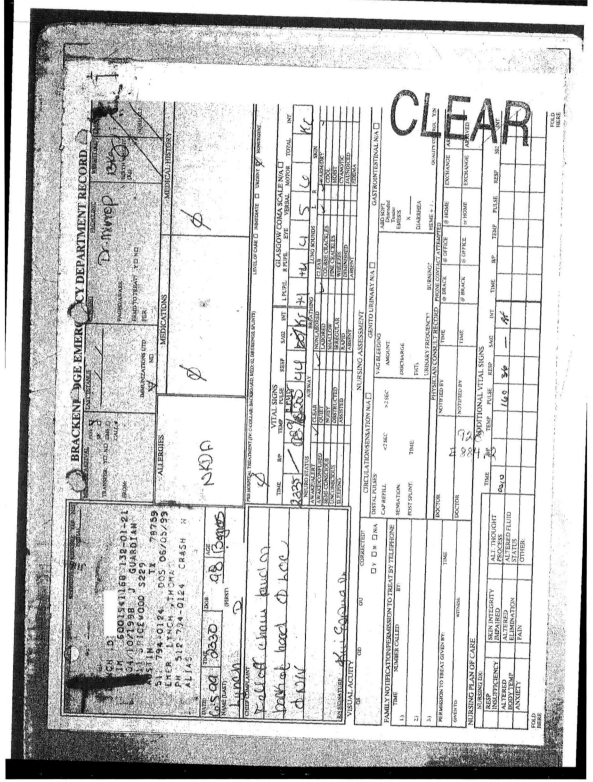

Figure 9: Hospital Report, "D* Fell Off Chair"

79

"D Hit the Wall"*

June 20 1999 it was a rerun. I was working upstairs, and heard the screams. This time H* explained that D* walked into a wall. He had a big bump on his forehead.

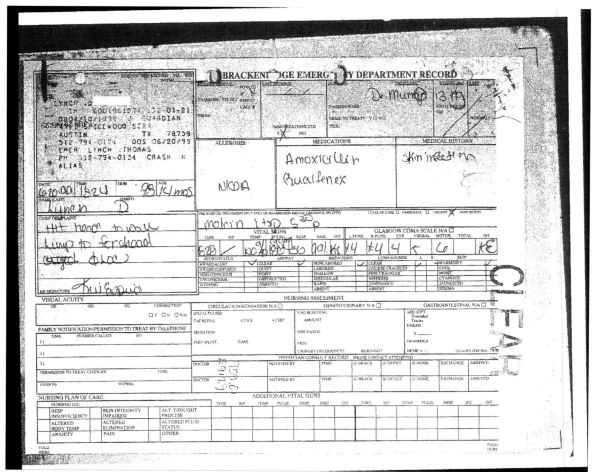

Figure 10: Hospital Report, "D* hit his head on wall"

"D Fell Down from the Dishwasher"*

August 8th 1999, H* explained we was screaming because he climbed up on the Dishwasher and fell off.

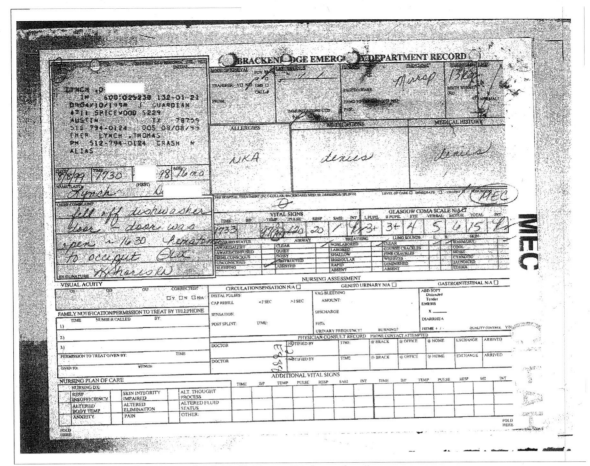

Figure 11: Hospital Report, "D* Fell From Dishwasher"

D* Climbs Stove for Boiling Water Pot While H* Watches TV

I came down stairs. H* was watching TV. I went into the kitchen. H* was boiling a pot of water, and D* was climbing the front of the stove to trying and get it. I blew a huge sigh of relief that I had caught him. I told H* what was happening, and she just said, "oh." She didn't even get up.

"D* Ran into The Cabinet Door"

H* now explained the baby had walked into an open cabinet door. I suppose an open cabinet door is a better explanation than an open door, for a one and half year old.

Indeed, by the time D* was two years old, we had been to the emergency room *eight times* for injuries which occurred while H* was watching the baby. It is possible that some of these incidences were due to neglect, as H*'s idea of watching the baby was to let him go free while she watched television - but that doesn't make them OK. Given what I know about H*, and what I had seen before, it seems probable that she had gotten in whacks when I wasn't there to see it.

When these trips to the hospital were presented to CPS and the social workers, H* claimed that I had made up the hospital trips in order to set her up, and those folks were satisfied with that explanation. I figure that CPS must use the following procedure.

1. Is the accused a man? If yes proceed to step 6, otherwise go to step 2.

2. Is the woman attractive? If yes proceed to step 7, otherwise go to step 3.

3. Is she likable? If yes, step 5, otherwise step 4.

4. Do you despise her, or has she challenged your authority? If yes, step 6, otherwise step 5.

5. The investigation is complete. The situation isn't worth my time.

6. Do everything in your power to destroy the predator.

7. She is vulnerable, now is a good time to make your move, if she is amenable, then proceed to step 8, otherwise 9.

8. Investigation results: The accuser has made false allegations, and we should consider punishing him. The accused is not only innocent, but she has to persevere a great deal.

9. Really up to you.

10. Oh, don't forget to comment on how precious the children are.

It would really be more accurate to call this organization LPS, Lesbian Police Services. 'What better group of people could there be for protecting women and children from men? ' The funny part is that of the social workers I have asked this question to don't see anything wrong with it.

Each time we went to the doctor H* provided excuses, and I tried to get the doctor into the discussion. I asked one doctor if it was usual for a baby to run into a cabinet door, fall backwards off a chair, or tumble from a table - the doctor said it was typical. "You know how active those little boys are." No one was very concerned that a baby would have accidents while mom was watching him. If father lifted a finger - well there was federal funding to cover that. One doctor went so far as to say it wasn't a good idea for the baby to have bumps and bruises, and that each time it occurred, we played a gambit. I thought to myself, "Yeah, doc, come to think of it I agree with you. No shit. You learned that one in medical school?" Today, D* seems to have some issue with his forehead. Crying gives him shooting pains. Apparently he lost the gambit, though it could be worse.

Looking for A House

H* and I had been searching for a house for years. If I liked the house, she didn't. I required that the house have a large yard, and be set away from busy roads. H* required that the house be 25 minutes driving distance to her office. Out of frustration, I finally agreed that I would let her search by herself and she would pick four houses she liked. I promised to agree with at least one of the four. Indeed she narrowed her selection to four houses. One of the four had a lot of maintenance issues. A second one was setup badly due to stair case leading from the front door to the living room, a large Southern exposure, and a yard on a hill. The third house looked great. I agreed to it. After I agreed, H* requested to see the house again. She came back and said she had changed her mind, "*the owners have a dog, so the house is dirty and I can not live in it.*" Our agent dropped us.

I called a broker friend who had done relocations for AMD. She dutifully resolved to find us a place. No case was too hard for Donna. She really ended up working hard for that commission. It must have been equivalent to single digits per hour of work. We found a place in Round Rock. It was a corner lot with a large yard. I set to fencing it in with a white picket fence, so that D* could not wander into the street. The house had only one floor, so I could keep a closer eye on the baby. We turned the dining room into a play room, so D* could sit in relative safety while H* watched television. If the neglect theory was correct, this would solve a lot of problems.

H* set up the closing. She was really into it, so I didn't see much cause to get involved. We met at the title company to sign the papers. I was presented with a deed of trust to sign. This document obligated me to pay for the house. However, there was another deed that was discussed, but I was asked not to sign. I called an attorney friend, and he advised me to not get cold feet and to just follow the title company's directions. The other deed turned out to be the ownership of the house. After closing I became obligated to pay off the loan, but I did not own the house.

Dad Became the Primary Caretaker

After H* had weened him, I was D*'s primary care taker. I feed from formula until he was on harder food. I changed his diapers. I took him for doctor's appointments and his shots.

Vaccine Administration Record

D.   98

Patient Name _____   Birthdate _____

"I have been provided a copy of the appropriate Centers for Disease Control and Prevention Vaccine Information Material(s) and have read, or have had explained to me, information about the diseases and the vaccines listed below. I have had a chance to ask questions that were answered to my satisfaction. I believe I understand the benefits and risks of the vaccines cited, and ask that the vaccine(s) listed below be given to me or to the person named above (for whom I am authorized to make this request)."

VACCINE	Date Given	Vaccine Manufacturer	Vaccine Lot Number	Initials of Vaccine Administrator*	Site Given	Signature of Parent or Guardian
DTP 1	6/10/98					
DTP 2	8/11/98					
DTP 3	10/12/98					
DTP/DTaP 4	7/15/99	Connaught	P0770AA 7316AB	LV	(R)thigh	
DTP/DTaP 5						
DT						
DTP-Hib 1						
DTP-Hib 2						
DTP-Hib 3						
DTP-Hib 4						
Hib 1	6/10/98					
Hib 2	8/11/98					
Hib 3	10/12/98					
Hib 4	7/15/99	(all	above)	patient present		
OPV/IPV 1	6/10/98					
OPV/IPV 2	8/11/98					
OPV/IPV 3	4/30/99	Lederle	0796B12	LV	po	
OPV/IPV 4						
Measles						
MMR 1	4/30/99	Merck	1981 1f	LV	(R)thigh	
MMR 2						
Hep B 1	4/98					
Hep B 2	5/11/98					
Hep B 3	10/12/98					
Varicella	7/15/99	Merck	04237	LV	(R)thigh	

*Signature of Vaccine Administrator

Lin Vieth, RN

Carolyn Schulze, RN

_____

Use reverse side if more signatures are needed.

Pediatric Associates of Austin, P.A.
1500 W. 38th Street, Suite 20 • Austin, TX 78731

Ellis C. Gill, M.D.   David E. Gamble, M.D.
Stephen R. Griggs, M.D.   Leslie R. Aiello, M.D.
Samuel A. Mirrop, M.D.

(512) 458-5323

84

TB Skin Tests	Type of Test	Date	Manufacturer	Lot Number	Reaction ·	Initials of Administrator

OTHER VACCINE	Date Given	Vaccine Manufacturer	Vaccine Lot Number	Initials of Vaccine Administrator*	Site Given	Signature of Parent or Guardian
Influenza	11/12/98					
Fluzone	11-11-99	PMC	U0144AA	JBS(0.25)	LT	
Prevnar	9-29-00	Lederle	471-211	C.S.	(R)thigh	
Fluzone	12-12-00	aventis Pasteur	U0400AB	L.S.	(R)thigh	

Figure 12: Vaccine Records All Signed by Dad

D* was a very good natured toddler. Where as other children would scream if you tried to take a toy from them, if I pulled on a toy D* was holding he would offer it to me. D* was a very curious and engaging child. In addition to his other toys I gave him a one inch diameter bolt that had washers and nuts on it. He would stare while I unscrewed the bolt. We had an air purifier due to all the Austin allergens, and D* would just stare at it on occasion. So one day while he watched I completely disassembled it and put it back together. He did not take his eyes off the process for one second. After it was over he laid down and slept for twelve hours. The constituent parts and construction of the machine were completely internalized. I also gave him geometric shapes cut from plywood.

Figure 13: Toddler D* Eating

Figure 14: Toddler D* with Truck

Of course I bought him a lot of toys. I got one of every animal in the zoo collection, a full set of construction vehicles, and farm equipment. He was also given a number of toys. We had no shortage. When we separated and after the temporary orders though D* was with me, H* kept the toys.

Figure 15: Toddler D* at San Antonio Zoo

You see that look in his eyes in the shot at the zoo? That is how I know I have connected with a topic, whether it is disassembling the air purifier, zoo animals, pumpkins, principals of mathematics, or sailing – that is the look of engagement that I work for.

Figure 16: Toddler D* at Laguna Gloria

We spent a lot of time outside hiking. D* road in the backpack. We used the mode of travel at big bend, at the San Antonio Zoo, and at local parks. The following shot is of D* in front of the beautiful oak tree is on the Shelton tract, which has since been developed. This tree is probably now in someone's back yard. I took D* to watch the construction of houses and buildings. We watched the condos next to Whole Foods from the point of a hole in the ground to the opening of the front door, and all stages in between.

Figure 17: Toddler D on Shelton Tract*

D* and I have been a team from the beginning, and it is beyond our understanding and the understanding of those who know us why any good intentioned person would interfere with such a vibrant father son relationship. Perhaps the answer is that no good intentioned person would.

Figure 18: Toddler D* Helping Out

Moved to Round Rock, June 2000

The In Laws are Back, Mr. Choi Watches "Total Recall" With D*

By 2000 the in laws were watching D* again. I had found a new pediatrician. Kretchman had me waiting, and H* was back to threatening me, and she told me she was going to divorce. I took my attorney's advice, and started to protect myself from false allegations. In addition, I plainly didn't trust Mr. Choi. I started taking D* to regular exams, especially if he had babysat by Mr. Choi. After Mr. Choi had him September 09 2000 Dr. Mirrop wasn't available, so I took D* the same hospital that we had taken him to for all of the "accidents." I asked for a wellness check. The nurse pried suspiciously. "Why would you want a wellness check?" I told her honestly that I didn't trust my in laws, they had been watching him, and that I wanted him checked out. "Checked out for what? She replied?" I told her "whatever." "Sexual Abuse?" she suggested. "Yes, make sure that hasn't happened," I said. They then ushered us into a room to talk to a social worker. I was told I couldn't leave. D* remained unexamined. I explained I was going to walk out, and that I would see my pediatrician the next day, and if they physically stopped me I would consider it kidnapping. I left. *Then* the hospital made a CPS report, and it was against me as a suspicious character. They still did not consider the prior ER visits.

Over two years had passed since Mr. Choi was thrown out of our place. Yet he was still in Austin. H* insisted that I let bygones be bygones. Apparently he had said "the words" just to get her riled up as he had been upset. I relented. They were to occupy the guest bedroom. I really wanted an extra pair of eyes for watching D*, but I didn't trust the in-laws. I was watching D* during the day, and working in the evenings and late at night. I was relieved to find out that everyone seemed to ignore D*. Often he waited outside my office until I finished working. On more than one occasion I walked out of the office at four in the morning to find him standing there waiting for father. I wasn't pleased that no one put him to bed, and I was concerned about his development, but the flip side was that I didn't have to worry as much about him early in the morning. One night I emerged from the office to find D* watching *Total Recall* with Mr. Choi. "See you at the party Rick," the TV blared.

More H*-isms:

"D* Ran Into The Counter" 2000 07 15

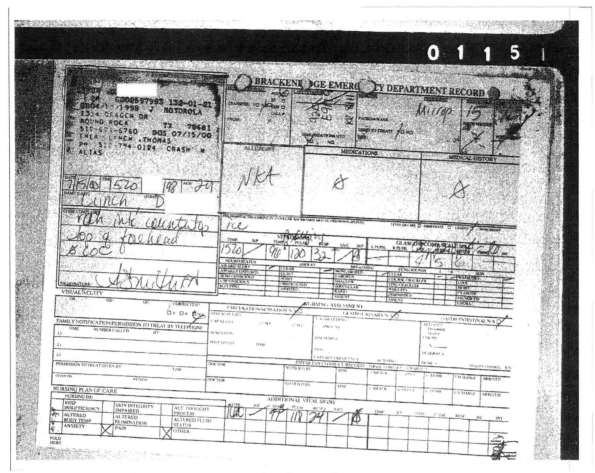

Figure 19: Hospital Report, " Ran into the Counter"

"Eat It Off of The Floor!"

H* feeding D* was the exact image of that "Jackson Polluck's Mother" poster. She would typically stand, sometimes while D* was also standing, and then try to spoon the food in from a bowl. Though D* was a very well tempered baby, It was still frustrating for both of them,

On one occasion D* was in a high chair, and H* had made Ravioli and put it in a bowl on the table of the high chair. D* attempted to use a spoon, but dropped some of the food on the floor. I was watching from the living room. H* then blew up and started screaming at D*. She picked him up out of the high chair and put him on the floor and told him to eat it off the food. I intervened at that point.

91

On another occasion, D* spilled a can of soda on the floor in the kitchen. H* scrunched up her face and started screaming at him. She picked something up from the counter, then saw I was there, she got on her haunches and started to wipe the floor. She explained that D* was out of control.

Dumps Dog Do-Do on Dad In Front of D*

Grandma Choi had paid for a puppy to be given to D*, which H* and I chose from a breeder. The concept was that when D* grew older, he would have a companion to run around the neighborhood with. As puppies will do, it made a mess in the house. It was in the playroom. D* had been using his dump truck to move dry dog food from a pile at one end of the room to the other, and he and the puppy were having a great time, when the puppy relieved itself on one of the piles. It was a grand mess which was strewn some distance over dog food and a few little plastic toys. I discretely placed the toys in the plastic bag with the urine soaked dog food and the paper towels. Just as I was completing the clean up, H* came home. She was furious that the dog had made a mess in the house and she started screaming at me. I saw no reason for her to be upset, as the mess wasn't even there anymore. I had already cleaned it up. The only indicators there had been a mess were the cleaning supplies and the trash bag, which I was about to take outside.

D*'s eyes were big like saucers watching her. She picked up the plastic bag. She was screaming that the mess was my fault and she was going to get even by messing me up. She poured the bag over my head, right in front of D*. She took one of the soiled toys and wiped it on my shirt. I did not move a muscle, or say a word. I just stood there. The whole time D* was trying to distract her by singing his ABCs.

H* was sleeping a lot. When she was awake, she was more aggressive than at earlier times. She was now slapping and scratching me, often times in front of D*. The nagging was constant, and the fits were closer together. Kretchman had insisted that I document her fits. At first I tried to hide the camera and recorder, but then I struck upon the idea that they might settle her down if she saw them. There was no discernible difference when I showed her the camera and recorder, she just went right on as before. I took pictures and made recordings of her blowing up at D* for spilling a sprite. I got recordings from the time she tried to make him eat off the floor in retaliation for having dropped food. I got a recording of her nagging, including a death threat. I recorded her declaration that she was going to divorce me and that I wouldn't see D* again. And the list goes on.

T> [jokingly] Thank God you are here H   , there has been a disaster.

H> What?

T> D   had Laika in the play room and was feeding her.

H> really

D> dog!

T> yep and she peed

H> you idiot!!!

D> ??

T> and there is some dog food there, and I am cooking so
I couldn't clean up.

H> why how could you let the dog inside

T> I didn't let the dog in, D   did.

H> That is why you let the dog in.

H> ?

T> no I didn't, well I turned my back and he let her in. I didn't
notice she was in

H> look at this   [shrieking] Why did you do this to me?

D> great, great! that great, great

T> [talking to D]

D> its doggy doggy

H> I'm sick of it sick of it

D> go to office

H> You did this on purpose right, Tom?

T> no I didn't do it one purpose

D> its dark here, its doggy, there is doggy, go to office [good advice]

H> every where! every where!

T> not every where

H> what is this what

T> most of that was already there, this isn't the mess

H> this is new one just now!

H> I hate the dog, really. Its stupid dog. Look at the back yard.

H> Why do I see grape seed everywhere?

T> grape seeds?

H> yeah

T> actually right now, while you were screaming at him, he spilled the grape bowl over here.

H> [shrieking] You are useless, why I help clean it? You clean it!

T> Ok, after I finish cooking.

H> [shreiking] clean up this mess!!!

pause

T> can I take your picture?

H> Shut up!

pause

H> you are ... you know that Tom?

long pause

H> ... stay clean inside?

T> don't know

H> you don't know so don't blame me.

T> I didn't blaming you

H> .. idiot

T> I wasn't blaming you.

long pause

H> useless! sick of it. [Shreiking] sick sick sick! Exactly like you, exactly like you! Is this the way. Shut up Tom I'll divorce you! That is why you broke. You always being me stick to you. You want ...

T> H

H> I don't have anything at home. No matter nothing.

T> H   it is just a little accident.

H> [Shreiking] It is not an accident!!! Look at those ...

T> It is just a little accident.

H> Who is going to clean up .. I am not going to clean that up.

T> [exasperated] I told you I would clean it up, just let me finish cooking.

H> [muttering and shrieking]

D> A, A, ABC [singing the ABC song] pizza lets go get pizza.

T> I 'm cooking fish. ...

H> [throwing stuff, things crashing, T took camera to take picture]
[shreiking] no! no! huh! You are doing this on purpose make the
evidence whatever. You are done. You are done. To make the evidence
whatever. [grabs the camera and starts pulling at it].

T> no no H

H> [screaming] I know you are doing this thing. It is the obvious
thing. huh? Out of context. You are done. You are done. what is
this? what is this?

T> don't break the camera

H> why why?

T> because it is $500 dollars

H> a huh $500 is so important. huh?

T> relax it is a small accident

H> why are you taking a picture, tell me!!

T> don't break the camera

H> why? to support me, you're trying to kill me right?

T> no I am not trying to kill you

H> you are trying to ruin my life.

T> no I am not ..

H> you are, why are you taking picture, explain that to me

T> I'll turn the camera off, just give it back to me

H> no no, why are you taking the picture? You want to aggrevate my
anger?

T> I would like to share it with other people.

H> why Tom? Out of context, what is this? You make a mess and I am
cleaning. and you are taking a picture. what is this

T> what you are doing is not cleaning

H> I am separating stuff

T> you throwing things

H> [shreiking at the top of her voice] of course how else would one
do this? I got collect all this stuff

T> I thought you said you were going to let me clean it up?

D> [muttering]

H> I'm told you whatever, .. bye Tom [stuff being tossed all over]

T> [talking to D] you stay in this other their and you will be ok. ok?

D> stay there

T> yeah you stay right there

D> [singing]ABCD I am staying in my .. I am staying in my chair!

H> [stuff still crashing] and you threw this away huh? [H holding up a small metal toy bus] why you throw this away? You going throw all those .. ah why did you throw this away?

T> well, because the wheels are broken off, and the dog peed on it.

[H hits T with the bus, and then wipes the pee off on his sweater.]

T> ouch!

H> you are just going to sit there, you know that [T wasn't sitting] [H strikes again]

T> ouch

H> and ...

T> and .. no I am going to clean

H> you can not clean, it is dirty already, all you can do is treat it chemically thats all [?] ... It is not possible. What is it you did? You slept?

T> no

H> what an idiot

    [H takes the garbage bag and hits T over the head with it. The stuff can be heard in the slam.]

T> you hit me

H> and you threw it away

T> ..

H> on purpose I know. You did it on purpose I know. It is not possible. .. you did it.

T> actually most of the mess is your stuff now that you have been throwing around.

H> This is pee dog , dog pee .. dog shit!

T> There is no dog shit there. That is dog food.

H> That is dog food there, yellow stuff?

T> No that is where the dog peed.

```
H> right.  Shit and pee is the same thing.  You think pee is cleaner
than shit, huh?

T> no, but what ? [H starts vacuum running to pick up the dried dog food.]

H> This is not possible.  I know! I know!  Now everything is
simple. ok .. You are collecting evidence.  That is your next step. I know!

T> H     you have hit me three times, and you wiped dog pee all
over me

H> no, prove it, prove it, prove that! How can you prove anything?  You did
this, evidence I have cleaned up, I am cleaning up actually.

D> [singing] ABCDEFG ABCDEFG

H> [still shreiking] what are you doing ... cooking ... taking my
picture ... idiot! ..

T> [heavy sigh] burned my fish [it was black]  Come on D        , lets
go for a ride.

D> ...

H> [still shreiking and clanging stuff]

D> ABC! [siging] ABCDEF,  ABCDEFJ, that way! that way! it is better
ABC ABCDEFG    I want my ABC!
```

Figure 20: Tape Transcript of H* Dumping Dog Mess On Dad in front of D*

Return from Indian Pow Wow

My friend Didi invited us to come to an Indian pow wow along with Sigfried and Isabel, and their daughter and her friend. H* had taken to sleeping a lot, and was on the couch in front of the TV, on or off, most of the time. She was in that position that morning. She didn't want to go, so D* and I went.

The event was setup at the high school off of South Lamar. There were booths selling leather goods, drums, flutes, velvet paintings and various nick nacks. D* was enthralled by the candy trailer, and after visiting it he walked around with a soda in one hand and a lollipop in the other. There was an area set up where Indians continued the oral tradition of telling stories. We sat and listened to a story about a bear hunt. D* had his picture taken with a man wearing the full garb of a chief. Inside the gym we watched a war dance, not unlike the one occurring in our very home on a daily basis.

Isabel asked us over for dinner. I called home and aroused H* from the couch. Miracle of all miracles, she answered the phone. She didn't want dinner, nor did she want us to have dinner. We went with our friends, and had an early dinner at their house. Afterwards we went directly home, and were early enough to go out for dinner if that ended up being necessary.

When we got home, H* growled from the bedroom. She was mad that we had gone to the pow wow so she was now on the war path. I grabbed the camera, then went to the bedroom to try and appease her. She grabbed D* and stuck his head into a pillow, and then gave one of her exorcist nags. These pictures became exhibits. The judge held up one of them while he read the decree after our first divorce (the temporary orders hearing).

The Indian pow wow became the pattern for our life. Whenever H* would start down the war path, D*, the dog, and I would retreat out of the house, get in the car, and go to the park. Usually we would manage to disengage, but on one occasion H* hit me in the face while I was in the car door way. D* was in his car chair in the back seat.

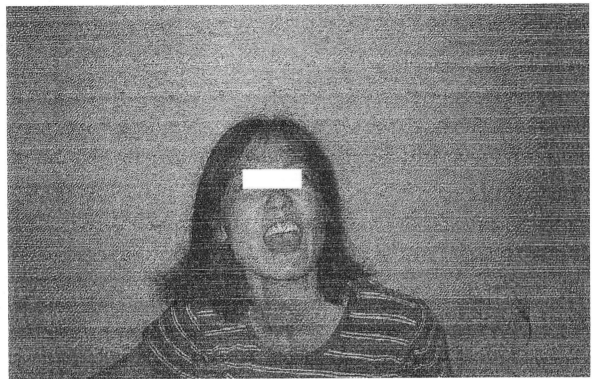

Figure 21: Court Picture 'the scream' From Incident H* Pushing D* Head

Puts D* in Water with Live Power Line

The house we moved into had an underground power feed. The feed came out of the ground on the side of the garage, directly next to a water faucet. Under the water faucet there was a flat rock, so that the water didn't splatter in the mud. H* had discovered a problem, she lifted the rock and showed me that the conduit had corroded all the way through. It was a little suicide arrangement. If one were to turn the water on, the water would collect under the rock and then run down the conduit over live 240VAC power lines. The saving grace would be if the 40 year old insulation remained in tact. She tossed the rock aside.

I wanted to call a plumber and have the faucet removed right away, but H* would not allow it. She said she couldn't do without the water softener, which was hooked up via some jury rig, and would be affected at least temporarily. I explained that we could take care of the water softener next, but this had priority. She wouldn't have it. The next day I heard water running in the back yard. There was more than one faucet in the back yard, but I decided to check and make sure. There was D* standing in a puddle of water next to the live conduit, with the faucet on full blast. H* was a safe distance away in the middle of the yard. I grabbed him out of the puddle and asked her what the hell was going on, and she replied, *"His will was stronger than mine, I could not stop him."*

I called OSGOOD plumbing and had them remove the faucet. Afterwards I happened to use the hole left by the missing faucet to run more telephone wires into the house. I contacted a contractor about fixing the conduit. They quoted me thousands of dollars. They said they would have to dig up the old conduit with a backhoe and replace it etc. I was collecting quotes, when Mr. Choi changed the course of events.

CPS spoke to H* about the conduit. They looked at it, and decided that standing in water pouring over 240VAC power lines was not dangerous. Something was said about telephone lines not posing a danger – but the telephone lines had not even been there at the time. An electrician came by and reiterated that poor little H* had not done anything dangerous, and he patched the conduit gratuitously. I want to see a demonstration. I challenge Lisa Osborne and the technician to come by my place, sign a release, and stand bare foot in a puddle of water along with live 240VAC lines. Isn't it funny that a CPS investigator would find something safe for a two year old, but not for herself? Recently a Round Rock policeman who is now working as a private investigator repeated the assertion that the 220VAC lines in the water puddle were not dangerous for D*. Apparently he was familiar with the incident, as he had this answer prepared when I started into the explanation. He gets paid $70 and hour, so I offered him $200 dollars to sign a release and stand in water with 220VAC. I noted it would only take a few minutes. He said he wouldn't do it. He didn't have enough time. I upped the amount to $2000. He asked, "Why would I do that?" Why indeed. In the opinion of the Round Rock police, it is safe for a bare foot 2 1/2 year old, but too dangerous for a grown policeman.

I considered that the sexist CPS biases that so many people spoke of might be avoided if I spoke with a male case worker. I called CPS 'hot line', but I wasn't put through, and no one returned my calls. On the *eighth* attempt I finally got someone, and I made a request for a male case worker. I wonder how many times a woman with abuse issues must call before gettting a return call, or if she isn't just put through directly.

The female LPS worker who eventually returned the eighth call demanded to see me personally, and refused to consider transferring the report to a man, though she said that she could arrange for a man to be present. She explained that a man could not handle my call because there was only one man in the entire division, but most importantly in her view there was simply no reason for it. It simply could not be allowed.

We discussed an appointment time. I told her my schedule which was free for most of the following weeks, but there was a day I would be out of town. She insisted on setting the appointment for the very day I would be out of town, and no other. She pretended to be nice about it and said it was OK because it was a tentative appointment, and she didn't really expect me unless I happened to be able to make it. However, later she accused me of having purposely stood her up on that day. It was a cute little setup that demonstrated CPS is a misandrist organization.

Hey, Lets Just Put Father in Jail - and Get Paid For It

The only person giving H* any grief over trying to fry toddler D*, and her other fits, was me. My pile of tapes was out of her reach so she could not destroy them. The solution must have seemed clear to the Chois. On Hiroshima day in 2000 I awoke before D* and started to work in the office. Later when D* got up, I moved him to the play room. Mr. Choi was in the kitchen. About 10 in the morning I heard a siren going off down the hall. No, it wasn't a siren - it was Mr. Choi calling in a sort of winding whistle, "Tom! Tom!" I grabbed my tape recorder off the desk. Mr. Choi was very upset about something. I put D* in the play room, and addressed Mr. Choi in the living room.

Mr. Choi was trying to pick a fight. He said to me, "You are not a man." I nearly laughed. The line was right out of a documentary we had reviewed in an anthropology course years ago. The primitives were sticking out their chests and picking fights to establish a pecking order while crowing that very line, just like birds establishing a pecking order. He did his best to get me riled.

He tried another line. He told me it was not my house, so I would have to leave. Quizzically I asked him to explain this statement. According to Mr. Choi, the wedding gift they had given us was actually still his money, and part of it had been used in the down payment. Later I would discover that I had been tricked by H* into signing the deed of trust, and not the warrantee deed. So in fact, the house was entirely hers, though I was obligated to pay for it. It seems that she had made some plans along with her father that I was not privy to.

I replied that he was a guest, but his welcome had expired. He would be leaving. It was a re-run of the day baby D* came home. Mr. Choi was aggressive, and it appeared to be only the three of us at the house. I called the Round Rock police and asked for help. I compare this to an incident that occurred when I was in college. A man had over stayed his invite and was occupying a room at the co-op. We called the police and they ejected him. I used the same words to ask the police to help me eject the visitor who had over stayed his welcome but refused to leave, but the events unfolded differently. The receptionist at the police department asked if I was married. When she found out that I was, she said, "*You have to have your wife's permission before we can send anyone.*"

With foreboding, I called H* at the office to ask for permission from that honored and special member of the American Brahman class. She came home, and told me off. They double ganged me. I created some space by pulling H* out of the house to have lunch at the Vietnamese restaurant up the street. We discovered that Mrs. Choi, was home, and out in the yard. She watched D* while we were at lunch.

Mrs. Choi didn't speak English, and even considering that, she was usually quiet. It was easy to not notice she was around. She did not appear to fit the stereotype of the feisty Korean woman. H* had said that her father had once cheated with a younger woman, and Mrs. Choi was much younger than Mr. Choi. Was this his second marriage, and now Mrs. Chois was the transgressor H* referred to? Supporting this hypothesis was the fact that H* fought heatedly with Mrs. Choi. There was real hatred in her voice, like when she did her exorcist act. On one occasion H* screamed at her for several minutes in the parking lot outside of Dan McKluskie's, because her mom had "bought garlic salt at the store."

At lunch H* only fanned the flames. She said that I had thrown away a prized possession that belonged to her parents, *a plastic water pitcher.*

The plastic water pitcher was from Walmart. It had a carbon filter in it and had cost about $14. I had asked for permission the night before to toss it while I was cleaning. I had tossed a bunch of other junk too, most of which came from my office and the garage, and had never been taken out of boxes after we moved. This stuff shouldn't have been moved in the first place, but we had been in a hurry while packing. We were using purified water for the baby, so the pitcher served no purpose but to create confusion. The evening before when I asked H* if she minded if I tossed it. I explained that carbon filters make the tap taste better, but the result wasn't as good as the drinking water we were already using. H* had said it was OK to toss the pitcher; now she was saying the opposite.

She was not at the top of her game as she had been when arguing against counseling, or perhaps she just did not have as much to work with while creating this travesty. She admitted that the pitcher also came from our apartment, and that in fact we had bought it. "So then,'" I asked, "How is it your father is so upset about it." "I gave it to him," she cleverly replied. She then attempted to switch the conversation to the telephone I had thrown away. Angrily she accused me of tossing a telephone. I pointed out that the telephone in question was mine since long before the marriage, that it had always lived on my desk - and it had ceased working. She dropped the phone plank, and the reality the artifice dropped into view like an big boob lost from a bra. She stuffed it back in and went back to being angry over the loss of the precious pitcher.

In hindsight it is apparent that I should not have argued with her, as I was only providing the test vehicle for her fabrications. The prized water pitcher was a ridiculous story, but as it turns out, it doesn't take much.

Back at the house instead of settling things down, H* accused me of being *violent* because I had *violently* compacted the trash the evening before to get all the junk to fit. She said it made her mother *afraid* the way I stomped and pounded on *the garbage*. This was trial balloon number three. Stupidly I pointed out the problems with it. The trash container was on the side of the garage out of sight of any windows, and there had been no one in the yard when I heaved that so special and dear water pitcher on to the top of the pile. I pointed this out. "Well," she said, "Mom had peeked around the corner."

I offered to buy another pitcher, but was told, "that is not the point." Indeed, it wasn't the point. No one cared about the pitcher. What was wanted was my blood. That was the point. H* left to go back to Motorola while her father picked up the slack.

From this date until now about six women involved in the divorce have repeated word for word the phrase "I think you are violent and you make me feel uncomfortable," no matter how inappropriate the situation. Most police departments in the U.S. have adopted policies that removed police discretion when this is said. Policemen are instructed they must make an arrest. This has been done as part of an education program on domestic violence, which in turn, has been paid for with VAWA money (Congressional grant), which in turn stipulates the money must be spent on protecting women.

Except for the couple of times when D* toddled over to see what the fuss was about, he stayed in his playroom. Late in the afternoon he dozed off and Mrs. Choi put him in the crib I had made for him. Mrs. Choi had sewed the mosquito net that went over it.

Mr. Choi yelled and made digs at me for another three or four hours. I had long hitherto run out of tape for the recorder. It was five o'clock in the evening and I felt sick that I had gotten nothing done all day. My opportunities to get work done were precious and few. I repeated that his welcome was over, and added that he would be leaving that evening. Since the police wouldn't help, I started moving his stuff out of the house myself. I told him I would put it in the yard, or garage, and that he could return later to get it. I went into our guest room and got the little TV we had bought, and started taking it out. I would make a gift of it while simultaneously making a symbolic gesture. He met me in the hall, he was tense, and it looked like he was going to slug me. He shoved me. The jolt loosened my grip, and the TV fell to the stone floor. I did not mind, he could take his gift in any form he wanted it, and as far as I cared at that moment, the rest of their stuff could go the same way. I went back for something else.

H* magically reappeared. I don't know who called her, or if she ever really left. There had not been enough time for her to have driven back from work. Mr. Choi met me in the doorway of the guest room, and yelled something in Korean using his sergeant style ejaculation method. His eyes were bulging. My head smarts as I write this just remembering the way he hopped up and head butted me. It felt like a big boulder had hit me on the forehead. I heard a crack like an egg. He then reached over and tried to stick his fingers in my neck. I jerked back. I staggered and H* jumped on my back and started biting me. Mrs. Choi had been standing there ready, she said something, they looked up, and she took a picture. It was a trophy shot. They could frame it and put it next to the one H* took of me after she created a scene at the Moulin Rouge. I was like a big fish strung on a line. I reached for the camera, and Mrs. Choi stumbled out of the room. H* took the camera, and Mrs. Choi crossed the hall, grabbed D*, and ran out of the house.

I left the house muttering, I said I was going to see a divorce attorney, but drove to the hospital. I was given a cat scan, and dressings. Then some policemen came. I requested to make a complaint, but was blown off. I wasn't among the special classes of people they serve, so their other, more important social work had to take priority. You see, when the Brahman woman speaks, the police listen, so they arrested me. It didn't matter that I had a concussion, lacerations on the neck, bite marks on the back - and they were without marks. I hadn't hit or done anything to anyone - but this did not matter. I had made the innocent, weak, and all so peaceful woman *uncomfortable*, and that is all that matters under modern municipal law enforcement, as it was written directly into the RRPD duty statement hanging on the wall in their lobby. To repay for this sin I was to give H* all of my worldly possessions and forfeit my liberty.

Later when I was shown one of the policeman's notes about the incidence, my hitherto positive opinion about policemen was shattered. The officers had rewritten my statements to make me look guilty, and thus make it easier to prosecute. My attorney told me that this was a common practice. I can now say, from experience, there is a good reason for the right to silence; although when the police came to the hospital they never said 'you have a right to remain silent' like is shown on television. In fact, if I had remained silent I got the distinct impression that I would have been charged for non-cooperation. My fate had been sealed the moment a complaint had been filed against me saying that I had made a woman feel uncomfortable.

I had thought that the Chois had complained to the police about their water pitcher, so I was babbling about that in my defense. Many months later a person who witnessed the Chois talking to the police explained to me that the Chois and the police worked together to find a better story. They decided to claim that I had beaten up grandma Choi. Later they showed pictures of her with bruises on her arms. They claimed I harbored some resentment of her. I was never told what the resentment was supposed to be. They said I had blown up at her and beat her up for no apparent reason, and that they were beating me up just to stop me from beating her, and apparently they just got a little carried away, which was OK with the police because I don't belong to a protected class, so it is OK to beat me up. No charges were filed on Mr. Choi for that, even though he had confessed to it. But at the time I wasn't told what I was being accused of, so I babbled about the water pitcher. The police interpreted this to be a non-denial. How clever of them.

Though their story didn't fit in with the earlier call I made to the police, the setting, or the facts – all of that did not matter. They didn't bother asking me if it was true. They used so little critical analysis that *they found Mr. Choi to be their best choice for an official Korean translator!* We live in a city of over a million people, there is an active Korean population here, and professional Korean translators advertise in the book. Yet, the Round Rock police used Mr. Choi to interview Mrs. Choi. It follows that we have no idea what she thought was going on, what she really said, or even if she had been asked the questions posed by the police. Mr. Choi was providing the answers.

Another attorney later explained another problem, that criminal attorneys are typically anxious to plead their clients guilty. Criminal attorneys get paid a fixed rate in Texas, independent how much time they spend. It follows that for these attorneys to increase profits, they must turn over as many clients as possible. Guilty clients go through their office much faster than innocent ones, so it is in their best interest to plead their clients guilty. And as a bonus, those found guilty go into the private jails that are run for profit, into education programs that are run for profit, and into the office of private practitioners who support their families on the profit. This system has been feeding on the lower classes for many years, but through divorce it has made its way into the middle class. Divorces are a growth market demographic for all social programs.

Social workers came to the house. *They had standard forms.* They urged H* to check the box that said I had a drug or alcohol problem. But something had changed. She refused. An officer was brought in to coerce her her further. He told H* that he saw these things all the time, and that if she didn't check the box and follow through so that the police could throw me in jail, that she would be murdered by me. It was a crime in the abstract, and *he guaranteed to her that it would happen.* I had only trouble to look forward to if the officer's profile was taken seriously by the police department – and why wouldn't it be?

A friend found another attorney. After he talked to the police, they decided to destroy the arrest records.

One has to wonder why, when they were on the brink of getting exactly what they wanted, the final solution as you would have it, why did everyone change their minds? H* would have the house, the paid for luxury car, the good job in America, the parents naturalized, and me gone. My career would be destroyed and I would probably never able to return. God help D*. H* was nice. Mr. Choi was talking about family honor, and then *finally* decided to leave.

Perhaps the police didn't want that little call in the morning to become public, the one where the police woman told me I needed my wife's permission to ask for help. Or perhaps it was because of the inconsistencies in the grandma story. But logic and reason didn't have anything to do with it before.

Perhaps what happened that an attorney friend wondered about Mr. Choi, and did what the police and the first attorney avoided, he checked Mr. Choi's background. He discovered that Mr and Mrs. Choi appeared to be wanted felons in South Korea. It appeared that they had stolen at least some hundreds of thousands of dollars, and he and H* had laundered it. The money may have been sitting right here in Austin in an AG Edward's account controlled by H*. Perhaps they didn't want to risk the money.

The Korean Stocks Turn Out To Be Stolen

The investigator came back with a letter from the U.S. Embassy FBI legal attaché. I had a separate account with the investigator so that Ted didn't pay him out of the retainer. It was for this reason I was copied on them via fax directly. This investigator would cost me another $15,000. I used the fax machine out of the box without setting the date on it. I didn't know the machine was going to write headers on the documents, so they got all of the default settings. The hand written note at the upper right is that of Ted's legal assistant noting they got a copy of the fax via hand delivery. The embassy's fax banner is accurate.

Received Mar-05-98 12:14pm   from 4046592265 → TOM LYNCH   page 1
      01/18/1994 21:54   4046592265   AALLSTATE BONDING   HAND DELIVERY

MZ 6/11/01 142pm

Southeast Recovery Service
165 Peachtree St. SE
Atlanta, Ga. 30303
Phone: (404) 659-5855
Fax: (404) 659-2265

Dear Mr. Terry,

The following letter is a result of months of investigation , telephone calls , and negotiation with The U.S. Embassy in Seoul, Korea along with the Korean authorities. Instructions from Mr. Seungkyu Lee who is the legal attache at the embassy for the F.B.I. State not to divulge the information contained within the letter that would in any way be harmful to the case that is now in the hands of the I.N.S. and should be close to the deportation stage. Should you have any questions please feel free to give me or my office a call and we will assist you any way possible.

Thank You,
Darin D. Strader

Embassy of the United States of America

Office of the Legal Attache
United States Embassy
Seoul, South Korea

File No.

8 May 2001

Darin Strader
Worldwide Detective Agency

RE: CHOI Tae-Yung
      MOON Song-Ja

      Mr. Strader.

      This letter confirms that you have provided information on the referenced individuals as illegal alien residing in the U.S. and may be wanted by Korean law enforcement authorities for fraud. I have relayed the information to the Korean National Police Agency (KNPA) on Choi and his wife MOON Song-Ja. The KNPA recently confirmed that they are indeed wanted for fraud committed on 3/15/98 in Korea.

      I will provide this information to our Immigration and Naturalization Service (INS) for further action. I thank you for the information your agency has provided on this matter

                                Sincerely,

                                Seungkyu Lee
                                Legal Attache, American Embassy, Seoul

TOTAL P.02

Figure 22: Letter from Embassy's Legat's Office that Mr. and Mrs. Choi are Wanted

Father in Hospital 2000 08

I did not feel well so I set an appointment at the Mayo Clinic in Scottsdale. They biopsied and found tissue damage in my gut. They said it did not match Celiac disease, but suggested I try a glutton free diet. It helps.

D* Fear of Sirens

While concentrating hard to pick his words, D* asked me, "Why do the police work for mommy?" He was very concerned. He was studying the problem. He had seen all of the people who came to the house after the 'lets throw father in jail' incident. He saw his father taken away in a police car. For some years after the incident D* would become agitated upon hearing a siren. On one occasion we were at Home Depot when a fire truck came into the parking lot with the siren on. He became very agitated and shook. "Lets go!" he insisted.

Father and D* And Our First Pumpkin

H* did not want to do Halloween. We were on our own, so we got a big pumpkin, and had a blast carving it.

Figure 23: D Carving Pumpkin*

H* Feeds D* Several Bottles of Triaminic

On November 6, 2000 NPR had an article on the radio that said that Triaminic could cause strokes in young women and children. Triaminic went on sale at Walgreens, and H* came home with a whole bag of it. There were at least five bottles, perhaps seven in the bag. A couple of days later I noticed a couple of empty bottles on the counter. I looked around for the bag or its contents. They were no where to be found. She had given it all to D*.

H* Tells Me To Leave, Announces Separation, Cancels Thanksgiving, "Take Your Dirty Bird" 2000 11 19

Since she got her citizenship H* asked me to leave often. The problem was that she always said she wanted D* to stay. I wasn't going to leave him to grow up in that environment. She also made allusions to a boyfriend, but insisted that she meant girlfriend. In either case the person was not identified. I think she didn't want to initiate the divorce for fear it would look bad at the INS.

```
                       Tom>was it a good book
              H        >I don't care.  [[it was something]]


              H        >Leave Tom Please
H      explodes        At least leave me one favor
                       leave me!! leave us!!  This week.
                       it doesn't cost anything you just __leave__
                       did I miss anything, don't give you?
                       it is very difficult to rent a place because those
                           illegal immigrants come and sit there and never
                           leave.
                       you are just like that! those parasites!
slamming               I should thought more careful when I get married to you
                         I don't know why it goes into me
                       to be divorced from you!!!

                       I call all your friends.  I talk about you if
                       you don't do this.  I will ruin your social life.
                       you want that?

(time 2000 11 19 11:19:56)  (elapsed 1136 seconds)
                       Tom>you're going to call my friends?

              H        >all of your friends.  About what you did.  I'll call your mom,
                       you will be in the dog house for the rest of your life.
gingerly               I'll do that.

                       Tom>what 'd'ya going tell them?

              H        >The rest of your life ..
                       I don't want to look like a saint
                       you are not.
                       because I don't have any .. I mean

                       Tom>what could you tell them?

              H        >why not?
                       because you're not using me
                       you want me to do that?
                       if you don't do it
                       I'll call
                       I'll start from today
                       huh?

                       Tom>and what are you going to say?

              H        >we we are going to divorce but you are leaving
                       I don't know why
                       And I'll tell them what happened ...
                       huh?
                       Are you worried, a little bit?
                       Are you worried?

                       Tom>no mainly I just kinda feel a little bit sick

              H        >what?
                       you think I'm threatening that I'll call [[three words]]
                       I'm just I just want you to leave easy

                       Tom>so your threats should be taken seriously?
```

```
         H      >this one?
                 on on the divorce?
                 yes!
                 I want a divorce.
                 I want a divorce. Period.
                 Period. No compromise.
                 No reconsideration.
                 There is no room for it.
                 I decided.
                 That's very bad, I mean bad thing actually
                 Effecting baby
                 I'll do it
                 I'll arrange that
                 it takes a long time, but I'll do that Tom
                 any how, really I am serious Tom

         Tom>[[mumbles]]

meek voice  H   >I might call the police
                 serious If you believe that thing
(time 2000 11 19 11:22:05) (elapsed 1265 seconds)
         Tom>Like what H       ?

         H      :>I'll tell them
                 I want a divorce he doesn't leave
                 I wanted him to leave from my house

                 you have a criminal record there they might think you are haras
                 so get real!

         Tom>would you tell them that I am harrassing you?

         H      >you are
                 because not leaving here
                 you're not out
                 and smirking something!
                 you're not harassing me though?

         Tom>smoking something??

         H      >smirking!

         Tom>smirking oh, I'm not smirking, I just feel sick.

         H      >I don't care! leave somewhere.

                 [[something in the background]] you never care

         Tom>heavy sigh

         H      >[[mumbles]]
                 leave
                 go to work
                 leeeeave!  leeeave!

         Tom>yes I think I will go to work

         H      >leave
                 you are free, really free
                 if [[two three words]] over I don't care
                 we are done, ok?
```

```
                            from today we are separated
                            but we er I give you give you divorce notice
                            decided
                            and then it will be over

(time 2000 11 19 11:24:10)  (elapsed 1390 seconds)
                   Tom>last time you got upset like this you changed your mind about
                            an hour later

          H        >this is not last time.   no no no
                            no it is not last time
                            I think abou er I thought over, about 10 days.

                            leave us now
                            you think you are
                            I'm very very so find it so weak because I love you
                            [[incomprehensible]]
                            If I were you I could have left long time
                            because your not because your not me
                            you don't know what you .. it is like my boss
                            you don't know what is some priority in your life
                            you want to do everything
                            [[incomprehensible]]

                   Tom>so you say your boss is stupid?

          H        >he is stupid, because he he does everything,
                            but he is one person.  he is [[word]]. He doesn't help
                            anything. he is rediculous.

                            if you want your life back, you should leave
                            [distracted] ah shoot
                            [[incomprehensible]]

                   Tom>always do my best


more to transcribe ...
     H        accuses Tom of experimenting with the baby
     H        tells Tom to leave with the turkey, as it won't
        be cooked in her house

          H        > doing your best doesn't mean much Tom, it is a very
                            irresponsible thing.
                            you don't leave us Tom, it is a very irresponsible thing


                   Tom>what do you mean

          H        >you experimented with him no?

                            and bring your stupid bird with you

                   Tom>I was going to cook it
```

Figure 24: Transcript, H* Nagging, She Announces The Separation, 2000 11 19

H* On The Floor With Broken Glasses

My friend Dan and I had gone out. When we came back we found H* on the floor laying among broken glasses. I said, "hello?" she answered slowly. She wasn't cut or hurt. She got up ok, but she was slow to respond. D* was in the other room.

Almost Hired Attorney Jim Piper November 2000

Given at that had happened, how hard could it be to divorce her? Still I wanted to make sure it was done cleanly. I got into the car drove downtown to meet an attorney of great experience and skill, Jim Piper. We met in a conference room where Jim explained what could be expected. I replied that I hadn't decided to use him for the divorce yet, but was thinking about it seriously. I would let him know when I had reached a decision.

Before talking to Jim, I had tried to contact Karen Kretchman, but her old number was no longer valid. I got her new number from an attorney friend. She had moved to Phoenix where she was practicing with her husband. Her voice mail came on, but she refused to return my calls.

Jim said Kretchman was wrong, as there was no particular age one had to wait for, though obviously, there were additional issues for younger children. He said two was fine. I explained I wanted to make the divorce go as quickly as possible. I wanted thorough up front planning, followed by a review. That is when he collected the retainer.

I went back to the house, and H* was home. On the answering machine was a message from Jim's assistant. She left her name and number, and requested that I contact her or Jim to "discuss the divorce further." Surely H* had heard the recording. I went back to Jim's office and requested to see the file. I checked the contact information, and the home phone was clearly marked as such. I requested to speak with Jim. I asked him why the assistant had called and left a message on the home recorder where H* could hear it, when I hadn't decided to divorce yet. Jim said dryly. "We didn't do it."

"So this isn't your legal assistant on the tape?"

"Nope didn't happen.'"

Initially I thought the message was an accident. All I wanted to hear from Jim was an acknowledgment that his office had made a mistake, so it wouldn't be repeated. I was concerned about what H* might do should she know I hired an attorney. One could never predict what she might do.

As we talked further and he continued the bald face lie denial even while he knew I was holding the tape, and doing so without even checking with his legal assistant, I realized three things. First off, he had no respect for my sensibilities. Secondly, the man could lie without even flinching a muscle on his face, and thirdly, he had left the recording for the purpose of expediting my decision to go forward. This was not the kind of person I wanted to work with. I managed to encapsulate my conclusion in a single sentence that blandly repeated a basic truth about him. If I had said it to another person, he or she would probably not have considered the words to be insulting. Jim was speechless, perhaps for the first time in his life. He turned red, but had nothing to say. You could have cooked an egg on his head. He took a step backwards and forwards, but still had no reply. I wondered if he was going to

112

have a heart attack or a stroke. I have never seen such a reaction to such simple words before. I walked away. I requested my retainer to be returned from the office, and got a small part of it. Jim kept thousands of dollars for an initial consultation and an initial conference discussion.

H* Cancels Christmas

Then she refused to have Christmas. She explained that there would be no tree in her house. She said it was superficial for everyone to go out an buy gifts. It was nothing more than a commercial boon that only benefited shop keepers. She said they were trying to introduce it in Korea, but she didn't like it. I surprised D* by setting up Christmas with gifts at my office downtown.

Figure 25: Dad and D* Christmas 2000

Separation from H*

As I thought about it further, I realized I had been thinking incorrectly that H* would make a big deal out of D*. H* wanted everything, so she added D* to the list, but there was no evidence that she was attached to him. The was a second problem as all the attorneys were telling me that in Williamson County, where the house happened to be, that the three judges in the county all believed that children belonged with their moms independent of all other variables. Laurie Nowlin recounted a case of hers where a mom was torturing her kids with lit cigarettes, but her client, who was the father, still lost custody. After I told the goings on at our house to attorney Ed Walsh, he replied in his Calvin Coolidge simplicity "you'll lose." So I decided to separate as she had ordered me to, and we moved to Travis county. We would then divorce in Travis.

I packed up D* and Laika the Dog, and we moved to the south side of Austin, which was in Travis County. We went back every week or two when H* requested. I could then watch her with D*. It was really a great arrangement, and if I had been more aware of American social ills, I would have stuck with it. I was purposely discrete about leaving so as to avoid a big confrontation that would surely have piqued her ire and caused a vindictive reply. A part of me really wanted my son to have a normal relationship with his mother, although I knew that to be impossible. I hired a nanny to take care of D* while I was at work. I gave her specific directions to concentrate on him, but she also cooked and cleaned. She said she had nothing better to do when he napped. It was really nice to come home to a clean apartment with food waiting, and to have nothing with higher priority than to spend time with D*. After three months, we had most of our clothes moved, but some of D*' toys and books, my books, major possessions, and most of my office, remained at the house. What I didn't know at the time, was that the few personal possessions I removed at that time would be all that I would ever get. Also, very little of the office material would be returned. I took an off site contract so I didn't need the material at my home office all the time. Although it was not ideal, the periodic visits to the house were sufficient for keeping up with the office. In between visits I left the office at the house locked.

Figure 26: D* at Apartment after Separation

After work D*, Laika the Dog, and I would go exploring. The apartment complex was built next to undeveloped woodland. Some older boys had build a tree fort in the woods, and we played on it. We came across some wild blackberries, and made fantastic dessert sauce from them. Down the street at Dick Nichols Park, D* made friends with two other boys,

Austin and Dylan. Their mother was also an adventurous type, and she invited D* to play with the boys at a number of parks around town. We continued to visit our favorite park at Cypress Creek. Laika was famous at that park. The kids would throw things for her to fetch. One day some older boys got into a keep away the Frisbee war with Laika. They would run and try to tackle her before she got the Frisbee. Laika returned the favor and tackled one of the boys and took the Frisbee. The boys were amazed by Laika. She sure was a good breed for the kids.

Of all the attorneys I interviewed, I actually liked Richel Rivers the best. Richel later said she heard that I didn't have enough money, which is why she turned down the case. We had never discussed the amount of the retainer. This was my first experience with the attorney gossip network. There would be many more. The attorneys were a very close knit group, and they loved to trade labels and sound bites. Richel didn't stipulate who had given her the information. There were a couple of possible sources, both attorneys. I was irked. What was Richel doing calling around anyway? All we had done was a short initial consultation, but still she had to be looking for the *cheat*, the *angle*, or the *inside story*. This turned out to be another hallmark of the attorneys. My second attorney choice was Ted. Mom put in fourteen thousand dollars, and I put in twenty-one, to make up Ted's required amount of $35,000. Mom was very concerned for D* after what she had seen.

In the spring of 2001 D* and I took a vacation to New Mexico and Colorado. H* was fully expecting to go along. I had to tell her she wasn't invited. This was the first time she had been excluded, and the first time she didn't get her way. It simply wasn't appropriate for us to go together after the papers had been served. Besides, I hoped to have fun on the trip, and bringing H* would exclude that possibility. We had two tickets for the Silverton Line that went between Durango and Silverton, via steam engine. One for me, one for D*.

Figure 27: D* With Steam Train Engine

We had a great time. In Silverton, we bought two matching T-shirts with a picture of the steam engine on the front. On the way back from Durango, we stopped and camped in the mountains in New Mexico. It was here that I decided to settle the potty training matter. We were having problems with the concept. The mothers play group mailing list gave me the idea. A mom suggested dressing the child only in a shirt while we were in the house. She said it worked out much better when the boy could see what was going on. I didn't want to do this in the house, but here was our chance outside. I gave D* a big T-shirt, but nothing else. We went for a long walk up an established trail that went though beds of mountain flowers. Part way, D* had to go. He wanted a diaper. I told him we didn't have any more diapers. Then I told him the flowers needed watering. He really liked the concept. He watered the flowers. We went further along the trail. On the way back, again he needed to go. I told him the trees needed watering. He found this to be fantastic idea so he watered a big oak tree.

D* and I were hiking. He was wearing his T shirt. He found a pine cone, he had never seen one before. He ran over and asked, "what is this?"

116

Figure 28: D* Discovers Pine Cone

On the drive back while going through Santa Fe D* had to go. He wanted to know where the trees were. The only trees directly visible and accessible were in a big line along a plaza heading up to some government building. We parked and D* walked up to a tree and went. It was very funny. He never asked me for a diaper after this. Though mom continued to use them because she didn't want to chance any accidents.

Later when D* was back at the Lycée in school, he went out on the playground and pee-ed on a tree. He got in big trouble for it. Alas, the natural method had a drawback. They pointed him at the restroom.

There was one interesting event, when we were driving through the downtown area of a small town in New Mexico, we got caught up in a traffic stop. The policeman had all the cars lined up down the road and were checking everyone for sobriety. I pulled up and rolled down the window, the policeman asked me so questions and looked us over. They also ran the plates, just as they did for the cars in line in front of us, and those behind us. We were near an Indian reservation, and this was their method of controlling drunk driving. Later H*'s attorney would have a habit of reporting me for abducting D* based on a technicality she created in the exchange schedule. Had this traffic stop incident occurred later, and our name was on some list, our vacation would have been a horror.

On H*'s next visit she was very upset. D* was still insisting on wearing his T-shirt from Silverton with a picture of the mountain and the train. She disposed of it. It went the way of the clock and the baby clothes.

D* and I decided to get a house. D* and I both suffer from Austin allergies, and he played on the floor a lot, so I made hard floors a requirement. We found a house in town that had a hard wood floors in all rooms except what would be the playroom, and a yard. However, when it came time to move in, the house wasn't ready. Luckily, there was another house for

117

rent just up the street that also had hardwood floors, and that house also had a large den in it. I paid to have the carpet changed to linoleum in the den and we used it for a playroom. I hired a decorator, and the end result turned out very well. I picked the location because it was just down the street from a French international school. The school taught Spanish and French. Also, the parents and students were an interesting group of folks. I thought it would be a good experience for D*, so he was on the list to begin in the fall.

H*: I'm going to come to the Birthday Party and Tell Everyone How Bad of a Person You are. 2001 04 10.

I had arranged for a party at Dick Nichol's park, and drove by to pick H* up. She started nagging, and told me she was going to come to the party just to tell all my friends what a horrible person I was. This was not the first time she had made such threats. I really didn't want the scene on D* birthday at the park. I wasn't going to exclude her, but I sure wasn't going to deliver her either. I told H* that in that case she would have to drive herself, and I left. It was a very nice feeling being able to leave knowing that I did not have to return to sleep there. We did not see her at the party.

Figure 29: D* at Birthday Party 2001

Many of my friends, knowing how difficult things had been, came to D*'s party. Most of these people appeared at the temporary orders hearing to testify for D*. The woman in the red hat was a mime who performed.

Filing for Divorce 2000 – 2001

The Leviathan is a Type of Sea Monster

The philosopher Thomas Hobbs says government naturally tends to grow. Accordingly, colleges and universities are graduating tens of thousands of people every year with specialties in the self involved people services of law, mental health and social services. These graduates are finding employment. Once employed, each person in the organization wants promotions, expanded purvey, and interesting and important work. Consequently departments grow, purviews expand, budgets go up, and service providers all declare each other to be ever so more important. As they are all so important, *everyone* needs to use their services.

If the economy is like a ship, then growing government is like a great sea monster, the Leviathan, that rises out of the sea, wraps the ship in its tentacles, and pulls it down.

According to this metaphor the Lynch family must be composed of some sort of live stock, whether they be sheep or cattle I'm not sure. We are Leviathan food, not Leviathan slayers. I hadn't thought much about it until writing this book, but my family and friends have inherited a stereotypical American frontier cultural ethic, which is not surprising as that is their roots. We are soldiers, farmers, small businessmen and engineers. After bad weather, we will still be standing. After being served with a law suit, one is left scratching one's head as to what to do. Bullets, bombs, cannons, clever products, tractors, mowers, earth movers, fast motorcycles, boats, airplanes, radios, wrenches, solder guns, nuts, bolts, building knowhow, and love for one's neighbors are all useless weapons against the Leviathan. The Leviathan is fought within the legislator and the courtrooms of law and public opinion – places we have never been. Now that Grandpa Seibert passed, decades ago, there is not a politician, lawyer, or journalist among us.

Hired Attorney Ted Terry

I interviewed another divorce attorney. Ted Terry roosted atop an old house in downtown Austin. Ted was a large man in good shape. He had black hair, dark complexion, and wore conservative black three piece suits. The reception area and offices were decorated conservatively, and his office was towards the back of the building, overlooking the park. One might imagine that he had a pistol in his pocket, and a bottle of whiskey in the cabinet. The day I visited there was a freezing rain. The southerners were sliding around randomly on the roads like hockey pucks during a power play. We spoke briefly but curtailed the conversation so folks could leave early and join the fray outside. Ted dispensed a business card, and said that if we should go forward that he would need a $35,000 retainer. I considered that the difference between Piper's retainer and Ted's might be due to the difference in caliber of their work. D* and I left the office and managed to make it home safely.

Surely H* had heard the recording Jim had left, but she never mentioned it. Perhaps dumping the dog mess on my head was her way of getting even for it. Late one night I saw her going through the pockets of my suit jacket. She pulled out Ted Terry's card. It was curious she didn't mention that either. Obviously she wanted to get rid of me anyway, but I didn't imagine that H* would put up with me divorcing her, as she demanded to be in control. Surely it must go the other way. Perhaps her immigration attorney had told her it was bad form to initiate.

Preparing for the Hearing

Ted had a legal assistant by the name of Jodi Welborn. She had no experience, but he gave her the case. He had another legal assistant who I had initially spoken to, and I was really impressed with, but Ted insisted on Jodi. It was a bait and switch routine. I gave Jodi my journals, audio tapes, pictures, and a list of witnesses.

My friend Gopi called. He was on the witness list. He said, "Tom, you are a person of means, why don't you hire a professional attorney?" I was surprised as Ted had a good reputation, but then again, he wasn't really the attorney, Jodi was. Jodi had contacted Gopi, and he hadn't been impressed. Gopi was a VP at a multi-billion dollar revenue company. His father was an attorney and state senator. He knew what he was talking about. I relayed the comment to Ted. Unknown to me at the time, Ted gave my letter to Jodi.

Then Dan called me. Dan was also an experienced executive. He did not mince with words. "Your attorney, Jodi, is as dumb as larks vomit," he said. Again I relayed the comment to Ted, and again, he relayed the letter to Jodi. Jodi was pissed. This time I heard back about it directly from Jodi. I complained to Ted. He initially said he would use a different legal assistant, but then it was Jodi who called back and who continued on the case. I asked for the other assistant, but was told I had to work with Jodi.

Ted asked me to say in court that I saw H* hitting D* repeatedly on multiple occasions. I told him I had personally only seen it once. He insisted, and I replied, "Christ don't you have enough material. After all, she tried to electrocute him, and I gave you pictures of her pushing his head into a pillow." I also pointed out the eight emergency room visits, and that my mother, grandmother, and one of my friends had seen her hit him also. He said that mom and grandma could not be used in the divorce court. There is a contradiction here because he also expected to see my father in law come to the courtroom; although as it turned out he remained in hiding.

I told Ted I would only stick to exactly what I saw, and that I would only describe the one incident where I personally saw her hit him, and that I would not embellish. I felt it was convincing enough by itself. He pushed me to make it graphic, and say that I had seen her hit him repeatedly on the side of the head. I stressed it was just once on the side of the head followed by a harsh spanking on the butt, and that is all that I was willing to say. In my opinion, there was more than enough real evidence, so nothing had to be embellished.

Now that I have been through the system I can see what Ted was doing. The courtroom is a show palace of relationships and emotions. If I were to dryly describe D* being hit, it wouldn't have much affect. On the other hand, if I balled like a girl and spouted purple prose, no matter the contents of what I said, I would win friends and probably the case. The courtroom is now a completely feminine environment. Only emotions are communicated, not facts. I couldn't do it. I didn't know how. Ted called me his worse witness.

There is another possibility, Ted may have been trying to see if I was telling the truth by giving me an opportunity to change the description. Though I did not get this impression at all. Among other reasons, the worse witness insult was delivered out of frustration. Ted asked me to work with a body language coach. I asked for a good book on the subject to read beforehand. He said there were none - but that is not accurate. That was a turn off. Using a coach to learn how to communicate better didn't seem like a bad idea in concept, but the coach turned out to be useless in practice. The one and only session was too short, and there were no exercises or reading materials.

Initially Jodi was ambitious. But her demeanor changed with the letters. It appears to me that she told Ted that I was lying. She called me in to Ted's office to drill me over facts. "Was the blow up at Casa Acapulco before or after the marriage?'" she asked. "After," I said. That event had been 6 years prior, towards the beginning of the marriage, so I fail to see the salience of a person being able to make that distinction. Still, I had answered correctly. Jodi rolled her eyes and looked at Ted.

Later I heard an accusation that I had sat in front of a computer and made it all up, including the pictures and audio recordings. Accordingly, I own a voice synthesizer that sounds just like H*, and I am a plotting genius. But plotting to get what? I already had a means to buy a house and was a U.S. citizen upon entering the marriage. However, H* was lacking all of those things, and gained them and more - in the divorce.

Have you noticed that people who are dishonest get lost in events told by an honest person? Dishonest people's mental framework and logical thought processes handicap them to the point of not being able to see the forest for the trees. While they are looking for the *angle*, or the *catch*, they miss the point. A dishonest attorney has no chance of making use of incremental knowledge to make sense of factual material. Indeed that is not even such a person's objective. I learned from watching H* and the attorneys that there is an alternative way of communicating. I communicate with other people in order to convey a message that augments our awareness of reality. I.e. I want to give the listener something they didn't have before, and can value. In contrast, H* and these attorneys communicated in order to manipulate people. I.e. they wanted to take something from the listener.

While I was concentrating on indexing my journals and tapes, and giving factual summaries to my divorce attorneys, they could not hear me, as that was not the way they thought or worked. In fact, the concept of telling actual facts was so alien to them, that they only imagined that I was synthesizing the facts.

Meanwhile H* was summing the people up to see what she could say to get them mad. She hit upon a brilliant stroke when she delivered a document accusing me of being a sexist. I am not a sexist. I have never used gender as a criteria for anything non-social. I have never considered gender when making a choice for inclusion on a team, in merit evaluations, or determining the source of my research. But this misses the point. Jodi wasn't looking for the truth. She did not research the accusation to see if it was true, because she didn't care. Her objective was to find ammunition to overcome the insulting letters, and H* had provided it. *Sexist towards women*, that is something people are conditioned to get angry about. Jodi could then say she hadn't handled the witnesses incompetently, rather my friends and I were sexists. And then, building upon the incremental knowledge approach to debate, she held up the ultimate weapon, she said, "*And everyone knows it.*"

The Thesis of Misandry, According to Isabel

Ironically Ted simultaneously explained that the courts were sexist against men, especially in custody cases, and that the testimony of a female housewife friend was so much stronger than that of an experienced male psychologist friend, that we ought not bother bringing the psychologist. Hence, I asked my friend Isabel to testify, but not Sigfried.

Isabel agreed, but then canceled due to having to help her mother who was sick. Though she buttressed this excuse with some misandrist views. She said, "Men have dominated women for 600 years so now it is time for Women to have a turn." She explained that her family donated money to Central American business funds for women only. She said it was important to put capital in the hands of women and not men, as men were lazy and corrupt, so they just wasted money. She continued to explain that in her travels in Central America she learned that men just lay around all day while women work the fields. She rejected the idea that CPS was biased, and pointed out the problems her adopted daughter had in another county.

Isabel explained that all the social, political, and economic barriers humanity has experienced are due to men. Men are by nature aggressive, territorial, and violent. If only it were the case that women were in control these bad men would be punished and we would live in a utopia.

I couldn't imagine what this had to do with my divorce. Are we to reason that D* mom should have what she wants because and only because she is a woman?   That seemed to be the message. Didn't D*'s life matter? I really felt prejudiced against.

Isabel didn't explain where she got the '600' years figure from, but this is immaterial. There is some similarity between Isabel and that of Naomi Wolf's in "Fire with Fire". They are both misandrist pieces. I see some serious flaws, the most eerie one is if you replace the word 'men' with 'Jew' it reads just like Hitler propaganda. All the worlds problems are due to men. All the worlds problems are due to Jews.

In the book *Pedagogy of the Oppressed* the political scientist Paulo Freire postulates that in the absence of enlightened leadership all successful movements turn into supremacy movements. The radical elements and esteem building forces that provide enough energy to propel a success movement to fruition continue to bare influence and this inertia carries the movement into a supremacy movement. Is this the answer to "who stole feminism?" The continued popularity of books such as Faludi's "Why do We Need Men," would indicate so.

H* Threatens: "I Can Touch Him" 2001 06 11

A month prior at an exchange near town lake, right in front of me, H* said, "you don't like your father do you?, to our child, who was just three, and strapped in his care seat. On May 18, 2001 a judge issued a restraining order banning her from making disparaging remarks. The next exchange was no different. This conversation and the Rhade deposition occurred simultaneously. This comes from Ted's file. The check mark's are Jodi's.

2001 06 11, 18:47 Dropping off D at Fresh Plus

[Taking D out of his car seat.]
T > Ok, D   here you go.
[T and D walk to H's car. D holding baloon from CM.]
T> Do you have my mail?
H> Yeah I do
T> D   ' Tee shirt? [referring to the Durango Tee shirt]
D> [in background] Yeah.
H> No I don't.
T> Are you planning to bring it?
D> [in background] Yeah.
H> I guess so.
T> You guess so?
H> D   - [Korean] - you're going home, soon. D   ' home!
T> How is it that you have some of my PO box mail?
H> What? Which PO box mail? Where is the dog? I have to carry the dog. I don't know. It is there, it is probably old mail. I never opened it.
T> There is another envelope there on the chair, is that mine?
[H shows the envelope and it is empty.]
H> What time 8:00? The dog should sit in the front.
T> I didn't bring the dog.
H> Where is the dog.
T> At the apartment.
H> You can get evicted. That is your problem. I don't know.
T> Across the field, same place?
H> yep
T> ok
[T starts to walk to car, then comes back to talk with D, leans over the back seat:]
T> Be good D   . Be sure to pee in the pot. Ok?
[the baloon from CM is in the way of kissing D on the forehead. T moves it aside.]
D> No!
H> He doesn't like you. D   come on.
T> What did you say?
H> That's nothing. Lets go.
T> What did you say?
H> He doesn't like you.
T> You said that right in front of him?
H> go ahead, I can touch him, why don't you record? Somehow I have to go. Your going to [keep, kill?] me?
T> what??
H> I don't know Tom, I have to go!

[T goes back to the car, turns on the radio.]

Figure 30: Tape Transcript, H*: "I can touch him."

Temporary Orders Hearing, 2001 06 14

We met in court a first time, and H* asked for a continuation. She had a victimization story while saying she had no expectation of a divorce, rather it had just come out of the blue and that I had completely tricked her by moving to Travis county. She asked for two more weeks. It was granted.

H* appealed to Sandy for help. H* had talked to Sandy once at a barbecue party three years prior. She showed up at their place crying and complaining about domestic abuse. She told Sandy that I was a violent person who she had put up with for years. Sandy introduced H* to Alicia Browner. Brian described Alicia as a person who "liked to help women get divorced." Although I had known Sandy's husband for years, Sandy decided not to consult me to get the whole story. By the time Brian called a great deal of damage was already done.

There is a fund created by a Congressional act called the VAWA (Violence Against Women Act). The fund must be renewed every four years, and was renewed at 8 billion dollars on the last round. The money can be used for a variety of things related to domestic violence, provided it is spent on women. That the money must go to women is stipulated right in the bill. Many organizations have applied for grants against this fund, so the money gets matched and expanded, and in some way now affects most all localities. VAWA funds have been used to raise awareness of domestic violence issues, though at times that awareness is one sided. Legal Aid in Austin, which provides attorneys to lower income people, accepted VAWA grant money. Because of its 'women only' constraint, they then turned away men who came with domestic issues, though they didn't tell men that this was the reason. The VAWA grants have probably had many positive affects, but in addition the organizations which receive them need customers to justify their next grant filings against. This may in part explain the existence of a person who goes around 'trying to help women get divorced.'

I was raising D*, so his friend's parents came to speak for us, as did the nanny. H* didn't even know who D*'s friends were. In my opinion there isn't really anything wrong with this, not every adult has to also be a parent, even if she is a woman. This is in fact a feminist plank – i.e. that a woman does not have to be locked to children or the house, and that men should carry some of the domestic burden also. However, they sang the misandrist tune instead. They sang, "A woman should have it all."

Rhade had survived the trip to Big Bend. She was willing to testify, but she had moved to California. Jodi had difficulty hooking up with her, so I pushed the process of a video deposition along. I was surprised that Heidi, Austin and Dylan's mom, wanted to testify, as most folks avoid divorces unless they have an external motivation, such as a political activists slant, sore ears from an eight hour car ride with a nag, or a close friendship that implied duty or obligation, or a subpoena. Heidi's reason was simply that she saw how well D* and I got along, so she wanted to help people understand.

Doctor Mirrop said he would be glad to testify. He added that he hadn't even met H*. I had been the only person taking care of D*. I had no problem talking to Dr. Mirrop, but every time I checked with Jodi she said she couldn't get a hold of him.

Long time friends, including Jo and Dan testified. Ted didn't want Jo's husband to testify because, as he explained, men's testimonies didn't mean much.

I did not front load anyone with information. Those who spoke did so sincerely and from a point of view of their own personal experiences.

During testimony the nanny got a bit carried away. "Takes him fishing," she repeated three times. Rosa has such a big heart. She would have done anything to help us, and it wasn't out of consideration for her job. D* was going to be attending a French school in the fall after we vacationed, so it was her final week. I had chosen to let her go now in part so she could speak, if she chose, without being conflicted, and in part I did not want it to appear I had let her go because I was unhappy with what she said. Ted was pissed when I told him. He lectured me on being more patient. "Jeeze, Tom, couldn't you have waited until after the divorce was over." He continued that it was part of the burden of proof to show continuity in D*'s life.

During the hearing, Ted did not ask for supervised possession. He refused to show the embassy letter because, as he explained to me, "it was not official." I asked him "if the U.S. Embassy seal on a letter does not make it official, then what does?" He just looked at me funny. He played one tape of H* screaming, but not the death threat tape. Though H* admitted to making a death threat so it was moot. He also showed a picture of H* screaming and pushing D*' head into a pillow after the Indian Pow Wow.

Ted explained to me that he held back because it was important to win by only a small margin. He said that otherwise we would open a Pandora's box after the hearing. I was baffled, but followed his advice because he was my attorney. However, in any case this objective failed, as future events demonstrated, the box would be opened by his own legal assistant.

H*'s side called two witnesses. Sandy the divorced woman rescuer, who lied about having lunch with H* "several times," and a neighbor woman who said H* had canceled a dinner invite so they had never got to meet. The neighbor emphasized that H* had been polite in canceling the dinner.

During the hearing H* said that we had agreed on splitting our property - however, she did not uphold her side of that agreement, I would never see the majority of my possessions again, and my professional possessions would be taken and used to destroy my livelihood. I did not receive any of the joint property.

On the morning of the second day D* had a fever. For obvious reasons day cares don't take kids with fevers, so I couldn't use our existing arrangement. The nanny was to be in the courtroom that day, so I couldn't call her back in. I had to find someone else. I also had to take D* to the doctor. Consequently I was late getting to the courtroom.

While I was gone, H* had an argument with the judge. It was related to our being late, but I wasn't there to see it first hand. I was told that she told the judge he had no business telling her what to do, and screamed at him. The judge commented on it in his ruling, he held up the scream picture and said he had seen it in this very court room.

Highlights of H*'s Testimony 2001 06 14 (D* turned 3 in April)

These notes are relative to the page numbers on the transcript, which is shown in its entirety in the next figure.

Page 139 line 18 she says she never put a hand on the baby because no mother could do such a thing. On page 160 line 14 she changes her testimony and says that she spanks baby D*, and she can't do it more often because dad hates it.

Page 128 she admits screaming at D* and says she does this because dad doesn't allow her to spank the baby, the "what is a scream" banter extends until page 153 when the picture (see Figure 21) is admitted into evidence and page 163 when a tape is played into evidence. Afterwards there is no doubt as to what word *scream* means in English.

H* goes over the incident where she blew up at D* over spilling a sprite. Page 135 says she calls dad stupid in front of D*. Page 136 she points out that dad has been making audio tapes of her fits.

Page 126 line 17 she admits to calling dad a dog and episode when she dumped the dog mess on my head(see Figure 20). She says that she did not call D* a dog, but fails to mention he was present during the incident as demonstrated by the fact he can be heard on the tape.

Page 139 she talks about the time Dan and dad came in to find H* on the floor in a pile of broken glass. She gets tripped up when trying to explain where D* was at the time. She claims that Dan and dad were business related [so he lied]. [There was no such relationship.] Page 137 line 14 starts the discussion about the money her parent's allegedly stole and she allegedly helped keep in the U.S.

Page 149 line 6 she admits canceling Christmas for D* when he was two. The attorney brought out that she bought herself something.

Page 148 lines 16 to page 149 H* admits telling dad that she wished he was dead. Page 151 line 16 also she admits to making a death threat. She defends herself by saying she only threatened to kill dad once.

On page 152 line 8 forward she claims that the picture of her apparently pushing D*'s head into the pillow while screaming was because he was tired and lying down. In his ruling judge pointed out her screaming was incompatible with her explanation he was sleeping.

Page 141 she corroborates the big bend trip hysteria where she ruined our trip (see chapters 'H* Nags and Screams On An Entire Vacation to Big Bend' and 'Rhade Ganaphathy Deposition'). Page 146 she corroborates the incident with the windshield though she said she broke it while "sleeping in the car."

On page 159 line 13 she says, "he is a good father, I don't deny it." She will repeat similar statements at other hearings. This is yet more evidence that the intensity of the opposition has been due to the attorneys.

H* denies kneeing me in the groin or elbowing me in the neck. She admits to scratching but says it doesn't matter as I don't care about scratches.

At the bottom of page 155 she corroborates the Moulin Rouge incident, but said that I threw the money at her instead of her throwing it in the air. Terry is incorrect in his question about her standing on the table, she was standing on the floor at the time. It was after she threw the money I told her to go alone and she asked for cab fare. Anyway this establishes the event, which turned out to be important as later she flatly denied it occurred.

(Page 149 there is an error for "beers" the $20,000 and $30,000 she alleges were for the "business.")

Page 163 describes the tape played for the court where she is screaming hysterically at me.

Years later D* was looking at pictures on my laptop and saw the picture of him laying on the bed next to H* that was shown and discussed at temporary orders. The picture without the context is not readily questionable. He started yelling "liar, liar, liar ..." On a later visit D* volunteered that his mother was pushing his head in a pillow so that he could would not see something bad that I was doing. He also assured me that he didn't really believe his mom's explanation that I was doing something bad. Thus, it is another evolving story from D*. At our most recent hearing on 2007 10 10 H* testified about this again, saying that I told D* that she had pushed his head in a pillow, and she said that if she had really pushed his head in a pillow, then why was I standing by doing nothing but taking a picture. This was six year old material and already adjudicated, so I didn't pursue it. It is a peculiar circle of events for me, as I hadn't suggested this was what she was doing in the first place but now it seems likely.

1 Terry, your next witness?

2   MR. TERRY: H

3   THE COURT: Ms. Lynch, if you would come up

4 and take a seat, I would appreciate it.

5   H

6 having been previously duly sworn, testified as follows:

7   CROSS-EXAMINATION

8 BY MR. TERRY:

9   Q.   State your name, please, ma'am.

10   A.   H   H-

11   Q.   Mrs. Lynch, is it accurate to say that you have

12 called both Tom Lynch and D   Lynch the family dogs?

13   A.   No.

14   Q.   So you completely deny that; correct?

15   A.   No, I'm denying it.

16   Q.   You are denying it?

17   A.   I called Tom one occasion he's a dog, like a

18 dog. Because he let the dog inside and put the dog food,

19 D   was playing with the water, he doesn't do

20 anything. And so I called him as a dog, if you -- not

21 toward D   .

22   Q.   And have you equated D   and Tom to the

23 dirty dog?

24   A.   No.

25   Q.   Who is the dirty dog, ma'am?

```
1       A.    I don't know what "dirty dog" means.
2       Q.    Who is your dog?
3       A.    Lyka (phonetic).
4       Q.    Lyka?
5       A.    Lyka is my dog -- our dog my parents bought for
6    D        ' birthday.  It's for I think second -- two years
7    old.
8       Q.    You don't deny do you, ma'am --
9       A.    What do I deny?
10      Q.    You don't deny do you, ma'am --
11      A.    Could you --
12      Q.    -- screaming --
13            THE COURT:  Let him finish his question.
14            THE WITNESS:  Okay.
15      Q.    (By Mr. Terry)  Screaming at D         ; do you?
16      A.    I don't understand the definition of
17   "screaming."  Because I'm not by nature English speaker.
18   When you say "screaming" what does mean?
19      Q.    I'm talking about screaming in unintelligible,
20   high pitched, for long periods of time, voice.
21      A.    Okay.  My voice is high pitch, even though I
22   have sore throat.  Can you hear the difference?
23            If I emotionally upset, my voice is getting
24   higher.  I'm aware of that.  People think I'm sure
25   whatever voice I'm using, but that's not it.  It's just my
```

1   voice. From my -- from throat. I'm not very upset right

2   now, you think I'm upset; right?

3   THE COURT: Wait for his question.

4   Q.   (By Mr. Terry) Do you yell and scream at

5   D   , yes or no?

6   A.   No, I scolding him. That's different.

7   Because we have tile floor when we moved in new

8   place. He's three years old, I mean now he has to learn

9   how to behave. And the thing is the tile floor is

10   slippery. And there is a refrigerator, and we have a

11   water button. Tom always worry about the water quality,

12   so he likes play with the water. That's natural.

13   But that causes danger, because he make the

14   floor slippery. I always have to tell him that you should

15   not do that, it makes your head hurt. And I have to be

16   firm.

17   But Tom doesn't -- I mean I cannot spank him.

18   Tom doesn't allow me do anything. Even whatever diaper, I

19   talked to my colleague I know about parenting thing, small

20   kid you have to use your bod (sic), whatever. But Tom

21   doesn't let me do anything, so I have to use my voice.

22   What can I do?

23   Q.   And the way you use your voice is to scream at

24   D   ?

25   A.   It's not screaming at. It's up, but it's

```
1  subjective/objective I don't know.  It's from my opinion
2  it was I'm trying to make him learn something.  He should
3  not play with the water around that slippery tile kitchen
4  floor.  That's all what that is, to make him safer.
5       Q.   Did you tell Tom, yes or no, after he'd taken
6  D        to the emergency room several times last year
7  that D        hurt himself on purpose just to get
8  attention?
9       A.   No.
10      Q.   Never said anything like that?
11      A.   No.
12      Q.   Did you -- do you deny becoming hysterical when
13 D        spilled a Sprite?
14      A.   Never hysterical.
15      Q.   Never been -- let me be real clear.  Is it your
16 testimony that you have never been hysterical and upset?
17 Do you understand what "hysterical" means?  I just want to
18 be real clear?
19      A.   Okay, what does it mean?
20      Q.   Let me rephrase the question.
21           You've got -- what is your education, first of
22 all?
23      A.   I have Master's Degree in South Korea and then I
24 came here for studying.
25      Q.   And you have Ph.D. from the Univers --
```

```
 1        A.    Ph.D. Electrical Engineering at Amherst.
 2        Q.    Okay.  Have you become extremely upset in
 3   D          ' presence where you were screaming at him?
 4        A.    I never scream at him.  I screamed at my
 5   husband, if you call it screaming.  I raise my voice.
 6        Q.    Well, then, let me ask you this, did you scream
 7   at your husband in front of D        ?
 8        A.    I raised the voice.  What can I do, my husband
 9   is head strong is strong, he has a violent behavior.
10        Q.    Listen to my question, ma'am.
11              THE COURT:  What's the question?
12        Q.    (By Mr. Terry)  The question is this, do you
13   scream at your husband when D        is there, yes or no?
14              MR. CALABRESE:  Asked and answered.
15              THE COURT:  You can answer the question.
16        A.    Never.
17        Q.    (By Mr. Terry)  Never?
18        A.    Uh-huh.
19        Q.    All right.
20        A.    It depends on definition of screaming.  I raise
21   my voice.
22              THE COURT:  Next question.
23        Q.    (By Mr. Terry)  Do you recall when D
24   spilled a Sprite can?
25        A.    Yes, please, there are many, many things.
```

1   Q.   Do you recall becoming extremely upset over him

2 spilling a Sprite?

3   A.   I never been upset.

4   Q.   Never been upset while he spilled a Sprite; is

5 that your testimony?

6   A.   Uh-huh.

7   Q.   Okay.

8   (Petitioner's Exhibit 2 was marked.)

9   Q.   (By Mr. Terry) Let me show you what's been

10 marked Petitioner's Exhibit Number 2 and ask you if this

11 is D   holding the Sprite can that he has just

12 spilled, and is that you?

13   A.   Who I looking at? Is it D   or the person

14 who's taking the picture. What do you think? Tom is

15 taking the picture --

16   THE COURT: Ma'am, hang on. The question

17 is is that a picture of D   holding a Sprite can with

18 you in the picture?

19   A.   Yeah, I am. That's me.

20   MR. TERRY: We'd offer Petitioner's 2.

21   MR. CALABRESE: Object for relevance, Your

22 Honor.

23   THE COURT: Well, Petitioner's 2 is

24 admitted.

25   (Petitioner's Exhibit 3 was marked.)

1   Q.   (By Mr. Terry) Now, right after that you began

2 screaming at D   ; did you not?

3   A.   No.

4   Q.   You recognize this picture?

5   A.   I don't remember, but he took the picture, it

6 made me upset.

7   Q.   Is this your picture?

8   A.   It's me.

9   Q.   Okay. Is that your kitchen?

10   A.   Yes, it's mine.

11   Q.   Okay. Do you have any reason to believe it's

12 been altered in any way?

13   A.   It's not, but he has digital camera, so I don't

14 know.

15   Q.   Well is this --

16   A.   It's me.

17   MR. TERRY: We'd offer Petitioner's 3.

18   MR. CALABRESE: I'll try relevance again,

19 Judge.

20   THE COURT: Petitioner's 3 is admitted.

21   (Petitioner's Exhibit 4 was marked.)

22   Q.   (By Mr. Terry) And Petitioner's Exhibit 4 is

23 you with the Sprite can in the back and the Sprite on your

24 shirt; is that correct?

25   A.   I'm not sure that's Sprite or water. I was

1   cleaning, so I don't know.

2   I don't know when this incident happen. I'm

3   crying, that's all that I know.

4   Q.   Are you testifying that you weren't mad in that

5   picture?

6   A.   How could I mad, Tom is taking picture --

7   MR. TERRY: We'd offer --

8   A.   -- for what?

9   MR. TERRY: We'd offer 4.

10   A.   Someone is making --

11   THE COURT: Hang on, ma'am. Just wait for

12   the question.

13   MR. CALABRESE: No objection.

14   THE COURT: Petitioner's 4 is admitted.

15   MR. CALABRESE: I may be a slow learner.

16   Q.   (By Mr. Terry) Have you told or have you said

17   to people that D   is making you a bad mother, yes or

18   no?

19   A.   No.

20   Q.   Never said anything like that?

21   A.   No. Making me a bad mother?

22   Q.   That D   is making you --

23   A.   A bad mother?

24   Q.   -- a bad mother?

25   A.   I don't even understand. That doesn't make even

134

```
1    sense.  I don't understand the meaning of that.
2        Q.    You don't understand the meaning of --
3        A.    Bad mother.  How could he make mother to be bad
4    mother.  I don't understand.
5        Q.    Have you told people, have you told D
6    that D         is making you a bad mother?
7        A.    No, it doesn't -- I don't even think that's a
8    sentence, correct sentence.  My English is not good
9    enough, so I don't know.
10       Q.    You have told D         -- you've told him,
11   "You're a bad boy, can't you see I'm busy".  You've told
12   him that sort of thing; have you not?
13       A.    Probably I said like, "If you do this, you're
14   bad.  Don't do that.  Can hurt you".
15       Q.    No.
16       A.    I don't know whether I said "bad boy" or not.
17   Because my English is not very perfect, as you see.
18       Q.    When you scream at D        , ma'am, what he does
19   is go "Da da da," does he not, calling for his dad?
20       A.    No.
21       Q.    That's never happened?
22       A.    No.
23       Q.    You've called him an idiot; have you not?
24       A.    Tom, yes, once.
25       Q.    D        .  Have you --
```

136

```
 1      A.   No.
 2      Q.   You've never called D        --
 3      A.   "D        , you idiot", did I say that?  No.
 4      Q.   Well, did you call D        an idiot, yes or no?
 5      A.   No.
 6      Q.   Did you use that word in connection with
 7   D        ?
 8      A.   No.
 9      Q.   Never have?
10      A.   Never have.
11      Q.   And did you call him stupid?
12      A.   No, he's very intelligent boy.  I'm proud of
13   him.
14      Q.   I'm asking you --
15      A.   Never.
16      Q.   -- if you ever called him stupid?
17      A.   No, I called my husband stupid because of all
18   these things.
19      Q.   You call your husband stupid in front of
20   D        ?
21      A.   Sometimes, possibly, if he irritates --
22      Q.   Okay.  If he irritates you you will call him
23   stupid in front of D        ; right?
24      A.   Because it's the way he's acting, like taking
25   pictures, whatever.  Trying to prove something.
```

1   It's been like this seven years, our marriage.
2   He's making tapes, audio tapes. I mean, the facts are
3   there, and it's so stupid, it's so obvious someone to look
4   at, he's making some study out of it. I always think
5   that's stupid.
6   Q.   Have you called Mr. Lynch a dog in front of
7   D   ?
8   A.   Not in front of D   .
9   Q.   Not in front of D   ?
10   A.   Uh-huh.
11   Q.   You're very, very careful not to get upset in
12 front of D   ; is that your testimony?
13   A.   You agree, yes. Most of time, I think. I don't
14 know when I'm -- I don't know, really. But most of time
15 I'm very careful about D
16   Q.   Now, you heard Mr. Issen this morning talk about
17 your hysterical, loud and sometimes violent behavior with
18 D   ; correct?
19   A.   Yeah, I heard that. I don't know why he has
20 that opinion. Really don't, no idea.
21   Q.   That's just a complete fabrication, much like
22 your friend up here on videotape was just lying?
23   A.   It's possible. Because they're business-related
24 people. He's writing patent with Daniel Issen. If you
25 break the connection with him, his future is not very

1   stable. So is business connection in California.

2   Q.   Okay.

3   A.   They're very business connected with him. They

4   are -- they are -- I mean, I'm out of picture. They don't

5   care about me. But he's very important for their lives.

6   Q.   Mr. Issen also said that you slapped D   on

7   the head and yelled at him "you're a very bad boy".

8   A.   How come if anyone sees that why don't call the

9   police. I should be arrested at the time.

10   If Tom is so concerned about boy -- baby, he

11 should have done that. Doesn't have to make this all part

12 of evidence, he could have called the police right away in

13 front of Dan because he knew I'm bad mother.

14   Q.   Speaking of the police, it's my understanding

15 that your parents who lived in your home --

16   A.   Uh-huh.

17   Q.   -- are wanted for felony fraud in Korea, yes or

18 no?

19   A.   I don't aware of that, no.

20   Q.   Your testimony under oath is --

21   A.   They're broke. Yes, they're broke, completely

22 out of business.

23   Q.   Broke, well they --

24   A.   Yeah, several years ago.

25   Q.   They embezzled and you hid for them a large

1   amount of money in your bank account; did you not?

2   A.   No.

3   Q.   You did not?

4   A.   I don't accept as far as I'm concerned, and Tom

5   was happy with that.

6   Q.   You're saying that you did not have a large

7   amount of money?

8   A.   I had money, yes. It's a gift. My father, my

9   dad was very rich. He had a business in Korea.

10   (Petitioner's Exhibit 5 was marked.)

11   Q.   (By Mr. Terry) Is this a copy?

12   A.   That is my copy.

13   THE COURT: Let him finish his questions.

14   Q.   (By Mr. Terry) Is this a copy of an A.G.

15   Edwards account in your name with total account value of

16    $282,000?

17   A.   Yeah, that's first I got the money from them.

18   Q.   Okay?

19   A.   That was arranged because -- oh, sorry.

20   Q.   Where are your parents now?

21   A.   In Italy.

22   MR. TERRY: We'd offer Petitioner's 5.

23   MR. CALABRESE: It is totally irrelevant,

24   Judge, and I object on that ground.

25   THE COURT: Well, it's admitted.

1   MR. CALABRESE: I'm sorry, what was the
2 date of that, Your Honor?
3   THE COURT: Statement is dated September
4 12, '96 to -- excuse me -- June 12, '96 to June 28, '96.
5   MR. CALABRESE: Thank you.
6   Q. (By Mr. Terry) You also heard Mr. Issen talk
7 about coming home and finding detergent on the floor in
8 the play room. You remember that testimony; do you not?
9   A. I remember. But I don't know what you're
10 talking about, actually. I mean what -- this detergent
11 thing you're talking about, really. From my is total
12 fabrication.
13   Q. Do you remember coming home last New Year's
14 Eve -- or, excuse me, them coming home, Tom and Mr. Issen
15 coming home and finding you sitting in the floor in a pile
16 of broken glass?
17   A. Yes. I don't remember who broke it. The glass
18 is broken. I was cleaning on the floor, and Dan stop by
19 with wine bottle. I remember I was cleaning.
20   And then we had a good time, we drink wine after
21 that.
22   Q. And where was D   when you were sitting in
23 the pile of broken glass?
24   A. He was not even there close to that.
25   Q. Where was he?

1   A.   He was in play room. Probably play room is
2 connected to kitchen.
3   Q.   Who was taking care of him?
4   A.   I guess Tom.
5   Q.   Who?
6   A.   Tom because I'm cleaning.
7   Q.   Wait a second.
8   Mr. Issen testified that he and Tom walked in
9 the door, found you in a pile of glass?
10   A.   Okay. I don't remember what happened. Actually
11 I think Dan was visiting, I don't remember.
12   Q.   You said what?
13   A.   I think only Dan was visiting from -- he knows
14 our house. But was he not? This is not very clear from
15 my memory. But I was cleaning the, what, glass.
16   Q.   Now, what do you do -- he testified about you
17 slapping D   on the head. You remember that; right?
18   A.   I don't remember. I don't remember. I never
19 put a hand on the baby.
20   How come any mother can do that? I can't
21 imagine that. How come those --
22   Q.   Now, you also heard -- you heard Radhe, your
23 friend -- and she was a good friend of yours; was she not?
24   A.   No, she's not.
25   Q.   Well, she testified you-all socialized four five

1 times a week.

2   A.   Okay, if she is a good friend -- if she is a

3 good friend how come she is so mad at me? She never

4 called me.

5   Q.   Okay.

6   THE COURT: Wait for the next question.

7   Q.   (By Mr. Terry) You heard her testify about you

8 becoming upset and yelling out at Big Bend; right?

9   A.   I was upset because we had a fight.

10   Q.   Were you yelling at Tom in front of that couple,

11 yes or no?

12   A.   That is raising my voice, yes.

13   Q.   Were you yelling?

14   A.   I was raising my voice. No, I was not yelling.

15 But from my definition I was raising voice.

16   Q.   Well, give the Court an example of what you

17 definition of raising your voice is. The loudest that

18 you've ever yelled --

19   A.   Yelling means with curse word, I guess. That's

20 my understanding of English.

21   Q.   That's not what I'm talking about. Tell the

22 Court and describe for the Court how loud you talk to

23 D   when you're mad at D   . Give the Court an

24 example of what you're doing?

25   A.   Just like I talk to you with a firm voice.

```
 1        Q.    Give the Court an example of what you do to
 2   D          ?
 3        A.    D          you should not do this.
 4        Q.    So there's no yelling?
 5        A.    Is this -- that yelling?
 6        Q.    There's no high pitched scream; is that your
 7   testimony?
 8              MR. CALABRESE:  Your Honor, this is getting
 9   a little repetitious.  We've talked about yelling and
10   screaming for about ten minutes now.
11              THE COURT:  What's the question?
12        Q.    (By Mr. Terry)  There's no yelling and no
13   screaming at D        ;; right?
14              MR. CALABRESE:  That question's been asked
15   and answered three or four times.
16              THE COURT:  You can answer.
17        A.    No, I raise my voice.
18        Q.    (By Mr. Terry)  Okay.  Now, with regard to
19   Carmen Blockus?
20        A.    Uh-huh.
21        Q.    You heard her testify --
22        A.    Uh-huh.
23        Q.    -- that when you called up and were asking about
24   the nanny --
25        A.    Uh-huh.
```

1   Q.   -- and when she said she was born in 1950, you
2 said she was old; right?
3   A.   She's too old for D   for to take care of
4 hyper -- I mean, he's very active. That's what I meant.
5   Q.   Did you tell her, yes or no, that you did not
6 like Rosa?
7   A.   I don't like Rosa for D   ' day care. That
8 doesn't mean I don't like her. I don't even know her.
9 That's why I don't like her to use as much D   '
10 nanny. That's why I told her.
11   Q.   You had never met Rosa; right?
12   A.   There was no chance to. She was not giving me a
13 chance. Tom doesn't tell me where do I go to meet.
14   Q.   Well, how in the world did you know he was
15 interviewing a nanny, he told you that?
16   A.   Tom called me while I was at work. Okay.
17 D   got kicked out of day care again, so we don't
18 have any choice to use nanny. And I was object to using
19 nanny for three year old. I mean, there's no social
20 activities, why then.
21   And he said he found someone from Peru. "Peru,
22 can she speaking English", I asked him.
23   "No. But it's temporary".
24   So I went, "Did you check the background"?
25   Tom said no.

1   "Then I have to check the background. So where
2   is the agency", I talked to him. So that's why I got the
3   phone.
4   He said "Nanny Solution, it's in the phone
5   book."
6   Q.   Did you threaten to call the police on Carmen
7   Blockus, yes or no?
8   A.   It's not threatening, I --
9   Q.   Did you threaten to call the police on --
10   A.   No.
11   Q.   -- Carmen Blockus?
12   No is you answer?
13   A.   I said --
14   Q.   Okay.
15   A.   I said "I'm going to call the police if you
16   don't let me know. I have parenting right. I can prove
17   myself with my ID everything. If you don't trust me as
18   his mother, I can stop by there and show that identity.
19   Please tell me where is nanny's place".
20   Tom is putting D   in nanny's place, I
21   didn't even know until today nanny's place is Tom's house.
22   Q.   Ma'am --
23   A.   So that's why I asked the policeman -- I called
24   Carmen.
25   Q.   Did you actually call the police?

1   A.   Now, I said if you don't do this -- if you don't

2   let me meet you and tell me about where nanny is located,

3   then I need help from outside. There's legal right.

4   So I call the police. And nanny said -- no,

5   Carmen said, "oh, wait a minute I have to talk to your

6   husband".

7   Q.   Have you hit Tom Lynch in the face in D   '

8   presence?

9   A.   No.

10   Q.   Ever?

11   A.   Never.

12   Q.   Never hit him in the face?

13   A.   No.

14   Q.   Ma'am, as a matter of fact, your temper gets

15   pretty out of control on a regular basis; doesn't it?

16   A.   I don't think I have temper. I'm very

17   emotional.

18   Q.   You're very emotional?

19   A.   That's all. Because I have been through -- I

20   mean, I don't want to defend myself.

21   Q.   Well, let's talk about the Volvo. Do you

22   remember when Tom was driving the Volvo and you kicked out

23   the windshield. Do you remember?

24   A.   No, no never.

25   Q.   You don't remember getting --

1   A.   I was sleeping in the parking lot while waiting
2 for Tom I kicked a little and there's a mark. That's all
3 that happened.
4   Q.   Do you recall?
5   A.   I remember the windshield is broken.
6   (Petitioner's Exhibit 6 was marked.)
7   Q.   (By Mr. Terry) Do you recall this bill that
8 you-all got from Roger Beasley Volvo --
9   A.   Uh-huh.
10   Q.   -- after you kicked out the window in the -- the
11 windshield in the car?
12   A.   I broke --
13   MR. CALABRESE: Judge, multifarious, two
14 questions.
15   THE COURT: Hang on. Why don't you break
16 it down.
17   Q.   (By Mr. Terry) Okay. Do you recall receiving
18 this bill from Roger Beasley?
19   A.   Yes, I fixed it.
20   MR. TERRY: Okay. Then we offer
21 Petitioner's Exhibit Number 6.
22   MR. CALABRESE: Objection, hearsay.
23   THE COURT: That's not admitted for the
24 truth of any charges. Petitioner's 6 is admitted.
25   Q.   (By Mr. Terry) All right. Now, what happened

n't

d,

s'

1   was you kicked out the windshield of the Volvo; isn't that

2   correct, ma'am?

3   A.   I didn't kick out the windshield of Volvo.

4   Q.   Okay. Let me ask you --

5   A.   I just made the --

6   Q.   What happened was Tom was driving down the

7   street in the Volvo; right?

8   A.   Lying. I -- it didn't happen that -- it happened

9   in parking lot while I was working for Austin -- Austin

10   Suite. I have tempered hardware, software, I actually

11   worked for a year for Tom.

12   Tom wanted to have a business for his life. So

13   as soon as I finish my Ph.D., nothing was -- two days why

14   I'm not getting a job, because he wanted me, Tom wants me

15   involved in business. So we rented an office suite --

16   Q.   Ma'am.

17   A.   It's related though.

18   THE COURT: Hang on.

19   Q.   (By Mr. Terry) Listen to the question.

20   You're denying completing injuring, cracking, or

21   in any manner harming the windshield of the Volvo; is that

out 22 correct?

23   A.   Is not correct. I broke the window because I

24   was sleeping in the car while I'm waiting for Tom. That's

25   what I told to the insurance company, too.

1   Q.   All right. Do you recall two separate times

2 breaking down doors in the home?

3   A.   Breaking down in the home. Rephrase that again.

4 I don't understand.

5   Q.   Yes, becoming extremely upset and breaking down

6 doors in the house?

7   A.   I don't understand.

8   Q.   You don't understand what breaking down doors in

9 the house means?

10   A.   Breaking down toward the house?

11   Q.   I'm talking about going up to a door and

12 breaking the doors in the home. Do you understand that?

13   A.   I never broke anything.

14   Q.   Never broke anything?

15   A.   Never.

16   Q.   All right. And you also told D   , quote,

17 "You bother me, I wish you were dead", didn't you?

18   A.   To D   ?

19   Q.   To D   .

20   A.   How come any mother can say that.

21   Q.   I'm asking if you said it?

22   A.   No, no, no. Never.

23   Q.   Have you ever said that to Tom, that you wished

24 he was dead?

25   A.   Tom said to me I wish --

1   Q.   I'm asking if you ever said it to Tom?

2   A.   Why, because D   got sick so often, yes,

3 once.

4   Q.   All right. And was D   there?

5   A.   No, he was in the car.

6   Q.   Last Christmas you told D   that he

7 couldn't have Christmas because it was a Christian

8 holiday; didn't you?

9   A.   No, we were broke. That's what -- that's my

10 excuse.

11   And Tom was doing those beers and everything

12 because we are so broke we spend like 20, 30K for Tom to

13 get from that incident, and Tom wanted to get -- I mean

14 these papers are our lives, so I don't want to spend

15 money.

16   Q.   Did you or did not, December of 2000, spend $400

17 on French lessons for you?

18   A.   French lessons for how much?

19   Q.   Four hundred.

20   A.   Never.

21   Q.   Never. Okay.

22   A.   I spend $60.

23   Q.   Did you go to D   ' birthday party that Tom

24 threw for him, yes or no?

25   A.   I couldn't go, Tom --

1   Q.   Yes or no?

2   A.   No.

3   Q.   All right. Thank you.

4   You agree, do you not, with the other witnesses

5   that said after D   was born that Tom stayed home at

6   the house; right?

7   A.   He stayed home at the house because his business

8   was not doing well.

9   Q.   Okay. And he was the one, for the most part,

10   that took care of D   for a lengthy period of his

11   life; isn't that correct?

12   A.   No, it's not correct.

13   Q.   All right. So is it your testimony that he did

14   not take care of D   in the first year of his life

15   when he was home working out the house?

16   A.   Okay I --

17   Q.   Just yes or no, did he take care of D   ?

18   A.   Did he, no.

19   Q.   Never did?

20   A.   Maybe 20 percent of all taking care of time, 20

21   percent. 80 percent is me and my parents.

22   Q.   You were working full time at Motorola; right?

23   A.   Yes, I spent two hours for lunch time breast

24   feeding him for seven months as a working mom.

25   It's pretty flexible, and sometimes I can go to

1 work during weekend. This urgency, up it's to the work

2 load.

3   Q.   Do you recall hitting D   on the check bone

4 while in the bathroom. Do you recall that?

5   A.   It never happened --

6   Q.   Do you --

7   A.   -- how can I recall.

8   Q.   Do you recall having a fit and breaking down the

9 screen door?

10   A.   Screen door? What are you talking about?

11   Q.   Do you recall that?

12   A.   No, I never -- our screen door is broken because

13 of the dog and you --

14   Q.   Because of what?

15   A.   Which screen door are you talking about?

16   Q.   How many death threats, if any, have you made

17 during the marriage to Mr. Lynch? Answer in numbers if

18 you would.

19   A.   One.

20   Q.   Just one?

21   A.   Yeah.

22   Q.   All right. Did you promise Mr. Lynch to quote

23 "give him your shit", did you ever say that to him?

24   A.   Give him your shit?

25   Q.   Yes, did you ever say that to him?

to

n

$400

Tom

1   A.   It doesn't make sense to me. I don't

2 understand.

3   Q.   Did you ever say "I'm going to give you my

4 shit," to Tom Lynch in front of D   ?

5   A.   I don't understand. I don't think so. I don't

6 understand the sentence.

7   No. As is, no.

8   Q.   So in these times when you've been pretty

9 calm --

10   A.   I don't know.

11   Q.   -- when you've been upset with D   --

12   A.   I remember that picture taken after sometime I

13 was playing with D   , and then I was tired and lie

14 down, he took a picture.

15   Q.   You were playing with D   in that picture?

16   A.   D   not showing there; right?

17   MR. TERRY: Well he's in the next picture,

18 so let's go ahead and mark these two, then.

19   THE WITNESS: Why do you even use these?

20   THE COURT: Hold on a second.

21   MR. TERRY: Mark all of these

22   (Petitioner's Exhibits 7 - 9 were marked.)

23   Q.   (By Mr. Terry) Petitioner's Exhibit Number 7 is

24 what?

25   A.   That's me.

1   Q.   Okay. Would you say that you're calm in that

2 picture?

3   A.   I'm not calm because Tom is taking picture.

4 What do you think?

5   Q.   Plaintiffs' Exhibit 8, is that you being very

6 upset around D   , screaming?

7   A.   Yes, D   was sleeping with me and Tom's

8 taking picture.

9   Q.   Were you screaming in that picture, yes or no?

10   A.   I think so.

11   Q.   All right. And Petitioner's Exhibit Number 9 is

12 the end of that sequence; is it not?

13   A.   Yeah, D   ' sleeping.

14   MR. TERRY: We offer 7, 8 and 9.

15   MR. CALABRESE: No objection.

16   THE COURT: Petitioner's 7, Petitioner's 8

17 and Petitioner's 9 are admitted.

18   Q.   (By Mr. Terry) Now, ma'am I'd like to play for

19 you a portion of a tape, or all the tape that we have, and

20 try to refresh your recollection about what goes on in

21 D   ' life and I'll represent to Counsel and Court

22 that my client is going to testify that he made the tape.

23   MR. CALABRESE: Your Honor, perhaps this

24 should be -- proper predicate should be laid for it.

25   THE COURT: Wait a minute. Stop it. And

1   the objection is?

2   MR. CALABRESE: Lack of authentication.

3   THE COURT: Sustained.

4   Q.   (By Mr. Terry) Okay. All right. Do you

5   recall -- you have a problem controlling your anger in

6   public, your anger toward Mr. Lynch; don't you?

7   A.   If I'm angry with my husband.

8   Q.   My question is you have problems controlling

9   your anger in public; do you not?

10   A.   When Tom pushes me, pushes the button, he's very

11 good at it, yes.

12   Q.   And you have, on numerous occasions during the

13 marriage, some of which your friend testified to --

14   A.   Uh-huh.

15   Q.   -- screamed at him, correct, in public places?

16   A.   When I hear "I wish you're dead", yes.

17   Q.   You've yelled at him in public places; correct?

18   A.   I raise the voice.

19   Q.   Just raise the voice?

20   A.   Uh-huh.

21   Q.   Do you understand that yelling cannot -- don't

22 necessarily have to involve cursing, yelling is a raising

23 of the voice.

24   You understand that; don't you?

25   A.   I didn't know.

```
 1      Q.    You didn't know.  All right, well you know now.
 2            You understand that now?
 3      A.    Okay.
 4      Q.    Yelling means screaming, the same thing.  You
 5   screamed at him in restaurants; right?
 6      A.    Without any reason?  I raise my voice.
 7      Q.    I'm asking you have you screamed at him in
 8   restaurants?
 9      A.    No, in restaurant, no.
10      Q.    You didn't scream at him at Casa Acapulco;
11   right?
12      A.    What is that?
13      Q.    You didn't scream at him at Moulon Rouge when
14   you were in Paris; right?
15      A.    You want to hear about that?
16      Q.    No, I'm asking you if you screamed at him at the
17   Moulon Rouge in Paris, France?
18      A.    He made me cry, that's all I know.
19      Q.    Ma'am?
20      A.    He made me cry.
21      Q.    And you remember standing on the table and
22   throwing all the money, all the trip money up in the air;
23   do you remember that?
24      A.    I don't remember that.  He gave me money, he
25   threw money to me because I don't have money.  We have an
```

1 argument in the Moulon Rouge. He was complaining that the
2 show is not ever picking up, and he doesn't want to move.
3 And waiter wanted us to leave so I asked him to leave.
4 And he stood there. Say, "then you go" and he threw all
5 the money.
6   And I asked him "I don't have money to go, how
7 can I go"?
8   He threw the money towards me.
9   Q.   All right. Do you recall a couple of years ago
10 him going upstairs and locking the door and you pounding
11 on the door until the door knob mechanism fell apart.
12 Back in 1999. Do you remember that?
13   A.   No, I don't remember. He lock the door because
14 he wants to keep his business up. He doesn't trust
15 anyone, so.
16   Q.   Do you remember -- do you acknowledge kneeing
17 him in the groin area?
18   A.   Kneeing him?
19   Q.   Kneeing him with your knee in the groin area?
20   A.   What is groin?
21   Q.   In the private area?
22   A.   Groin area?
23   Q.   Groin area. Do you acknowledge kneeing him near
24 the penis?
25   A.   Never.

```
 1      Q.    Never?

 2      A.    Yes, he scratches me with toenail.

 3      Q.    What about the scratches on the face?

 4      A.    Never happen.

 5      Q.    Never happened?

 6      A.    Tommy's not --

 7      Q.    Okay, do you remember --

 8      A.    So he got a cut sometimes.  He doesn't mind, he

 9  doesn't even put antibiotic.  He says it naturally

10  healing.

11      Q.    Do you remember elbowing him in the neck?

12      A.    Never.

13      Q.    Do you remember hitting him in the face and the

14  side?

15      A.    Never.  He hit me.  How can I fight with a big

16  guy.

17      Q.    Let's talk a little bit about what has happened,

18  ma'am.  He and D         have been out of the family home

19  for how long?

20      A.    Okay.

21      Q.    Might February sound right?

22      A.    No, I think it's March sometime.  He's saying

23  that he got an apartment from his contracting company.

24  That is -- because once in awhile he has to work late

25  because he has to pay all the debt out.
```

1   Q.   Okay. Ma'am, do you have --

2   A.   From March I aware he's having apartment, mid

3   March.

4   Q.   And is it accurate to say that prior to March

5   there was a time when you-all were separated or in the

6   process of separating when he was pretty much exclusively

7   taking care of D   . Would you agree with that?

8   A.   He never give me any chance to be involved in.

9   He goes to doctor without letting me know. So how do I

10   know?

11   Q.   Has Mr. Lynch taken D   to the pediatrician

12   the vast majority of the times?

13   A.   Yeah, now I see is the medical reports about how

14   many visit he made last year.

15   Q.   Okay.

16   A.   And I really worried about D   because he

17   got sick so many times. He didn't even tell me.

18   Q.   And you've been to the pediatrician once with

19   him and D   and once by yourself and every other time

20   in D   ' life Mr. Lynch has taken D   ; is that

21   correct?

22   A.   That's not correct.

23   Q.   So how many times do you say you've been up

24   there?

25   A.   Dr. Samuel Mirrop or before? From '98 to 2000

1   where are right now?

2   Q.   To the Pediatric Associates, yes, to that group?

3   A.   After Samuel Mirrop doctor you talking about,
4   almost half.

5   Q.   Almost half. Why do you say that, you just said
6   that you just saw how many times he had taken him to the
7   doctor last year?

8   A.   Last year from my understanding he's trying to
9   make an evidence as primary take care. That's why he's
10   making unnecessary visits.

11   Q.   You heard Ms. Grover today talk about what a
12   good father he was. You remember her?

13   A.   He's a good father, I don't deny it. I worried
14   about when he grows up D   ' having opinion, and I
15   don't know he's answering that. He's very, very
16   attentive, I know that.

17   Q.   You also heard her say that he wasn't the type
18   to badmouth you to her, at least in her hearing. You
19   heard her say that; did you not?

20   A.   I'm sorry?

21   Q.   To talk negatively about you, you heard her say
22   that?

23   A.   Right there, I'm sorry?

24   Q.   Ms. Heidi Grover.

25   A.   I don't know which Ms. Heidi Grover.

```
 1       A.    No, he said I cannot come there.

 2       Q.    Let me finish.  And tell everybody about

 3  you-all's marital difficulties; did you not?

 4       A.    I didn't threaten him.

 5       Q.    Didn't do that.

 6             How much money do you make per year, ma'am?

 7       A.    Okay, I am earning 74,500 plus bonus.

 8       Q.    And how much is the bonus, how much was it last

 9  year?

10       A.    Last year I have a detention (sic) bonus for

11  three months extra bonus, so.

12       Q.    How much was your bonus last year?

13       A.    I don't even remember.  Tom has all the records.

14  He removed everything December from our house completely.

15  He claims that he had to get out his work out, I don't

16  really know, I don't have any information with me.

17       Q.    Okay.

18       A.    I guess, so 5,000 I make per, per month.  More

19  than 5,000.

20                  MR. TERRY:  I pass the witness.

21                  THE COURT:  Mr. Calabrese, any questions at

22  this time?

23                  MR. CALABRESE:  I don't think so, Judge,

24  we're going to reserve.

25                  THE COURT:  Thank you, Mrs. Lynch, you can
```

162

1 step down.

2   And, Mr. Terry, your next witness?

3   MR. TERRY: Yes, I call Mr. Lynch.

4   (Petitioner's Exhibit 10 was marked.)

5   THOMAS_WALKER_LYNCH,

6 having been previously duly sworn, testified as follows:

7   DIRECT_EXAMINATION

8 BY MR. TERRY:

9   Q.   Mr. Lynch, let me hand you what's been marked

10 Petitioner's Exhibit Number 10 and ask you what it is.

11   A.   This is a tape recording of one of H   's

12 fits.

13   Q.   And did you make this tape recording?

14   A.   Yes, I did.

15   Q.   Okay. And did you make it -- and was it

16 produced on a machine which is capable of recording this

17 sort of tape?

18   A.   Yes.

19   Q.   Okay. And is it accurate, to your knowledge?

20   A.   Oh, it's completely accurate.

21   MR. TERRY: Okay. We'd offer 10.

22   MR. CALABRESE: I have no way of knowing if

23 it's relevant, Judge. I haven't heard any of it.

24   THE COURT: And Petitioner's 10 is

25 Admitted.

```
 1              (Mr. Terry played part of Exhibit Number

 2              (10.

 3       Q.    (By Mr. Terry)  Mr. Lynch, what does that tape

 4  depict?

 5       A.    This is H       's usual way of communicating

 6  with D       and I.

 7       Q.    Okay.  What was going on there?

 8       A.    I'm not sure which segment you cued up.  But I

 9  do think I remember that episode.  We came back from the

10  park, and H       was upset for a reason that I don't

11  know, and then there was something with water and D

12  towards the end.

13              Often when she talks like that, I can't

14  understand what she's saying.

15       Q.    There was discussion by Mr. Issen this morning

16  regarding the high-pitched screaming and this

17  unintelligible.  Is that an example of what he's talking

18  about?

19       A.    That is an example, but it gets worse than that.

20       Q.    Okay.  And do we have a number of tapes that

21  depict this sort of behavior?

22       A.    Yes, we do.

23       Q.    All right.  Mr. Lynch, I want to talk a

24  little -- before we get off the tape, D        in the

25  background was uttering a phrase or a part of a phrase,
```

```
 1   did you hear that in the audio?

 2       A.   Yes, I heard it.

 3       Q.   What was he --

 4               MR. CALABRESE:  I object to the hearsay.

 5   Judge.

 6               What is this, you bring a tape recorder and

 7   then you start playing it for the court without any

 8   proper --

 9               THE COURT:  Hang on.  Hang on.  Hearsay's

10   sustained.

11       Q.   (By Mr. Terry)  Was D          saying anything

12   that -- well, let me try it this way.  Was D

13   uttering any sort of complete sentence at all?

14               MR. CALABRESE:  Objection to hearsay.

15               THE COURT:  Just answer that question.

16       A.   I can understand my son, and he is usually calm,

17   and in this particular case he's --

18               THE COURT:  The question was was he --

19       Q.   (By Mr. Terry)  Was he uttering a sentence?

20       A.   Yes.

21       Q.   A sentence?

22       A.   Well, a one-word sentence, two-word sentence, so

23   technical.

24       Q.   Okay.  What does he call you, sir?

25       A.   Da Da.  Well, at that time.
```

Figure 31: Temporary Orders, H's Testimony*

After H* stepped down from the box, and was walking across our side to her seat, she turned while walking with her back to the judge, and she smiled a fuck you grin. I was so accustom to H* vile nature that I barely noticed it. Our nanny was sitting behind us and she was exasperated. "Did you see that?" She said. "Can you believe that?" Rosa was convinced that H* was an evil person.

When the judge made his concluding remarks, he held up a picture of H*'s exorcist fit after the Indian Pow Wow, and he said, "I saw this face in this courtroom," and he held up the picture of H* shown further down in this document. He also questioned H*'s explanation that D* face was stuffed in the pillow because he was sleeping. He noted he couldn't be sleeping if she was screaming. Judge Hathaway gave me sole managing conservatorship. He commented that he didn't know why we hadn't asked for supervised possession, but since we hadn't, he wasn't going to order it. But I had asked for supervised, but Terry didn't want to request it, because, as he explained, he didn't want to win by too much. The following is the ruling:

1   REPORTER'S RECORD

2   NO. FM102879

3
     IN THE MATTER OF   *   IN THE DISTRICT COURT
4   THE MARRIAGE OF   *
                               *
5   THOMAS WALKER LYNCH   *
     AND   *
6   H   *   TRAVIS COUNTY, TEXAS
                               *
7   AND IN THE INTEREST OF   *
     D   *
8   A MINOR CHILD   *   98TH JUDICIAL DISTRICT

9

10

11
                     ****
12
                       COURT'S RULING
13
                     ****
14

15

16

17   On the 14th day of June, 2001 the

18   following proceedings came on to be heard in the

19   above-entitled and numbered cause before the Honorable

20   John Hathaway, Judge presiding, held in Austin, Travis

21   County, Texas:

22   Proceedings reported by Machine Shorthand.

23

24

25

1 | is saying D   is awake and you had put him to bed
2 | and holding his head down. And you are telling me that
3 | D   is asleep. Petitioner 7, whether he is awake
4 | or asleep, you are going to tell me that after this?
5 | And I have no reason to believe it is a silent scream,
6 | in fact the evidence is that it was not a silent scream.
7 | You are telling me he stayed asleep?
8 | So, these pictures coupled with the
9 | testimony of the other witnesses, coupled with the tape,
10 | it is not an appropriate response to whatever
11 | provocation Mr. Lynch was initiating. Absolutely
12 | without question presumption of joint managing
13 | conservatorship has been overcome. I cannot have a
14 | joint managing conservatorship, it is not appropriate at
15 | this time. I hope one day it is. But right now there
16 | is just no way. Which means, that when you both lobbed
17 | your grenades and fired off those missiles and tripped
18 | the wire that always kept mutually assured destruction
19 | as a safe doctrine, it means I have got to choose one of
20 | you as temporary sole managing conservator but I can't
21 | choose both. And so based on the evidence presented Mr.
22 | Lynch is appointed as temporary sole managing
23 | conservator. Because, Mrs. Lynch, at best I cannot get
24 | past the pictures, plus the testimony of the other
25 | witnesses, plus the tape.

168

1   Mrs. Lynch is appointed as temporary

2 possessory conservator with possession according to the

3 standard possession order as requested by Mr. Lynch and

4 as represented by Mr. Lynch as being in D   ' best

5 interest. That standard possession will start not today

6 but on Friday, June 15, 2001.

7   MR. TERRY: That is Father's Day weekend?

8   THE COURT: Well, it would be according to

9 the standard possession order so I guess whatever the

10 standard possession order says.

11   MR. TERRY: Okay, I just wanted to make

12 that clear.

13   THE COURT: And I had momentarily

14 forgotten it was Father's Day weekend. So the

15 possession starts on Friday but subject to the standard

16 possession order which will not happen this weekend.

17   You-all cannot be together during

18 exchanges. The only place, the only time you can be

19 together during an exchange is inside the Austin Police

20 Department headquarters at 8th Street and I-35. There

21 are no exceptions. You can never be together during

22 exchange. So exchanges first will take place at the day

23 care while the day care is in session. But again,

24 remember these temporary injunctions. You-all can't get

25 within 200 yards of each other except in those very

Figure 32: Temporary Orders, Ruling

H* gets a New Attorney, Sara Brandon

H*'s new attorney was Sarah Brandon. Brandon had a reputation of doggedly following up on her cases, provided that she was well paid. She bragged that she only took one case at a time. She was also reputed to be crazy and marginally competent. Her phone number differed by one digit from that of Legal Aid, who administered VAWA grants. The rumor was that she had lost custody of her kids when she was a young mother, so her profession was a blood sport. Also, something I didn't know at the time, was that Brandon had worked for Jim Piper, the attorney I had fired over the answering machine messages left at the house. Attorneys told me that going up against Brandon was always a lot of work, some charge more money when she is on the other side, some simply avoid such cases. She had a bag of dirty tricks, and one of them was to bury the adversary in paper. She referred to H* as "Poor Little H*."

Father's Meeting Notes With His Attorney Stolen from the Car

My attorney notes from Ted were taken from my car. Ted was pissed.

Jodi: Give Us $35,000 OR No Summer Agreement and No Case File

Shortly after the hearing Jodi called me. I was in an attorney friend's office at the time, Bill Jang.

> "Tom, we are not doing *anything* more unless you give us another $35,000 this week.

> Not even return my records?

> Not even the records.

> What about our agreement with H*'s attorney about the summer possession schedule?

> That has been lost for now, but [if I was working] I could try and get it back.

> I can't pay you all off this week Jodi.

> Then we are withdrawing. Oh, and by the way, I have found a great ad litem for you. You are really going to like her. Good bye."

This was a very bizarre thing for Ted to have done. I could have added more to the retainer, but I didn't have $35,000 that very week, and to be holding a threat behind it, and then instantly loosing the agreement. It was strange. Ted died 5 years later. The paper says it was a heart attack. It is rumored that he had a dependency problem. I have also been told he was showing up in court while out of it. The attorneys tell me it was "sad." Sad as they thought it was, they still didn't do a thing to help the clients who paid, such as myself.

The example I set by allowing H* run over me for so many years was recognized by Ted, and others, as an invitation to do the same. In effect, Ted held D* for ransom.

The tone and phrasing of the ad litem recommendation raised questions.

After the call, Bill Jang just shook his head. He called Jodi back and spoke with her about taking the case. His purpose was only to close the case out, as Bill didn't normally do divorces. At that moment it appeared to Bill that we were about done.

Jodi apologized to Bill about the records, and did send something. Though the summer possession agreement remained lost, as promised. We called H*'s attorney, Gary Calabrese. He said, "I don't think it is appropriate for me to provide you with a copy, as there is a new attorney on the case." Alicia Browner, Sandy's friend "who liked to help women get divorced," had found a new attorney for H*, and this new attorney said she knew nothing about any summer possession agreement.

Ted's final invoice landed at an astonishing $35,000.00. I called him to discuss it. The conversation became exasperating and I blurted out, "If the bill is so accurate, then what an amazing coincidence it is that the total is exactly $35,000 point 00." Ted then invoiced for sixteen hundred dollars and some odd cents more, although I hadn't seen him in the interim, the bill was itemized. I called back again. The tone of his voice became low and grumbling. He growled, "Give me my money!" I paid him. I didn't want the baggage of Ted becoming an adversary.

Poor Little H* Tells Dad: "When I am done, you will never see your son again. You will never have a penny in your life. I will make sure this happens if it takes me a life time." 2001 07 03

H* had a new attorney and although she had lost everything she had a new found confidence. At our next exchange just before the July 4th weekend H* told me she was going to get even, and she threatened that she would make sure I would never see my son again, and she guaranteed that I would never have a penny in my life. Furthermore, she said that she would make this happen even if it required the rest her life to accomplish it. She started working on her promise that weekend, and has done a pretty good job of continuing it for eight years now.

H* Does Not Return D* after July 4th Weekend 2001

D* was not returned after the weekend. Bill Jang contacted Sarah Brandon, and Brandon told him that the ad litem had recommended that H* keep D* so she could observe mom with her child. The official sound of the explanation assured that the police would not get involved. Only a judge could overrule their ad litem, but Hathaway was on vacation for two weeks. The funny part was that we hadn't met the ad litem yet, so how could she be making recommendations?

Bill recommended waiting. Because the ad litem was being quoted and we had never met her, I insisted that he call her on it. Bill sought TRO with Judge Jenkins.

Sarah Brandon arrived at the just 10 minutes to the close of the session. She requested we go into chambers. Stupidly we agreed as there was no court reporter. On the wall was a framed photo of Judge Jenkin's father. Sarah explained that she had been at the zoo with her kids. Karen Phelan came in with us. Sarah explained to Judge Jenkins that she had the ad litem's, Lara Nixon's permission to keep D*. She continued that she would be glad to meet and talk about it in two weeks time when Judge Hathaway returned from his vacation. Judge Jenkins elected to let the matter wait for two weeks.

We had not met the ad item yet, and here the other side was acting on recommendations she claimed to have made. In two weeks time Ms. Brandon was not available to meet. Ms. Brandon happened to have a conflict after two weeks. After that Ms. Brandon *said she was on vacation for the month of August*. "Everyone knows that I take August off," she said. H* kept D* for almost two months. H*'s sister came from Italy and watched D*.

There was an emergency room visit with D* to the ER in Round Rock for a dislocated elbow during this period. He was said to have fallen out of bed.

Peggy Farely Doesn't Answer or Return Father's Calls

Peggy Farely was appointed by the ad litem to be the child psychologist. She simply refused to answer my calls or return messages. I went into my attorney's office one afternoon. He was incredulous, so I called from his phone in the afternoon, and got the recording. I left a message to call me back, and gave the attorney's number. She did not call back. Lara then sued me for not seeing Farely. My attorney asked her, then "you deny getting a message to call back at my number?", "yes" was the reply.

H and Sarah Brandon Take Dad's Business Files Negotiate to Trade them For a Favorable Settlement Agreement*

H* entered my locked office at the house, took all of my papers, and gave them to Sarah Brandon. Most of these predated our marriage, none of them belonged to her. The papers contained a lifetime of my proposed architectures, designs, mathematical work, and business plans, and I could not do my job without them. Due to my consulting practice the papers also contained intellectual property work and the concomitant secrecy agreements. All of this was now sitting in Sarah Brandon's office.

Ted Terry initially requested the material be returned, then Bill Jang sent a series of letters where Brandon violently agreed to return the material, and then forgot she had agreed, but Jang never filed a motion to force the issue. Bob Luther, strangely, refused to do anything to help me get my files back. This, the conflicts issue, and his refusal to issue with Lara Nixon, lead to the conclusion that he was not my advocate, rather something else.

It wasn't until after Brandon accused me of kidnapping D* in the spring of 2002 did my attorney at the time finally wake up and decided there was an issue, and then filed a motion to force the return of the property.

172

EDWIN J. (TED) TERRY, JR.
BOARD CERTIFIED - FAMILY LAW
TEXAS BOARD OF LEGAL SPECIALIZATION
FELLOW - AMERICAN ACADEMY
OF MATRIMONIAL LAWYERS
FELLOW - INTERNATIONAL ACADEMY
OF MATRIMONIAL LAWYERS
AMERICAN BOARD OF TRIAL ADVOCATES

805 WEST 10TH
2nd FLOOR, SUITE 300
AUSTIN, TEXAS 78701
TELEPHONE (512) 476-9597
FAX (512) 476-6106

JAMES A. VAUGHT
BOARD CERTIFIED - FAMILY LAW
BOARD CERTIFIED - CIVIL APPELLATE LAW
TEXAS BOARD OF LEGAL SPECIALIZATION
MEMBER, ASSOCIATION OF ATTORNEY - MEDIATORS

KARL E. HAYS
BOARD CERTIFIED - FAMILY LAW
CIVIL APPELLATE LAW - CIVIL TRIAL LAW
TEXAS BOARD OF LEGAL SPECIALIZATION

June 26, 2001

VIA CONFIRMED FAX

Mr. Gary Calabrese
Attorney at Law
808 Nueces
Austin, Texas 78701

Re: Cause Number FM102879; In the Matter of the Marriage of Thomas Walker Lynch
        and H   and In The Interest Of D   , Minor Child

Dear Mr. Calabrese:

Here is a summary of what I have gleaned about current issues between the Lynches:

Electrical Conduit.

I have spoken with Mr. Lynch regarding the dangerous exposed electrical conduit. As you face the house, on the left of the garage is a gate. You walk through and on the right, attached to the house, is the power meter, from which a conduit pipe leads to the ground. The pipe has a hole in it, which is Mr. Lynch's safety concern. He already spoke with one contractor (informally, not an actual bid), who estimated the work with a back hoe and replacing the conduit would cost around $2000; another contractor estimated it might cost $500. Presumably the actual cost will be somewhere in between those two figures.

Tom Lynch's Property at Dragon Drive

Mr. Lynch would like to pick up the following items from the   house: (1) his files (in the file cabinets); (2) his books; (3) any other research or paper that is not filed in the file cabinets; (4) all office furniture–desk, chair, file cabinets and any other furniture belonging to Tom in that room. Mr. Lynch needs these items in order to do his business. We must set up a time for him to retrieve these items within the next two days, or we will file a motion before Judge Hathaway, asking for orders to be able to do it.

LAW OFFICES OF SARAH K. BRANDON, P.C.
508 WEST TWELFTH STREET
AUSTIN, TEXAS 78701

(512) 477-4707 OFFICE
(512) 477-2770 FACSIMILE

SARAH K. BRANDON

APRIL PERRY
LEGAL ASSISTANT

July 13, 2001

1 pages sent by fax 323-2338

William Jang
314 Highland Mall Boulevard, Suite 406
Austin, Texas 78752

Re: Cause Number: FM102879; In the Matter of the Marriage Lynch and in the interest of D
a child; In the 98th Judicial District Court of Travis County, Texas.

Dear Mr. Jang:

I read your letter dated July 12, 2001 to Ms. Brandon. She has instructed me to forward your letter to the client immediately, so that we may address the property issue as soon as practicable. Ms. Brandon also inquired as to how Mr. Lynch has managed so well without these files and the contents so long if they are in fact of such vital importance. He never mentioned these issues in the Temporary Orders hearing and he moved out of the residence over 90 days ago. Please advise.

Ms. Brandon will give the property matter her attention on Monday.

Ms. Brandon will have a proposal of "visitation time" for Mr. Lynch during Dr. Lynch's extended period of summer possession of D   on Monday.

It is our understanding that you will now be making additional changes to the Temporary Orders to include a "Standard Possession Order" and the place for the exchange, among other things. Please send us a draft of the corrected Temporary Orders for our review.

Are you still requesting a meeting? If so, when and what is the scope of the meeting? Please advise. Please keep us posted if you are still requesting a meeting, because Ms. Brandon's calendar and schedule fills up fast.

Thank you for your attention to the above matters.

Very truly yours,

Michelle Gonzalez
Assistant to Ms. Brandon

cc: client
Lara Nixon   473-9818

174

LAW OFFICES OF SARAH K. BRANDON, P.C.
508 WEST TWELFTH STREET
AUSTIN, TEXAS 78701

(512) 477-4707 OFFICE
(512) 477-2770 FACSIMILE

SARAH K. BRANDON

APRIL PERRY
LEGAL ASSISTANT

July 31, 2001

VIA FACSIMILE and Regular Mail   *36 pages sent*
323-2338

William Jang
314 Highland Mall Boulevard, Suite 406
Austin, Texas 78752

Re: Cause Number: FM1-02879; *In the Matter of the Marriage of Thomas Walker Lynch and H_____ In the Interest of D_____ a Child*; In the 98th Judicial District Court of Travis County, Texas.

Dear Mr. Jang:

First, I want to apologize for not getting back with you concerning your July 25, 2001 letter with respect to Temporary Orders. I have been in Court or mediation every day since, including this morning. I worked late last night reviewing your last draft at the Temporary Orders and in all candor was a little frustrated with it. Then I have to remind myself that you do no routinely practice family law and some of this is a little different from the Orders you usually prepare. I prepared them rather than attempting to mark up the copy.

I read the Order thoroughly, as I suspect you will read the draft I prepared throughly. I assumed that you were not trying to "trick" me by inserting property language in a draft of an Order, when you knew that there was no such Order in place. I have deleted that portion of the Order in my draft. Because you thought I was trying to "trick" you in the one page Rule 11-Agreement, I have highlighted portions of the Order that were not specifically Ordered in the Judge's Orders in the transcript or standard language.

In addition, I suggest that you look at the family law drafting/practice manual, since it appears you are without the language. In addition, it appears that it would be in the best interest of everyone for the visitation exchanges to be at the day care. You are certainly aware by now, that the possession schedule is determined by the school district in which the child resides.

Not that I think you would act in bad faith, but sometimes clients either abuse the system or do not understand it, thus, in the event, your client attempts to do something other than standard visitation and withhold the child under the standard possession order (for which I have drafted), I will file a Motion for Contempt and Sanctions.

July 12, 2001
Page 2

With respect to the "documents" we have been contacted by Paul Drake, Attorney for AMD. (apparently at your client's request) concerning the documents. My client will bring the documents here to my office. We will not look at them, We will then contact Paul Drake to come and retrieve those documents. In addition, we are concerned about the "confidentiality of other such documents and in all candor do not trust your client with them either. Our client, will give us the corporate address of all the companies in question. (Or your client can do the same) We will write them, and copy the letter to you, and notify them that we have such documents and do they want to retrieve them. We will give them 10-14 days to respond. Thereafter, any remaining documents will be divided by a neutral; mediator (either Jan Lindeman or Bob Bowman whoever is available first on an agreed upon date to divide any remaining documents and that person will list all documents taken by each party and will take into his or her possession any unagreed documents. This person is not to view or read such documents. Please advise us if this is a satisfactory compromise on the dispute over documents and then contact April or Michelle to set this up.

It is my understanding that Lara Nixon would like for us to agree on a neutral play therapist for D   . Please send my a list of names.

If you are interested in sitting down to discuss this case, meaning just the lawyers, I would happy to entertain that idea Simply let my office know so they could schedule the same for a mutually convenient time for both of us.

I hope this letter finds you well

Very Truly Yours,

Sarah K. Brandon

cc: client

cc: Lara Nixon

176

Exhibit H2
p1

LAW OFFICES OF SARAH K. BRANDON, P.C.
508 West Twelfth Street
Austin, Texas 78701

(512) 477-4707 OFFICE
(512) 477-2770 FACSIMILE

Sarah K Brandon

APRIL PERRY
LEGAL ASSISTANT

August 1, 2001

VIA FACSIMILE
323-2338

William Jang
314 Highland Mall Boulevard, Suite 406
Austin, Texas 78752

Re: Cause Number: FM1-02879; *In the Matter of the Marriage of Thomas Walker Lynch and*
H_____ *and In the Interest of D_____ a Child*; In the 98th Judicial
District Court of Travis County, Texas.

Dear Mr. Jang:

WOW!, is my response to your July 31, 2001 letter. A simple, I don't think that proposal with
respect to exchanging files would have done; however, my client will be boxing the files up and we
can discuss other possible solutions. What do you suggest that would protect my client in the event
that these files got disclosed to the wrong person. You communicated to me and did Mr. Drake that
these were confidential files and should not be disclosed to the wrong persons. How do we know that
Mr. Lynch would not disseminate these documents to the wrong person. Right now, the documents
are in my clients possession of control; therefore, she can prevent these documents from falling into
the wrong hands.

With respect to my conflict dates they are as follows:

    A. She will be on vacation for the entire month of August.
    B. Our office will be closed on September 3, 2001, for Labor Day.
    C. She will be in a hearing in Tarrant County on September 4-5, 2001.
    D. She will be in a Final Trial on the Merits on September 11-13, 2001.
    E. She will be in a Final Trial on the Merits on September 17-20, 2001.
    F. She will be on vacation from September 26-October 2, 2001.
    G. She will be in a Final Trial on the Merits in Williamson County on October 8-10, 2001.
    H. She will be in a Final Trial on the Merits on October 29, 2001-November 1, 2001.
    I. She will be in a Final Trial on the Merits on November 13-16, 2001.
    J. Our office will be closed on November 21-23, 2001, for the Thanksgiving Holidays.
    K. Our office will be closed on December 20, 2001-January 2, 2002, for the Holidays.

EXHIBIT
H

177

Exhibit H2
p2

August 1, 2001
Page 2

       L. She will be out of the office on January 3-4, 2002.
       M. She will be out of the office on January 18, 2002.
       N. She will be out of the office on January 21, 2002.
       O. She will be in a Final Trial on the Merits on January 22-24, 2002.
       P. She will be out of the office on February 22, 2002.
       Q. She will be on vacation from March 11-15, 2002.
       R. She will be out of the office on March 29, 2002.
       S. She will be out of the office on April 1, 2002.
       T. She will be out of the office on April 29, 2002.
       J She will be out of the office on May 24, 2002.

Please also find page 21 and 23. I apologize that those did not get sent to you.

If you do set a hearing to enter these Orders with the Court, please also set it for longer than three hours, as we will have additional request and sanctions in that Motion. Moreover, you do not have any problems with Ms. Lynch, because she has not violated any court order. Thus, what could you sanction her for? Moreover, she has not violated any rule.

Sending me a two page fax full of question is counterproductive.

Very truly yours,

Sarah K Brandon /MG.

Sarah K. Brandon

SKB:mg

cc: client

178

LAW OFFICES OF SARAH K. BRANDON, P.C.
508 West Twelfth Street
Austin, Texas 78701

(512) 477-4707 OFFICE
(512) 477-2770 FACSIMILE

Sarah K. Brandon

APRIL PERRY
LEGAL ASSISTANT

September 10, 2001

William Jang   Sent by Fax 323-2338
314 Highland Mall Boulevard, Suite 406
Austin, Texas 78752

Re: Cause No. FM1-02879; *In the Matter of the Marriage of Thomas Walker Lynch and H____
          ____ and In the Interest of D_____ a Child*; In the 98th Judicial District Court
      of Travis County, Texas.

Dear Mr Jang:

I am sorry that I missed your call on September 7, 2001 with respect to some property issue. That
is the only message that I received, in that you called on a property issue.

I attempted to call your office on the evening of September 7, 2001 and I obtained your answering
machine and I left a message.

Perhaps it would be best if you sent your request in writing or the issue concerning the property in
writing so that I can forward it to my client.

Thank you for your courtesy and cooperation in this matter.

Very truly yours,

Sarah K. Brandon

SKB:mg

cc: client

179

john f. campbell
lawrence j. morgan
mark w. clemens

December 27, 2001

Ms. Sarah K. Brandon
508 West Twelfth Street
Austin, Texas 78701

RE: Cause No. FM1-02879; IMM Lynch

Dear Sarah:

Thanks for your recent letter concerning the Lynch closing.

I do not recall that there was any condition precedent to the right of Mr. Lynch to get his property.

Nonetheless, I have written Mr. Lynch and I am going to try the very best that I can to get this finished up before the end of the year.

Yours very truly,

John F. Campbell

cc: Tom Lynch

campbell & morgan, p.c.
attorneys and counselors
805 West 10th third floor
austin, texas 78701

512/476-6036   fax 512/478-8919

180

NO. FM1-02879

IN THE MATTER OF	§	IN THE DISTRICT COURT
THE MARRIAGE OF	§	
	§	
THOMAS WALKER LYNCH	§	
AND	§	98TH JUDICIAL DISTRICT
H‾‾‾‾‾‾‾‾‾‾	§	
	§	
AND IN THE INTEREST OF	§	
D‾‾‾‾‾‾‾‾ ,	§	
A CHILD	§	TRAVIS COUNTY, TEXAS

MOTION FOR TURNOVER OF PROPERTY

Comes THOMAS WALKER LYNCH, Movant, and would show the Court the following:

On or about the 13TH day of December, 2001, the parties were divorced and as a part of that Divorce Decree, Respondent, H‾‾‾‾‾‾‾‾‾‾‾‾‾, was to turn over the contents of Movant's office and all of his personal belongings within five (5) days.

Instead, Respondent has refused to turn over the contents of the office and personal belongings and thus Movant is requesting the Court to set a time specific when Movant can retrieve all of the contents of his office and his personal belongings from the residence at ‾‾‾‾‾‾‾‾‾‾‾‾‾‾‾‾‾‾‾‾‾‾‾‾‾‾‾‾.

Movant further requests that such retrieval be without any interference from Respondent and Movant requests that he be allowed to provide whatever security and assurance he may deem appropriate to accomplish a peaceful turnover.

Pleading further, Movant would show that it was necessary for him to secure the services of the undersigned attorney to represent him in this Motion and for which he requests that Respondent be ordered to pay a reasonable attorney's fee.

WHEREFORE, PREMISES CONSIDERED, Movant prays the Court grant this Motion so that Movant can retrieve his office and personal belongings as stated herein. Movant prays for attorney's fees.

Movant prays for general relief.

FILED

2002 FEB -3 PM 3: 25

Figure 33: Letters Documenting Brandon's Theft of My Work Files

181

Guardian Ad Litem Lara Nixon, "Lost the Evidence"

Lara Nixon declared to my attorney Bill Jang that *"all the evidence has been lost."* The audio tapes and pictures from the court file showing H* abusing D* had been sent to her, and she now claimed to have lost them. She said that since the evidence was lost, none of it would be considered for her final report. She had not been given the originals, but she would not except new copies. She never made any formal accusations about the integrity of the evidence, rather she simply brushed it all aside.

If I were to guess at a reason for Lara having lost the evidence, I would say it was out of a sense of injustice related to the expungement (see chapter "Hey Lets Just Put Dad in Jail"). Lara may well have thought that H* was telling the truth about this, and it was unfair that H*'s evidence against me would not be available to the court, while my evidence was. Independent of her motivations, it was an abuse of power as she had not only lost the evidence, but she had also dismissed it. Instead of starting a search for the material, it was to simply be left out of the report.

Lara Nixon requested a meeting with me alone without my attorney. Bill told me that since the ad litem had the power of the court I was obligated to be cooperative. He explained that the ad litem made a final report which for the vast majority of cases was followed. I interpret this in layman's terms to mean she was the de facto judge.

At the meeting Lara explained that attorneys just got in the way, and that I should tell her everything, including what I had discussed with my attorney. She wanted to know the *real story*. It was very awkward. She was an officer of the court, I was obligated to cooperate, she had just screwed me out of my summer with my son, had in affect unplugged our case by losing the evidence, and now she wanted to know what I discussed with my lawyer.

While Lara was talking I looked at her calendar which was hanging on the wall by her desk. It was open to July. It showed her first appointment with H* was not until three days after she met with me. I pointed at it and asked her if it was true that her first appointment with H* wasn't for three days. She said it was the case. I then asked if she had ordered D*, my son, to stay with his mom like Brandon had told Judge Jenkins. She didn't say yes, but she also refused to deny it. Indications are that Ms. Nixon had ordered my son to stay with his mother, in contradiction to the original judge, without having met the mom and without having seen any of the evidence. It also meant she had been working with the attorney on the other side before even contacting my attorney.

I asked around about Lara Nixon and a friend of a friend warned me that she was bad news, and in his opinion he had a penchant to making false allegations. I started taking D* to Dr. Mirrop and his associates for regularly wellness examinations.

Lara scheduled a home visit, and came by the house. Initially she was very nice, and seemed to be implying that she was on my side. She looked over the house approvingly. We took a walk down the sidewalk. Surprisingly she brought up Dr. Mirrop. I told her, "Yeah, D* sees him often." Lara wanted to know what we did during the examinations. I told her that I asked Dr. Mirrop to check that D* was not being sexually abused. Lara, who had been the master of composure, became very frustrated. She blurted out, "Well you are abusing him by taking him to the doctor too often!" I was taken back by the change in her face. I asked her to explain. "Doctor's examinations are not good for kids," came the reply. Then she recovered her composure and asked to know specifically what procedures had been done in the examinations. I told her I didn't know.

Lara Nixon requested that H* be given a sole managing conservatorship.

I asked Bill to write the ad litem department head explaining what had happened. He didn't really want to do it. There was no benefit for his career in such a move. After some deliberation Bill signed a complaint letter, only because he felt it was the right thing to do. When I called and asked the director, Katy Kapple, about the letter, she actually laughed. "So what," she told me.

Given the circumstances, I felt bad about having given Lara one of D*' best paintings when she came by the house. It was a painting of a lighthouse next to the sea during a storm. It was fashioned after a photo hanging in the living room. After Katy laughed, I asked for the painting to be returned. Katy Kapple's told me triumphantly, "it doesn't even look like a lighthouse anyway." It was amazing how emotionally connected and petty she was. After the final decree was signed, Katy sent a letter saying that the evidence had been found, but wouldn't be integrated into any reports, as they had already been published.

I pressed Mr. Jang to document the lost evidence, and he made the following calls and notes. He then provided a letter, which follows. Following that is Katy Kaple's reply:

Call Notes

12/13/01 Called Lara Nixon and left her message letting her know that we sent her approximately 10 audio tapes and inquiring about her statement that she only received 3 audio tapes.

12/13/01 Called John Campbell to let him know information regarding the alleged missing tapes and left him a message.

12/17/01 Called Lara Nixon and discussed the alleged missing tapes. She stated that she went back and looked and only found 4 tapes and stated that she could have misplaced the rest. She stated that she no longer needed the tapes because the parties settled and added that she "disposed of them all."

12/17/01 ~~They told me~~ Mr. John Campbell called me back and gave me some information regarding what happened at the contempt hearing. He told that the judge ruled that proper notice of contempt was not given by Sarah Brandon's office and therefore dismissed that part of

[editors note, chopped line reads:
the motion right away. He also mentioned]

184

that two therapists testified at the hearing. Specifically, Dr. Peggy Farly testified that Tom Lynch never tried to contact her when in fact Tom Lynch tried to contact her many times, including one time at Mr. Campbell's office, in his presence. When I ~~was~~ He agreed to my statement that Peggy Farly lied on the stand. He ~~also~~ also stated that Peggy Farly was getting ready to close down her practice. In addition he stated that Dr. Izzell ~~and~~ did not like Tom Lynch.

12/27/01 Called court reporter Sandra Lawson to inquire about the transcription of the contempt hearing. Her voice mail stated that she won't be back until 1/7/02. I left a message

185

Tom Lynch
POB 10199
Austin TX 78766-1199

Attorney Il Jang
301 Highland Center Blvd
Austin TX 78757

Mr. Jang,

Although the divorce is over, I feel that I can not leave the actions of the ad Litem unaddressed as others
will then be open to the same abuses. I hope you will consider answer the following questions, the
answers to which I will supply to the Travis County Probation office.

1. Are you currently retained by Mr. Tom Lynch?
2. Did Lara Nixon receive the evidence relating to the case (17 tapes, over 50 photographs, and other
   material.) What indications did you have that she had/or did not have the evidence?
3. Did this evidence show Ms. Lynch to be a good mother? Why or why not?
4. Did Lara Nixon want to use Peggy Farley as a child psychologist?
5. Did Lara Nixon ever mention Ms. Farley's qualifications?
6. Was Lara Nixon alarmed by the repeated large bug bites/ bumps which D   would have after
   visiting his mother? What did she do about it?
7. Did Sarah Brandon tell you she and Dr. H   were working with Lara Nixon at the TRO
   hearing on July 5th?
8. Did you have an easy time contacting Ms. Nixon?
9. Do you have, or did you have, US embassy documents showing that Mr. and Mrs. Choi are wanted for
   fraud in Korea?
10. Did Dr. H   open a bank account at AG Edwards with 300 dollars of stock from a Korean
    company after the Choi's arrived in Austin?
11. Did Mr. Lynch assault Mr. Choi.
12. In the CPS material you received from Ms. Nixon, did you find any occurrence of an incorrect address
    for Mr. Lynch?
13. Did Ms. Nixon desire to use a different school schedule than for the school D   attended.
14. Did Ms. Nixon ever express a concern about Dr. H   behavior, or about D   well
    being? What did she say?

Thank you for time.

Sincerely,

2002 02 01

Tom Lynch

186

WILLIAM JANG
ATTORNEY AT LAW
314 Highland Mall Boulevard, Suite # 406
Austin, Texas 78752
Phone: (512) 323-2333 Fax: (512) 323-2338

January 31, 2002

Tom Lynch   Via Hand Delivery
PO Box 10199
Austin TX 78766-1199

Re: Thomas Lynch vs. H
        FM1-02879

Dear Mr. Lynch:

    I am writing to respond to your letter requesting me to answer several questions. I will respond to each question as to the best of my memory. But before I do so, I ask that you reconsider submitting any complaints against Ms. Nixon. Your divorce is finalized, and it's probably in your best interest to put everything associated with your divorce behind you as much as possible.

    In addition, please be advised that if you allow a third party to read this letter, then it may act to defeat any attorney-client and attorney-work product privileges claims in the future. This means that another person may be able to compel information and documents that would have otherwise been protected as privileged materials. Therefore, extreme caution should be used before showing this letter to others.

    The following are my answers to your questions:

1) Question: **Are you currently retained by Mr. Tom Lynch?**
    Answer: I have not provided legal representation to you since Mr. John Campbell substituted in your divorce case sometime in December 2001. I am still providing legal services to Enregal, Inc. which you are a shareholder, director and officer but my representation is limited to drafting documents for Enregal, Inc.'s dissolution. In addition, per your request, my office has taken possession of your files and I have ordered transcription of the contempt hearing of December 13, 2002 but both of these acts were done with your clear understanding and agreement that my office is not providing legal services to you.

2) Question: **Did Lara Nixon receive the evidence relating to the case (17 tapes, over 50 photographs, and other material.) What**

happy, healthy etc." When I asked Ms. Nixon about possible mosquito bites, she stated that they were common at time of the year and that as long as D   got proper treatment it probably was nothing to worry about.

7)   Question: **Did Sarah Brandon tell you she and Dr. H   were working with Lara Nixon at the TRO hearing on July 5th?**

        Answer: On or about July 6, 2001, during the TRO hearing, Ms. Brandon represented to the court that she and Dr.   ·Lynch had communicated with Ms. Nixon and that Ms. Nixon supported the extended summer possession of D

8)   Question: **Did you have an easy time contacting Ms. Nixon?**
        Answer: I initially had difficulty contacting Ms. Nixon. However, after the initial period, Ms. Nixon either returned my calls fairly promptly or let me know in advance that she would not be available.

9)   Question: **Do you have, or did you have, US embassy documents showing that Mr. and Mrs. Choi are wanted for fraud in Korea?**
        Answer: My office has one letter from the US Embassy that states among other things, "The KNPA (Korean National Police Agency) recently confirmed that they (Mr. Tae Young Choi and his wife Song-Ja Moon) are indeed wanted for fraud committed on 3/15/98 in Korea."

10)   Question: **Did Dr. H   open a bank account at AG Edwards with 300 dollars of stock from a Korean company after the Choi's arrived in Austin?**
        Answer: We have several AG Edwards & Sons, Inc.'s account statements, which is under "H   ." However, I don't have any personal knowledge regarding the bank account at AG Edwards nor the time frame when the Choi's arrived in Austin.

11)   Question: **Did Mr. Lynch assault Mr. Choi?**
        Answer: I don't have any personal knowledge of the incident. However, I have documents that show that Mr. Choi accused you of assaulting him. But a Judge dismissed and expunged the records and files associated with the allegation, prohibiting "the release, dissemination or use of the expunged records and files."

12)   Question: **In the CPS material you received from Ms. Nixon, did you find any occurrence of an incorrect address for Mr. Lynch?**
        Answer: The CPS materials were provided by the Custodian of Records for Child Protective Services pursuant to a Deposition on Written Questions by Sarah Brandon's office and not by Ms. Nixon. As far as I can tell, only the following addresses are listed on the CPS

188

indications did you have that she had/or did not have the evidence?

Answer: On August 10, 2001, my office hand delivered 13 original audiotapes, a CD which contained several pictures, and documents, to Ms. Nixon, pursuant to our Response to Respondent's Request for Production. On August 14, 2001, my office and Ms. Nixon exchanged, via hand delivery the 13 original tapes with copies and we also delivered a few additional tapes and documents pursuant to Supplemental Response to Respondent's Request for Production. On or about December 12, 2001, you contacted me and stated that Ms. Nixon claimed that she only received 3 audio tapes and asked me verify that we sent all the tapes. I called Ms. Nixon on or about December 13, 2001 and left her a message concerning the tapes. On or about December 17, 2001, I discussed with Ms. Nixon concerning the tapes. She stated that she went back and looked and found four audiotapes and that she could have misplaced the rest. She stated that she no longer needed the tapes because the parties settled. I did not discuss with Ms. Nixon regarding the CD that contained the pictures nor documents.

3) Question: **Did this evidence show Ms. Lynch to be a good mother? Why or why not?**

Answer: I believe that there was some evidence that indicated Ms. Lynch may have been abusive. Some of the pictures and audiotape showed her unaccountably yelling. In addition, testimonial evidence was provided during the Temporary Hearings that indicated possible neglect and abuse of D .

4) Question: **Did Lara Nixon want to use Peggy Farley as a child psychologist?**

Answer: On or about August 29, 2001, at the Hearing to Enter Temporary Orders, Ms. Nixon supported the appointment of Dr. Peggy Farley as a child psychologist.

5) Question: **Did Lara Nixon ever mention Ms. Farley's qualifications?**
Answer: Ms. Nixon and I have not discussed Dr. Farley's qualifications.

6) Question: **Was Lara Nixon alarmed by the repeated large bug bites/bumps which D   would have after visiting his mother? What did she do about it?**

Answer: I remember you raising concerns about D   having mosquito bites, when he returned from Dr.   Lynch's residence on several occasions. In addition, I later received a CD with photos of D   with mosquito bites. I also have medical records that indicate mosquito bites. About the same time, July 18, 2001, Ms. Nixon stated in a fax that "everything seems fine, child looks

documents: '   Round Rock, Texas 78681 and
                    '   Austin Texas 78759." I
have other documents that list these addresses.

13)   Question: **Did Ms. Nixon desire to use a different school schedule than for the school D   attended?**

      Answer: Ms. Nixon supported the use of the A.I.S.D. school schedule. D   was attending Lycee' Francais d' Austin which had a different schedule.

14)   Question: **Did Ms. Nixon ever express a concern about Dr. H   l's behavior, or about D   well being?   What did she say?**

      Answer: Ms. Nixon repeatedly expressed concerns about D   well being. As for Dr. H   's behavior, Ms. Nixon's statements were mainly that she would investigate our allegations.

If you require further information please let me know. Thank you.

Sincerely,

William Jang
Attorney

Figure 34: Jang Notes and Letter, Documenting Nixon's Losing the Evidence, and Other Points

To: Travis County Juvenile Probation Department
From: Tom Lynch
Date: 2002 02 01

I am writing to make a formal complaint about Ms. Lara Nixon, the Guardian ad Litem assigned to the divorce between Dr. H   and myself in June of 2001.   Much of what occurred happened while the attorney Mr. Il Jang was handling my case. Mr. Jang has worked for the ACLU and now practices in Austin. He now handles adoptions and works with ad Litems. Hence, I hope you will appreciate the extraordinary nature of his attached letter.

When Ms. Nixon proposed reversing Judge Hathaway's decision she also began denying having received or even knowing of the case evidence. This evidence consisted of over a dozen tapes of Dr. H being abusive, photographs of the same, and medical records of ER visits for our son. Mr. Jang's legal assistant had hand delivered this evidence directly to Ms. Nixon, and Ms. Nixon had discussed it previously. [reference attached letter from Mr. Jang]

Lara Nixon forced the issue of using a child psychologist by the name of Peggy Farely. Ms. Farely had also been a client of my wife' attorney [reference court records of Farely divorce]. Peggy Farely was not listed in the phone book, did not have a regular office, and she was not listed in a guide of child psychologists. When I asked if she was a psychologist? a counselor? did she specialize in children? was she even licensed? - the subject was always shifted to a different psychologist - a very well qualified Dr. Ezel. After I posed the question to Ms. Farely, she no longer returned my phone calls. Ms. Nixon assured me that Ms. Farely was just "out of town for a while" and would call me back within the month. During this period Ms. Nixon wrote me a letter containing a complaint for not seeing Peggy Farely. Ms. Nixon then backed sanctions where Peggy was produced to testify. Ms. Farely perjured herself and was caught stating that she had not received calls from John Campbell's office on my behalf. [reference court transcripts from December hearing]

Ms. Nixon worked with my wife's attorney in order to change Judge Hathaway's temporary orders before she was willing to contact myself or my attorney. This became apparent at an emergency TRO in early July when my wife's attorney explained to Judge Jenkins that Lara Nixon had already met with her, and Ms. Nixon was working with my wife. Ms. Brandon explained that she had broken the court order due to Lara Nixon's recommendations. At my first appointment with Ms. Nixon two days after the emergency TRO, Ms. Nixon told me that she had not yet met my wife. Ms. Nixon then refused my direct request to say she had not made the statements represented to Judge Jenkins, or even to repeat that she had not yet met my wife. [reference attached Jang letter, reference Judge Jenkins notes, reference Lara Nixon's calendar, reference August hearing.]

I had an appointment in October to have my son see a pediatrician at the Mayo Clinic in Rochester because of indications that he shares a hereditary problem. I asked Ms. Nixon to secure permission for him to go to the Clinic. I gave her the dates I would be there.   She said she would take care of it. The complaint letter referred to above arrived while we were at the clinic, and it also contained a statement that she was alarmed that we had not made prior arrangements. [reference attached Nixon complaint letter].

When my son came back from a visitation yet again with mosquito bytes the sizes of quarters, and which left scabs, Ms. Nixon suggested that the problem wasn't that my son had been left unattended, but rather it was because he was allergic to bugs. She suggested that I should have this checked while I was at the Mayo clinic. [reference attached Jang letter].

Ms. Nixon provided a CPS report to my wife's attorney. She claimed that I filed it and had given an incorrect address. I had not filed that report. The report was produced at a convenient time and used to convince Dr. H   to abandon an already agreed upon settlement. [reference attached Jang letter].

There are other irregularities I will not go into here. I made these complaints to Ms. Nixon directly, but it is my understanding that she has not shared them with her management. In addition it is my opinion that some of her actions were in fact in retaliation to my complaints.

2002 0701

3/4

Figure 35: Complaint Letter to Domestic Relations

ESTELA P. MEDINA
Chief Juvenile Probation Officer

CECELIA BURKE
Director

February 12, 2002

Mr. Thomas Lynch
1217 Arcadia St.
Austin, TX 78757

RE: Cause No. FM1-02879, In the Matter of the Marriage of Lynch

Dear Mr. Lynch,

I have completed the investigation of your complaint regarding the Guardian on your case, Ms. Lara Nixon. I believe her investigation was objective and within the standards for Guardian ad Litem performance.

Her early involvement with visitation issues was due to problems in the development of an order to conform to the Court's decision of "standard visitation". Her support of the use of the AISD school schedule is consistent with Texas law. She did misplace some audiotapes around the time that copies were exchanged with the original tapes that had been sent to her in error. The tapes were subsequently located.

Attorney Jang's letter indicates Ms. Nixon did not provide incorrect addresses for you to TDPRS. At the time that Ms. Nixon recommended Peggy Farley, she was highly regarded in the therapeutic community for her work with children of divorcing parents. I am sorry that you were not impressed with her work.

Thank you for coming in with your concerns. I hope that your agreed settlement of your case works out for the best interest of your child.

Sincerely,

Katy Kappel, M.A.
Family Court Services Manager

Figure 36: Domestic Relations So What Reply

An interesting thing occurred last Friday, now the second of May in 2008. Another party who had Lara Nixon as an ad litem had a similar experience and they called her up before the social work review board. I was invited as a witness. The board ruled that she wasn't a social worker and therefore the case could not be heard. It turns out that the Travis County Domestic Relations office, who sent Lara to me to do a home study for the divorce in 2001, does not require people they hire to be licensed social workers.

Normally if an area of practice is licensed there are two parts to the regulation. In the first part the practice must be only be done by someone who is licensed, in the second part the person must follow the regulations of the license. For example, if you want to drive a car on public streets in the first part you must obtain a license, and then as a license holder you are obligated to follow the rules of the license. In Texas the social work license does not have a first part. Anyone may act like a social worker. Lara Nixon who has no license and not even a social work degree, but rather a degree in African American studies, routinely comes to houses and does a home studies. She does social investigations and provides reports to the courts, and the reports are almost certainly followed. She can do all of this in Texas without having a license. Now as the second part, since she doesn't have a license, she does not have to follow any social work regulations. If this same approach were used for drivers licenses, then the policeman would let everyone they stopped who did not have a license go without a ticket, because they only had the authority to regulate licensed drivers.

I went over this in front of the social work board. I pointed out she worked for the county's social work organization and did everything that a social worker would do. I pointed out that a person divorcing had a presumption that the person sent out to act as a social worker was qualified, and that in fact one would expect a social worker to come from the social work department of the county. The board pointed out that statute that gave them the authority to regulate people who had a license and that is all that mattered. No license, no regulation. Independent of any verbal claims the board required to see "LSW" written down to act, for example on a business card, letterhead or resume. One of the board members had a habit of speaking for the board without conferring with them. This could have been by agreement for efficiency sake, no one said. He wasn't the chairman. He and one other board member went over this during a break with the complainer off record, when I brought it up during session so that what he had said would be put on record, he became flustered and said 'we have heard enough from you!' I suppose this is not the only sensitive spot for this board. Most of the cases they heard that afternoon were dismissed because the person who filed the complaint was not present. It seemed strange that someone would go through all the trouble to make a formal complaint just to have it dismissed at the hearing because there was no accuser present. Having remembered my experience at the bar with my lost complaints, I was left wondering if there wasn't an endemic reason for the poor attendance.

This means that the Travis County Domestic relations office typically doesn't have to follow any social work regulations because their workers are typically not licensed. The most that can be done is what I did, write a complaint letter to DRO, so then they can reply with a so what.

Mayo Clinic Visit 2001

D* had loose stools from being very young. I even took him to Dr. Mirrop's nurse to show her once. Dr. Mirrop's nurse said they were normal. I showed them to Grandma, she disagreed. D* continued to have loose stools, and he had some mixed antigliden tests results at the pediatrician. I took him up to the Mayo Clinic in Rochester. According to Amber the nurse, they found some tissue damage in his gut. Nurse Savanna Borne confirmed this, and also said that it did not look like a fructose issue. What does this mean? No one has explained it. There is a bit of a coincidence with the biopsy I had, but no one has ever compared them. I suggested this be done, but they want it to be recommended by a psychologist, and D* psychologist sees no need. I have no idea if this type of thing is common or rare.

Summer to Fall 2001

As a first step towards making an agreement Bill Jang asked Sarah Brandon what she wanted for a settlement. She refused to say, which indicated to us that the law suit was not about settlement, but about punishment. The events that would follow buttress this view.

Brandon played games with all of the letters and proposals, by changing wordings between revisions, and adding little barbs. In one settlement agreement she had H* exchanging in the morning, but had me exchanging in the evenings before. Mr. Jang had to shut down his law firm for periods of time and just concentrate on exchanging words with Brandon. Brandon was always hostile at times even threatening to report Mr. Jang to the bar.

Mr. Jang and I asked Brandon to return my office papers, and she violently agreed - but never sent anything. On July 19 2001 she replied in a letter that they were gathering my records to return them "as we speak." I count 27 letters on the subject in the file. The bulk of records would not be returned until after the extortion demands to give everything to H* were met in March of 2002.

We asked Brandon to simply confirm she hadn't shared the materials with others, as that would have been sufficient to meet the criteria for my secrecy agreements, at least for the time being. She wouldn't. The police refused to get involved because "it was a divorce matter." We mulled it over and decided that we needed to follow the contracts and inform the other parties that the records were clearly no longer under our control. My consulting practice came to an abrupt halt. It would be five years before I would get another consulting contract.

At the time I was working for a partnership based design consultancy firm. Due to the divorce issues and intellectual property issues, I was asked to leave and that is putting it euphemistically. I was given an offer letter at another processor design company, but then the company bought the offer letter back. I had already declined an offer from another startup, and I went back to them and said I had changed my mind. They had been put off when I turned them down, as they had met my requested salary. The second company honored their original offer, but I had a political enemy in the company even before entering the door on the first day at the job. A few months later, with help from John Cambell, I would be asked to leave this company as well. The money from the offer buy back and the few months at the second startup constituted all of the money I would have for the next year.

I asked Lara Nixon to help me resolve the possessions issue. The files were part of my livelihood, so they obviously affected my son. My off site contract was over, and I needed my office materials. Lara said that her job was only to oversee the welfare of our son, and whether I could work [or lived or died] had nothing to do with that. This probably explains why my son had never come up as a topic of discussion with her. She added, that I shouldn't worry, "I saw all of your office records in garbage bags."

I called AMD and spoke with Paul Drake. I told him my office records had been taken. I have twenty patents with AMD, had been employed at AMD, and had contracted with their legal department to help write applications. Paul Drake replied dryly, Tom you shouldn't have any AMD related material. I don't think Paul realized that I had contracted with their legal department, and had been given material to work with. In addition I had legitimate publications on my AMD work. Paul only knew me as an employee. I asked him if he could help with recovering my records. He said no, and we got into an argument over obligations. He did call Brandon, and she told him that she had found records belonging to AMD in my files, i.e. she admitted to having my office files, admitted to going through them, and furthermore was willing to accuse me of stealing from AMD.

Paul requested that anything belonging to AMD be sent to him, as obviously, it belonged to AMD and not to Brandon. Brandon sent nothing, but a great deal of damage had been done just because she controlled the documents. I was obligated to notified Chromatic, they were considerably less happy than AMD.

The Brian Walters Agreement – H* and I Settle, Sara Brandon Cancels the Settlement

I called H* and proposed we meet and just talk between ourselves. It was really my only chance for a reasonable settlement. We drove to a park and talked. I figured we were both being screwed to some extent. I had heard Brandon had charged H* a lot of money. I pointed out to her all the damage that was being done, and how self serving the people involved were. Nobody cared about D*. Although H* lost control during her fits, and we couldn't live with her, I did, and do believe, there is a part of her that cared. I was also heartened by the rumor that she had tossed her father out. It was a hopeful sign. I proposed going back to the situation when D* and I had just moved out. That arrangement had been comfortable for all of us. We could work out where to go from there.

H* agreed.

We drove to the attorney Brian Walter's office, and had him compose a letter to fire both my attorney, and Brandon. We paid Brian Walters with separate checks to demonstrate that we were acting independently. We signed the letters, and Brian sent them out.

After Brandon received the letter, she contacted H* and persuaded her to continue the suit. H* contacted me and said she had only signed the letter *"because of your eyes."* I asked Brian Walters to press the original letter. Brandon then spun it and attacked Walkers. Unfortunately he was not up for the fight, and he dropped the matter.

195

LAW OFFICES OF SARAH K. BRANDON, P.C.
508 WEST TWELFTH STREET
AUSTIN, TEXAS 78701

SARAH K. BRANDON

(512) 477-4707 OFFICE
(512) 477-2770 FACSIMILE

APRIL PERRY
LEGAL ASSISTANT

September 10, 2001

Re: Cause Number: FM102879; In the Matter of the Marriage Lynch and in the interest of D_____
       a child; In the 98th Judicial District Court of Travis County, Texas.

Brian Walters
Walters & Turquand
812 San Antonio St., Ste. 507   Sent by 457-8399 **URGENT**
Austin, TX 78701

Dear Mr. Walters:

       It is my understanding you met with my client last week whereby she signed a document
either dismissing the lawsuit or dismissing her lawsuit against Tom Lynch which would allow her
to see her child whenever she wanted. I know of no such document and she tells me that you and
Tom Lynch told her it would be best not to contact me. She was not clear what to do. She has called
me and told me stop whatever it is you are trying to do until we have established what she as signed
and has me, her legal counsel approving the document. It is my understanding that you were hesitant
about filing the same.

       PLEASE DO NOT FILE WHATEVER IT IS SHE SIGNED. YOU DID NOT PROVIDE
HER A COPY OF THE DOCUMENT. PLEASE SEND ME A COPY ASAP.

       As an officer of the Court, I would tell you that she has represented to me that she has
revoked any such agreement.
Very truly yours,

Sarah K. Brandon

SKB:

CC: William Jang by fax

Figure 37: Brandon Independently Continues Law Suit

196

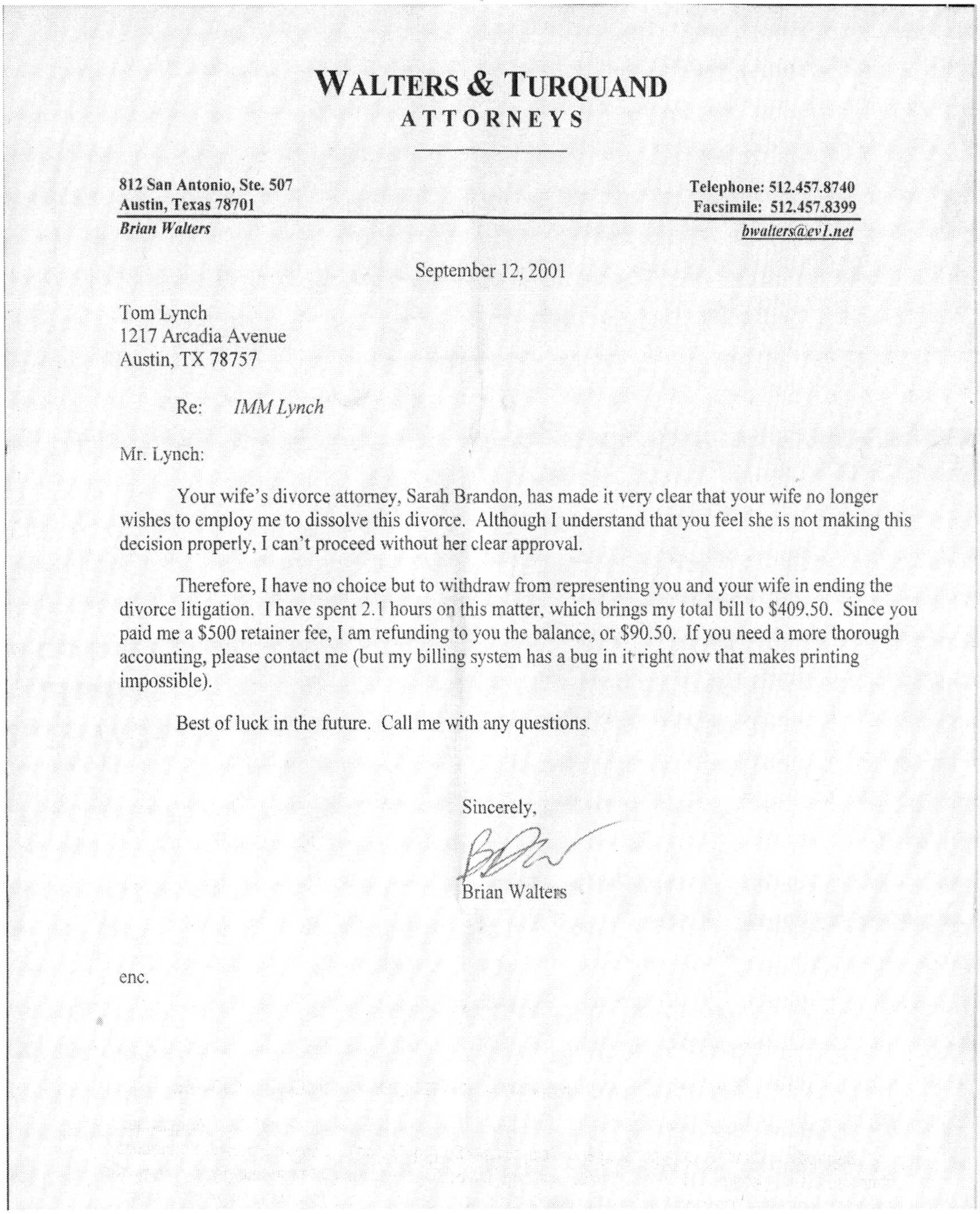

WALTERS & TURQUAND
ATTORNEYS

812 San Antonio, Ste. 507   Telephone: 512.457.8740
Austin, Texas 78701   Facsimile: 512.457.8399

Brian Walters   *bwalters@ev1.net*

September 12, 2001

Tom Lynch
1217 Arcadia Avenue
Austin, TX 78757

     Re: *IMM Lynch*

Mr. Lynch:

     Your wife's divorce attorney, Sarah Brandon, has made it very clear that your wife no longer wishes to employ me to dissolve this divorce. Although I understand that you feel she is not making this decision properly, I can't proceed without her clear approval.

     Therefore, I have no choice but to withdraw from representing you and your wife in ending the divorce litigation. I have spent 2.1 hours on this matter, which brings my total bill to $409.50. Since you paid me a $500 retainer fee, I am refunding to you the balance, or $90.50. If you need a more thorough accounting, please contact me (but my billing system has a bug in it right now that makes printing impossible).

     Best of luck in the future. Call me with any questions.

              Sincerely,

              Brian Walters

enc.

Figure 38: Walters Withdraws

Attorney Bob Luther Takes Over from Bill Jang

My friend Daniel offered me some advice. He said never fight with an attorney. He explained that the community was close, and that one never knew when one might need an attorney.

I asked Mr. Jang to prepare for a dirty fight. I suggested to him to make sure as many people knew what was actually going on as possible. He refused. He said it was unethical for an attorney to do anything except gather information and plead the case. He also felt he didn't have time to deal with Brandon, so we searched for another attorney.

I had an initial consultation with an attorney named Jim Ferris. He appeared to be anxious to take the case, but then called out of the blue and said he couldn't do it. When a mutual friend prodded, I heard back through the contact that Jim had explained that my criticism of Ted Terry's use of Jodi indicated that my priorities were not correct.

Yet, another attorney told me that he didn't want to take the case because he didn't want to be punished by Ted. He said he might be doing something simple like an adoption and then get punished in some sort of tit-for-tat in the other case, and he didn't want someone innocent to suffer.

An attorney who has a reputation as a maverick told me that the forces arrayed against me were such that he would have to shut down his whole practice and just work on my case full time if we were to prevail. He continued to say that he didn't have the time or energy to do that, and I probably couldn't afford it anyway. He explained that the women I was dealing with were indeed organized, that the attorneys were a clique, and that there was a familiarity between some of the attorneys and some judges. He said that familiarity would not work in my favor. I was stunned at hearing this, though very thankful that someone would be frank. There was no advantage for himself in giving me this information.

It was clear that since I had not paid off Ted, it was going to be difficult to get another attorney. The attorneys in the click were going to make me pay one way or the other. Though, surely among the about 40 professionals listed in the book, there was someone who would not be concerned about moving in on Ted's road kill. Though, upon closer study, it turned out that among the 40, there were about 10 who were highly respected. Those 10 were all on polite terms with each other.

William Travis, a long practicing attorney in Austin, said he wouldn't take the case for less than a $20,000 retainer, but he suggested Bob Luther. Based on Travis's recommendations, I retained Luther.

I was short of cash, so I was worried that Luther might not take the case, or would quit at a bad time, like Terry had done, so I stressed both how important my son was to me and how much of a bad deal he was getting. I also stressed that I was respected in my field, and made good money. Later I saw Bob's notes from the meeting. He had written down a few facts, but mainly he had analyzed me. While I discussed the bad deal my son was getting, he wrote down "histrionic." When I tried to allay fears he wouldn't get paid by explaining I was respected in my field, he wrote down, "narcissistic." As for most family practice attorneys, facts did not matter much to Bob. So, instead of recording the facts while I went through the case history, he was gathering tidbits of psychoanalysis.

I requested that Bob get a court order to have my office materials returned, so that I could work. He refused. I asked him directly for information about the child psychologist, Peggy Farely, who was be the psychologist for my son. I wanted to know if she was qualified, and if she had a relationship with Brandon or Lara. Lara had not impressed me as being impartial, and she had appointed Peggy.

Initially Bob said Peggy was *his friend* so I shouldn't worry about it. I found little solace in that reply, so I pressed again. I didn't even know if she was actually a psychologist, and I wanted to know. He then replied "Jeff Ezel is a fine man." I thought he hadn't heard me, so I repeated the question. "Is Peggy Farely a psychologist?" "Jeff Ezel is a fine man," he repeated. I guessed it was some sort of code, and I didn't like it. I wanted things to be above board. Because Bob would not tell me information, I requested a copy of Peggy Farely's resume. Surely, if she worked for the court, something with her qualifications was written down in a resume somewhere. I refused to all the conversation to move to Ezel.

Peggy Farely did not return my phone calls for making an appointment to see her, at the same time Lara Nixon was pushing me to see her. I felt like I was caught in some sort of slap stick comedy. I went back to Bob. Again, I asked him to get a court order to get my office material back. He did nothing, again. I again outlined how the three women involved, Sarah Brandon, Lara Nixon, and Peggy Farely, seemed so facile with each other. I wondered aloud to Bob if some of the women have a conflict of interest. I explained that I didn't like how some homosexuals took advantage of the court's indulgences of keeping stigmatic relationships secret, at the expense of tolerating the presence of conflicting parties. Bob took great offense at this suggestion. Another Austin attorney later suggested that perhaps this was because Bob himself was homosexual and Jeff Ezel had been one of his liaisons. If this is why he was upset, then he misinterpreted what I said, I did nothing more than an issue of team work that shouldn't exist.

Bob insisted again that I see Jeff Ezel. I didn't want to hear anything more about Jeff Ezel until the Farely thing was straightened out, and I told him this, yet again, and again asked him to call out the conflicts. That is when Bob said, "I can't do that, they are my friends." *He angrily added that if I didn't co-operate with him that things would turn out very badly for me.* I understood it as a threat. I felt beaten. I had been through four attorneys, and it was clear no one was going to work for me. The only thing that was happening was that my money was being spent at an accelerating rate. I had had enough. I told him. "Just get me out." He said that we had to go through it. I was heading into attorney five.

I came back with Will Jang who had not yet withdrawn to see if Bob Luther would do his Jeff Ezel switch thing in front of him. I asked Bob to conflict out Peggy Farely. Bob changed the topic to Jeff Ezel. I repeated I would not speak with Jeff until he addressed the Farely issue. He told me if I didn't see Jeff he would withdraw. I told him that I could not accept an ultimatum in place of a discussion about Farely, and that he was fired because he was issuing ultimatums, effective that moment. I have heard that Bob Luther then withdrew on the grounds that I would not see Jeff Ezel, and did not mention he had been fired.

Luther had never scheduled a hearing, had not tried to get my property returned, did not point out any conflicts or complain about the ad litem, in fact did nothing at all. He kept the retainer and sent me another invoice for $4,000 beyond the retainer. The final invoice is the attorney's coup de gras.

Attorney Campbell Takes Over From Bob Luther

Worse for the wear, I went back to William Travis. I trusted his recommendations because of the source of the referral for Mr. Travis, I was hoping he would change his mind about the size of the up front retainer. I asked Mr. Travis if there were not any family practice attorneys who had ethics or morals, who would just do what was right. I thought he might say, "Yeah me," but he didn't. Instead we discussed a laundry list of referrals. We came up with the name of John Campbell as someone who had a strong Christian faith.

In our first meeting after the initial consultation I asked John directly to get a court order to have my office material returned, and to figure out the nature of the conflicts and have the conflicted parties removed. I explained I didn't know exactly what the relationships were, but obviously there was something amiss.

John replied that everyone in family practice knew everyone else, so conflicts didn't matter. I wasn't sure how his conclusion followed. He continued to tell me about working a case in the courtroom of a judge who he knew well as a friend. He emphasized that the attorneys handled the conflicts responsibly. He said that the problem was that I didn't like anybody, and he listed them, you don't like Lara, Peggy, and not even Sarah. He then repeated the Bob Luther line, that these people were his friends, and to not like them simply meant I was paranoid.

It was getting late. I told John I had to go. While I was leaving, and just outside the door, I said, "Goodnight." John replied, "You are like the snake from the Garden of Eden." I was stunned and felt numb all over. "What do you mean by that John?" I asked. He replied, "That was pretty slick how you changed jurisdiction to Travis County." I left holding back tears. My attorney was insane and thought I was the devil. I had given him the 2001 11 19 recording of H* telling me to get out, but he hadn't to listened to it, and he didn't believe me when I told him. Instead his primary source of information that was the basis of a conclusion he obviously found to be very important came from someone else, the attorney gossip grapevine, and the word out there was that I had tricked poor little H* into a divorce.

The 'truths' that attorney's trade about a case are much more difficult to overcome than any other type of evidence because the attorneys behavior often determines the result. And now my attorney wrap sheet was to be modified by John's opinions.

John even borrowed Sarah Brandon's name for H* and called her a poor little girl. He wanted me to give her everything. Later when we discussed the success of the first divorce (temporary orders), Campbell told me that "Rain also falls on the evil man's garden."

I began wondering how far Campbell had actually gone. He surely wasn't advocating my professional or personal interests. I requested to see my file and related documents in hopes of answering these questions. I was hoping to see where John got the story that I had cleverly tricked H* and surprised her about the divorce, because it sure as hell didn't come from me. I was also especially interested in seeing his notes. I wanted to know if they looked like Bob Luther's notes, or if he actually practiced what I had hired him for. Attorneys are hired vendors and advisors, so I felt that these requests were completely in line with convention. In my experience, engineers make a point out of keeping notebooks and calculations in order to justify their work, and as a starting point should something go wrong. Accountants regularly audited books. Operations managers keep spreadsheets of inventory and shipments. Contractors make a point of documenting services, procedures, and materials. My world view was shaken when John Campbell refused to show me *anything*. I

200

showed up at his office one day when he wasn't there and asked the legal assistant to pull my file and show it to me. The file was nearly empty. On his desk there was a thick CPS report he had never shown me or told me about. I asked the assistant where the rest of my papers were, and she told me that "John has a green filing cabinet in his office where he keeps his own records. Yours are in there, but I don't have a key for it."

I pressed the issue through the State Bar CAP program for attorney client relations, and they asked John to produce my records. After a few weeks of going back and forth, John finally claimed that I already had everything because copies of the correspondence had been sent to me as they were mailed. Though it is funny that he hadn't thought of saying that in the two month interim since the issue had arisen. It is true that his office had sent copies of some faxed letters that went back and forth between him and Brandon, but I never saw other documents, and I had no way of knowing which letters he had. He never showed me the interrogatories, the discovery, or reports that came from various offices such as the ad litem and CPS. I do not know to this day if there had been discovery, but it appears there wasn't. It turns out there was a great deal of damaging and false accusations in those documents, which I never had the opportunity to reply to. Apparently I was being accused by H* of raping my son, of being a violent person, and being a domestic abuser. (One should take note of these allegations relative to the Dr. Thorne document subpoena issue that arises in a later chapter.)

Not replying to those allegations made me look guilty, but I couldn't reply, as I did not even know the allegations had been made. Luckily, I had taken the precautions of having D* examined, so the physical evidence pointed the other direction. There was nothing the other side could act upon. In a sense I was lucky. There was another engineer going through a divorce who was sent to jail for abusing his kids. He served two years. He claims the accusations were fabricated, but everyone has doubts. Even I have doubts, thus I write "He claims," while simultaneously my experience indicates that his claims are not just possible, but also quite likely. Nobody wants to go out on a limb. Cute little girls who apply their charm towards intrigue are far from innocuous, especially with people like Lara Nixon in official offices, and federal grants like VAWA.

After a couple of months, the Bar's CAP program told me I would have to enter a formal grievance or sue Campbell if I wanted to go further. They gave me a list of malpractice attorneys. All of the malpractice attorneys on the list, and then some, refused to take the case. One rather colorful attorney in Houston told me he had been married four times, and in each case had given the ex everything, including the kids, and walked. He told me I would come out ahead doing that. I would avoid all of the ugly fighting, and it would be cheaper in the long run. In fact, I would probably remain friends with my ex if I did so. I must say, as things have turned out, he was right, but what about D* interests? They had not been discussed since the Temporary orders hearing.

In general, friends, attorneys, relatives, and even my father, told me to walk away. My dad claimed that if I walked, H* would soon be requesting that I come back. He believed that H* was only pressing the issues out of a sense of entertainment. After all, it cost her nothing to make accusations, other people did the leg work, she was probably spending her dad's or my money, and in practice there is no penalty for doing it. He pointed out that if I capitulated the entertainment value would evaporate.

Campbell pumped me for information about where my money was. He wanted me to sign over my patents pending to my ex, although there is no legal precedent for doing such a thing in a divorce. When he found out I had competed in a math contest, he wanted to have the prize money handed over to my ex also. I informed him, that sadly I hadn't won the contest, but I appreciated his presumption. Then, I told Campbell that he was fired and that I wanted my retainer back. He told me that he refused to be fired, that he would not return the retainer, and that he would continue to invoice. I needed the retainer back in order hire another attorney. I had even sold my car to make the rent that month. Ted Terry had taken all of my savings and some of my mothers money as well. The money I had was what I could raise on the spot, and as John wouldn't return that, I was stuck with him.

Campbell took up where Luther left off, and insisted that I go see Jeff Ezel. However, Luther was pissed at me, and knowing that Ezel was ready to do Luther's bidding did not exactly motivate me. I finally asked Campbell one day, if you really think that I am paranoid and controlling, why do you feel so strongly that it is in your client's best interest to be analyzed? John, had a high pitched drone when he talked. It stopped. He refused to admit he wasn't working in my interest, but he couldn't think of a single word when I asked him how his advice was supposed to be helping me.

Eventually he said that I should trust him because he knew more about what was in my interest than I did, though he didn't bring up Ezel again. I suppose this is lawyer talk for saying he had a back room deal. It is hard to say.

Strangely, after some months and a few more incidences, he began to change his tune. Instead of referring to *that poor little girl*, it changed into *that girl can hold her own,* and other such references to her not being so innocent.

John's legal assistant, Cherry, told me that Mrs. Brandon hung one of my college degrees up in her office. I never did get it back. Brandon was brash about not returning my belongings or my office material. One of my patent attorneys called Mrs. Brandon asking for papers back. I don't know what was said in the conversation, but he called me and lectured me on the importance of telling one's attorney everything. To this day I am baffled as to what he meant by this.

Campbell was wrong about my hiding money, the truth was I was broke, could not get clients, and could not get a job. I had a stack of reject letters.

When we discussed the standard decree I explained it was unworkable as I had to find work elsewhere and that meant traveling. I explained I had never intended to live in Austin, I just came here for school and got stuck. Campbell said there was no problem with my moving. I perked up a bit, and asked him how it would work. He said it was simple, I should just leave without my son.

Mediation 2001

We mediated at Brandon's office, which was in an old house. The room we were in was the dining room. Our backs were against curtained glass paneled double doors that did not quite meet in the middle. One of Brandon's assistants sat just on the other side of these doors. We started with all of us in the same dining room. The mediator, Bob Bowman, explained the game theory matrix to us, i.e. win-win, win-lose, lose-lose. He was sincere and careful as though talking to school kids instead of two graduate degreed researchers.

He then asked if I had a picture of D* in my wallet. I didn't, so I guess he decided I didn't love him. I was being stared at. I pointed out that I often left my wallet in my pocket when SCUBA diving, and that all my pictures had been ruined more than once, so I stopped putting pictures in my wallet. I don't know if that meant I loved my son after all, or not.

We were then to separate. My attorney, John, and I were to have our confidential attorney client prep talk there in the dining room, while the others went to another room. Lara got up and went with H* and Brandon.

I pointed out the lady sitting behind us to John. He shook his head. We sat silently waiting for the others to return. When they came back in, I told Bowman I could hear him, and added that everything I said to my attorney could also be heard. Brandon pulled Bowman out to another room, where for a change, nothing could be heard. Bowman came back and called off the mediation without giving me any explanation. He did not want to reschedule, it was over, though he still charged for it.

The only good thing that came out of mediation, was that Campbell began to soften. At one point he said, "this little girl can take care of herself."   One thing about John Campbell was that he didn't always remember quite where we had left off.

Brandon's rifling through my files and destroying secrecy agreements made it such that no one wanted to do business with my company. One client actually negotiated and bought out his contract rather than continue with me. Without income, my cash was drying up quickly. Although it was clear that the family law circle in Austin was a pretty tight clique, I simply couldn't afford to bring in someone from out of town.

Brian called and told me that Ms. Brandon and H* were arranging little meetings to show people papers saying I was a violent criminal. Brian believed that even a Round Rock policeman was helping out. Perhaps it was the policeman who had told H* that it was sure I would murder her. Though I had no idea at the time, they were also stuffing the official case file with that bullshit, and more. An attorney friend sent a letter to Brandon warning her to stop the slander, but this only incited her further, and then the friend dropped the issue. Brian defended Brandon, saying that she couldn't be a female bigot because she had had a male client. I have been able to identify two male clients Brandon had, TL and SR. TL said that Brandon screwed him, and she ought to be sued. SR says he had to fire her after she had lost all of his property in a no-fault divorce with no children. Taking male clients just to screw them is not a testament of non-bigotry.

There were a lot of parallels between being married and working with Campbell. As Campbell was not working in D*'s interest and I was broke. I reasoned that the best thing I could do was come back another day. The other side had said they would return my office materials if I capitulated everything, so I told Campbell what I had told Luther when he refused to advocate my position: "Go find out what capitulate everything means."   I knew I could not win under the circumstances, so I wanted to exit with the least amount of damage.

Although I couldn't get anyone to act upon the conflicts of interest, they must have known I was trying to do so. Wouldn't the other side prefer to avoid this risk by just ending the suit? What was in it for them? I must have been naive or desperate, as that analysis had two glaring holes. First, the conflict information was just a nuisance to them, as Campbell, Ms. Brandon, and Lara Nixon were confident because the conflicts went up the ladder and not just across it. Secondly, my situation was ideal for people in the Divorce Industry. They were making money hand over fist. It was in their best interest that the situation remain in stasis.

The first proposed agreement came back. Brandon asked for all of the property and cash. She asked for the house and the paid for car. The retirement account had never been disclosed. She requested that H* have exclusive medical, so that she would never have to explain any bumps or bruises. She requested that I assume all debt in the marriage. They claimed that the money H* spent in the divorce had been borrowed and wanted that repaid.

I told John Campbell to contact my patent attorney, Bruce Garlick, and my accountant, Ron Meyers, to make sure the financial settlement was 50/50, and that the pending patents would be protected. Just to make sure Campbell followed through, I told both Bruce and Ron to call Campbell also. Both of them left messages for Campbell to call them back. After a couple of days, Campbell told me he had drafted an agreement to return to the other side. I asked him if he had run it by Ron Meyers to check the financial numbers. He said he had. I asked if he had spoken to Bruce Garlick. He said he had.

Sarah Brandon's and Lara Nixon's Sanctions Hearing 2001 12 13

The court appointed misandrist, and de facto judge surrogate, had ordered Peggy Farely to be the neutral court appointed child psychologist, and for Jeff Ezel to analyze the adults. Of course, by this point, I was suspicious of anything Lara Nixon might order. Thankfully, I had no choice but to not see Peggy, as she wouldn't talk with me, but it appeared I was going to have to see Ezel. I called and made an appointment. Ezel wanted me in his office for an entire eight hour day - nonstop. He explained that most of his analysis is based on the long subjective interview he conducts. I told him I couldn't take a whole day from my work to talk with him. We arranged for two half days. It turned out that I would never make those appointments, as Lara Nixon sued me for not seeing Ezel while putting the hearing date the week before the appointment time. After the hearing there was no point in keeping the appointment.

Conventionally an analyst would see both parents before making a report, but during the appointment call Ezel tried to make me feel like I was slow by telling me he had already published his report on H*. When I suggested I might provide new information, he said, "I never make mistakes," so he concluded that it was not possible that anything that might come up in our conversation would cause him to have to make any revisions. Clearly Ezel was trying to hatch his own egg. Also, apparently, he had given H* a clean bill of health; so it was clear that either he wasn't working to find the truth, that he had made a mistake, or *perhaps it is the case that sanity has nothing to do with whether someone is a bad spouse or parent.* Plenty of sane people are mean or otherwise awful spouses.

The court appointed misandrist ordered me to use the services of the company she had helped found and had been a director of, Kid's Exchange. When I went by Kid's Exchange, and saw steel doors and men holding guns next to children playing, I was filled with apprehension. Then the Kid's Exchange manager told me I had to sign a liability release in order to use the service. According to the Kid's Exchange contract, and Lara's order, I had to leave D* by himself with them, while they took no responsibility whatsoever for what might happen. The reasoning was that since the court, or rather, the official misandrist, had ordered me to use Kid's Exchange, I had to sign any paper put in front of me. Still, I refused to sign. Kid's Exchange refused to let us use their facilities, and then Lara Nixon sued me for this too.

We had a second option of exchanging at the police station on a temporary basis. In order to cut this possibility off also and foment the Kid's exchange issue, Brandon subpoenaed the policeman who worked in the reception area. The police department then refused to let us exchange there.

MEMORANDUM

TO: Control Booth Officers
Austin Police Department

FROM: Sgt. Bruce Boardman, Special Operations
Austin Police Department

DATE: November 29, 2001

SUBJECT: Witnessing Custodial Parent / Child Exchange

As of this day, November 29, 2001, the Control Booth Sworn Personnel will no longer be allowed to witness the exchange of children, to and from, the custodial and non-custodial parents. In the past, we have provided this service to citizens, as a means of bridging the gap between the parents of children. If the parents of the children have difficulties in resolving their differences, the Domestic Relations of Travis County has a program with Kids Exchange to provide this same service for a fee. Again, the Austin Police Department Control Booth Officers, will no longer be able to mediate the exchange of children to their parents or guardians. If you have any questions, please contact me at 974-5850.

Sgt. Bruce Boardman
Special Operations Unit
Austin Police Department

Cc: Cmdr. Duane McNeill
Lt. Van Cearley

BB:sc

Figure 39: Letter from Police Stopping Exchanges There

206

Alas, we were forced to exchange at Starbucks. Poor D* had to witness all of those people drinking coffee instead of policemen with guns. Clearly it had been the goal of the ad litem and Brandon to create the appearance of a great danger to H*.

Mr. Campbell refused to talk about our court appointed misandrist's law suit. Instead he kept changing the subject and telling me not to worry. When we got to the courtroom and were standing in front of the doors before entering, he said, "Get ready to take your medicine." I asked if he had talked to any witnesses. He hadn't. I asked to see any documents or notes. He had none. When we got into the courtroom, he did ask witnesses some questions.

Peggy Farely repeated the mantra, she said that she had interviewed the grandparents, and she had gathered that I was a violent person, and that the reason the grandparents were in hiding was because they were afraid of me. John asked Peggy if she was aware the grandparents had any legal problems. She said, "No." Then John dropped the line of questioning.

Peggy claimed I had never called for an appointment - but I had documented some of the calls, including from Campbell's office. Campbell asked Peggy if she would deny having received a phone call for an appointment from his office. She said she would. She said she had an assistant who always answered the phone even when she wasn't there. He then dropped the line of questioning.

I asked John to call her a liar, as calls from his office were clearly documented. He replied, "I think I just did." But he hadn't, as the question was phrased in the conditional. Perhaps he had communicated to her to back off for *her* sake, but he certainly hadn't done what would have been best for D*.

Ezel took the stand, he provided an analysis of me *based on our short phone call when I had finally made an appointment*. I had never actually seen him before, nor did I ever end up meeting him. It was a striking hypocrisy that the man who obstinately said that analysis of a person could not be done in less than 8 hours, was now satisfied with the results from a five minute phone call on the topic of matching calendars. Gleaning from our phone conversation, Ezel testified that I was manipulative because I didn't take the first appointment time he offered. Then he said something weird. He said that Bob Luther called him and told him that I had requested his resume. He used it as an example of my being controlling. I had never done that, rather I had asked for Farely's resume because Luther would not tell me who she was or even if she was a psychologist. The only discussion of Ezel we had had was that I wouldn't talk to him until the Farely thing was straightened out. In any case, Luther had no right to be flaunting an attorney client conversation to Ezel.

Then the representative for Kid's Exchange got on the stand. At this point, I had had enough. I requested to speak for myself. The Kid's Exchange director called me rude and said I was aggressive and made her feel uncomfortable. This was a direct lie. I had been very polite at Kid's Exchange, if for no other reason, due to the proximity of the police. I had politely refused to sign, without any show or pretense. I told the judge about the liability waiver. The judge asked the Kid's Exchange director if Kid's Exchange had required the liability waiver, and she said yes. The judge asked if Kid's Exchange would be responsible for the children if the roof collapsed. The director said she did not know. That was a enlightening answer, as it demonstrated that Kid's Exchange did not think about the kids or their well being. Judging from what she knew and didn't know, apparently a higher priority for the women who ran Kid's Exchange's was to generate witnesses for the mothers than to take care of kids. The director's first words about my being rude and aggressive had exposed their approach. They knew they didn't have to answer to fathers, but didn't know if they were responsible if a child was hurt. This indicates that their liability waiver's true purpose is to prevent men from suing Kid's Exchange after the staff slandered them. The judge ruled that I could not be forced to sign the liability waiver.

We took a break. While walking out John said, "That was fun." I suppose the old man hadn't been in such a spirited debate for years, though I wish he had done it of his own volition. We had come out on top. Kid's Exchange had virtually held up a baby in front of them to deflect bullets. Ezel had admitted, perhaps inadvertently, that Luther had shared attorney client privileged information with him. And though she didn't get penalized for perjury as she should have, it was obvious to everyone that Farely lied on the stand.

The Final Decree Agreed Upon 2001 12 13

In the hallway during the break, the other side, i.e. Lara Nixon, the court appointed misandrist, and Brandon, wanted to know if we could work out the agreement that had been started. I told them that I would only sign if there was a joint conservatorship, that the line where Brandon had put in saying that domestic violence had occurred would be removed. Also I required that there be joint medical. H* very much wanted me to be prevented from taking D* to a doctor. Although we crossed this language out of the decree, some of the secondary statements were not chased down and edited out while we were there in the hallway. I did not realize this at the time.

The decree meant that my son was going back to live with H*. I did not think that the agreement would last for a second as what they did to get the agreement was nothing less than extortion. They had lied about the financial statements, they did not provide discovery. No agreement gotten through extortion, fraud, conflicts of interest, and subterfuge can be valid. I fully intended on bringing the conflicts of interest involved, the fraud, and extortion be brought to light. All I was doing was buying time so I could find an attorney to represent my interests so that the truth could come out. I needed someone who wasn't more interested in "my friends" than in my son's well being. It turned out to be a tall order. Eventually I hired Larry Schubhut senior to do this.

Although the agreement was changed to joint medical, a clause went unnoticed that said I would not take D* to a doctor. Of course, this would be very convenient for H*, as then there would be no one to call her on her, 'father did it', accusations. However the other language contradicted this clause, and the meaning remained clear enough that H* later admitted she did not have exclusive medical. In addition, there was a clause that said she could pick the doctor. I agreed to this latter clause on the grounds that I could fire the doctor. I found it to be an interesting balance of power. If she picked someone who was biased, then we could move on to the next doctor. I didn't believe there were very many biased doctors out there. Lastly, she insisted that Caryl Dalton be the new child psychologist in order to replace Peggy Farely. The other side saw that Farely was done. However, I was allowed to mediate clauses, so I reasoned that if Farely did not work out, we could mediate the issue.

I also agreed to the injunction of not going by the house. Although this was unpleasant, if I was not allowed to go by the house, exchanges would be at the school. With exchanges at the school D* and I would get a few more hours of time, and she wouldn't have to be present when I picked him up or dropped him.

After we wrote all over the agreement, Brandon ran down the hall with the original. I called to her to come back, and I told John that I didn't want her to be alone with the original. He told me not to worry. Brandon never turned around, she was gone, with the original covered with handwriting changes. It was never retyped, and was filed directly by Brandon.

I negotiated this agreement solely to get my records back. I had full intentions of making some money, finding another lawyer, and having the fraud and extortion pointed out. This agreement would prove to be as butt tape placed on a cat. And while I spent years scooting around to get it off, one attorney after another would stand around and do nothing but laugh at my expense.

Conflicts Confirmed

A friend called and suggested that I run into JW and get to know his family history. With some trepidation I called JW and struck up a conversation. I guessed this had something to do with my divorce, so I steered the conversation in that direction. I told him I was having a difficult divorce. He said he could empathize, as he had been through one himself. He spoke about his ex wife. "Peggy could be difficult," he said. I thought, "Nah, couldn't be." "So JW, what is Peggy's last name now?"

"Her name is now Peggy Farely."

"Oh," I commented. "Hey, I'm curious, who was her attorney."

"She employed Jim Piper, though Sarah Brandon did most of the work for her. Sarah was working for Jim at the time."

"Really? Do you happen to know Lara Nixon?"

"Oh yes, the three of them are thick. They are good friends and work in family practice together on a lot of cases. Those folks are bad news. So, why do you ask?"

"Well Lara is my ad litem, Sarah Brandon the opposing attorney, and Peggy is the neutral psychologist appointed by Lara."

"Ah, Tom, I have to get along with Peggy still, and I don't want to be sued again, so I hope you will forgive me if don't talk about this anymore."

"Sure JW."

Before this conversation I had only surmised the existence of conflicts based on people's behaviors. The approach of balancing conflicts with more conflicts would surely have been expensive and damaging for both H* and I, though as things turned out, trying to get an attorney to actually point out a conflict was even more expensive.

Attorney Campbell Forces Closure, Runs Out Clock On Appeal

H* kept the house and equity, all of the dressings and utensils that went along with the house. She kept the paid for car, the complete retirement and savings accounts. In the decree she specified that everything that belonging to D* was hers, so she kept everything from his bank account to his dog – even though she hated dogs. (The dog was supposed to go back and forth, but at first opportunity she kept it.) She kept the television, the stereo, the kitchen devices, all of my ham radio gear, my bow, my clothes remaining at the house, my books, gifts from my friends and relatives from even before the divorce, and everything else. Her attorney kept my framed diploma on her wall at the office. Sara Brandon still has it as of the time of this writing. The only thing H* didn't keep was all of the debt from the marriage. That was assigned to me.

I wanted Campbell to appeal but he said there was no reason to do so. I suspect this wasn't accurate, and I wanted to get another attorney, but I didn't have any funds to do so. I asked Campbell to return the balance of the retainer so I could hire someone else. He refused to do so. Then one day replied that the deadline for appeals had passed. He had waited it out.

Because of Brandon's subpoena's and pressures she had mounted, I had been forced out of the consulting house where I worked. I found employment with a processor design house, but they bought the offer letter back after hearing something through the grapevine. I hadn't even started yet. I then went to work for a startup outside of Austin. They were not happy with the time I missed during the day. I was busy interviewing potential new attorney's, and because of the driving distance, it took large chunks out of my morning or afternoon each time. They tolerated this because the divorce was going.

I had been at a startup for just a few months by January 2002, still walking on egg shells because of the time I was missing and the way I came in, when Campbell sent a fax to the general number saying that the divorce was all finished as of December 13, 2001. The fax was picked up by someone and not given to me. When I took off during a day for a meeting with a potential new attorney to replace Campbell, I was asked directly where I was going. I explained it was divorce related meeting. I was fired. While I was cleaning out my desk, the chief financial officer came over and set Campbell's fax on my desk. The fax made me look like a liar. Though, the startup later changed the status of the termination, the damages caused were immense.

Brandon and H* did not honor the deal they made as part of the extortion. They kept all of my papers, and my personal belongings. When the ad litem suggested that H* at least return my power tools, because she didn't know how to use them, H* replied, *"I know how to sell them."* Though Campbell had told the startup that the divorce was over, he finally did something and on February 8th and filed for a motion to turn over my office records and personal belongings. The other side produced some of the bookshelves I had made for my library, boxes of papers, and some power tools.

When my accountant, Ron Meyers, saw the decree he was horrified. Campbell had just given all the money to H*, and left me with $120,000 in debt. Campbell had lied, contrary to what he told me about working with my accountant, he had never returned Meyers' phone calls. I called my IP attorney and discovered Campbell had lied about calling him also. The IP language in the agreement was not from the IP attorney as he had claimed. H* had fraudulently not disclosed her retirement account, nor an account she had opened under D* name. I believe that she had faked debt by sending money to friend's and relatives and then having them 'loan it back' to her on paper. My account would have caught this, as he had bank records up to the divorce, but he was denied the opportunity to comment on the financial claims by Campbell. So in point of fact, H* had not only gained everything, but *she turned a profit.*

After The Divorce, Summer 2002

When read from this point it is important to remember that H* already 'won' everything. She has D*, and I was only visiting. She has the house, the car, all the bank accounts. She had not declared the retirement accounts or her stock investments, so she has those untouched. I did not get any equity in the house at all. She has it free and clear. I was awarded all the debt.

D*: "Why Have You Forgotten Me?" 2002 03 22

D* was very mad at me. He wanted to know why I had forgotten him. I wasn't missing any visitation periods, but before the order we had seen each other every day, since he was born. We had a lot of fun together, and now it all came to an end. I could have shriveled up and died. I can't begin to describe how horrible this felt. D* had a lot of questions about why he went back to his mom and I couldn't answer them. What could I say? Extortion can not be explained to a four year old. One of the pictures he refers to was his painting of a light house. It eventually was placed on the main bulkhead in front of the Salon.

211

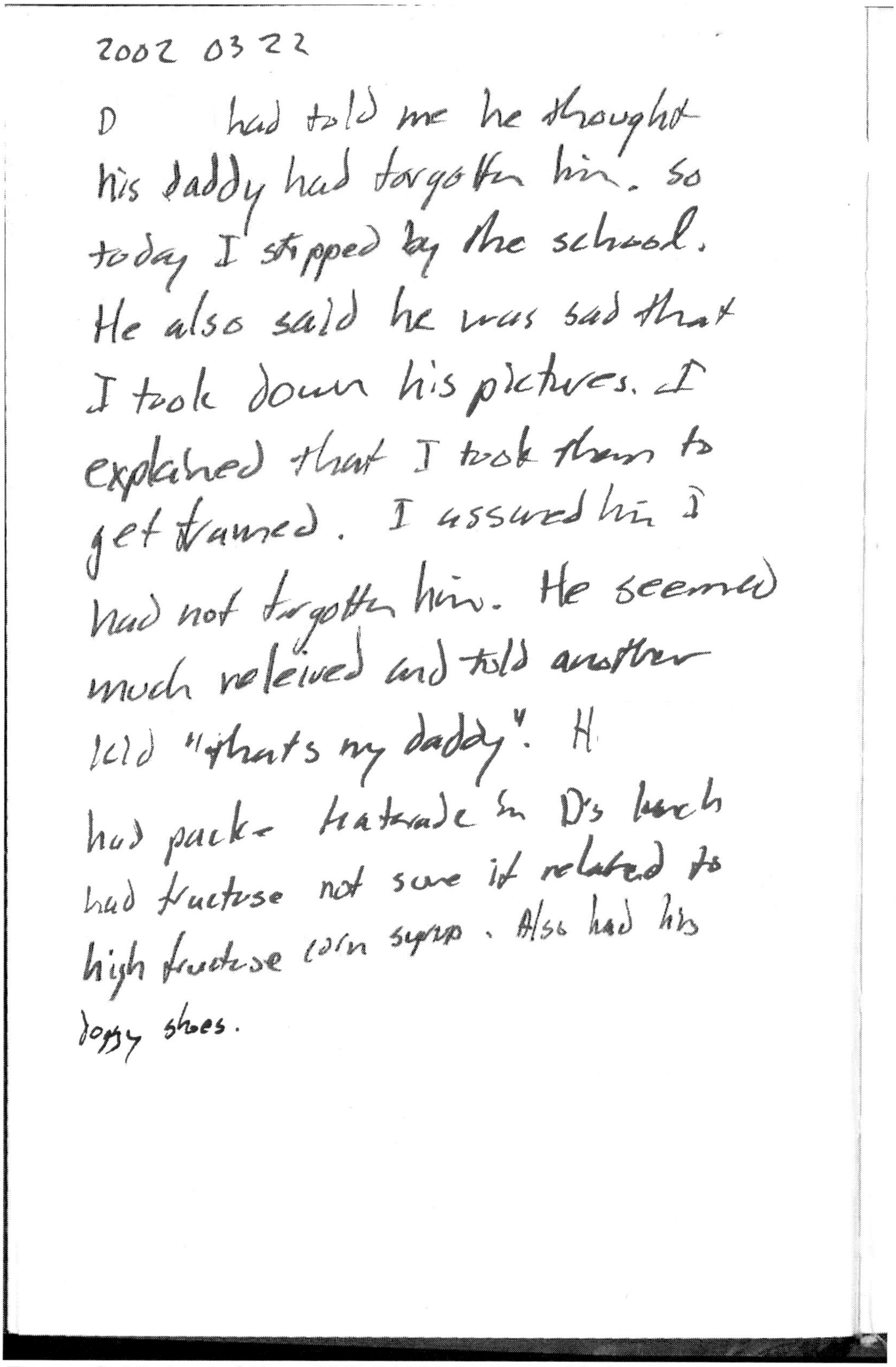

2002 03 22

D   had told me he thought
his daddy had forgotten him. So
today I stopped by the school.
He also said he was sad that
I took down his pictures. I
explained that I took them to
get framed. I assured him I
had not forgotten him. He seemed
much relieved and told another
kid "thats my daddy". H
had packe treatrade in D's lunch
had fructose not sure it related to
high fructose corn syrup. Also had his
doggy shoes.

Figure 40: My Journal Entry 2002 D* Thinks His Daddy Has Forgotten Him

212

Looking for Others and Meeting Consultant Pangborn

As Sarah Brandon did this for a living, I reasoned there must be other men who had been screwed. I went to Travis county to do a records search, and was disappointed to find that the search capabilities were limited. They had over a million records on file indexed against 'cause number'. So the question reduced to how one to find the cause numbers. Cause numbers are given to the plaintiff and respondent when a case is opened, but that doesn't facilitate research. There was a computerized search engine which allows one to find a cause number from the year and the exact spelling of the plaintiff or respondents name. Note this is the exact spelling as entered by the clerk from a form provided by the attorney. For example, H*'s name is misspelled, so someone who know the year of our divorce and looked under the correct spelling of her name would not find any records. This might cause a person to question whether they were looking in the correct year, and then repeat to repeat the process five to 10 times, perhaps with three variations of the spelling of the name for a 30 total traversals through the menus. Some people, often attorneys, have managed to get their records entered with variations of their name, or under their initials. The county did not support searching records by the name of the judge, consultants, experts, or witnesses.

So I went ahead and did a freedom of information act request for the whole data base. It was declined on the grounds that some of the records were sealed. I offered to pay for programming time for the sealed records to be filtered out. It was only a half bluff, though I couldn't afford to do this I was willing to bet I could find an investor. They gave me a run around at the data center. First they tried to snow me technically, and soon found out that I knew more about tape formats etc. than they did. Then they just got slow. My requested had to be put on a form. The form had to take time to process. The next time I inquired, no one knew what form I was talking about, nor why in the world I had submitted it to Linda when it should have gone to John. "Why don't you fill out another."

In the meantime I went to the Internet and searched. It is more common now, but at this time there were only a few attorneys specializing in men's issues. There was a web page called the A-team. It was run by Ken Pangborn.

Even with all the support from friends, I couldn't put together anything that would help me afford an out of state attorney with all the travel time hours, but Ken arranged meetings with an attorney and a psychologist in Wisconsin. I couldn't afford these people at the prices they quoted, and he knew it. He said we would work something out. I thought that perhaps after hearing about what had been going on, they might provide a discount. It was curious that the psychologist in Madison was in a large office building and had an FBI insignia on his wall. None of these people were willing to lower their rates. The entire trip had been for nothing. Ken charged me thousands of dollars, a significant fraction of the total I needed to hire the attorney in the first place.

Even the Clerk Who Does the Car Titles

Robin from Whiteside Motors called from his cell phone. Robin had bought my Volvo. He was at the tax office trying to get the title for the car I sold him transferred, but the lady at the desk refused to accept the power of attorney. She insisted that my ex wife come give permission for the transaction in person. Robin called for a couple of reasons, he wanted to make sure the power of attorney was legitimate, though he didn't really have any doubts about it. Mostly he called because he was so amazed that he wanted to share it with me. I told him they could double check the power of attorney with H*'s attorney if they really wanted to.

Robin put the clerk on the phone. The clerk told me that they didn't transfer titles for divorced men, and she reiterated that my ex wife would have to come and give permission in person. I explained that was what a power of attorney was for. She repeated the same thing. It was ridiculous, so I asked for her manager. The woman laughed and said sure, "You want to talk to *my* manager. *She* will tell you the exact same thing." Another woman got on the phone and told me to listen to the what the clerk said.

Robin called back a few days later to say he had gotten a court order for the ladies to do their job.

Also at about that time, the female manager at the apartment complex where we lived near Motorola, before moving to the house, sent a letter requesting payment beyond the deposit, which they had not yet returned. The nanny had kept the place immaculate. The woman manager at the complex was adamant, she said she had even taken pictures of "The mess." I replied, "Oh this I gotta see." She promised to send the pictures, but didn't. Instead she filed a bad credit report. I called a higher level manager, explained I was divorcing, that a nanny cleaned the place spotless, and that no pictures were ever sent. The credit report was removed, though I never got my deposit back.

Bankruptcy

After having spent so much money on attorneys and having received all of the debt from the marriage, but none of the assets, not even equity in the house, and not being able to work, there was no other option than bankruptcy. The job was the big killer. Sarah Brandon and company, and the stink they made, followed me around so I couldn't work. For example I found a descent job offer at Centaur Technologies doing design work for $150,000 a year plus bonuses. I felt this was a step backwards, as my usual work at the time was in building intellectual property and creating opportunity for startup equity, but that was out of the question at the time. It took about two weeks for the rumor mill to catch up with Centaur, and they withdrew the job offer.

CENTAUR TECHNOLOGY

August 27, 2001

Tom Lynch
P.O. Box 10199
Austin, TX 78766-1199

Dear Tom:

This is to confirm that your offer of employment with Centaur Technology, Inc. has been withdrawn.

We wish you the best of luck in your future endeavors.

Sincerely,

Christy Wolter
HR Director
Centaur Technology, Inc.

Figure 41: Dad's Client Buys Back Contract

Many companies who were sent notices of debt dismissal went ahead and added more bad news to the credit report. Frost Bank, Chase, and Citibank, all did so. The only credit card company who respected the notice was First U.S.A. Some years after the bankruptcy I happened to type the wrong PIN number for my ATM card, and the card was canceled. The Frost Bank customer service people then conveniently forgot who I was between phone calls. I had a long time business relationship with the bank, and called a VP who I knew. She explained that any bank would do the same thing to someone who had a "charge off" I.e. she explained that banks don't just limit loan decisions etc. based on credit, but they even punish such people by giving them poor customer service. In the banks view, and in many other business peoples view, someone with bad credit is plainly a thief who should be rebuked at every opportunity. The VP spoke with the customer service people on my behalf, and finally the ATM card was replaced, but frost made the issue clear enough, and I was forced to repay the charged off.

All car insurance companies refused to give me car insurance, due to "bad credit". My old insurance company, State Farm, had not lost a penny due to the bankruptcy raised my $60 semi-annual liability on one car to $750. They have not lowered this amount now in six years. It is funny, a company who is in the credit business, FIRST USA lost an amount on bad debt that is equal to what State Farm has picked up gratuitously.

A credit report is in fact a sort of hunting license for accounting write offs. Based on the principle that past history is the best predictor of future behavior, those who have marks, cannot defend against new marks.

The tech bust had started, so only the top contenders were finding good jobs. In terms of technical ability I was a top contender and had the stats to back this assertion, but I had a millstone around my neck, bad credit, vicious gossip circulating, and involvement in a contentious divorce.

In the U.S. large corporations consider credit when hiring. And even interviews are difficult because expense reports and car rentals are paid against credit card charges, but I couldn't get a credit card. The security departments at large companies share security information, and that information does not have to meet the threshold of any particular law. In this context, being accused of something is information all by itself. All that combined with the startup firing in February 2002 assured I could not be hired. I applied all over. And there was no looking back to doing my own business or continuing my consulting practice, as the burned bridges were still smoldering.

Then the next horror came to light. Apartment complexes take bankruptcy into consideration, so I couldn't rent a place to live. In 2003, STA, a company in San Jose who had leased me a place but over charged by hundreds of dollars. The manager threatened to add another line to the report if I didn't pay the extra amount. I folded and paid her when she said it was my lost opportunity or STA would make a report. STA filed a report anyway.

Moving home to Iowa would have been hard on D* and me. H* refused to take D* to an airport, and this raised the cost of travel considerably. H* was supposed to help with travel expenses, but she refused, and my attorney refused to press it. D* and I would not have been able to meet nearly as often if I went to Iowa, and my missing visitations could easily be used against us to make it even harder yet to gain back what we lost. There is no work of the kind I do in my home town in Iowa, so recovery would be even more difficult. Also, God I love them, but being unemployed, and living in my folk's house, especially given the financial phobia of my depression era father, would have been miserable.

H* Accuses Father of Abducting D*, Spring Break 2002

I picked D* up for spring break. The French curriculum starts younger than the in the U.S. The school had their spring break two weeks later than the Round Rock school district. According to the decree it was our turn for spring break. After I picked D* up for spring break I got a call from the Round Rock Police department on my cell phone. The officer asked if I had D*, and when I said I did, he requested that I return him to his mother. I explained that it was my spring break. I also told the officer, "you may think that is a cute young girl and sequestered house wife you have been talking with, but in point of fact she is 40 years old, has a PhD, has worked at two well known labs (one in Korea), and is now an engineer at Motorola." There was silence on the line. We hung up. I didn't hear anything more from the Round Rock police on the issue.

216

john f. campbell
lawrence j. morgan
mark w. clemens

VIA FACSIMILE NO. 477-2770

April 22, 2002

Ms. Sarah K. Brandon
Attorney at Law
508 West Twelfth Street
Austin, Texas 78701

RE: Lynch

Dear Sarah:

Mr. Lynch called me yesterday evening to report that this week is Spring Break for his son's school which would make sense that he keep the child during this Spring Break.

Please confirm that to us as quickly as possible and if your client has a contrary view let us know what she perceives the schedule should be since there will not be a school for the child to be delivered to and returned.

Yours very truly,

John F. Campbell

JFC: ma

C: Tom Lynch

campbell & morgan, p.c.
attorneys and counselors
805 West 10th third floor
austin, texas 78701

512/476-6036   fax 512/478-8919

217

LAW OFFICES OF SARAH K. BRANDON, P.C.
508 West Twelfth Street
Austin, Texas 78701

(512) 477-4707 OFFICE
(512) 477-2770 FACSIMILE

Sarah K. Brandon

April 22, 2002

VIA FACSIMILE   *1 page sent*
478-8919

John F. Campbell
805 West 10th St., 3rd Fl.
Austin, TX 78701

Re: Cause Number: FM1-02879; *In the Matter of the Marriage of Thomas Walker Lynch and
       H_____ and In the Interest of D_____ a Child*; In the 98th Judicial
       District Court of Travis County, Texas.

Dear Mr. Campbell:

As you're aware, the Order provides that the Spring breaks, Christmases and the other vacations
are designated by the School District for which they live in. Dr. Choi lives in Round Rock;
therefore, the vacation schedule shall be determined by the Round Rock School District To my
knowledge, the Round Rock Spring break was over two weeks ago.

If your client attempts to exercise any unauthorized periods possession, my client will have no
other choice but to call the police and we will file a Motion For Contempt and Interference With
Child Custody.

Please give this matter your immediate attention.

Very Truly Yours,

Sarah K. Brandon

SKB/so

cc: client

john f. campbell
lawrence j. morgan
mark w. clemens

VIA FACSIMILE NO. 477-2770

April 23, 2002

Ms. Sarah K. Brandon
Attorney at Law
508 West Twelfth Street
Austin, Texas 78701

RE: Lynch

Dear Sarah:

Thanks for your response to my fax.

I don't disagree with what you say about the Decree. What I was trying to inject was a little common sense and avoid having to file a Motion to Modify.

I am not exactly certain what any of us were thinking about when we spent all that time negotiating over the schools and more particularly a private school.

Does it make any sense at all to have a Decree that gives a person Spring Break at a time when the child is in school? I think you know as well as I do that the intent of these Decrees is to follow the holiday schedule of the school where the child is enrolled and I would think that next year when Spring Break rolls around that your client would prefer to have the Spring Break coincide with the child's Spring Break than to coincide with a few thousand children in the Round Rock Independent School District while her son is in school every day in his private school.

Also, I would call attention to the fact that we believe that the Courts encourage the parties to govern their behavior and their decisions by what is in the best interest of the child and I certainly don't think it's in the child's best interest for his Spring Break with his parent to be at a time when he is still going to school. Furthermore, the policy of the state of Texas is to encourage the parents to work out their own agreed schedules and use the guidelines as a backup.

campbell & morgan, p.c.
attorneys and counselors
805 West 10th third floor
austin, texas 78701

512/476-6036 fax 512/478-8919

219

Page 2
Ms. Sarah Brandon
April 23, 2002

I don't always agree with my clients and when I think they are being unreasonable and out of line, I have no hesitation to tell them but this is one time I have a real hard time telling Tom that his position is nonsensical and in this case I am almost certain that had this matter been brought to the attention of the Court by either one of the lawyers, the Court would certainly have sided with the lawyer who was advocating for the parent to have his Spring Break with the child when the child has his Spring Break. Am I missing something here?

Yours very truly,

John F. Campbell

JFC: rna

C: Tom Lynch

Figure 42: Brandon Insists On Using Schedule Different Than That of the School's

Dad Moves to Dallas

A friend suggested I move up to Dallas, do some consulting on his startup, and house sit. Another friend opened a bedroom up to me at his house in Austin, so I split my time between the two places. When in Austin I could visit D* daily. Times were tough then, and I didn't have much money. Mom sent some cash, and I fasted to save money for visits with D*. One friend commented that I "got skinny." Another said I looked healthy.

At least my friend's condo in Dallas was comfortable. Between looking for a job and another attorney, I worked on solving the RSA cryptography problem. I'm sorry to say, I did not find a solution. I say I'm sorry about this, as John Campbell wanted me to give the prize money to H*. He quizzed me over it, as though I might be hiding money. On the one hand it is nice that someone would have so much confidence in my to solve such problems, on the other hand it sure was a sinking feeling that my attorney was so suspicious of me.

When we negotiated the final decree I traded my off week visits for a longer summer vacation.   This made the summer break 42 days, which is less than half of the summer. We hand wrote the changes on the draft that Sarah Brandon had brought with her to the sanctions hearing. This draft was supposed to have been based on a standard decree, but Sarah had made changes. Where in the standard decree it said that summer visitation is 30 days, it instead read two weeks. It seems we had not fixed this. A big surprise came when I provided H* with my summer schedule with D*:

H   Lynch

April 8, 2002

Tom Lynch
1217 Arcadia
Austin, TX 78757

Dear Tom,

This is to respond your letter dropped to me on March 31, 2002 regarding your 42 day summer break
notification. We both had agreed on your 2 week summer vacation when we live less than 100 miles
apart. There is nothing wrong with our agreement about this in our divorce decree. Guardian Ad
Litem recommended this way for D   's best interest so that D   can be with both parents
without a long period of separation. 42 day separation from either parent for four year old boy is
definitely too long. Please talk to D   's therapist, Dr. Caryl Dalton if you wish to have an expert
opinion.

Since your notification of 42 days from July 15, 2002 is invalid, I assume your vacation will start at
6:00 pm on July 1, 2002 and end at 6:00 pm on July 14, 2002. Under this assumption, I will
exercise summer weekend possession right from 6:00 pm on July 4, 2002 to 6:00 pm on July 8,
2002.

In the case when you claim your summer vacation from 6:00 pm on July 15, 2002 for two weeks,
my summer weekend possession will be from 6:00 pm on July 18, 2002 to 6:00 pm on July 22, 2002.

Please let me know as soon as possible which two week vacation you are going to take.

Sincerely,

H

Figure 43: H* Blocks Dad's Summer Possession Time

222

I looked it up. There were hand written changes on the greater than 100 miles section, but the less than 100 mile section was unchanged. It was a mistake. However, by the standard decree, which should have been the default, it should have been 30 days, not two weeks. It was a Sarah Brandon gotchya. When I tried to discuss it with H* she would have none of it. I explained I was going to be in Dallas during the summer, which is more than 100 miles away. She just ignored me. D* explained that his mom told him that I was being punished for doing something bad, which was why he couldn't see him as much. He didn't know what that bad thing was.

Instead of spending time with father, D* spent his time in a day care center.

The Horologist's Wife

One evening I was out sitting in the hot tub at the condo complex in Dallas. A young couple came and got in the tub. I asked him what he did for a living, and he replied he was an *horologist.* He explained that meant he repaired watches. He worked for a Rolex dealership. He said they didn't have any children.

He was rather quite, but she was animated. She gabbed away and in midstream brought up the subject of domestic abuse. She seemed to have bragging rights for some story. She said that her mother had been abused by a man for many years. She described a cycle where her mother had been beaten, lived in an abuse shelter, and then went back to husband. Apparently her mother repeated this cycle a number of times. The horologists wife then said, "Then she had him sent to jail." Her manner wasn't sad or mad, but triumphant. Apparently this was a trophy event.

I asked for confirmation, "Over a period of years?" That was the case. "Anything broken?" Apparently not. I asked if her mother had been responsible, "*at all*?"

The young woman replied "*not at all.*" Her mother had the temperament of the Virgin Mary, and her father just slapped her around without provocation. I thought to myself that if the mother shared this young woman's arrogance, there were no Virgin Marys involved. She talked about her father as though he was no relation to her. Perhaps I was mistaken in assuming that it was her father. I wondered, is this what happens to a father after the kid grows up with mom telling the kid that father was being punished for 'doing something bad'. May be D* will be talking about me this way when all of the false allegations are told to him as real, and he is given the *explanation* of why doesn't see his father more.

I asked the young woman why her mother hadn't left him. She answered it was because her mother was sacrificing herself for the cause of fixing him. "A noble deed," I replied, and pointed out that there must have been many people involved. She agreed that it was a noble deed. There had been shelter people, social workers, policeman, anger management teachers, and some relatives. Over the years her parents lost a great deal of time that could have been applied to more constructive activities. Later there were attorneys, experts, judges, court recorders, more officers, and clerks. It was unclear if the father had been convicted of anything, but if he had, then there would be jail keepers, parole officers and the damage to her father's career.

I pointed out such battles in the United States were easily costing over $100 billion dollars a year. She was indifferent. I suggested that it would be better, perhaps, to use such money to pay for college tuition for people like herself. This apparently was not the reply that she expected, and she was starting to steam like the hot tub water. I added something that would surely give her pause, "That would pay for about 5 million students each year." But there was no pause, she simply snapped out that *getting dad was a better use of the money.*

"Well then," I said, "I really think that it is your mother's business if she wanted to go back even after knowing what was likely to happen, but she should have done so at her own expense, and not that of society's. I should not have to pay for other people's noble deeds." I delivered my comments slowly and sincerely. The horologist was helpful by saying I had a point here or there, though this may have been to delay the imminent tongue lashing. They exchanged glances, then the young woman stormed off without using a towel. She was literally steaming. I wondered how much time they had left.

H* Accuses Dad of Abducting D* Christmas 2002

My aunt and uncle in Dallas loaned me their old car. I was broke and I not eating every day in order to have money to spend on D* during our weekend visits. I used the old car to drive from Dallas to Austin, and to pick up D*. We would then stay with my friend Dan in Austin, go camping, or return to Plano. We spent time at Lost Maples park in the hill country, and on South Padre beach.

On the way to pick D* up at Christmas, the car overheated. The temperature gage on the dash gave no indication of a trend, rather, around Troy on I35, steam billowed out from under the hood. I removed the thermostat completely, added water, and went down the road another stitch. Steam billowed out again. The problem wasn't a stuck thermostat. I called for a tow. After repairing a hole in the radiator, the car burned oil and trailed a big cloud of smoke behind it. The car was clearly finished. I called my uncle and apologized. My aunt exclaimed surprise that it had gone that far. I smoked a path to Austin to pick D* up at school and take him to the Amtrak station. We were heading to Iowa for our Christmas break.

According to our final decree, we exchanged through the school. Consequently I didn't see H* when I picked D* up or dropped him off. However, her attorney, Ms. Brandon, insisted that we use Travis County public school schedule instead of the private school's schedule where D* attended. It was an impractical suggestion, and she pushed it only to cause trouble. H* threatened that she would report abductions if I used the school's actual schedule. Indeed I had gotten a call from the Round Rock police that prior spring break asking me to return the child. She had rationalized the abduction request in the same manner based on schedule differences. When I took D* out of school on that day, the day when the private school was out for the Christmas holiday, Ms. Brandon again called it 'kidnapping'. I was under such a threat when I arrived at the school to pick D* up.

I parked a bit down the street so that the smoke wouldn't be visible from the school. I didn't want us to be embarrassed. I gathered D* up and put him in the car. We would miss our train if I borrowed money for a cab. If we missed the train we would be in court over the school schedule instead of having Christmas holiday in Iowa.

We left a smoke trail down Lamar on the way to the station. I hoped the police wouldn't stop us, mainly because that might make us late. I parked the car on a side street off of 5th next to an abandon industrial building. It could stay there a long time. I got our bags and D* and I crossed the tracks to get to the station. The train arrived a few minutes later, we boarded and were off.

The train made its way north from Austin. Out the window D* could see the Texas countryside of limestone flats and scrub. Farther north there were more trees. The woman sitting in front of us was Iranian, and she thought D* was cute, and she talked for an hour. At night in Oklahoma or Kansas the train stopped, and a man got into our car and sat in the chairs opposite us. D* was asleep in spread across the chair and in my lap. My eyes were closed and I was thinking about a engineering problem. To all appearances I was asleep.

The man got up from his seat and stood behind the divider leading to the door and made a telephone call on his cell phone. He may have thought it private, but I could hear him clearly enough. He said the helicopter had dropped him off on time to make the train. He said that he "found his roommate," and would be in Illinois in the morning. He then complained about his vacation being interrupted.

After hearing this I remembered a lesson from psych class. In the class room they showed a large number of people arriving on a train, and being met by a crowd on the platform. It was just a coincidence that a train was used in the film, though an interesting coincidence. The caption read, "the angry crowd of demonstrators meets the strike scabs arriving by train". Indeed the crowd appeared angry. I could feel the betrayal. The class stayed glued to the film in anticipation of what would happen next. Then the film jumped back. We were once again watching the same train arriving at the station. This time the narration was different, "soldiers returning from the war are given a jubilant welcome by their families." I remember looking at the film, the exact same scene, and not being able to shake the emotion of happiness that the soldiers were being met by their families. A girl in the class shed tears of joy. This was an education film designed to show the role that suggestion plays in our interpretation of what we see. The exact same scenes had opposite emotional interpretations when the viewer was cued with different one sentence prefaces.

My inclination was to assume that there had been an 'amber alert' set off by Brandon for my picking D* up at school, as on the prior spring break. "An abducted child is everyone's child, " how convenient for the leviathan. If so the man could be an FBI guy who had caught up with our train to make sure I didn't get off before Illinois or hurt D*. But then I took into account the cue I was working with from H*'s over zealous attorney. Perhaps I was reading into the picture. I considered trying to make it fit other scenarios. The man was an oil worker and he had stayed an extra day on the job because his negligent roommate didn't show up for a shift. The company then dropped him at Amtrak so he could visit his family for the holidays. As yet another take, even if he was a cop, and I would be arrested in Illinois, what could I do about it? This was no adventure movie, I wasn't going to be hopping off trains or anything.

I shouldn't have been listening anyway. I noted that the fact I was listening meant that I was nervous. I considered just forgetting what I heard, and going back to enjoying my holiday with my son. Then I happened upon a better idea. I would just strike up a conversation with the man and discuss our trip and my ex's nutty interpretation of the school schedule. Then I thought I would probably come across like the crazy woman on the bus coming back from California. I would have to say something that would appeal if he had a professional opinion, yet be interesting if he was a regular passenger. It must have been 4am. I went to the restroom, and came back. "Hello," I said on my return. "Well I didn't see you get on, we must have stopped." That was probably a give away that I did know he got on, because he could have come from another car. Oh well. There were no scores for form. I explained to him how difficult my ex had made it to get away for the holidays, and that we were going to visit grandma and grandpa. I made it out as a father son Christmas story. Independent of the reason, the man was attentive and asked questions. He sure didn't approach the topic with the diffidence one might expect from a random commuter.

When dealing with such a well funded vindictive person such as my ex, I never knew what to expect. I applied this cue to the events around me in order to increase the chances of things not going wrong. This was an example. Had this been an amber alert of some sort, then I had just diffused a sticky situation. And like all human beings policeman do not like to be wrong. Should a person be arrested, they will instantly be put in a position of justifying their actions. The police call this, "making it stick." It is common for a person to be charged with many things at once, this has the effect of creating the appearance that the person being arrested is a very undesirable person, so if it turns out the person didn't do the root thing he is being accused of the arrest still appears justified. Hence, though a kidnapping charge may not 'stick', a flight, resisting arrest, violating a judges order, child endangerment, or a child neglect charge might.

Given all the suspicion surrounding divorcing men, it is my opinion that they are justified in being careful, and a person who is cued to be careful is a person who lives in fear. As Naomi Wolf points out in her new book, *The End of America: Letter of Warning to a Young Patriot,* living in fear is a horrible thing. How ironic that the fear that many men live in was in part created by Naomi Wolf in the first place.

In the morning D* woke up and saw snow and trees out the window. He was excited at the sight of snow. There were rolling hills and a creek could be seen in the woods. I felt like I had returned home. There is no other feeling like it. When we stopped in Illinois D* and I had a snow ball fight, though we weren't wearing gloves neither of complained about the cold. Later I found a pay phone and called a charity and donated the car to them. I explained I was out of state but the title and keys were in the glove box. I gave them my uncle's number in case they had any questions. They picked up the car.

D* Finds Jim Hawkin's Treasure in a Graveyard by Duck Creek

When we arrived in Davenport, mom told me that my attorney had called and I was to call him back immediately. My father told me what a good guy my attorney was. He was impressed. They had discussed raising children, and had agreed that I should grow up in a responsible manner. No matter that I was in my 40s and already had a career, or what was left of one. They are in their 70s, so I'm a kid to them.

When returning the call the first thing I noticed was that John no longer called H* "that poor little girl." At one point he even said, "that girl can hold her own." It was too bad the change came so late. I wished to God he had acted more strongly in getting my office records back as I had requested at the beginning, or even had returned my retainer so I could have afforded an attorney who would go to court to get my papers back. Now Campbell told Brandon that he would be glad to go to court. He said that he was confident that he would win an argument that the child should follow the school schedule of the school he was attending. This was the first and only time Campbell had shown any fight. It was a welcome

226

and satisfying. My understanding from the negotiations was that we were rotating Christmas breaks year by year. This was negotiated to give H* enough time to travel internationally and visit her family in Korea. Campbell informed me that the decree said we were splitting Christmas and that I was to be back on the 27th December.

While in Davenport I read Treasure Island to D*. Jim Hawkins from the Admiral Benbow Inn and all. He stared at me while not missing a word. The stories magic unfolded as the boy Jim avoided pirates, and then took a ship to seek treasure. After three days we had read past the point that Jim recovered the treasure map, and that Dr. Livesy had purchased a ship and rounded up a crew, and they were off sailing. I said to D*, "did you know that Jim Hawkins lived in this house before Grandma did? " His jaw dropped. "It is true. And rumor is that he left stuff in the attic."

The house I grew up in, had a finished basement, two floors, and a walk in attic. In 1969 cousin Calvin had signed the back of the attic door, "luv for all – Calvin, 1969", and then he proceeded to explain to me about the ghost that lived in the attic. I had nightmares for a week. The house was located on a hill, and had been the original farm house before the surrounding land was developed in the 1930s. From the roof top one could see the whole of the city. Looking south one looked over the old neighborhoods, the Mississippi river and then Arsenal Island. To the north one could see some houses, a large cemetery, Duck Creek, and then old Mo's land. Old Mo was a crazy hold out farmer still growing corn though he was now completely surrounded by city. North of old mo was a highway and a grocery store. Old Mo once met me with a shot gun when I had attempted to cross his land to get to that store. He made me walk all the way back instead of finishing the crossing which was just a stitch farther. To the east was residential going to Jersey Ridge and then to 'The Heights.' To the west was residential leading to the old elementary school.

D* rotated the old fashioned switch that turned on the light to the attic. One could see the cotton covered wire that was horse shoe nailed to the side of the stair make its way to hanging lights in the peak of the roof. In the attic there was a collection of forsaken items, some forgotten for decades. This box, I pointed out, was already here when grandpa and grandma moved in. D* dug it out. He looked in and with great curiosity suggested he had found a map. "You don't suppose it belonged to Jim?" I asked. "I don't know." "Here look here, it leads from the garage, going North."

D* and I went out back to the falling down old garage and fashioned some swords just in case we ran into undesirables. We put pins in for the blades. I carried the shovel. We read the map together. It lead us down the hill along a road next to the cemetery. I corrected D* at a few points when he went in a different direction than indicated by the map. Down at the bottom of Belle Avenue where the cemetery ended at the woods, and the bridge leading to old Mo's place could be seen up ahead crossing the creek, the map showed a left turn into the cemetery. D* paced it out. Sixteen steps from this gravestone, turn right, five more steps, we are standing on the X. I suggested his steps were a bit short, as he was shorter than Jim Hawkins, perhaps he ought to add a couple more steps. He did. We dug a hole, and D* found a chest. D* lifted the bread loaf size chest from the hole and opened it. It was full of coins and jewels. His eyes sparkled.

Upon our return, more accusations were to follow, though it seems the Austin police became jaded, but the Round Rock police were still willing. For example, D* brought his dog with him on two visits, about a year apart. Both times H* called the police and reported me for "stealing the dog." In the original agreement the dog was supposed to travel with D*.

227

Dad Moves to California and Works for Quicksilver January 2003

In January of 2003 I went to work for Quicksilver technologies on the west coast. Each month I gave my pay to Larry Schubhut senior so that he could point out the conflicts and the fraud in the agreement.

A Woman and Her Wannabe Daughter

While working in California, I rented a condo in South San Jose. It had a pool area, and once in a while I would go for a swim. On a Saturday afternoon there was a woman and her son in the pool when I arrived. He must have been about 7 years old. He was preening over his mother. He stared at her and grinned that big artificial grin that kids that age will sometimes make.

She was divorced and proud of it. I struck up a conversation with her. It didn't take long to discover that she was very nice, but not very sharp. I explained that I was also divorced. We talked about the difficulty of making bills. I commented that my divorce hearing had been very expensive.

"Oh?" she perked up. "Why is that?" She couldn't understand why anyone would pay for a divorce. "All you have to do is go to the legal aid office downtown, and tell them your spouse is abusive. Then they will pay for everything."

The case is, that the federal legal aid money for domestic violence is legislated to be spent on *women only*. Indeed the legal aid group in Austin was turning men with domestic abuse cases away, but not by saying they didn't have funds for men, rather they told the men that their cases didn't warrant Legal Aid's help. She was a nice woman, I didn't want to get into the politics of divorce with her. I told her that I would look into it first thing, and feigned some excitement over her helpful tip.

I got out of the pool, and started drying off. Her son swam over close to her and gave her the eyes. He said, "I'm going to grow up to be a woman like you." She glanced up to see if I had heard. She did not look happy. My face said it all, and she felt obligated to reply, but she just stammered, "No, ah, no, ah ..."

Exercise in Futility, Bar Complaints 2003

I filed complaints at the Bar in Austin. The complaints were returned to me with a form letter that had a wrong number and address on them. The letter said that they needed to be sent to Dallas. I called the head of the Bar in Dallas, to ask for an explanation. She gave me information on how to FedEx the complaints to Steve Malleke. After he signed for them I called him. Steve first told me that they were not accepted because they weren't on the correct forms. I pointed out in their rule book, that it was stipulated complaints could be filed as letters. Then, Steve apologized and said the complaints should not have been returned. However, he complained that my letters had not been written in a lawyerly fashion. He also complained that I hadn't done an investigation to amass evidence. Basically, he said that since I wasn't a lawyer I couldn't complain about lawyers, and because I hadn't done an investigation I couldn't request one. I got upset and called him a snake eating his own tail.

Mr. Malleke put me through to his 'chief investigator,' 'John,' to explain further. John told me that he had no intentions of investigating any of it. He said there was a committee I could appeal to, but that committee could only send it back to him, "and I already told you what I'm going to do."

After a couple of years past, I reasoned that there might have been a change of staff at the bar. I called and gave a quick review of the complaints on the phone. A Ms. Murphy returned my call. She said that she would investigate and get back with me. Initially she said her investigation would not cover everything, but would be limited to answering the question of whether I had been told something incorrect. When I suggested that this was futile she revised her purpose. She would not accept any material from me. It was some stylistic thing. There had been no change of staff. A few weeks later she called and left me a message that most of the records had been destroyed, but that the "two" Bar complaints had been handled properly. There had been nine complaints. If all the records were destroyed, then how did she know they were handled properly? Why didn't she accept my copies, and why did she not want new information?

Having Fun Introducing D* to Sailing

We started sailing on a Catalina 18 on Lake Travis.

One day J a good friend wanted to show his gratitude for an introduction I gave him to business associate, and offered to pay for a sailboat rental on Travis. We all went out and had a good time. It was a typically calm day on the sheltered lake.

We let D* sail the boat. When he grabbed the tiller his face became serious and he got that look in his eyes. Clearly we will be doing a lot of boating.

D* Cries About Needles In His Candy

One evening I was reading at the Barnes and Nobel book store. When I was leaving a stranger accosted me. He stood directly in my walking path. When I veered he veered. He said I needed to listen. He told me he had an Asian ex wife. I had never met the man in my life, but he just started in. He was clean cut and didn't appear to be crazy. As I backed off, he politely pinned me against the wall by artfully standing in the wrong place. He said that his Asian ex was always late to take his child to school, had run a red light one morning, and gotten in a car accident. He had my full attention. I stared and said nothing. Then he told me that his ex wife left needles on the floor where his child played, an the child had gotten into them. He concluded by saying that he knew someone so lazy he hadn't worked for a year, and then walked away. I stood there for a little while trying to absorb what had just happened. Was he telling me about H*? What a strange way to do it.

H* had run a red light, and also had gotten into a car accident – both while trying to get to the Lycée in the morning. So I added up the coincidences and extrapolated.

D* didn't usually answer questions I asked him. So the next time I had D* for visitation I made up a word game. I told him to say the first thing that came into his mind after I said a word. I learned that the car had been broken. Once I found out about that I pressed him to tell me more. He was hesitant, but said that mommy had a new one. I brought up needles. He was silent. "Carpet," I said. He started crying. Later I tried again. I brought up the needles. Tears welled in his eyes and he sobbed. He told me that mommy's candy bag also had needles in it. "Why don't you do anything about it?" He balled and accused me.

As in most incidences with H*, there are ways to rationalize what has happened here. H* started sewing, and she used the toy room as her work room. She could have left needles in the carpet. But, as I just mentioned, when I asked D* about this incident, he didn't talk about needles in the carpet, he talked about needles with his candy. It seems from D*' description that H* has a sewing kit, and she stored candy and needles in the same bag, and D* got into it without knowing better. I'm rationalizing here based on the further input from D*. However it is now clear that the story is becoming more detailed, but instead that it is *changing*. D* says his mom has been working with him on the couch to get him to change what he says about the incident, and he says it hasn't been just for the needles incident. He says she used the same method on his recounting of watching her kick the dog, which is described in a later section. He says she did not succeed in that case.

It was also at about this time that D* volunteered from the back seat of the car that he was upset that his mother was giving him naps. There is nothing unusual about this, as D* hated to nap, and never did it voluntarily except on one occasion, as described a couple of paragraphs further down. The unusual part was that he also said that he knew the naps weren't really 10 minutes long like she said, but rather they were only 10 seconds long. He explained he knew this because he could hear counting to 10 when he woke up.

D*'s story about the needles and the candy bag changed very slowly over a period of years. He told another story that changed in a much shorter time. D* told me that he took baths with his mother, and that he had pulled on her breast, and asked why nothing came out. He said his mother explained it was because she was out of milk. I found this story to be innocent enough and didn't think much about it. A week later I was at the school. We were standing by the wall just outside the cafeteria door, and he said he needed to tell me something. He said, "you know I told you mom was out of milk?" "I explained it wrong." "See, she was out of milk because there was none in the refrigerator, and she had to go to the store." I replied with just an "oh," and dropped it.

There are more examples. D* was mad at his mother as he wanted to live with his dad. I worked with him to try and teach him to communicate better. He had told her out right, and she said that it was his dad that was talking. D* wanted to break something so that she would know he was serious. I read him a short biography of Ghandi which had some passages about non violent protest such as simple refusal. He went home and flushed her toothbrush down the toilet as a 'protest.' The next time he came to visit, we got back to the apartment I kept in Austin at about three in the afternoon. He said he wanted to take a nap. That surprised me. "Sure," I told him, and he went into my room and laid on the bed. A few minutes later he got up, walked to the refrigerator, and peed in it. I stopped him. He apologized profusely.

Hired Attorney Larry Schubhut Sr., 2003 02

Ken Pangborn gave me the name of a woman in Leander, Trish, who was also having difficulty with Lara Nixon. Trish's second husband was getting roasted by Lara Nixon and Trish was not happy about it. Trish spoke highly of Larry Schubhut Sr.. So I gave him a call. Since talking to Trish I have since met two other people who had Sarah Brandon as an attorney. We all four have similar experiences.

I found employment by going to California. I used my first paycheck to hire Larry Schubhut Sr. I asked him to point out the fraud and conflicts related to the divorce decree. I agreed to pay him two thousand dollars a month. I paid him mainly from cashiers checks drawn from Downey Savings and Loan. I started with zero balance each month, I got my paycheck, paid for my next ticket to Austin, went grocery shopping, paid the rent, and withdrew Larry's check, and then had a zero balance again. The airlines reservations were especially frustrating because if I didn't have quite enough to make a fare one week, the price went way up the next week. If the price hadn't gone up, I could have paid ahead, but I could never get ahead because I was already behind. Apart from meeting the costs of living, I did little else to spend money.

Schubhut was a short man who talked quickly. He liked to push back in his chair behind his desk. He spoke in friendly tones, as though I had been invited to his place for a scotch, rather than to work out a custody issue. Schubhut started by telling me he did a lot of murder cases. He talked at length about a client he had who owned guns. He told me his ex wife had broken into his house and taken much of his collection. One day when I was leaving he even introduced me to the client when we passed in the doorway. I told Larry I didn't care to hear about his clients, but he insisted that I should listen, and he assured me he wasn't charging, and reassured me that all of the information could be gotten from public court records.

Larry had a legal assistant who kept a pair of fighting beta fish. They were in separate bowls placed next to each other on the receptionist's desk. When the invoice arrived, every minute I had been in the office, and then some, had been charged for. I took it up with Larry, and he apologized. He argued with her. She took the hard line that time in the office had to be charged for, and Larry hadn't told her about any exceptions. Larry reassured me not to worry, that the invoice would be fixed. It wasn't.

The one thing we weren't talking about much was D*, so to make things easier I put a whole bunch of information about it on a DVD ROM, and gave it to him. He could just put it in his computer and clique around, thought because he was a bit older and might not be computer literate, I thought I better check. I asked him if he knew how to read the disk. He said that he did.

I tried to tell him about how my son was doing, and when that didn't work, I brought D* to talk with him in person. I told Larry about the strange thing my son had said while riding in the back of the car, that his mother was giving him 10 minute naps, but he knew they were only 10 seconds, because he could hear counting to 10 when he woke up. D* was upset that his mother had mislead him about the length of the naps, and he thought it might be helpful information for rectifying the living situation. (This occurred on 2002 09 09. It was a very advanced locution for a child his age. I wondered if he had picked it up from television.) Larry perked up. He was interested in this.

Larry talked to D*. He said he was very experienced with kids, and he had never seen any kid respond to questions about home life the way D* did. D* refused to say anything about it. Larry said most kids blab on and on about what goes on at home. He continued that he had a friend he had grown up with who was a psychologist named Steve Freitag who specialized in hypnosis.

The next time I saw Larry he said sarcastically, "those letters you sent to the Bar were really something." I had filed some bar complaints, though I had not given him copies of the letters. Larry Schubhut continued on to tell me gossip about some of the players in the divorce. He also told me that Ezel had stopped doing custody cases. Larry said that Peggy Farely had left town and no longer practiced. He said she was in her fourth marriage and was off with her new husband on a ranch in south Texas where she shoots cattle from a helicopter for entertainment.

Checking as of 2005, Ezel no longer does custody evaluations. Apparently there was also an attempt to remove Lara Nixon. She left the department but still practices independently.

I asked Larry how review of the DVD was going. He said he had read it over fine, but when I tried to discuss the contents with him he hadn't a clue. I suggested that we put the disk in his machine and that I point some things out. We got out the envelope I had given him, and slid the covered DVD out. I opened it and put the DVD in his machine. The machine could not read DVDs. It was a CD player only. Initially Larry had said he had read the disk on the machine we put it in, but after I explained it could not read DVDs, he volunteered that it was really the machine in the next room in his legal assistant's office. I walked over to the next room and put the disk in that machine. It could not read DVDs either.

The California startup froze over very quickly when the company ran out of funding. I walked out the door with the founders. I told Larry that I was no longer obligated to stay in California, and that I didn't expect to be unemployed long. He replied that he was withdrawing, "Because all of the information you have given me is old." He was keeping the full $12,000 retainer, although he had never filed a single paper.

I called and told him that he could not keep the retainer without having done the work. He replied, "Tom those are fighting words." He then sent me a letter accusing me of "attacking" his legal assistant.

Psychologist Steve Freitag Says Hypnosis is Being Used On D*

Larry Schuhbut wanted the PhD psychologist Steve Freitag to see my son. Larry said that Steve was a master hypnotist. I agreed on the condition that he would not hypnotize D*. He could observe all he wanted to, but I did not want the situation to become one of battling hypnotists, if indeed there was anything to this concept.

Dr. Freitag came and saw D* at Schubhut's office. He then told me that it was beyond a doubt that something had been done. Apparently D*'s father was to be gotten rid of like a bad smoking habit. Dr. Freitag said for one thing, D* had been conditioned not to answer questions that I asked. Also he pointed out that when asked any questions about home or his Korean grandfather when I was present, that he would just get quiet. He said this may have been done using "subliminals", but that there were other methods. He wanted to know if D* was listening to music recordings. At this time the Korean grandfather, who was mentioned in the embassy letter presented earlier, had disappeared but was believed to be in the U.S. He may even have been at the house.

232

Dr. Steve Freitag provided a letter to Larry saying that he believed that D* had been "mentally coerced," and that it was not good for him. However, he did not sign the letter. Though when we came to litigation some years later, Dr. Freitag provided a sworn affidavit as shown on the next page.

Steve said he wanted to talk with me, but he was busy, and wanted to do it at the Denny's on I35. At the Denny's Steve explained to me that he often worked for the police. He explained that he had a PhD in hypnosis, and that he could release repressed memories. He explained that hypnosis was done by distracting the conscious mind, perhaps by telling a person something so awful that it caused them to reel away mentally. He then said he would give an example. He launched into a story where he was working as a police interviewer and he got testimony from an old woman who's husband had been killed in a hit and run accident. His voice was monotonous. He said that he had hypnotized the old lady, and gotten the plate numbers and color of the perpetrators car. He described the accident in detail, and told me that the old man had been decapitated when struck by the other car while changing a tire.

We left the restaurant together, but after Steve got in his car, I turned around and went back in. I did this because the timing didn't add up. We were there for a rather long time given the change of crowd, but it seemed like a short time. Our waitress was at the counter. I asked her if she had seen me eating. She said she had, of course. I asked if she had seen anything unusual. She said she hadn't. I asked if she was *really* sure she hadn't seen *anything* unusual, though I didn't say at all what that might be. She said, "Well, yes it looked like your were in a trance of some sort.." Those were her exact words.

B. 26. 2007 11:29AM NO. 091 P. 2

DR. STEVE FREITAG'S AFFIDAVIT

STATE OF New York §
§
Delaware COUNTY §

Before me, the undersigned authority, on this day personally appeared STEVE FREITAG, who after being duly sworn, stated upon his oath that the following are true and correct:

1) My name is Dr. Steve Freitag, I am of sound mind, capable of making this affidavit, and personally acquainted with the facts herein stated, the following facts are true and correct:

2) I hold a PhD in Psychology, and a master's degree in hypnotherapy. I am the Founder and President of the International Institute of Hypnosis and Complementary Therapies. I am also a member of the National Guild of Hypnotists and the International Hypnosis Federation. I am on the Advisory Board for Chris haven Foundation, a not-for-profit organization for children in need I've practiced hypnosis for over 10 years.

3) In 2003 I examined D and recently reviewed audio files of D . It is my expert opinion that psychological and hypnosis techniques of coercion have been used and is still being used on D which could cause irreparable harm. Such techniques are most likely to be introduced by a trained professional such as a psychologist.

STEVE FREITAG – AFFIANT

SWORN TO AND SUBSCRIBED BEFORE ME ON THIS 22 DAY OF February

NOTARY PUBLIC, STATE OF New York

My commission expires on 1/23/2010

LINDA J. SCOFIELD
Notary Public, State of New York
Greene County, # 01RE4646118
My Commission Expires 01/23/ 2010

*Figure 44: Psychologist Steve Freitag's Affidavit Stating Hypnosis Being Used On D**

Steve's conclusions gave me a lot of stress, confusion, and incredulity. It took a few years to undo this knot, and it really wasn't until reviewing drafts of this book that I came to understand that Dr. Freitag provided a correct read on the situation. Since I am a researcher, the first thing I did was go to the local university library and research the subject. I had expected to find references to hypnosis as a quack science. However, this was not what was in the library. There were a number of serious volumes in the psychology section dedicated to hypnosis, and many more with chapters on the subject. Hypnosis is now taught as part of the standard curriculum in psychology.

A recent book by Marcia Degun-Mather is a serious work on the subject, "Hypnosis Dissociation & Survivors of Child Abuse". In the first chapter she explains there is a localized part of the brain that performs critical analysis of what we hear or say. Hypnotic states are induced by dulling this part of the brain while simultaneously leaving other parts active. Degun-Mather reports that this state is not just a theory – it can be seen on brain scans. She shows pictures of scans in the book. When the critical analysis part of the brain is suppressed a person becomes gullible and loses track of time. I think of this as being analogous to the reduced inhibitions, losing track of time, and forgetting that can accompany experience alcohol consumption, though instead of reduced inhibitions, the patient has reduced critical thinking.

Once a person is in the so called trance state the practitioner may converse with the patient in a more direct manner than if the patient carefully analyzed what was said. Analysis is turned off in both directions. The patient is likely to remember what suggestions made by the psychologist without questioning them, and the patient is more likely to tell the interrogator about memories that would otherwise be repressed perhaps due to psychological trauma, such as abuse. If the hypnotist says to not remember the session or other things, the patient is likely to comply without questioning, and later will not be able to remember. The hypnotists I have talked to have all pointed out that some people are naturally gullible and it is much simpler to put them in a trance state. They also say there are some people where nothing special need to be done at all to make suggestions or to gather information. Children are more likely than adults to be highly susceptible. According to the DSM, histrionic personalities are naturally gullible. The hypnotists also point out that there are limits to what can be suggested. When the patient 'wakes up' and finds that some new assumptions don't make sense, the patient may just discard them. Dugun-Mather points out that it is best to use hypnosis along with other methods, such as cognitive therapy. Hypnotists say that the best suggestions are those that already fit within the persons belief framework. When there is some distance to be spanned between the current belief framework and where the hypnotist wants to take the patient, they lead the patient through small steps perhaps combined with other therapies, and cause the patients non-repressed memories to evolve into place over a period of time. In "The Manipulated Mind" Denise Winn points out that given enough time anyone will succumb to just about any new idea.

A gifted hypnotist working with people who are highly susceptible can induce a state of gullibility quickly. The following article talks about a man who is both talented at inducing hypnosis, and talented at picking those who are susceptible. The problem is, he is using his skills to have the subjects hand over money.

'Hypnotist' thief hunted in Italy

Police in Italy have issued footage of a man who is suspected of hypnotising supermarket checkout staff to hand over money from their cash registers.

In every case, the last thing staff reportedly remember is the thief leaning over and saying: "Look into my eyes", before finding the till empty.

In the latest incident captured on CCTV, he targeted a bank at Ancona in northern Italy, then calmly walked out.

A female bank clerk reportedly handed over nearly 800 euros (£630).

The cashier who was shown the video footage has no memory of the incident, according to Italian media, and only realised what had happened when she saw the money missing.

CCTV from the bank showed her apparently being hypnotised by the man, according to the reports.

Italian police believe the suspect could be of Indian or North African extraction.

Figure 45: Article on Hypnotist Thief

In "Hypnosis, Dissociation And Survivors of Child Abuse", Dagun-Mather notes "In the early 1990s there was an outbreak of adults who claimed to recover memories of being sexually abused as children. There were many cases, especially in America, of adults accusing their parents of having sexually abused them as children and taking them to court." What Dagun-Mather didn't mention here is that some of this was occurring through CPS on younger patients, and some men went to jail due to the accusations. When it was proven that some of the recovered memories could not possibly be true, in the true American style, those who had been hypnotized to recover memories turned around and sued the clinics that had performed the hypnosis. According to one hypnotist I spoke with some of the settlements were large, and a clinic in Houston was sued out of existence. These incidences, combined with the stigma of hypnosis have caused hypnotists to become very careful when talking to people, especially those who are writing books.

One hypnotist relayed a very important incident to me, and he repeated it again, though after I requested his permission to publish it he has backed off to some degree. He said he doesn't want to be sued. I will repeat his recounting here, though without attribution. Lets say his name is Fred. Fred said he was teaching a class. The students in the class had a lab where they worked with patients who had phobias. Fred went to check on one of the practice sessions and the woman who had volunteered to by hypnotized to recover from a phobia of horses was balling and crying. Fred was able to ascertain that the patient had been told by the student, probably while under hypnosis, that the phobia of horses was due to her having been sexually abused as a child. There was nothing else involved, simply that a phobia of horses meant sexual abuse; however there is no such link known. Fred described the student as young and an radical feminist, in the parlance used in this book, she was a misandrist. He felt that indications were that the student's actions had been

236

ideologically motivated. Fred tried to have the student removed from the course, but the student and apparently some friends went to the administration. Fred was then told by the administration that he had to get along with the feminists for political reasons, as one bad student wasn't worth the fallout that would affect the whole department.

The false sexual abuse allegations made in the 1990s as a result of memories recovered through hypnosis has been blamed on something called *false memory syndrome*. Two reasons are commonly given for false memory syndrome, and I think Fred's experience suggests a third. A first reason given for false memory syndrome is that the patient isn't thinking critically, by definition, and thus may just be spouting nonsense. A second explanation is that the hypnotist interrogator is cuing the patient with the questions. For example, asking "were you abused?" along with ten variations of this same question suggests a context of abuse to the gullible trance induced patient. The patient assumes that where there is smoke there is fire, and accepts the questions as a planted suggestion of abuse. After the session, the patient will take this suggestion just like any other and know there was abuse. This same affect occurs with patients who are not hypnotized. For example, false allegations made against me lead to investigations as all allegations of abuse of children must be investigated according to state law. This meant people came around and asked questions about dad. Not mom, but dad. It gave my son and other people who witnessed the questioning the impression that dad was somehow suspicious. Fred's experience illustrates a third cause for false memory syndrome, that an unethical, deluded, or ideological practitioner has taken advantage of the patient's gullibility and does not want others to know he or she has done this. Such deluded practitioners may feel they are making a sincere effort to help and to protect the patient but that other people just won't understand.

William Edmunston Jr. gives many example of how to induce hypnosis in his now classic book "The Induction of Hypnosis." The majority of this methods integrate counting to 10. Hence, counting to 10 isn't not just the stuff of the popular media, hypnotists really incorporate this. On p237 he lists modifications of the induction methods for use with children. He notes on p340, "Children are more receptive to hypnotic induction and suggestions than adults. There is a Children's Hypnotic Susceptibility Scale provided on page 340, it covers children from ages 5 to 12. Karen Olness and Daniel Kohen's book "Hypnosis and Hypnotherapy With Children" states on page 52, "Children respond to a large number of hypnotic induction techniques, strategies, and approaches, each with countless variations."

Because hypnosis works with children, and because it can be used to unlock repressed memories, CPS at times uses hypnosis in their investigations of abuse with children. A professionals accusations would have given a green light for such a process to be used with D*.

Identifying trauma is also important for therapy. On p21 of "Hypnosis, Dissociation and Survivors of Child Abuse," Dagun-Mather writes:

> Pierre Janet had considerable success with his patients when using hypnotic age regression .. if the memories were too distressing for the patient, he would deliberately change the memory into something else.

D*'s explanation of the needles changing over time has all the hallmarks of a therapist's handiwork. The therapist would change the memory in order to help him get passed the trauma and to recover form ill feelings that the incident may have created towards his mother. Such an interpretation makes the therapist out to be acting in the child's best interest. Perhaps the practitioner was protecting the mother out of a sense that the incident was an accident. If so she unwittingly hid part of a pattern of "accidents" from the court and investigators. Also, I, the father, was not informed of what was being done. These ethical lapses exposes a bias, and that bias begs questions. What is the source of the bias? What would such a biased practitioner be willing to do? These are especially salient question in a divorce context, in a milieu of misandry, and in the presence of Malicious Mothers Syndrome. A malicious mother is likely to find an ally in a malicious mother practitioner. A misandry divorce attorney is likely to have such contacts to refer an angry mother to.

After doing the research I decided to get a second opinion. Finding a second opinion turned out to be exceedingly difficult, which is ironic as many practitioners are listed in the various directories. I called and spoke with a men's movement activist and an attorney by the name of David Sibley, he pointed me to a psychologist who could provide a second opinion. I called her and told her what Steve said, and asked if she had the expertise to give a second opinion. She said she would be glad to. When I got there she said while looking at D*, "I don't want to talk to him." Turning to me she said, "I want to talk to *you*." I told her I wasn't interested in talking with her. She suggested we sit down to talk about D*.

We sat down, and she told me that Dr. Freitag did not exist. She said she had looked in the phone book and he wasn't listed. I will give her bonus credit as a practitioner for saying what she thought. I believe it is more common for psychologists not to share such 'insights.' I went into the other room, grabbed the phone book from under the table. Sessions Hypnosis was listed. I showed her. I dialed the number, and the recording came on, "This is Doctor Freitag, please leave me a message." She did not apologize, but continued on without hesitation, "so how long have you known that your ex has been controlling your son's mind?" I was still standing by the receptionist counter with the phone book. I said good bye. We walked out.

Dr. Freitag had described doing police interviews, so I typed in a Google search and found an academy that teaches hypnosis, mainly to police interrogators. They were located in Waco. The person I spoke with was excited to promote the school. He bragged that 1 in 4 police interrogators in Texas have training in hypnosis. He then gave me two names. I spoke with both of them. They both brought up the issue of his age. As one put it, it couldn't have been going on very long. This concurred with the library books that put the age hypnosis starts to work at 4 to 6, though one expert wrote that different techniques than used for adults may be effective on younger children. It was 2002 09 09 when D* was complaining about the length of afternoon naps. D* was 4 ½, so this actually correlates well. Because hypnosis wouldn't take well, he would be more likely to talk about the session, as he did.

I looked one up one of the authors of a book from the library. He was at a University in California. He knew a professional in Dallas who was an expert at working with children. This man had worked with the Branch Davidian children after the Waco siege. I called. The receptionist engaged me in a conversation about UFOs. I told her that I had never seen one, and frankly I didn't think they existed. Then she asked me if I had any memories of being in the military etc. She said that most of their patients did, and suggested this might be a way to get seen. "No, unfortunately, I guess, I don't have any of those."

238

"No military experience?"

"Nope."

"Every been abducted?"

"Nope. ... and I have never abused drugs either, if that is your next question."

"Hah," she laughed. "You seem normal enough to me, you would be surprised the calls we get." She let me through to the doctor. I spoke with him, and he referred me to a colleague.

I hadn't pursued the second opinion with much zeal. The events above span years. By this time it was 2005. Larry had quit long before, and I had more recently hired Gabe Guitierrez. In addition I was looking for an expert Gabe might use to try and come to grips with Dr. Freitag's feedback.

Unfortunately the psychiatrist in Dallas called back and said she couldn't consult, "because your attorney is just a personal injury attorney."

Later I would get a second opinion from Mike Boulch. Mike runs a small school that teaches hypnosis to police interrogators, he also travels as a consultant, instructor, and as an interrogator. He did volunteer work for a high school security firm and has a lot of experience working with children. He concurred with Dr. Freitag and suggested to Jim Wallace that he should question the motives of the mother (see Figure 75 p349).

D*'s New Child Psychologist Lists On Her Resume that She is a Student of Shamanism

After Peggy Farley lied on the stand about the phone calls, and certainly after it came out that she had divorced using H*'s attorney, Peggy was out of the picture. This seemed to be a win, but on the very same day Peggy officially quit, Lara Nixon appointed Caryl Dalton to replace her.

The very fact that Lara Nixon appointed her made me feel incredulous. What are the odds that a person who had accused me of molesting my son, and had appointed a conflicted party – a conflicted party who testified against me without ever meeting me – would appoint a neutral party the second time?

Caryl Dalton is the vice president of a non-profit called One Heart Many Rhythms. According to their website, "the primary focus of One Heart Many Rhythms is to provide assistance for young adults from indigenous cultures to continue their education beyond primary school in order to prepare for occupations such as teachers, nurses, and physicians." The 15 board members are all women. Her bio on the website explains she is a student of shamanism (I added the underlining.):

> Caryl is a psychologist in private practice in Austin, Texas and has been working with children and families for over 30 years. She holds a Doctorate of Educational Psychology from the University of Texas. As the founder of White Hummingbird Consulting, she created the Post Divorce Coaching program as a preventative intervention to help families make a successful transition to this change in their lives. Caryl is a student of shamanism and enjoys traveling and visiting indigenous cultures to learn about their healing traditions.

I have run into Shamanism on three occasions, first in a cultural anthropology course at the university, Dr. Chad Oliver taught that shamans used a lot of drugs and trance states to induce people to see spirits. In some cultures, if you don't see them, there is something wrong with you. In others, everyone will see them. The term 'shaman' has displaced the term of 'witch doctor'. True, occasionally the various plants the shamans use are found to have positive medicinal qualities, after all if one goes into the jungle and eats everything, one is bound to find a few good things. Shamanism is described in a number of books, and even on wikipedia. Here is the forth point describing shamanism on the current wikipedia page:

> Shamans engage various processes and techniques to incite trance; such as: singing, dancing, taking entheogens, meditating and drumming.

Just as *shaman* is a nicer word for *witch doctor*, *entheogen* is a nicer word for hallucinogen. Another term for entheogen is psycho hypnotic. Trances are are how hypnotic states are induced..

Another time I heard about shamanism was from my erstwhile uncle. He talked about taking hallucinogens and being transported to the spirit world. The transportation dropped him in a small apartment and a job at Walmart. It is hard to understand the benefit of that insight.

Really, is this someone you want to be your kid's child psychologist? Perhaps you are open minded, perhaps you would be ok with this, but take this another step, should this be someone your ex forces you to use as your child psychologist? We have a joint decree, but H* refused to change, if for no other reason, because I wanted to. Dalton refused to be fired. Now take this a third step, when one psychologist is telling you that your kid is being hypnotized, your wife hates your guts and periodically hurts your kid, and the child psychologist is protecting your ex – is this the person who should be the kid's child psychologist? And on top of all of this, there are many good practitioners in town who would have made father feel more comfortable, so why not use one of them?

I wanted to observe, but Dalton didn't allow that. I wanted copies of her records, it literally took years of gaming to get them. She initially told me that she was also H*'s psychologist and the notes were all mixed together, and though I had a right to see D* records, I didn't have a right to H*'s and therefore I would get neither. The records showed she was using tree and house diagrams for diagnosis. Tree and house diagrams were discounted a decade ago, because it was discovered a clinician could read anything into them she wanted to. One must ask, is she 10 years behind on her education, or is she crumbing up data so she could justify conclusions that are not true? Then there are the quotes attributed to D* in her records that were completely out of character. The following pages are drawings made by D* that come from Dr. Dalton's records:

T
8/30/04

241

104

Figure 46: Dalton's Records Showing Discredited Tree and House Diagrams

242

Robyn Dawes of Carnegie Mellon is probably our nations foremost expert on the efficacy of psychology methods. He has been involved in scientific evaluations of these methods and his work helps set the license regulations of psychologists. Here is what he had to say after looking at Ms. Dalton's records:

Carnegie Mellon

Department of Social and Decision Sciences
Porter Hall 208
Carnegie Mellon University
Pittsburgh, Pennsylvania 15213-3890

Fax: (412) 268-6938

February 21, 2007

NO. _____

IN THE DISTRICT COURT
395TH JUDICIAL DISTRICT
WILLIAMSON COUNTY, TEXAS

Tom Lynch v. Caryl Dalton

AFFIDAVIT

State of Pennsylvania
County of Allegheny

BEFORE ME, the undersigned authority, personally appeared Robyn M. Dawes, who, being by me dully sworn, deposed as follows:

My name is Robyn M. Dawes Ph.D. I am of sound mind, capable of making this affidavit, and I have been a researcher in the Social and Decision Sciences department at Carnegie Mellon University since 1985, belong to the Center for Behavioral Decision Research and Risk Perception, am a fellow of the American Statistical Association, and am author of many apropos papers and the book *House of Cards*, a work which explores the basis for the practice of psychology. Based on my expertise:

The techniques of tree drawings and house drawings were thoroughly discredited in the early 1990s; use of such discredited techniques will place a patient in harm's way

Affiant, Robyn M. Dawes

SWORN AND SUBSCRIBED before me on the ___21 day of ___Feb___, 2007

Notary Public

Notary's printed name:

COMMONWEALTH OF PENNSYLVANIA
Notarial Seal
Emma Jean Harpley, Notary Public
City Of Pittsburgh, Allegheny County
My Commission Expires Dec. 14, 2008
Member Pennsylvania Association Of Notaries

Figure 47: Dawes on House and Tree Diagrams

244

The basic issue is this. The psychologist who uses these diagrams may come to any desired conclusion, as the tests are not normed against any predictors. I.e. a little stick here in this diagram does not indicate what a little stick over there in that diagram made by another child means. When norming a test, a research scientists correlates interpretations derived form specific predictors for a large number of diagnosed patients. In contrast, for the diagrams the clinician is free to make up both the predictors and provide their meaning. For various reasons a practitioner may be intentionally or unintentionally biased to find specific results and is free to find them. This may be to subconsciously support intuition, to support a given theory, or unfortunately, to do a good job for someone who brings a lot of business to the practitioner. Once in court the clinician is considered to be an expert witness, so the results may be presented to achieve goals such as trumping the testimony of people who have known the child for years.

Dr. Dalton published that she was a student of shamanism, gamed me over records, continued on with father when there were other options, used discredited techniques. My concern was that Dr. Dalton was H*'s advocate rather than an impartial advocate for D* long term mental health. For these reasons I did not want to give her the ability to testify about me, so I was not comfortable in visiting with her, even if she did change her mind.

I spoke with Dr. Dalton and asked if she was the only person in Austin qualified to be D*'s psychologist. She said absolutely not, that there are many qualified practitioners in Austin. So I suggested wouldn't it make better sense to have a psychologist both parents were comfortable with? Gee. She never answered this question, and nor would she quit. Instead she worked with mom and D* for a period of years.

Dr. Dalton wrote in correspondence that she did not know Sara Brandon.

She testified in deposition that she knew nothing about hypnosis and had no training in the subject. In my opinion this was one of those over denials that beg questions, as with a PhD in psychology and a religion of shamanism it seems she should have had some exposure to the subject.

Broken Music Box, Broken Kid

In spring of 2003 D* was going to the Lycée Francaise private school. The idea was that he could learn a couple of foreign languages while he was young. It was also interesting that the curriculum was standardized. Hence, he could enter a school someday and be in the same place in the books. The Lycée also allowed divorced fathers to take long weekends provided that the child did his homework. Hence, I could pick D* up on Wednesday or Thursday, and then, drop him back on Monday.

When I went to Dallas, this made things infinitely easier.

I sent D* a gold plated crystal music box from California. I still remember mine from being a kid. I would see the sparkling crystals in my dreams. I sent it to the Lycée so that he would get it directly. At the next exchange I saw H* walking up with a shopping bag in her right hand. D* was at her left. Tears were running down his face. H* handed me a bag with music box parts. "Here is your music box, it is broken" she said, paused and then added, "Here is your kid."

D* balled that he had broken the music box. He said it was given to him to play with, and he had played with it until it broke. I explained to him that it wasn't usual for someone his age to be left alone with something so fragile, and it wasn't his fault at all. It was to be expected.

H* had difficulty waking up early enough to take D* to the Lycée on time. She ran a red light on one occasion, and had an accident on another. In addition she didn't get along with the director, who refused to limit my time with D*. The divorce decree said I would pay for the Lycée, so when my finances got tight, instead of kicking in a couple hundred dollars, H* moved D* to a public school.

D* Refuses to Go with H*

In 2003 D* discovered the telephone. He called me daily at Quicksilver, and would talk for an hour. The folks at Quicksilver were very good about it. I would excuse myself from meetings, or whatever, and take a conference room and talk with him. If necessary I would then work late. H* told D* he couldn't use her phone, so I mailed him a rather cool looking antique replica phone. H* claimed that it didn't arrive, but the tracking of the shipping said otherwise. I had told D* about the phone, and he started asking for it. He found it and opened it. H* curtailed the calls anyway. Between late 2003 and 2006 I made 100s of calls to the house, and to H*'s cell phone. All except a very few went unanswered.

Quicksilver allowed me to telecommute from Austin, so I got an apartment. For about two weeks out of the month, I would go by after he got out of school, and instead of going to the YMCA after school program, we would typically play soccer or Go.

D* was usually picked up late, so H* didn't know about the set up initially. We had a close call once, when she unexpectedly arrived before 6. As she walked in one door, I turned and walked out the other. However, the system fell apart in the late spring one evening because D* decided to refuse to go home with her.

I took him back to the gym and then left. I was walking outside by the gym wall when I saw he was under a cafeteria table. I paused to see what would happen. H* arrived and he refused to come out. He wanted to go home with his father. After a short exchange, she reached under the table, yanked him out, and drug him off.

We Had a Good Time in Iowa for Six Weeks Summer 2003

In 2003 D* and I spent six weeks in Iowa with my family. This was the only stress free vacation we were ever to have. I wrote during the day, and Grandma and D* settled into a routine. They did breakfast together, headed to the park, saw Great Grandma, and then went for violin lessons. D* also played with my high school friend's kids. The local school let him play soccer. He commanded the field. The coach was absolutely sure he was older than I had said and actually accused John of bringing a ringer. D* is athletically gifted.

I started the violin lessons with a promise from H* that they would continue when we got back. She said they would, but she stopped them when we returned. We tried very hard to convince her to let him play soccer, but she refused. During the next year he became overweight in part due to lack of exercise. It made no sense.

Mayo Clinic Visit 2003, D* Has Tissue Damage in His Gut

I didn't really know what to do on a *visit* with my son. I wanted him to feel good, so I took him directly to Amy's Ice Cream, and told him he could have anything he wanted. It was also the last thing he needed. I felt awful. Is this what things had reduced to? Had I replaced our good relationship with ice cream? It reminded me of the settlers buying Rhode Island from the Indians for a handful of beads. The Indians got a bad deal. D* was getting a bad deal. Were we really to trade a real father son relationship for a periodic ice cream and a game of soccer?

D* ordered a chocolate cone. He took a few bites and then threw up. There was only one other person there, with a child. They nodded understandingly and went outside. The staff was very helpful, they got towels, and we cleaned things up.

My first thought was that he must be getting a fever, but he wasn't hot. Nor was he acting sick. I didn't know what he had eaten before I picked him up. Perhaps he was already full of ice cream, and this had been one too many. We declined a replacement and went to the park to play soccer.

After D* went back to H*'s place, I started thinking about it. It reminded me of my wheat gluten problem, so I called the manager at Amy's. She knew about the incident. I got an ingredients list for the ice cream. It was cream, sugar, eggs, and chocolate. That was it. He hadn't gotten to the cone, so that didn't matter.

A couple of weeks later we went down town and walked around the lake. We went to TGI Friday and got a window seat so we could watch the bats fly out from under the Congress street bridge at sunset. The tourist brochures brag that Austin harbors the largest bat population of any city. We had pizza, and then D* had to urgently go to the bathroom. He threw up. Again he had no fever. I requested the ingredients for the pizza. They didn't know them off hand, but they had them mailed from district office. The ingredients list arrived in the mail a week later. It was very long. The only thing in common with the ice cream was the dairy – cheese and butter.

The decree said I couldn't take D* to the doctor, so I had to be satisfied with talking with them on the phone. Calling Dr. Mirrop's office was always problematic. They never answered directly. The outgoing recording made all sorts of caveats about unnecessary calls and then after a long hold would say no one was available and ask for a message to be left. This was true during the day as well as during off hours. The same nurse, Jeannie, always called back. She had become the official H* liaison officer. I told her that I thought D* was dairy intolerant. Jeannie explained that H* had told her that I was just making trouble, and that he had no such symptoms.

D* again got sick at McDonald's. This turned out to be very confusing, as he had only had french fries. The manager told me the fries were not just any potatoes, but potatoes which had been through a strict growing and quality tests. He said that McDonald's in eastern Europe was even having problems getting enough potatoes because of all the requirements. The manager may not have realized it, but it was a big lie. McDonald's is now being sued in a class action suit from the mothers of Autistic mom's. Despite their claims of purity, their fries have all sorts of stuff in them, including dairy and wheat gluten. But at the time, for me, it just added to the confusion, and caused me to ask more questions rather than taking a stronger stand.

What I decided to do was to take D* home to Iowa, and have my mother and Grandmother examine him. Due to family and working at the church day care, they have taken care of hundreds of kids. Describing things on the phone, just wasn't getting the message across. The next opportunity to spend time in Iowa was the summer of 2003. We stayed there for six weeks.

They agreed there was an issue. They said D* was dairy intolerant, but that there was "also something else." If D* was dairy intolerant, then I had a problem. H* had taken D* out of the French school, and placed him into public school. According to Texas law, the public school has to give kids milk at lunch every day. Though the kids are allowed to drink 'chocolate milk,' which is mostly corn syrup and water, it still has some dairy component. The only way to get out of the milk requirement, was to have a note from a doctor.

Dr. Mirrop handled the issue of 'H* saying D* had no dairy intolerance,' and my saying 'he does,' as though it was an academic debate. He wanted the answer from the parents, not from any sort of test or any other source. Jeannie had become openly sarcastic when I called, so I figured they had ruled on the debate, and H* had totaled more style points.

Apparently my mother's and grandmother's opinion was not enough to change the score, so I decided to hire a local nurse. A local nurse would be official, and unconnected to the family. It would be difficult to argue that she was just a troublemaker. I thought hiring a nurse would be rather easy, as my aunt, and mothers cousin both had been nurses. They were not practicing, and pointed me to the phone book. A source from the phone book would be the most unbiased. There were no individuals listed in the phone book, but rather a number of agencies. Those agencies dealt with me suspiciously, and told me they would not send a nurse out to feed D* and observe – unless I had a note from his pediatrician. I was tempted to get a local pediatrician involved, but D* pediatrician was officially Dr. Mirrop.

I called Dr. Mirrop's office to get a note. Jeannie called me back. Jeannie said that Dr. Mirrop would not write such a note, and I should drop it. She said this without even asking him, so I began to wonder if she had taken up the practice of medicine herself. I asked to speak to doctor Mirrop directly. She told me that he was too busy, so she would have to help me. Jeannie reiterated that H* had told her there were no symptoms, and that was all there was to it. I suggested there was no harm in checking. Jeannie lectured me about not wasting medical resources. I insisted on speaking directly to Dr. Mirrop. Jeannie would only relay a message. A little later, Jeannie called back. She explained she had spoken to the doctor, and that he saw no need for a nurse. There would be no letter of permission to hire a nurse.

I decided it was time to go around the decree. Technically, I suppose at this point it could be called an emergency anyway. It had been a year and a half since the last time we went to the Mayo Clinic. We made an appointment with Dr. El-Youssef.

The Mayo Clinic also had an instrument that measured dairy intolerance. D* measured as being very dairy intolerant. Earlier anti-gliden tests administered by Dr. Mirrop were also suggestive of wheat-gluten intolerance.

Dr. El-Youssef's head nurse struck up a conversation with me while D* was being biopsied. I was reading a book at the time, it was called, *Our Stolen Future*. It was a book claiming an environmental catastrophe due to artificial hormones in the environment. I'm not an environmentalist. Perhaps I should be, but I'm not. It just happened to be a book that was recommended to me, so I was reading it. We were making small talk so I explained the thesis of the book to her. The authors were claiming all sorts of ills due to pollution, all the way down to reduced intelligence of the population. The nurse explained that she had a degree in psychology, and then she started in on some B.S. about me not having to worry, and everything working itself out, and that the divorce would be fine. I felt like saying, "Look lady, I passed the 'worry' stage years ago," or making a snide remark about analyzing things you don't know about, but I didn't say anything.

When I met Dr. El-Youssef, he did not talk about D*, instead he told me that everything would work out with the divorce. His nurse stood by his side while he explained this. The other nurse was more forthright. Amber explained there was tissue damage.

Dr. El-Youssef sent a letter to Dr. Mirrop informing him of the dairy intolerance findings. Dr. Mirrop simply replied with a letter saying that he was quitting as D*'s pediatrician. Apparently he decided to quit as debate judge. There was no apology. According to the decree, H* got to pick the next pediatrician. She found a doctor with the Austin Regional Clinic, where Dr. Coldwater had been. The new office told me to take a hike. Basically, they weren't going to inform me of anything. They rejected the Mayo Clinic letter, as did the school nurse. With H*'s blessings, D* was being given milk at the school.

A series of letters between Dr. El-Youssef's office, the new pediatrician, and the school ensued. Eventually they agreed on a compromise. The school would continue to give D* milk, but he would take enzymes for digestion before hand. Furthermore, D* would not be allowed to carry the enzymes, although they are non-toxic, but rather they would have to be dispensed by the school nurse. In addition the school has gone on to teach the food pyramid, with milk and cheese as a corner stone.

This is a very selfish conclusion. It basically trains D* to rely on food he cannot naturally eat, when there are many good alternatives. The majority of people on earth can not digest milk, so there is nothing wrong, indeed not even anything unusual, with eating alternative food. Furthermore, it has been my experience that the enzymes do not always work sufficiently.

After the battle over diagnosing dairy intolerance, there was a battle to get D* his enzymes. I went by the school on several occasions, and he was at lunch without them. He would eat, and then go the restroom. It wasn't until second grade when the school started taking it seriously. I came by the school for story time, and D* was sitting with his classmates. He started farting, and the other kids said, "Ooo." I asked if he had his dairy enzymes with lunch, he said he didn't. I explained to the class that it was common to be dairy intolerant, and to the teacher what the symptoms were. Suddenly there was a aura of understanding. It had taken two years.

My mother's "other thing," has still not been addressed. I simply haven't had D* long enough during visits, nor the energy, to go around with it again. He is still running to the restroom after some meals.

The first year after the decree, I discovered that D* had not been to the dentist. I took him for an examination and he had cavities. I told H* about it, and she then took him to the dentist and had the work done. The next year I had to prod again. The next year yet again. Just before Christmas this year, I have taken him again. He has not been to a dentist since last year, and has a cavity.

It has also been the same with flu shots. Every year I find out late in the season that he hasn't had one, so I take care of it.

H* Can't Be Flexible With Even a One Day Schedule Variation November 2003

H* was not going to allow me to see D* for one more minute than she had to, and not even that when she could get away with it. In late November 2003 my visitation began on the 19th, and ended on the morning of the 24th. The next day, the 25th was my turn for Thanksgiving. I asked H* if she minded letting D* stay the night of the 24th so as to simplify my travel. Otherwise I would be an extra night in a hotel.

From: H* Lynch <------>_____
Date: Tue Oct 21 2003 - 17:22:47 CDT
To: <tom.lynch@ths.com>

Yes, I mind. I don't see any reason why this breaks your
visit in half because D*'s school is still in session until
the Thanksgiving
holidays.

--H*

Figure 48: H Won't Negotiate Even a Day Variation to Fit My Flight Schedule*

Return of the Indian Pow Wow

D* had an issue with my not taking enough pictures. Somehow he had gotten the impression this was related to where he was living. I opened my laptop, and pointed him at the picture database, and started making dinner.

I few minutes later he started screaming, "She is a liar, she is a liar, she is a liar ..." The Indian Pow Wow pictures were there. However, these pictures could not have meant anything out of context. Still when D* saw them he started yelling.

It turned out that H* had actually taken the time to defend against the evidence presented against her – to D*. It appears that Caryl Dalton has been involved in this also. According to D* his mother said that I had made up a story about Indian Pow Wow for the court, but it wasn't true, and that I was now being punished for having done so. She had explained to him that was why he was living with her and not me. When he saw the pictures, he realized she was lying, and everything he had done to rationalize why things were as they were collapsed.

He went home and called a liar. I received a phone call accusing me of having rehearsed him to accuse her of being a liar. D* then renewed his requests to live with his father. This was at the time he was kicking and screaming in the hall at the school not to go home with mom, but to go home with me.

H* then took D* back to Caryl Dalton. Ms. Dalton appeared as the child psychologist handwritten into the final divorce decree. Although she had not included me for years, refused to provide records, she also refused to be fired. It appears to me that she viewed her job as convincing D* that he should live happily with his mom, and that his true feelings had no baring on the mater.

Now four years after Judge Hathaway held up the pictures and gave me a sole managing conservatorship, H* has introduced a brand new explanation of what happened that day, and she felt compelled that D* should be the primary audience for this explanation. H* has explained to D* that she didn't want to tell him the truth in order to protect him from the *real story*. D* tells me, "Mom said that you were doing something horrible, and she needed to hide my face from you." He hasn't yet told me what that horrible thing is supposed to be.

D* told me a few weeks ago, that Caryl Dalton keeps asking him the same questions over and over again, until he gets so sick of it that he starts lying to her to make her stop asking. I think lying is very bad thing for anyone, but especially for children. It will not take long for his thoughts to start confusing what was just said to stop her from repeating questions, and what he knows to be factual. Caryl Dalton has become D*'s ministry of truth for an Orwellian rewriting all of history that has the point of making 'mom good' and 'dad bad', complete with a recurring new story of how pictures of mom screaming and suffocating the kid are really indications of some unspeakable abuse committed by dad.

H* Prevents Our Visitation for 7 Weeks Spring of 2004

H* has disturbed a number of legitimate vacation weekends by taking D* out of school or day care on days I am supposed to pick him up. Spring of 2004 I went seven weeks without getting a visit.

H* Tells D* He is Going to Six Flags With Her On My Weekend

In July of 2004 H* went so far as to tell D* that he was going to six flags with his best friend on my visitation period-- unless I insisted on picking him up in which case he wouldn't get to go. I came by the next week instead. When D* was older his mother also took him to Lego Land and Disney World.

Introducing D* to Buddhism

The divorce decree states that I have the "right to direct moral and religious training of the child" - and I have endeavored to do this.

My first exposure to Buddhism was actually in High School, though I hadn't realized it, as Sardartha is the story of the Buddha. I ran into again while studying Japanese language and culture in the college. Since then I have known many Buddhists from a number of countries, heard their points of view, and have been to Buddhist temples.

When D* was four I suggested he should chose a religion. At that time I still had the remnants of my library, and had many books on religions. I described to him briefly about Hinduism, Buddhism, Christianity, Islam, and Judaism. Though both sides of the family the only among these we did not have connections to were Hinduism and Islam. We did visit a Mosque. D* decided on Buddhism. I did have a lot of books on the subject. I think that the Budha's first lesson that the nature of living was struggle was attractive to him.

The first thing I taught D* was geared more to his situation than to directly to a sutra. I taught him what I called the "rules for keeping the ghost out of your heart."   These rules were: 1) remember you are a good person, 2) meditation, 3) be honest about the signs 4) remember that there are people who will take advantage of you if you let them. These were put in simple language for a four year old who was in a special situation.

The first point was to address his formation of self identity. He had a strong feeling that he had done something wrong and was being punished for it. I wanted him to know that what was going on was not because of anything he had done. Some years later I came back and reminded him when he was particularly feeling bad and explained that I had designed this lesson just for him. That the "you" in this remember you are a good person was meant to be him specifically, and that this was not a general rule. He started crying in relief. This was a well sown seed that came to fruition and kept us on course.

I taught him to meditate so that he could sort his thoughts out and also learn to relax. I used it to counter his 'bouncing of the walls' symptoms that he often had when I picked him up. I used to help him learn to control his emotions. Along with this I explained that when he communicated that he should keep his center, lest people lose the message in what he says, and just say he was behaving badly. He would mediated and then we would talk, often times with something nasty coming out. He was always relieved afterwards.

By telling D* to be being honest about the signs I wanted him to pay attention to people's actions and deeds, and notice the results when possible. In Buddhism this is related to dependent origination. In Christianity and Judaism it is known as you reap what you sow. But it goes much farther than this. I tried to teach him to see the emotion and body language behind the words he was told and to understand what it was that people really wanted when they talk. This laid the foundations for critical thinking and observation. He has now pondered many years about what a sign means. This is beginning to lead, and I intend it to lead, into a general discussion of semiotics.

This last rule was an explanation of the Buddhist concept of attachments tailored for a four year old. I explained to him many scenarios for attachments and how people may use each other. For example, I explained how people who are insecure will put on displays in attempts to balance themselves, and then reach for whatever is offered. I explained how two people can set each other up to need each other by hurting each other for the comfort of the apologies.

I didn't say it explicitly in the list, and probably should have, but at each of these steps I told him to approach all people with compassion.

When D* became five I taught him two forms of Mahayana meditation. The first form of meditation I taught him was that of thinking of silence. I mixed this with a discussion of Zen and the elimination of the ego. In the second form I taught him breathing meditation.

252

When D* was five I taught him the five folds of the one way path to enlightenment. I believe this is a concept of the Tibetan school. The Mahayanas call the first folds the "three learnings." I once saw a Theravadan teacher working with preschoolers teach the first three folds as "the thing that all Buddhas taught." I began to use a book that was a secular work rather than a religious one. It is one I studied many years ago, Buddhism, by Richard A. Gare. It is part of a series on many religions, and I plan to branch out. We will no doubt read the Bahavad Gita. D* and I read Hess's Sidartha while sitting on the cows at the Arboretum.

Namely the five folds of the one way path to enlightenment are, discipline and virtuous conduct, meditation, wisdom and learning, devotional practice, and faith. These words are translations of more general Buddhist concepts and we have discussed their meaning, now, many times. Accordingly, the first step is to obtain a sort of morality. This combined with meditation leads to a clarity of mind. Then observation and learning lead to wisdom as the next step. The wise person devotes himself to Buddhism and finally has faith in the dharma.

Oh but what is dharma? I explained it to D* like this. Dharma is that thing that makes a piece of paper different from a paper airplane. A piece of paper by itself is boring. But a paper airplane is many things. It is a toy to be played with. It is reminds us of the struggle of humans to fly, and their success. It reminds you of the story we read about the Wright Brothers. It is has embedded in it many great things. And how do you know to make a paper airplane from a piece of paper? Well you follow the directions I explain to you. It is this difference between the paper and the paper airplane which is dharma.

In 2006 we started talking about Buddha's first sermon on the four profound truths, the first being that struggle is a fundamental component of life and this leads to suffering. We then discussed the nature of suffering, the wheel of life, and the role of meditation in rising above the struggle and escaping suffering.

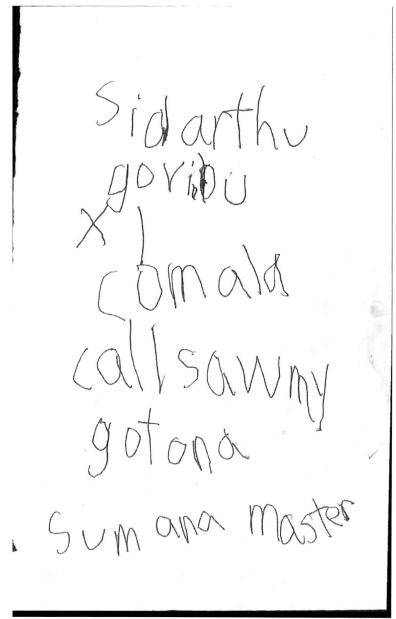

Figure 49: D* Completed a School Assignment Listing Characters in Story He Read

Math Lessons Etc.

When D* was a baby I placed plywood cutouts of a circle, a triangle, and a square, in with his toys. I carried them around with him, sometimes put them in where he slept. I would hold them up, variously turning them, and repeat their names. When he was five we discussed Euclidean geometry, and then moved into some simple number theory and arithmetic.

D* was showing off his math to Dr. El-Youssef at the Mayo Clinic in 2003, by telling him about prime numbers. By first grade D* was adding two digit sums in his head, and could do long hand multiplication. We were also working on language and music, but got side tracked because H* wouldn't let him practice, nor take him to lessons. Although she has put him in a Korean language school.

In my opinion, the most important thing for D* development in this last year has been being part of a team sport so he can experience working with others and winning and losing as team. I tried my utmost to get this point across and get his mother and get him into soccer or hockey. She took him to hockey practice for a few months, then stopped.

Figure 50: D Essay: "I love my dad be kus me dad teches me"*

H* Uses Five Hundred Dollar Fines Against D* Allowance for Bad Behavior

D* was in tears shortly after dinner. When this happens I know something awful has happened to him at home. Usually I can just ask and he tells me, there are two exceptions. First if he is embarrassed to tell me, and the second if he is under threat not to tell. Often during these fits he is also very ADD like, bouncing of the walls so to speak. This time it was because his mom told him that he owed her over a thousand dollars, and his allowance was $7 a month. He had figured out that he would be in debt for the rest of his life. At least in part the debt came from his mom having 'billed him' for hundreds of dollars each time he misbehaved. Now I knew why she kept using word consequences. *If you don't do what I say there will be consequences.* I told D* that I would reimburse him for what she charged so that he wouldn't be in debt. This settled him down.

This is a conversation between D* and father about his allowance fines. It is true, when D* was just learning to ride a bike, his mom fined him $500 for scratching her car, and then told him that he was in debt, and had him paying *her*. D* is talking:

You know that reminds me of something. One time I had $50, and this teacher she I accidentally touched her, like this. And she says I hit her <holding back tears>, but I didn't. My mom subtracted, $70, no $80, no $70 from my allowance. She took away the $70 and the 50. [Has she taken allowance for other things?] Yeah. Scratching her car, she wouldn't give me allowance for a year. [So what happened to scratch the car?] I was riding my bike. I accidentally, it was a while ago when I just got that bike, and I wasn't that good. I accidentally turned too late when I was going out of the driveway. And I accidentally bumped the car and made a little scratch. She said it was $500, she owed me because it made a little scratch. A little scratch. And she said it would be $500 dollars to do it. And she just bought like a ten dollar paint jar and painted over. [Does she take money out of your allowance for anything else?] Yeah, like doing these things. [Like something with the couch?] Yeah, that was one. You know how it was like winter. Close by winter, it was kinda cold in the house, so turned on this portable heater. I was still cold so I got closer to the heater. I was on one of the those <leg rests>, because I could move faster without much strength. I moved closer and closer and I touched. I got bored. I went to another room. Not quite to another room, I continued to play with Legos. It was touching, and the leather got burned. That was $200. … [how much debt did you have total?] $450 actually that was two, there was about $40 or $50 for some other minor … it was about $600.

D*: "I Want to Live With Dad"

D* continued to ask H* why he couldn't live with his dad. *H* told him that it was because I didn't have a house.* She then enrolled him in a self defense course. D* became emphatic that I buy a house, and he provided me with a number of designs. When he got older he talked about the "mansion" we would get. When I moved to California one had a landing strip on the roof so that I could commute to my job.

In first grade when he was asked to write an essay about what he wanted to be when he grew up, he wrote about being an inventor like his dad. He has been talking about this since he was old enough to formulate the sentence.

In second grade when the class did a New Years wish on a star. D* wrote that his wish for the next year was to live with his dad.

When D* figured out that the house wasn't the real problem, he was upset with H*. She revised her explanation and told D* that he was in danger. *She said that he couldn't live with his dad because if he did, then he would never be able to see her again, and that dad would hurt him.* She then enrolled him in a self defense course. The story has now changed again. H* now says to D* whenever he brings it up, "that is your dad talking," and she threatens to punish him by taking him to her child psychologist, Caryl Dalton.

According to D* Caryl Dalton explained that his father has done bad things. She told him that I lie, and that I break the rules. He has even been given an explanation of the evidence presented at temporary orders. D* doesn't believe most of it, but he is noticeably depressed about it. He seems to think I have done something wrong, perhaps by calling him at the house. For the first time this year, I see that his spirit has been broken. When he talks about living with dad, he mumbles.

Dimitris

258

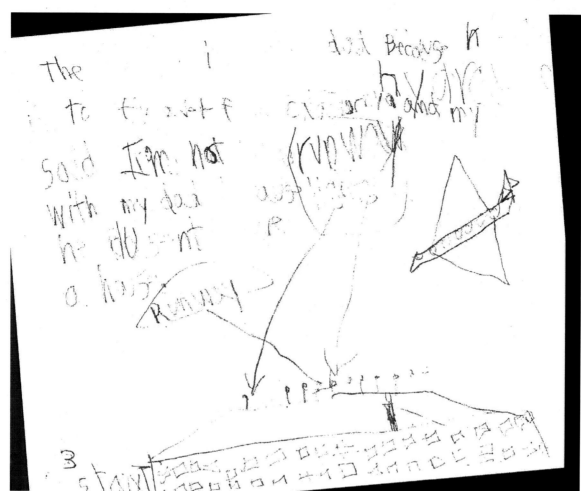

Figure 51: D* Art, Lots of Houses

259

Figure 52: New Years Wish Star from School, "I Wish I live with My Dad"

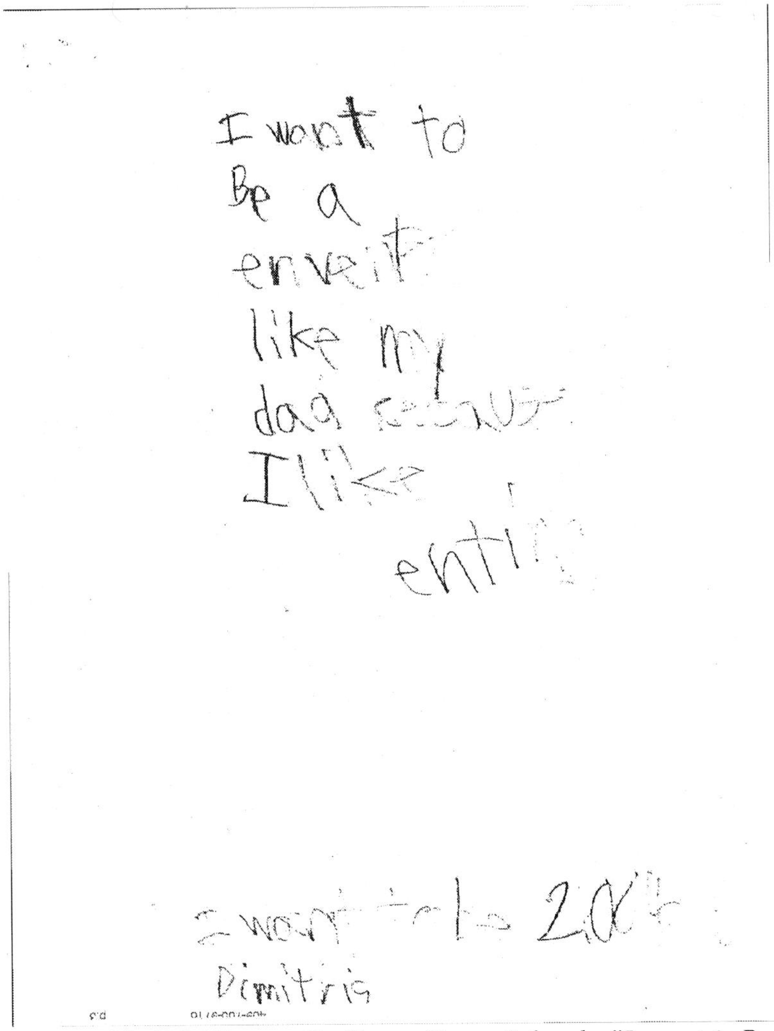

I want to
Be a
enventor
like my
dad because
I like

enti

I want to 2016

Dimitria

Figure 53: D* Want to Be Essay From School, "I want to Be a enventor like my dad"

Figure 54: A D* Invention

H*: No Soccer, No Boy Scouts, Hockey, Swimming, or Violin

After soccer and violin was killed, D* took an interest in Cub Scouts. The three of us were at school orientation for first grade. There was a demonstration setup for the Cub Scout's Pine Wood Derby. D* was very interested. He talked with Doyle Higgins, and asked if he could join. Right in front of Doyle, D*, and me, H* agreed that he could. Then she didn't show up for any meetings, she didn't answer any of Mr. Higgins telephone calls.

We gave the violin another shot. D* wants to play very badly. This time we hired a woman from the university who will be playing for the Boston Symphony next year, and got D* a wooden handmade instrument. H* says he doesn't have time to practice because of school work.

I worked very hard to get D* into the youth hockey program, as it was mid season. H* actually brought him for a few months, but then stopped. She says he doesn't have time to play hockey because of school work. D* said he would make time to play hockey by giving up swimming lessons. H* took him out of swimming, but still no hockey.

[2] Interrupted Dad Time Activities

Hockey

The program coordinator was Angie Schneider at Chaparral Ice. God only knows what she will say as she found herself stuck in the middle (like Mirrop, the YMCA both in Round Rock and Austin, Gritzka, Stepping Stone, Dalton, and the school). Here is email on the subject:

From: Lynch H
Sent: Thursday, August 17, 2006 11:33 AM
To: Tom Lynch
Subject: RE: Just a reminder that hockey is on its way!!
Hi Tom,

D   is now a third grader and his No. 1 priority should be the school work. Although D   is good at math, his writing skill needs improvement. We decided to dedicate about one hour for extra study at home and I have started to tutor D   on English Grammar and Writing and Math since Monday.

Attending four extracurricular activities (TaeKwonDo class, swimming class, Korean language class, and the unplanned Ice Hockey league) last year was very strenuous for D   and me to keep up with the regular school work as well as our one-on-one time.

D   and I talked about the extracurricular activities this year. He is determined to become a TaeKwonDo blackbelt (we are in halfway, so he will keep attending the TaeKwonDo class. He loves to do art work and he is happy with the one-hour art class once a week this fall. Hopefully this will teach him to appreciate the art. He will keep going to Korean language school where he meets his best friend, T   ' and learns something about Korean language and the culture.

I know D   loves skating, and the Ice Hockey is one of the many things D   likes to do. He can practice the Ice Hockey with you in an unstructured format when he stays with you, just like D   goes swmming and learns piano or guitar whenever he wants at my house. Let's see how this work out. Later, we can re-evaluate the extracurricular activities based on what is best for D   .

Thanks.

--h

From: Tom Lynch [mailto:tlynch@ths.com]
Sent: Wednesday, August 16, 2006 6:37 PM
To: Lynch H
Subject: FW: Just a reminder that hockey is on its way!!

H   , D   wants to play hockey, we have bought all the equipment, please start bringing him to practice.   (Surely you weren't serious on the phone when you said he couldn't play this year.   After canceling violin lessons twice – and then switching him to guitar which you said you didn't want, and now sticking me with the violin … after refusing to take him to soccer, and after saying right in front of D   and Scout master Higgins that you would take him to scouts but didn't do it – surely you are not going to continue this take away his hockey…)

From: Angie Schneider |
Sent: Wednesday, August 16, 2006 6:24 PM
To: Tom Lynch;

Subject: Just a reminder that hockey is on its way!!

Hockey is back and sign up start next Friday.

See you on the ice,
Angie
Question? Just call

H   told D   that he couldn't do both hockey and swimming. Then when she took him out of hockey, she jerked him around by also taking him out of swimming. Swimming was done by the YMCA who told her they couldn't stop dad from coming to see him, so she probably stopped it for that reason.

Cub Scouts

The scout master, Doyle Hudgins witnessed D   ask if he could join. She told both Hudgins and D   that he could, then she jerked him around by not bringing him. Hudgins tried to call her, but she wouldn't answer or return his calls. I have some email on this:

From: "khudgins"
To:
Subject: Pack 155 Open House Meeting
Date: Wed, 25 Aug 2004 22:48:20 -0500
Message-ID: <003301c48b1f$898c5920$1002a8c0@doyle>
MIME-Version: 1.0

264

Content-Type: multipart/alternative; boundary="----
=_NextPart_000_0034_01C48AF5.A0B65120"
X-Priority: 3 (Normal)
X-MSMail-Priority: Normal
X-Mailer: Microsoft Outlook, Build 10.0.2616
Importance: Normal
X-MimeOLE: Produced By Microsoft MimeOLE V6.00.2800.1106
X-Virus-Scanned: Symantec AntiVirus Scan Engine
X-UIDL: jS)"!-*-"!\)e!!LNA!!
X-Evolution-Source: pop://tlynch@mail.ths.com/
X-Evolution: 000002fa-0010

This is a multi-part message in MIME format.

------=_NextPart_000_0034_01C48AF5.A0B65120
Content-Type: text/plain; charset="us-ascii"
Content-Transfer-Encoding: 7bit

Just a quick reminder about our Open House this Thursday @ 6:30 p.m. in
the Deep Wood Elementary Cafeteria. We will have our Pinewood Derby
track set up and racing cars. There are also refreshments & information
about what Scouts can do for you & your son.

Questions? Please call my cell

See ya there.

Doyle & Kristen Hudgins on behalf of
Pack 155

From tom.lynch@ths.com Wed Sep 1 15:39:58 2004
Subject: cub scouts
From: tom lynch <tom.lynch@ths.com>
Reply-To: tom.lynch@ths.com
To: Doyle_Hudgins
Content-Type: text/plain
Organization: THS Inc.
Message-Id: <1094071198.3263.24.camel@box>
Mime-Version: 1.0
X-Mailer: Ximian Evolution 1.4.5 (1.4.5-1)
Date: Wed, 01 Sep 2004 15:39:58 -0500
Content-Transfer-Encoding: 7bit
X-Evolution-Transport: smtp://tom.lynch@mail.ths.com/;use_ssl=when-possible
X-Evolution-Account: tom.lynch@ths.com
X-Evolution-Fcc: file:///home/lynch/evolution/local/Sent
X-Evolution-Format: text/plain
X-Evolution: 000000c8-0010

Doyle, did my son get enrolled?

Tom Lynch

tom.lynch@ths.com

From Doyle_Hudgins   Thu Sep 2 13:33:16 2004
Return-Path:
Received: from ausc60pc101.us.dell.com (ausc60pc101.us.dell.com
          [143.166.85.206]) by ns1.webhosting4business.net (8.10.2/8.10.2) with ESMTP
          id i82IXGh01735 for <tom.lynch@ths.com>: Thu, 2 Sep 2004 13:33:16 -0500

          a="83625378:sNHT20313116"
x-mimeole: Produced By Microsoft Exchange V6.0.6527.0
content-class: urn:content-classes:message
MIME-Version: 1.0
Content-Type: text/plain; charset="us-ascii"
Subject: RE: cub scouts
Date: Thu, 2 Sep 2004 13:37:31 -0500
Message-ID:
<7B70D786CE211741BBAB5A609C972B0E07B41A@ausx2kmpc116.aus.amer.dell.com>
X-MS-Has-Attach:
X-MS-TNEF-Correlator:
Thread-Topic: cub scouts
Thread-Index: AcSQZDM4R71QTl8OSk6jX2qv01RjNQAt51Jg
From: <Doyle_Hudgins(
To: <tom.lynch@ths.com>
X-OriginalArrivalTime: 02 Sep 2004 18:37:31.0939 (UTC)
          FILETIME=[E838AF30:01C4911B]
Content-Transfer-Encoding: 8bit
X-MIME-Autoconverted: from quoted-printable to 8bit by
          ns1.webhosting4business.net id i82IXGh01735
X-UIDL: %O)!!2;d!!!"9"!"_!!
X-Evolution-Source: pop://tlynch@mail.ths.com/
X-Evolution: 00000350-0011

No, not yet. I have not heard from your wife. We will start meeting
next week. Should I call her?

Doyle Hudgins

From tom.lynch@ths.com Mon Sep 13 13:47:13 2004
Subject: RE: cub scouts
From: tom lynch <tom.lynch@ths.com>
Reply-To: tom.lynch@ths.com
To: Doyle_Hudgins
In-Reply-To:
<7B70D786CE211741BBAB5A609C972B0E07B41A@ausx2kmpc116.aus.amer.dell.com>
References:

<7B70D786CE211741BBAB5A609C972B0E07B41A@ausx2kmpc116.aus.amer.dell.com>
Content-Type: text/plain
Organization: THS Inc.

Message-Id: <1095101232.3156.6.camel@box>
Mime-Version: 1.0
X-Mailer: Ximian Evolution 1.4.5 (1.4.5-1)
Date: Mon, 13 Sep 2004 13:47:13 -0500
Content-Transfer-Encoding: 7bit
X-Evolution-Transport: smtp://tom.lynch@mail.ths.com/;use_ssl=when-possible
X-Evolution-Account: tom.lynch@ths.com
X-Evolution-Fcc: file:///home/lynch/evolution/local/Sent
X-Evolution-Format: text/plain
X-Evolution: 00000110-0010

Doyle,

It wouldn't hurt to remind her. D.   was sure interested.

Doyle called me back, he said he called her, and she hadn't returned his call.   H
did not show up at any of the meetings.

Violin

H   wouldn't let him practice, so the teacher gave up. Here is the email I
have:

From tom.lynch@ths.com Fri Dec 17 10:39:30 2004
Subject: violin lessons
From: tom lynch <tom.lynch@ths.com>
Reply-To: tom.lynch@ths.com
To: r-ando
Content-Type: text/plain
Organization: THS Inc.
Message-Id: <1103301570.14855.4.camel@box>
Mime-Version: 1.0
X-Mailer: Ximian Evolution 1.4.5 (1.4.5-1)
Date: Fri, 17 Dec 2004 10:39:30 -0600
Content-Transfer-Encoding: 7bit
X-Evolution-Transport: smtp://tom.lynch@mail.ths.com/;use_ssl=when-possible
X-Evolution-Account: tom.lynch@ths.com
X-Evolution-Fcc: file:///home/lynch/evolution/local/Sent
X-Evolution-Format: text/plain
X-Evolution: 000005b0-0010

Dear Ms. Ando,

D   my six year old son, appears to be receiving a handmade
European violin for Christmas - oo. Problem, is there is no teacher.
Perhaps you know something about teaching violin?

Tom Lynch

From r-ando   Sun Dec 19 10:04:12 2004

Received: from mx06.ms.so-net.ne.jp (mx06.ms.so-net.ne.jp [202.238.82.6])
        by ns1.webhosting4business.net (8.10.2/8.10.2) with ESMTP id iBJG4BM29571
        for <tom.lynch@ths.com>; Sun, 19 Dec 2004 10:04:12 -0600

Received: from [192.168.1.4] (p1068-ipbf37marunouchi.tokyo.ocn.ne.jp
        [220.104.127.68]) by mx06.ms.so-net.ne.jp with ESMTP id iBJFpemi018646 for
        <tom.lynch@ths.com>; Mon, 20 Dec 2004 00:51:41 +0900 (JST)
Mime-Version: 1.0 (Apple Message framework v619)
In-Reply-To: <1103301570.14855.4.camel@box>
References: <1103301570.14855.4.camel@box>
Content-Type: text/plain; charset=US-ASCII; format=flowed
Message-Id: <DDF71BC7-51D5-11D9-9CC5-000D9339EA3C@mail.utexas.edu>
Content-Transfer-Encoding: 7bit
From: Risa Ando
Subject: Re: violin lessons
Date: Mon, 20 Dec 2004 00:51:37 +0900
To: tom.lynch@ths.com
X-Mailer: Apple Mail (2.619)
X-UIDL: S!?!!"c)"!?HH!!#AP!!
X-Evolution-Source: pop://tlynch@mail.ths.com/
X-Evolution: 00001d82-0011

Mr. Lynch,

It is very good for D   to get a good violin! I am a doctoral
student at UT and teaching violin in UT music building. He may need 30
min. lesson once a week. I am happy to teach D   . Please let me
know if he needs lessons.

Risa

From tom.lynch@ths.com Sun Dec 19 21:29:34 2004
Subject: Re: violin lessons
From: tom lynch <tom.lynch@ths.com>
Reply-To: tom.lynch@ths.com
To: Risa Ando
In-Reply-To: <DDF71BC7-51D5-11D9-9CC5-000D9339EA3C@mail.utexas.edu>
References: <1103301570.14855.4.camel@box>
        <DDF71BC7-51D5-11D9-9CC5-000D9339EA3C@mail.utexas.edu>
Content-Type: text/plain
Organization: THS Inc.
Message-Id: <1103513373.17482.2.camel@box>
Mime-Version: 1.0
X-Mailer: Ximian Evolution 1.4.5 (1.4.5-1)
Date: Sun, 19 Dec 2004 21:29:34 -0600
Content-Transfer-Encoding: 7bit
X-Evolution-Transport: smtp://tom.lynch@mail.ths.com/;use_ssl=when-possible
X-Evolution-Account: tom.lynch@ths.com
X-Evolution-Fcc: file:///home/lynch/evolution/local/Sent
X-Evolution-Format: text/plain
X-Evolution: 000005b6-0010

Risa, yes, D   needs lessons. How much do you charge? When could
he start? The sooner the better for a first lesson and some pointers,
as Santa Clause came this morning ;-) (I didn't see any reason to let
gifts sit under a tree while he was on vacation from school.)

-tom

From r-ando(Tue Dec 21 10:04:23 2004

Received: from mx07.ms.so-net.ne.jp (mx07.ms.so-net.ne.jp [202.238.82.7])
          by ns1.webhosting4business.net (8.10.2/8.10.2) with ESMTP id iBLG4NM23258
          for <tom.lynch@ths.com>; Tue, 21 Dec 2004 10:04:23 -0600
Received: from [192.168.1.4] (p1068-ipbf37marunouchi.tokyo.ocn.ne.jp
          [220.104.127.68]) by mx07.ms.so-net.ne.jp with ESMTP id iBLFpwO2001963 for
          <tom.lynch@ths.com>; Wed, 22 Dec 2004 00:51:58 +0900 (JST)
Mime-Version: 1.0 (Apple Message framework v619)
In-Reply-To: <1103513373.17482.2.camel@box>
References: <1103301570.14855.4.camel@box>
            <DDF71BC7-51D5-11D9-9CC5-000D9339EA3C@mail.utexas.edu>
            <1103513373.17482.2.camel@box>
Content-Type: text/plain; charset=US-ASCII; format=flowed
Message-Id: <3F0A4BBF-5368-11D9-AE4C-000D9339EA3C@mail.utexas.edu>
Content-Transfer-Encoding: 7bit
From: Risa Ando
Subject: Re: violin lessons
Date: Wed, 22 Dec 2004 00:51:58 +0900
To: tom.lynch@ths.com
X-Mailer: Apple Mail (2.619)
X-UIDL: 4dJ!!T/="!j1K!!fJ<"!
X-Evolution-Source: pop://tlynch@mail.ths.com/
X-Evolution: 00001d98-0010

Mr. Lynch,

How lucky D   ! Does he like the violin?
I will be back to Austin on January 10th, so after that I can have a
lesson. Now I am in Christmas vacation and in my home town, Tokyo.
Usually I charge $20 for 30 min. and $35 for 60 min. $30 min. is for 45
min. I recommend 30 min. lesson. Is it too late for D   to have a
lesson next month? All of my friends in UT are going home now......

Risa

Soccer

H   just said no, so I went to the YMCA after school program and we played
together.   This was sort of the first one, and I didn't make a big deal out of it.

French

H   took D   out of the French school, I don't think you will get an
argument on this point, but it can easily be documented.   She took him to a French tutor
for a short time, then gave up.

[3] School Notices and Art Work not shared with Dad

Figure 55: H* Prevents Any Activities Involving Dad

269

D* Refuses to Go With H* Again, H* Threatens D* with Seeing Dalton

2005 04 18, Monday, I went to the school in the late afternoon to drop off a birthday card that had arrived in the mail. D* had just come from his class and we read the card. Frances Floyd, the assistant principal stopped and asked if I had signed in. I told her that I would sign in on the way out. She walked off. It was somewhat of a peculiar request, because signing in isn't required after school lets out.

D* got up to go out the front door where his mom would pick him up. He didn't want to go. I explained she would be waiting. However, H* didn't go to her usual place, but instead came in. She had never done this before. She walked over very directly and looking angry in a threatening manner.

H* complained I shouldn't be there. I replied I was within my rights to be at the school. D* said he didn't want to go with her. H* said she had a court paper that said he had to go. D* was clinging to me. I explained to H* that if she would just be patient, D* would settle down, and then they could go. She asked me to rip him off me and hand him over. I told her I couldn't betray his trust like that, but I could talk to him and work it out. She looked as if about to launch into one of her fits, and she did. D* hid behind me and the two exchanged screams with each other.

Mrs. Connie, D*'s first grade teacher in training jogged over. D* screamed at her "I want my dad." Mrs. Connie then ran to the office. H* started arguing. D* was clinging to me, so I asked if he could go with me. It would keep things simple. H* said no, and screamed that I would have to take her to court before she would give me more time with him. I asked H* to relax and be patient. She started tugging on D*. She said she had to be somewhere. Then she turned to D* and told him that he would have to go see "Miss Caryl" if he didn't come with her. That affected him, and he started to go. It made me feel sick to my stomach to threats to visiting Miss Caryl used as coercion or punishment. (see email/0137)

They were walking towards the door together when Mrs. Connie came back. Mrs. Connie insisted we go to the principal's office. So we did. Once we got there D* latched on to me again. We waited. Betty Carbonneau, the office staff, and Mrs. Floyd were there. They explained to D* he had to go with his mom. Apparently that is all they wanted, which is funny as he was going with his mom before they dragged us to the office.

After H* and D* left, Mrs. Floyd started saying that I had tried to take him from the school on a day that was not mine. I told her not to put words in my mouth, that I had come to give him a birthday card, and that I had also told him he had to go with his mom. Mrs. Floyd then said that D* was getting older and needed more time with his father. She suggested that I go back to court and get the order modified.

The next time D* came to my place he demanded that I go to court. He asked about the process, and then asked me to get a lawyer. Though this isn't the first time he had asked for these things; he now had a renewed level of demand.

D* Science Fair Project

In kindergarten D* decided he would do a science fair project. He had saved the plastic snap together spheres his toys came in, and used the halves as boats. To the bottoms he taped rocks, and to the tops cardboard fins. That project he wanted to know how much wind tipped one over, so he put them in a tub next to a fan and turned the fan on.

The following is from D* first grade science fair project:

1. wa
2. tinfe wall
3. tub water

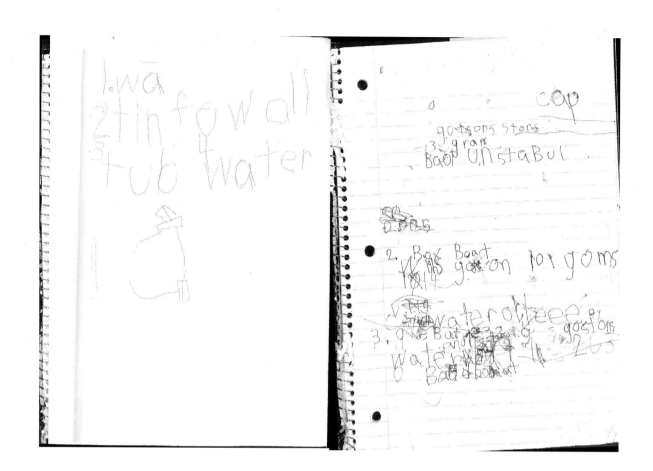

cap
gotgons stone
3. gran
Baot Unstabul

2. D2.5

2. Box Boat
gal on for goms

3. gne Boat water off
water gostons
Bad boat out

272

4 tiy goll Bat
water with go stons

5. 2 water ollee
  can
  2 3 water ollee
  can x water
  go stong ollee gams

an
mar llen brds water
pshing is up ot it

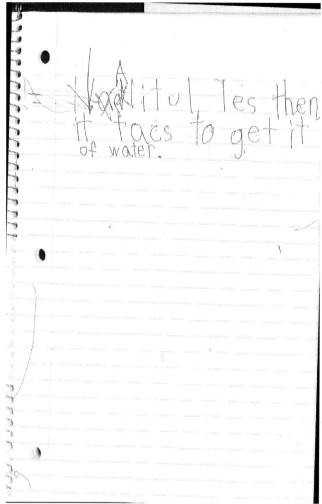

Figure 56: D* First Grade Science Fair Notebook

As in Kindergarten he did it all on his own because he wanted to. I told him that a notebook was used and what sections it had, but did not fill it out. I only watched from that point. He wanted to answer the question why boats float. He made little boats and filled them with stones until they sank. He found something close to the Archimedian principal. Though he was one of only few students in the first grade who made a project, *the teacher did not give him an award.* I went over to Teacher's Haven and bought a blue ribbon. I gave him "dad's first place."

The next year at science fair time, we decided instead to do a business. Business has its own built in reward system.

I got to be a consultant for D* first business. D* got the idea of making a whole bunch of bad fortunes and then selling "Miss Fortune" cookies for Halloween. With my direction he worked out a sort of business plan calculating costs, unit price, profits and required financing in a blue notebook. He found a custom fortune cookie seller on the Internet. We filled out the forms. I was the financier. He got 2000 cookies in the mail. They came in two big boxes full of plastic wrapped cookies. I really thought we were going to have Miss Fortune cookies for years to come. D* thought he would sell them to grocery stores, but the HEB manager rebuffed him. His second thought was Chinese restaurants. There the cookies were a big hit. The kids working in the restaurants bought them to give to each other. In one place D* sold a few cookies then we sat to eat. A little later we heard laughing in the kitchen, and someone came out and bought a dozen more cookies. Then we hit the coffee shops. The college student loved them. The last of the cookies were sold around the neighborhood. D* was stuffing the money in his pockets, an leaving a trail of money as a he walked. I followed picking up the errant dollars. In just the one weekend he had sold them all. After paying off the investor had had more than $200 in profit. This was perhaps more fun than the science fair projects.

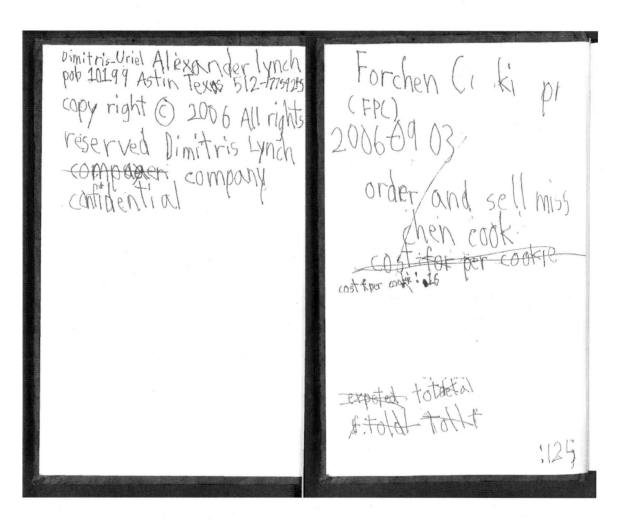

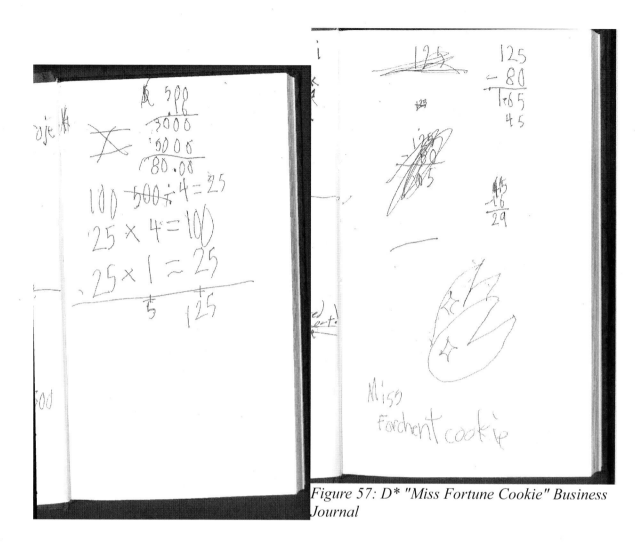

Figure 57: D* "Miss Fortune Cookie" Business Journal

The big question D* had about the fortune cookie business was why people would pay 25 cents for a cookie that cost only 16 cents. This question came up the first time after a college girl at one of the coffee shops came back and bought more cookies for a third time. I explained it was because he had taken *initiative*.

More H*-isms:

Won't Share Insurance Card

H* assigned a new pediatrician with the same organization where Dr. Coldwater had worked – the doctor who refused to comment after Mr. Choi said he had wrapped the baby in blankets in a hot room in order to "prevent colds." H* did not provide the new doctor's office with a divorce decree. This put them on the defense, and it contributed to the difficulty of getting the school to give D* his diary enzymes. When H* didn't do it, they didn't wouldn't to listen to me.

As per the decree, H* was carrying the medical insurance. This was related to her desire to control when D* would see the doctor. She refused to give me a copy of the card. I was still sending her notices about it in September of 2004. In this manner H* enforced a sole managing conservator ship in fact, though it wasn't one in name. On 2004 09 20 she came out and directly said as much, and claimed that the reason was that I was being punished:

From: H* Lynch <------>
Date: Mon Sep 20 2004 - 09:50:38 CDT
To: <tom.lynch>

Tom,

As for medical decision for D, I have an exclusive right.* Please
read the decree carefully. This provision was made because your medical
misuse over D* (changing doctors so many times, making D*
going thru x-rays on his head when he was not even one year old....).

Figure 58: H Asserts Exclusive Medical Rights*

The removal of exclusive medical was a key point enabling settlement. In the divorce decree on page 7 point 2 exclusive is clearly crossed off. In addition, my medical right is stated on page 5 point 3. I was not being punished for anything. Initially I had a sole managing conservatorship, and had only *agreed* to make her a joint conservator. After I pointed out that the exclusive medical was crossed off, she replied:

From: H* <------>
Date: Mon Sep 20 2004 - 15:41:32 CDT
To: <t----->
O.K., other copy shows that the word "exclusive" is scrached out. If I had
known this when we had reached agreement, I would never sign the
decree. Divorce agreement was made in very hectic and exhausting way,
so I had overlooked this. Well, the damage is done. In any case, the court
assigned Caryl Dalton to be a D*'s phychiatrist and I don't have any
intension to change the doctor at this point. If you don't agree with this,
you can initiate the mediation which our agreement says you will pay all
costs.

Figure 59: H Withdraws Assertion of Exclusive Medical Rights*

So she admits that the decisions are supposed to be joint, but at the same time tells me I'll have to pay to have any input. Indeed, she has never included me.

Blocks Dad's Visits, 2004

H* was not happy that the YMCA was allowing me to visit there in 2003. In 2004 she attempted to put a stop to it. She moved him to a different school with a different staff. When I showed up I was told I couldn't see my son. The counselor I was speaking with wouldn't tell me her name. When I talked to others they put their name tags in their pockets. When I went to the YMCA office it was late in the afternoon, and a woman was just leaving out the door of the building for the managers. I said, "Hello, I'm Mr. Lynch." "What are you doing here," she snarled. Then she said she was going to call the police. I pointed out that it was a public entrance, and as of this date it still isn't illegal to be a father, though some debate could be made on the subject. I spoke with her manager, and then to the CEO of the YMCA. I explained I had a joint managing conservatorship, and that they had no right to exclude me from seeing my son.

I went to see the CEO, and then the staff again. They had no father listed on the form. They said they only spoke to divorced parents if they had a copy of the divorce decree. H* was listed as divorced, and the YMCA had spoken to her for over a year without a decree. Apparently there is a different set of rules for fathers. I supplied one immediately.

It had taken the summer and the first month of school, but the YMCA relented. They had done their best but run out of legal options. All I had wanted was to be able to see my son. They YMCA told H* I could not be blocked from visiting D* at the program. H* responded by taking him out of the program altogether.

But H* wasn't done. We would do virtually the same drill at the Stepping Stone school. When she failed to block me she moved him again. The she put him in day care at the YMCA on the other side of McNeil road. This branch had a different manager's office. It was a virtual re-run of the previous time. Again I was denied access, but eventually H* was told I couldn't be blocked, and took him out of that YMCA also.

Officially Forbids Calls, 2004

Since the Edison phone incident H* refused to let D* call me, or vice versa. I didn't take long to figure out what was happening, but I called once in a while, just to make sure that not getting through wasn't my fault. After D* was taken out of the YMCA program we had no way of communicating between visits. I decided to document that H* was blocking the calls. There had been some times where she had obviously hungup. Between 9/12 and 9/15 I called 8 times at various times of the day. A few times H* answered and hung up. The other times I left a message for D* to call back. H* then answered and told me not to try and call for D* anymore. There have been a few times when D* has gone home upset, and I couldn't get through to the house on the phone, and the RRPD has stopped by and found them home. On one occasion I called and H* and D* were fighting. D* said he was afraid of her, and the RRPD went over to settle them down.

Accuses Dad of Poisoning D* 2004

D* showed up at my place with amazing 'consequences problems.' I assumed this was a method Dalton taught to H*. I called H* to discuss it. She was very rude, and accused me of trying to "poison D*". I recorded the conversation. We were back to the old H* who issued death threats. When I pressed the question of discipline, I then got back a very professionally written email saying how important it was that we communicate. When I tried to follow up on that, she didn't return my calls.

278

T> Are you informing me of all of his medical visits and such, or is there stuff I don't know about?

H> Stuff that you don't know about.

T> I'm asking you are you keeping me informed of his medical records?

H> Of course what ever it is I'm always I told you!

T> Ok.

H> I'm open. Unless easily pushed, you are poisoning D*.

T> Doing what to him?

H> You are poisoning him. Lots of times.

T> You are saying I'm poisoning him, and it is a medical issue?

H> He's outside, he is blaming. He doesn't lie. You are saying I'm lying. Its your level, and I'm going to tell his teacher.

Figure 60: H Accuses Tom of Poisoning D**

Asks Dad to Watch D* for Me. (huh?)

H* called me on the phone and made small talk in nice tones. It felt like I had woken up from some awful dream. She said that she was going away for the weekend with her boyfriend, and she wanted to know if I would watch D*. She said she knew it wasn't my weekend, but she wanted to know if I would do her a favor.

I shook my head and pinched myself. I tried to place the conversation into correct context. I'm the guy she has accused of abuse. I'm the guy she accused of kidnapping our son. I'm the man she had been at war with ever since she couldn't marry Ravi. Perhaps it was a trick? I would pick D* up from school, and take him home, and then the police would show up. Though, if I waited at the school until no one else showed up to pick him up, it would be difficult to make such an accusation. I calculated the risks, and decided she would have a weak platform for making accusations if she didn't show up to pick him up in the first place. Besides, there was a new element here, *the boyfriend*. Finally she had someone else to think about.

With some trepidation, I went to the school and waited. I made sure to strike up a conversation other waiting parents to tell them why I was there on an off week. D* came out. We stood around and waited until the crowd dissipated. No one else came to pick him up, so we went home.

On Monday, I took the precaution of stopping by the school after class and making sure he got picked up. H* did not show. I didn't have any choice, so we went home. Tuesday, again, she didn't show. Wednesday she didn't show. She didn't show up all week. There was no answer on the phone at the house. She did not call.

The next week, she picked him up. Come to find out, she had gone to England with her boyfriend. Though, I didn't mind about this little subterfuge. Compared to the others it was rather innocuous. I would have watched him for the week anyway. I viewed this as a positive development. Perhaps she would stop using day cares during her vacations and holidays. D* and I have a lot of stuff to work on. We have kits that have been unopened since the Christmas before last, we would still like to learn the violin. We need to practice hockey. We haven't played soccer in ages. D* and I can talk about mathematics for hours on end, but we rarely get the chance. More recently he has become interested in strategy. It would be fun to talk about general Chennault approaches, and others. On her next holiday, D* was back in day care at an undisclosed location. H* made a point out of knowing lots of people who could have watched D*.

RE: summer schedule

This message: [Message body] [More options]
Related messages: [Next message] [Previous message] [Maybe in reply to] [Next in thread]

From: H
Date: Mon Apr 04 2005 - 09:07:20 CDT
To: <tom.lynch@ths.com>

Tom,

When I went to England for my business trip for a week, I have several friends who are willing to take care of D   . Since you have been asking more time with D   , I was being considerate for D   to be with you, although I was a bit concerned like this which you are using that against me.

In any case, since you are feeling bad about it, I will take six days from your summer possession period. Please let me know which days you would like to give them to me.

--h

-----Original Message-----
From: tom.lynch@ths.com [mailto:tom.lynch@ths.com]
Sent: Sunday, April 03, 2005 6:48 PM
To: H
Subject: Re: summer schedule

You know I have been looking through this document, and I just can't find the part about "H   takes a vacation to England, and Tom watches D   for a week." At this point no one is forcing you to be fair about splitting D   's summer vacation, but I am asking you to be fair about splitting his summer vacation, especially since I have the time off.

On Sunday 03 April 2005 13:16, you wrote:
> *Per our divorce decree, page 10, for parents who reside 100 miles or less*
> *apart, with written notice by April 1,*
>
> *THOMAS WALKER LYNCH shall have possession of the child for two full weeks*
> *beginning no earlier than the day after the child's school is dismissed for*
> *the summer vacation and ENDING NO LATER THAN SEVEN DAYS BEFORE SCHOOL*
> *RESUMES AT THE END OF THE SUMMER VACATION IN THAT YEAR, to be excercised in*
> *no more than two separate periods of at least seven consecutive days*
> *each,as specified in the written notice. These periods of possession shall*
> *begin and end at 6:00 pm.*
>
> *School start on August 16 (Please see the attached calender) and this means*
> *that your proposed summer schedule from Aug 1 to Aug 14 should be*
> *amended, i.e., the last day of summer possession time should be on/before*
> *Aug 8.*
>

Figure 61 H* Asks Tom to Watch D* While She Goes On Vacation

281

Kicks Dog As D* Watches

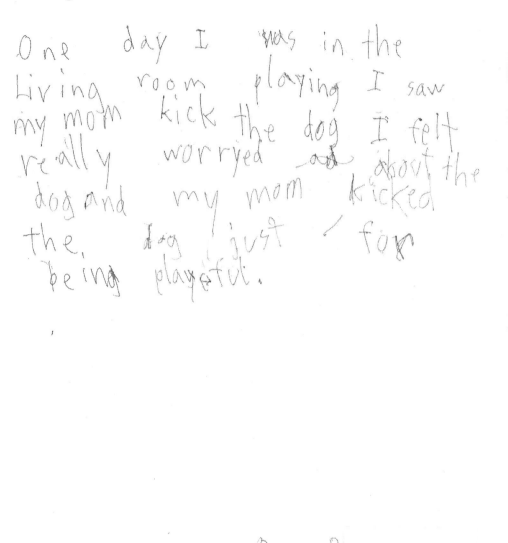

One day I was in the
Living room playing I saw
my mom kick the dog I felt
really worryed about the
dog and my mom kicked the
the, dog just for
being playful.

By D

Figure 62: D* Essay Describing His Mom Kicking The Dog

When we got the puppy in 2002 H* was afraid of it. She explained that her father had gotten her a dog when she was younger and that something had gone wrong that made her afraid of dogs. She didn't say what. She explained that she had agreed to the dog for D*'s sake. The in laws would tie Laika dog tight by her walking leash to a post that holds up the patio roof. When Laika would grew tired of holding her head up she would just hang there until I let her off.

At temporary orders H* insisted that she get everything, including Laika dog. I argued that it was not her dog. She argued it was not mine. And I said that was exactly my point, "it is D*' dog" we agreed that Laika would travel with back and forth with D*. On our very first exchange I did not have time stop by the apartment to pick up the dog, and showed up without her. On our second exchange, Laika went back to H*'s place with D*. H* never brought the dog for later exchanges. We were back to, 'its my dog because my mother helped pay for her as a gift.' She also said, "what is D*' is mine."

Nor did D* get to play with the dog. Laika dog lived in the fenced in area behind the house. She was not allowed in the house. And because she was a 'dirty animal' D* was only allowed to play with her when she had a bath, or when he surreptitiously let her out though the gate when he was outside. A bath for the dog was apparently a rare event, perhaps occurring twice a year.

In 2004 during our Christmas break we were at the school yard, and up came running Laika dog. She had no collar and no tags. We called H*, but there was no answer. We didn't know the state of her shots, so we took her to the Vet and got her updated. We bought her a new collar and put on tags.

After the holiday H* wanted the dog back very badly, and sincerely promised that this time the dog would really go back and fourth with D*. I told her the dog might have a torn ligament and asked if she would help pay for an operation to re-attach it. She immediately accused me of clipping the ligament just to make her look bad.

It was quizzical to me that she wanted the dog since she didn't like dogs, and D* didn't get to play with the her. So I asked D* what he thought, and he said it was because mom wanted to torture it:

Tom Lynch: Why does mom want Laika?

D* Lynch: Probably because she doesn't want us to have her.

Tom Lynch: You said something else before.

D* Lynch: Oh, she wants to torture it.

Tom Lynch: You think so?

D* Lynch: That's my first prediction, my second prediction is she doesn't want us to have fun with her.

Tom Lynch: Lets talk about the first prediction a little bit. So why do you think mom wants to torture the dog?

D* Lynch: Because she doesn't like it.

Tom Lynch: Did you see her see her do something?

D* Lynch: She kicked it.

Tom Lynch: She did what? Tell me about that. When did she do that?

D* Lynch: She wanted her to sit and she wouldn't.

Tom Lynch: Where were you when this happened?

D* Lynch: I was at home outside. On the weekend I think.

Tom Lynch: Why do you think that?

D* Lynch: Because it was in the middle of the day.

Tom Lynch: So what did she say when she kicked the dog.

D* Lynch: You bad dog Laika!

Tom Lynch: What did Laika do after she got kicked? Was she kicked very hard?

D* Lynch: I don't know that.

Figure 63: D* Describes His Mom Wanting the Dog to Torture It

In my opinion, the word torture shouldn't even be in my son's vocabulary. I sent D* home with the dog, and H* again broke her promise and did not return the dog with D*.

In 2006 D* insisted on picking his dog up. He said he had to save the dog. He went back to the house and got the her. She was huge! She walked in kind of a C shape, and limped. She had a name tag, but no rabies shot tag.

We took her to the vet, then exercised her and put her on a diet. She lost over 20 pounds and got a lot more frisky. Last time we were at the vet he said we can go a little farther. On this last trip to the vet, he X-rayed her hips, and discovered a torn ligament. This could be from being kicked, or it could be from being overweight.

Then I got the call from the police on my cell phone. "Hello is this Tom Lynch?" "Yes." "You have stolen Mrs. Lynch's dog, and it should be returned." Thank God the dog is papered in my name. I pointed out the dog was mine, and challenged the officer to ask H* for the papers. She couldn't, or didn't want to, produce them. I pointed out that the dog did not have tags on, so we couldn't determine if she had a rabies shot. He said I must be at fault because I was not polite to him. I said that maybe since she was so nice, that he might like to ask her out – though in my opinion it was much ruder to take advantage of someone and have them do their bidding than it was to be gruff on the phone to an unwelcome caller. He then wanted to know if the dog was dead on the side of the road. Then I understood his concern. H* had prepped him. "Oh gosh no," I replied. "We even had her at the vet, and had her shots updated because we couldn't tell if she had them."

Then a letter arrived from H*'s attorney saying that H* had produced the "shot records" for the officer. I shook my head, as I don't see the point. I wish she had told me that the first time we had asked.

The next time I saw D* he was depressed about it. He told me they had grilled him. He said they asked him over and over if I had come and taken the dog, and that he had finally said yes to get them to stop asking. He felt very guilty about it. He wrote the following essay on his new laptop:

It was a sunny day in my back yard. When I was looking out the window in the living room playing I saw my mom kick the dog in the year 2004 . And about two weeks later my mom said that my dogs leg was hurt to the vet and the vet sais that it is broken and mom sais that she would fix it .But she never has. Sents then my mom makes up esquses . [D* 2006 09 15]

Figure 64: D* Wrote Another Essay On His Computer About the Dog

I'm not sure what the year 2004 part is about, as I gather from D* that the dog needing protection is a recent event, or why else would saving the dog be an emergency? D* is eight years old, sometimes it is difficult to understand an 8 year old's logic.

Coppell Veterinary Hospital, P.A.
504 South Denton Tap Road
Coppell, TX 75019
www.coppellvet.com
972-462-1120
Listed in D Magazine "Best Vets" 2004

12 December 2006

Mr. Tom Lynch
P.O. Box 10199
Austin, Texas

Dear Tom,

Attached please find a copy of Laika's radiology report. Based upon the imaging report, it cannot conclusively be determined that trauma caused the likely ruptured cranial cruciate ligament. Her previous history of severe obesity, however, is a great risk factor for causing this type of injury.

Surgery is the recommended treatment for her ruptured cruciate ligament along with continued treatment of her degenerative joint disease using nutraceuticals and non-steroidal anti-inflammatory as were previously sent home with her. As a reminder, we need to recheck Laika's blood values 30 days post starting the Rimadyl to ensure she is tolerating the medication well.

As I mentioned to you yesterday, I will attempt to find a board certified veterinary surgeon in the Austin area for Laika. Please call me with any questions or concerns about Laika.

Best regards,

Dr. W.C. Stearman, III

286

Metro Veterinary Imaging, PLLC
2 Brook Hollow Lane
Trophy Club, TX 76262
(817) 542-4856
Debra S. Gibbons, DVM, DACVR

Date: 12/10/2006
Patient: Laika
Owner: Lynch
Breed: Aust. Shepherd
Sex: FS
Age: 06.00
Clinic: Coppell Veterinary Hospital
RDVM: Dr. Stearman
Fax: (972) 355-5340

Imaging Consultant Report

Pertinent History:	Laika was presented for a right rear limb lameness of several months' duration. She was overweight at 75 pounds, but now weighs 53 pounds. She remains approximately 5 pounds overweight. Cranial drawer motion is detected in the right stifle. Laika sits with the right rear limb in the air as many dogs with ruptured cruciate also sit.
Imaging Diagnosis:	Two views of the pelvis and two views of the right stifle, all dated 12/6/06, are available for interpretation. There is increased soft tissue opacity within the right femorotibial joint with cranial displacement of the infrapatellar fat pad and caudal displacement of the caudal joint capsule. Periarticular osteophytes have formed on the apex of the patella and on the lateral margin of the tibial plateau. There has been remodeling of the lateral condyle of the right femur. Muscle atrophy is observed in the right hind limb. The left femoral head is small, and has a remodeled, squarish shape. Periarticular osteophytes have formed at the site of joint capsule attachment on the left femoral head and on the left acetabular margins. The left acetabulum is shallow and flattened, providing only fifty percent coverage of the left femoral head. Images of the left stifle were obtained for comparison and are within normal limits.
Impressions:	Effusion and degenerative joint disease are diagnosed in the right stifle. These changes typically develop secondary to joint instability, such as seen with a ruptured cranial cruciate ligament. Unilateral dysplasia with secondary degenerative joint disease is diagnosed in the left coxofemoral joint.

Figure 65: Vets Imaging Report On the Dog

Uses D* to get the Only Piece of Art Given To Dad: 2005 03 11

I went by the school and had lunch with D* on a nice Friday morning, 03 11. D* was excited and wanted to show me a painting he had done. We went up the hall, and there it was, it was beautiful. He had done great. Then he said I could have the painting. It was part of an exhibit on the wall. I said it looked like it was part of an exhibit, and I didn't know if I should take it down. Ms. T was in her office behind us. She said that the exhibit was over, and that it was ok to take it down. I was absolutely thrilled. D*' art went home from the school on Mondays, and H* had not shared any of it with me in two years. I had given the art teacher self addressed stamped envelopes, but she never sent any art either. I thanked D* and took the painting back to the Austin apartment.

About a half hour after school let out this message was left:

> Message from H* Lynch 2005 03 11 3:09PM
>
> H* Lynch: Hi this is H*, D* is telling me that you are picking up the paintings. I enrolled D* in that after school class and I think that should belong here. If it is just the case that you want to take a picture it is ok, but you really have to leave it here. I suppose you are going to do that. Please call me back. Thanks Bye.

I was thinking I might have to take a picture of it, then my heart fell when I heard the next message:

> Message from D* Lynch 2005 03 11 3:13PM
>
> D* Lynch: Return the painting please. Bye,Bye.

She had actually set him up and made him ask for the painting back. I can't imagine what it would be like to be a happy seven year old giving something to one parent, just to have the other parent make you feel bad about it and have you reverse the decision. And then there was yet another message:

> Message from H* Lynch 2005 03 11 4:28PM
>
> H* Lynch: Tom this is ridiculous the painting is mine. This is from an after school enrichment program. I paid $25, I have check. (inaudible). I paid for that and expect to have it. I told D* that is our painting. I brought him home and now its gone. This is ridiculous, I just want the painting back.

Figure 66: Tape Transcript of H Has D* Ask for His Gift to Dad Back*

I felt kinda sick in the bottom of my stomach imagining what was happening to D*. I hadn't known about the after school program. H* hadn't/doesn't share any school information with me unless there is a special circumstance. I replied by email explaining that D* had given me the painting. H* could not believe this, and I got the next phone message:

Message from H* Lynch 2005 03 11 4:42PM

H* Lynch: Tom, I really think you need to stop the lie.Now you should be very careful, now that D* can read. Now I show the e-mail you sent to me. It is clear that it is not true. So please be careful. Now I really wanted D* to see the fact who is lying. So don't do that. You make me to be the liar, but that is not the fact. I have the after school contact person here and it is me. (inaudible) Please stop lying.

It was a typical H* message, with a veiled threat. Nobody tells H* what to do without repercussions. I wondered what my further punishment would be. The whole scenario probably transpired in front of D*.

'No You Can't Have Even One Extra Day With Dad' 2005 03 27

H* never allowed us a minute more than she had to. Even at exchanges, she would be 5 minutes late. Nor has she ever admitted to herself that D* likes spending time with his father. Note at the bottom of this conversation between us, H* accuses D* of repeating what his dad told him to say:

H*: Hello?

D*: Mom.

H*: Hi, D*.

D*: Can I stay longer with dad?

H*: No what are you talking about?

D*: Just one day?

H*: I was calling to know, how was the taco party?

D*: Good.

H*: Did you have taco party.

D*: Yes.

H*: You were crying when I left.

D*: I was not crying, I was disappointed.

H*: You were disappointed?

D*: Yes, Can I stay one more day with dad?

H*: No, you get see him all the time. He comes to school all the time.

D*: No, not all the time.

H*: Most of the time.

D*: Can I just stay one more day with dad?

H*: No you know the schedule.

D*: Just one more little day?

H*: Nope, D*.

D*: Just one day?

H*: No that is between me and your dad and you are not going to talk about.

D*: I miss my dad and I have lots of stuff to do, so can I stay longer?

H*: D* that is your dad talking.

D*: Bye.

Figure 67: H Refuses to Let D* Spend Any Extra Time With Dad*

Modification Attempt 2, 2005

Hired Attorney Gabe Guiterrez

I was having lunch at a Mexican restaurant in east Austin with some friends one afternoon. A friend and I were a bit early and started discussing my attorney experience. "You really ought to find a minority attorney, perhaps someone from the east side of town," my friend Steve suggested. "These guys know that the clique down town can be bad news, and are probably glad to help out." The concept was appealing. I was always taught in school that minorities had been given a bad deal by the system, so surely a minority attorney from the east side would have no problem understanding this aspect of my legal problems.

State Senator Gonzalo Barrientos happened to be sitting in the same restaurant eating lunch. "Now there is a guy who knows better," my friend commented. After lunch I called Senator Barrientos' office to get an attorney referral. The assistant said that Mr. Barrientos couldn't give out referrals, but Mr. Barrientos had a couple of attorney friends who might be able to answer my question. She gave me Gabe Guiterrez's phone number.

I recognized Gabe's name. He has the office in a house just off of the north bound IH35 access road. The sign on the side of the building facing the interstate bares his name. It now burned into the subconscious of everyone in the state. I called him, his daughter answered the phone and setup an appointment.

Other attorneys I worked with had teamed with their legal assistants, so this time I decided to get my own assistant. That way at least one relationship would not have a conflicting obligation to a dishonest attorney should things travel sideways.

I arrived at the house for my appointment. The house was covered in dark silt from the interstate. The windows had burglar bars, and there were matching bullet holes in the windows on opposing sides of the house. Gabe's office was conservative, much like any other attorneys. He told me he had just finished a rape case. His client was found guilty and got five years. After that he would be deported back to Central America. Gabe considered it to be a win. "It could have been 25," he said.

I explained that I wanted information from the school, such as a copy of D* cumulative folder, and some of his art work. I was also concerned about a dangerous fence at the school. Ultimately, I wanted to get custody of my son, but I viewed that we had a number of steps to take to get to the point where a custody hearing would be wise.

Gabe did very little for five months, and then kept the retainer. He sent one letter to the school asking for records, and when they weren't provided in full, he dropped the request. Guiterrez wasn't nearly as smart as Larry, so his exit wasn't quite as well executed. He called me to his office after five months and explained he had seen the light. After five months of not providing any legal advice whatsoever, he wanted to delve in. He let me speak my uneducated thoughts on what should be done. He asked my opinion, but provided no guidance of his own. He then called the next day and told me I was selfish, never thought of anyone besides myself, and that for those reasons he was withdrawing, i.e. he baited me. Later he said he had recorded conversations, and that Attorney's are allowed to do this in their own defense. Gabe not only kept the retainer, but he also kept the trust fund set aside for paying the assistant. The assistant was absolutely aghast, and can't imagine why I'm not suing for malpractice. What the legal assistant doesn't know is that no malpractice attorney I had spoken with would get involved over a few thousand dollars. Well, at least I proved one thing. Belonging to a minority or being active in a minority struggle does not imply integrity or empathy for another's plight.

To replace Gabe I interviewed an attorney in Round Rock who claimed to be ethical. Indeed she had worked on an ethics committee at the Bar. She said that she would never place a complaint on a colleague, as that was up to clients to do. This is lawyer speak for saying that she placed professional courtesy above advocating her client. She also said that it was better to wait until a modification hearing instead of doing any up front work such as sending any professional complaint letters or filing any injunctions. This was lawyer speak for saying she wanted to write a lot of letters without teeth, followed by a large expensive hearing. So I asked where the ethics were in that. She said, "I will always return your phone calls."

D* and I were eating barbecue at the Iron Works a while ago. The sisters who have been serving barbecue to me and my friends for ten years, were not there that day. We sat in the open upstairs area. We had a rack of pork ribs to split between us, and a couple of large ice teas. Some grackles flew over and perched by the table. D* reached in his tea pulled out some ice, and threw it and hit one. The flock flew off squawking and didn't come back. Wouldn't it be nice if this was prophetic. Children used to be able to have input into a divorce at age 8, but the legislator has moved it to age 12. Apparently, now child are not allowed to decide at all. A child may sign a letter of opinion. This can do little more than provoke the Divorce Industry for another go around.

D* and Dad Buy a Sailboat to Look for Treasure, Spring Break 2005

The treasure was becoming an issue. D* had been talking about it for two years and the kids at school were starting to question its authenticity. His mother out told him outright that it was fake.

I sold a patent and decided to buy a boat to live on. At least when I was broke I would have a place to live and a means to feed myself. In addition service never appears in the middle of large bodies of water. Then there was girl catching aspect.

D* would use his half of the treasure to pay for his half of the boat. We found an aluminum sloop rigged for single handed circumnavigation racing for sale in the Florida Keys.

The Turquoise trading post appraised D* treasure, all except for some jewels that had gone missing,and some coins moved to his collection, and it came out to just half the price of the boat. The appraisal cost us a pizza. You should have seen the look on the brokers face when D* dumped the treasure on his desk. "Your turn dad."

We stayed in Florida for a week, snorkeled reefs off keys.

Why can't experiences like this be the hallmark of D*'s raising?

292

Figure 68: Picture of Mystique

Along with the patent sale I had developed a relationship with a patent broker, and he wanted more of my work. Ironically, the reason I had patents to sell in the first place was because my business in Austin and the chances for my last business plan had been destroyed in the divorce. Who knows if the business plan would have succeeded if my reputation hadn't been smashed by the theft of my records, but why should other people be able to determine my destiny in such a fashion?   The fact that the IP was marketable indicates that the business plan had some merit.

So now I had a dream job. I could work anyway in the world, even aboard my boat. I could spend my time dreaming up new technologies, and then selling them to the patent brokerage. The only draw back was that I was paid irregularly. I did not receive a salary, it was purely pay for results. It would often take months to get a group of patents together. Then I would have to wait for the funds to be assembled. Sometimes there were commitments for purchase up front, other times there were not.

But is was all meaningless because my son could not participate. I couldn't bring D* along and it was impossible to make bi-weekly trips to Austin to visit him from the middle of the Gulf of Mexico or the Caribbean sea. And although I was paid enough to follow my dream, I was not paid enough to afford to live in two places and travel between them.

There have been two issues with the custody battle over D*. The first has been the questions of his relationship with his mother and all the accidents. The second has been the Texas standard decree. The Texas decree was set up so that the dad has to stay in the same locality, or spend an awful lot of money on travel, or must give up his child. If the court wasn't going to see the abuse issue, at least they could have allowed a parenting sharing arrangement where by D* would spend half calendar time with dad and half with mom. The current decree is a document of oppression that guarantees D* dreams to spend time with his father, and my dreams for a father and son relationship will be dashed upon the rocks.

H* Discusses Moving to Korea with D*

According to D*, H* sat him down asked what he thought about living in Korea. She explained to him that they could move their to get away from his father. She also said that it may not be necessary to move because of the Round Rock Police. She liked them a lot.

I called H* to discuss this and left a long message about it along with requests for medical records. There was no reply.

Day Care Instead of Dad, Summer 2005

I had just completed a long project. I set aside six weeks to spend with my son. I gave notice to H* by the April first deadline to take the second half of the summer.

H* rejected the schedule because it came within 7 days of the start of school. She then insisted that I take only two weeks because that was what the decree listed for less than one hundred miles, and I had given notice from Austin. She would put D* in daycare for the remainder of the summer. When I complained about this, she dictated that six days (?) be docked from my summer break for the time I had him when she went on her trip. She wanted D* to have 9 days vacation with his father in 2005, and then spend the rest of the time in day care. In all she changed the schedule three times for purposes of punishing.

I had to find another attorney. I had just had the Schuhbut experience. The summer passed by before I could find anyone willing to take action. D* stayed at daycare, while I stayed home and worked on a book.

Having Fun Sailing Thanksgiving 2005

The next Thanksgiving, just after hurricane Wilma passed, in the winds of dissipating Gamma, D* and and two crew sailed from Boot Key off of Florida to St Petersburg. We pulled our bikes out of the fo'c'sl, and road around downtown St. Petersburg. D* talks about this still. He wants to take our bikes down town Austin all the time.

Having Some Fun, Sailing Christmas 2005

I took the boat to Mississippi delta. Christmas I drove back to Austin in a rental car, picked up D*, and we drove back to the delta. The delta had been leveled by Rita. We then sailed back to Galveston.

H* Refuses to Give School Diary Intolerance Med Note

D* had diarrhea as a toddler. My mom and grandma had pointed out he was diary intolerant. I explained this to Dr. Mirrop. Dr. Mirrop talked to H*, and H* denied that there was a problem. Consequently I took D* to the Mayo Clinic in 2001, and then again in 2003, where he was diagnosed using an analytical machine by a world famous pediatric gastrointerologist, Dr. El-Youssef. This information was fed back to Dr. Mirrop, who threw up his hands and quit. He then apparently fire walled himself behind his legal department. H* chose a new doctor at the ARC who would agree with her.

Deepwood elementary school serves milk with lunch. They say it is a state law. D* should not be drinking that milk, or at least he should have a diary enzyme to aid in its digestion. The school refused to stop the milk in any condition. They refused to provide the diary enzyme without a note from D* pediatrician at the ARC, and it was not forth coming. Consequently D* just suffered.

H* refused to provide the note in K, 1, and 2.

Each year I engaged the school nurse and the pediatrician with the Mayo Clinic with a mini war of letters, and got the enzymes to the school.

H* Blocks dad From Seeing D* at the YMCA. The YMCA Helps Her.

When D* was in kindergarten, and I was in California working at Quicksilver as a computer architect D* would call daily. I would take a conference room and we would talk usually for about an hour. It was my daily executive meeting. Then H* put a stop to the calls. My management was understanding, and allowed me to start telecommuting more from Austin Texas. I would fly in for my alternating week visit, and then I would stay a couple of weeks and make the next weekend visit as well, then fly back. In the interim I would go to Deepwood elementary in the afternoons after school. H* had him enrolled in the after school program. It was at this time that I taught him how to play soccer, how to sight read, and how to play chess.

H* may have been unaware of my visits. D* was almost always the last boy to be picked up. So around 6:00 I would leave. We rarely crossed paths. Though after about a year of this an event occurred where D* did not want to go home with H*. I watched through a window from outside. He barricaded himself underneath one of the gym tables and refused to come out. He wanted his dad.

H* insisted that I stop visiting. The YMCA told her that there was nothing they could do because I had a legal right to be there. H* then elected to take him out of the program.

Some time went by, and she put him back in the program for the summer at Fern Bluff Elementary school. This time she conspired with Kacie Nesby to block me from visiting. They did this by leaving the blank on the enrollment form for the father blank. When I went over to Fern Bluff, and saw D*, I was asked by the staff to leave. I told them to check their records. They made some phone calls, and I had to leave. I asked who I had been talking to at Fern Bluff, and the woman would not tell me. The counselors took their badges off and put them in their pockets.

I went over to the Greater YMCA of Williamson County office. I had never been there before and had not met in of their staff. I was walking across the parking lot, still outside, when there was a woman standing by the entrance to the office area. She told me from across the lot that I would have to leave.

An exchange of letters and phone calls ensued. In the end they said they couldn't stop me from visiting. H* then took D* out of the program. Kacie Nesby had litterred the YMCA records with slander about how Kacie Nesby was afraid of me. Kacie Nesby provided a deposition. The YMCA has kept those records and distributed to them to H* so that she may use them in court.

D* Corrects his First Grade Teacher, Mrs. Hernandez, She is Pissed

In first grade they taught some basic Euclidean geometry. One of the lessons was that a shape does not change its name when it is rotated. This is known as rotational invariance, and it is a lesson I had been teaching D* every since he was a baby. I put a large circle, square, and an triangle cut from plywood in his crib. I would pick them up and turn them around while saying their names. When Mrs. Hernandez taught Euclidean geometry one of her shapes was diamond. When it was standing upright she called it diamond, when it was turned it was a square. D* corrected her, and explained that a diamond was a forty five degree rotated square. They had a big argument, and he was punished for having the right answer.

I explained what happened to the school principal, and told her that I wanted it explained to D* that it was wrong to interrupt the class, but that he had the correct answer. I emailed the principal a the description of a diamond from the Oxford English dictionary which explained the issue well enough. The principal talked to Mrs. Hernandez and D* was pulled aside, as planned, but, according to D*, he was given a lecture and told not to listen to his dad, that she was the teacher of mathematics. D* was in tears as the first grade teacher told him not to listen to his dad in mathematics.

The principal tried again, and again D* was told to listen to the teacher. It wasn't about mathematics, it was about Mrs. Hernandez. She was adamant.

The principal and I elected to let it go. The principal D* and I sat outside on a bench one day and we tried to explain the concept of pride to D*.

Mrs. Hernandez managed to undo five years of math education, and even out weigh the baby lessons with the plywood. In second grade when D* was tested for TAG, he missed the rotation invariance question, and in fact failed the math section. I conferenced, and the principal and she wrote a waiver to let him into the program.

This was not the extent of the damage. To D* Mrs. Hernandez now represented the reason that he could not live with his dad like he wanted to, and he let her know it. When the had an essay D* wrote he wanted to live with his dad. Mrs. Hernandez threw it away while he watched, and told him that he needed to change the topic. She suggested writing an essay on how much he loved his mother. D* responded by refusing to go home with his mother. Mrs. Hernandez then said that D* had social problems and brought in the school counselor, Betty Carboneau.

Betty Carboneau invited me to her office to discuss D* social issues. I explained to her that D* already had a counselor. I was trying to get across to her that I had my hands full already. She was divorced four times, she should have understood that. She insisted not talking about D* as a whole and she hung up on me. I went by the school not for an appointment in her office, but to explain to her that I did not want her working with D*. I sat in a chair in the main office. When she walked up the hall on the opposite side of the office, some 15 feet away and on the other side of two administrator's occupied desks, I remained seated and explained I did not want her working with D*. Ms. Carboneau was obviously very frustrated and she went through the standard lines, that I was making her uncomfortable, that perhaps I was aggressive. I was sitting in a chair 15 feet away with two people sitting between us. That proved it was a game to her. Mrs. Veach the principal invited us into a three way meeting, and I explained again that I did not want Mrs. Carboneau to meet with D*. That afternoon I was back at the school for another reason. D* was not in class. I asked Ms. Hernandez where he was. She said that he was meeting with Ms. Carboneau.

In second grade a much better teacher, Betty Coplin successfully resolved the situation. She invited me to the classroom to read and give a math lecture. D* then decided that his teacher wasn't so bad. It was amazing how simple the issue actually was, and how in the appropriate D* behavior actually was for child his age given the circumstances.

In my opinion, both Mrs. Hernandez and Betty Carboneau are unhappily divorced and have issues with men and when they act out they are creating a huge liability for the children in their school. Not all fathers are as patient and articulate as I am. Some fathers will respond to the bait, and after they take the bait the misandrists will cry about how evil they are, and that will just lead to yet more damage to the child and the family.

Modification Attempt 3, 2006

I hire Felix Rippy Feb. 2006, Margo Fox Takes Over for Sara Brandon

An attorney in Williamson county explained that I needed representation who was part of the good ol' boys network. She said that no matter how hard she tried, she would always be excluded from that group. "They play poker together with the judges." She told me. She listed a couple of names, her first suggestion being Felix Rippy.

I wasn't going to hire another attorney who ignored the case summary, so I loaned Felix an early form of this document. It was marked confidential, copyrighted, and we agreed it would not be copied or distributed before it was returned. I told Felix that I would only consider hiring him if he read the document over and agreed.

Felix called me back, he explained that he had been a judge. He said he was the kind of attorney I needed to handle the case. He said he had read over the document. He had with him some journal article showing how much money attorneys made from divorces, and he commented that all that money mentioned in my document wasn't going to the attorneys.

After working with Felix for some time I came to the conclusion that he had read only the first few paragraphs of the document, as he was not familiar with anything more. I was constantly running into things he had not heard that were in the document, and would then effectively read the document back to him. Hence, he received the information in bits and pieces. However, unlike any other attorney I have worked with, Felix did not over charge for the work he did, and he did do work.

Felix had the records moved from Travis county to Williamson county. Sara Brandon attempted to block this movement, and the next thing I heard is that Ms. Brandon had done something unethical in trying to stop the movement of the records, and had withdrawn from the case. Margo Fox replaced her. Margo Fox runs an all female law firm in Williamson county. Ms. Brandon was still listed as co-counsel but she never made an appearance.

The next issue was the summer break. It was February, and I wanted to inform H* that I had moved to Galveston, so that D* and I didn't get stuck with two weeks vacation. I had traded the off week visitation during the year for more contiguous time with my son over the summer. This was infinitely more practical as I traveled and worked in California. In past years we had had six weeks of vacation. However, H* had held us to two weeks vacation due to a clause in the 'less than 100 miles' section. She forced the issue, in 2005 D* sat in an undisclosed day care facility while I had six weeks off. I did not want a repeat of this.

Felix did not want me to send the address change notice. He pointed out that I could easily claim to still be living in Austin because I had an apartment, and received mail here. I was adamant about our vacation not being ruined. He told me we would end up with four weeks, and suggested that I give notice to H* that D* and I would be taking off the month of June. He coined the phrase, "You move, you lose," and it became his rejoinder whenever I brought the subject up. He was referring to the ultimate goal, custody. I gave her the notice, and copied Felix. H* refused to honor the notice, and replied that we would get two weeks in July. Later Felix told me that he had not suggested June, but instead said he had said July. July was a bit problematic for sailing, as it encroached into the storm season.

298

Along with the vacation notice problem, in February I wrote an email to Felix and informed him of the passport problem. I had D* passport, but H* would not sign the passport renewal papers. Felix didn't address the issue until it became critical when approaching July. However, he did address it then, and Judge Jergins ordered H* to sign the passport papers.

In addition there was the Caryl Dalton issue. I wanted D* to see different child psychologist. In my opinion Dalton had been brought in as mom's advocate, not as D* therapist. At that time I had not accepted Dr. Freitag's analysis, but I did know that Dalton refused to step aside in favor of someone who could work with the whole family, and she had given me a hard time getting records or in giving me any idea of what was going on. I felt that was enough information to show bias and justify a change.

Felix suggested Sally Ray. He said that she was a friend, and that she was conservative. He explained that she was married to one of the most conservative people in the county. Felix added this part about conservative because I told him I was tired of nanny state liberals who thought everyone should be processed through every department and office that needed to have funding. I later would find out that Sally Ray is both an attorney and licensed professional counselor, not a psychologist. Sally Ray's "conservative" husband is sitting judge of the Texas Court of Criminal Appeals Paul Womack, in place 4. Sally herself ran as a republican for Criminal Appeals Court in precinct 2 in 2000. One of the people she ran against was republican James Wallace, who was the son of a supreme court justice and would later be appointed our attorney amicus.

I called Mrs. Ray. Due to the Dalton experience I made it clear that I wanted access to records. Ray refused saying she could not do her job if the sessions were not secret. I took issue. I said I might be able to see that was the case if D* were a teenager or if we had a confrontational relationship, but he was too young to understand a records issue and we were good buddies. She insisted that she could not build up a rapport without secrecy. I then asked the obvious question, did this mean she would deny my legal right as a parent to see the records. She said of course she wouldn't do that. I told Felix that Ray didn't make sense and I didn't want her. I wanted a person who welcomed my presence.

We mediated with Mark Sim's in his office in downtown Austin. The building was located next to I35 off of 12th street, and was dirty with silt from the constant traffic on the interstate. Felix and I met on the noisy I35 side of the building. It was here that a pivotal conversation occurred. Felix brought up the proposal of using a psychologist to settle the matter. Felix explained that the fact I didn't believe in psychologists meant it looked like I had something to hide.

This was the very attitude that I had raised with Felix in the first place before he suggested "conservative" Ray. The letter of the Texas law is a presumption of sanity. The de facto presumption in the divorce industry is if you don't pay the piper, you lose. After Felix said it *looked* like I had something to hide, I asked him directly if he thought I *actually* has something to hide. He said, "yes." Felix said though it was nothing serious, nothing "a little medication" couldn't cure. I was flabbergasted. Here I came as a dad to help out my son who needs his dad, and I am treated suspiciously for being a good father. I do credit Felix for being honest, though this rather significant impression of his begged a the question of what his goal was in this mediation.

I thought he must have made a joke, and then I started contemplating his rather manic personality and considered the possibility that he had a different set of values than I did. No, he was serious. I smiled. Felix continued on saying that if we proposed to have a psychologist settle the matter, that we put them in a tight spot. If they really believed I was crazy to the level they claimed, then this would be an opportunity. Saying no would essentially call their bluff. If they agreed, we had a lot of evidence, and a psychologist would rule on our side. This latter part made sense, and for mediation I agreed to the proposal of a binding custody evaluation by one psychologist.

On June 13th Felix informed me that he had worked out a deal so that I would get four weeks of vacation in the summer, but it would not be the month of July (or the month of June), but it would be in two parts. The first two weeks would be at the beginning of July, the second two weeks would span the last week of July and the first of August. I was not happy with the arrangement, as our plans required more than two weeks, and by late July it would be too late to go at all. In addition I had assured the crew we would be leaving soon. Felix had not conferred with me before making this agreement. He explained that nobody got uninterrupted vacations, and that this was the standard. That brought up the question of what having custody would be like in general. I explained again that I wanted to talk about it, because it looked like having custody with a standard decree would be problematic. It wasn't what I was after. Though I was frustrated I understood his delay of this conversation to mean that we weren't ready for it yet.

It was now our vacation time, but the passport issue had not been resolved, so even a shorter sailing trip was problematic. I had discussed the passport with others. Perhaps D* didn't need one because he was a kid? In the past people could travel to Mexico and some parts of the Caribbean with just a drivers license. D* didn't have a drivers license, but perhaps a birth certificate would be good enough? Everyone told me that things had been tightened up since 2001, and also there was a lot more concern about child abduction. I would be running a great risk. Also, foreign countries are well known for creating trouble and issuing fines for any excuse.

At the passport office in Houston I tried to run the passport application through based on the divorce decree language alone. The divorce decree allowed international travel, and required H* to provide a letter. The local post office referred us to the passport processing center in Houston. D* and I made an appointment, drove there, waited through a long line, and spoke with a representative. It was a two day affair. The representative read the decree over, and apologized. She said it was clear to her that H* should have provided the letter, but she hadn't. The decree didn't say that the passport office could act without the letter, rather it said she had to provide one. So we went back to Austin.

Felix brought the matter to a hearing. He asked me to show up first thing in the morning, which I did. He put me in a little conference room, and that is where I stayed until mid afternoon. Felix came by the conference room periodically. At one point the opposing attorney came by. She wanted verification that D* had travel shots. Travel to the Caribbean requires them. I showed her the shot recommendation papers from the CDC, and the shot records. I assured her it had been taken care of.

Going into the hearing Felix spoke of attorney fee reimbursement and extra vacation time to make up for the fact we were sitting in court during my vacation. Felix came back with signed forms for the passport. That was wonderful; however, we were given no extension of time, and no attorney fees. After announcing multiple delays, I would now have to tell my sailing crew that the trip had been canceled. They were none to happy. No one ever asked for my agreement to the terms. I never left the small room until it was over. Felix thought it had been a good thing that the judge had never seen his client. I did thank Felix. I was thrilled to have the passport issue resolved. The vacation and passport were the first advances in the case since 2001, due to prior attorney inaction. How could I be completely disappointed? However I also expressed strong satisfaction that we didn't get reimbursed for trouble to my crew or the missed time, and that our vacation plans had been ruined. Felix told me that I had no "God Given" right to go sailing. This was placed in contrast with, for example, if I was holding canceled plane tickets – my expenses and crew be damned. Felix and I continued to have tiffs over the difficulty of communication. I just didn't feel like I was getting through.

It was too late to drive to Houston that week. The next week we managed to get the passport by paying a hefty expedite fee. We took a consolatory two day sail out to Stetson's bank. The guys were very disappointed, but nice about it. Mark the photography had rearranged his client schedule for no good reason. He was not happy.

In the second vacation rotation, we were too late to go sailing due to storm season, so we visited Iowa, and then Grandma and Grandpa in Sun City.

On August 9 Felix called and left a message that we had an agreement towards settlement. He said that I had nine days to contact two psychologists, one being Sally Ray. Over many days I tried to get questions answered, or to see the agreement but was rebuffed. I had been given no input into it, and certainly hadn't agreed to it. I was surprised by the call. I was told by his assistant that Felix was at a conference, and that she didn't know where the agreement was. He was unavailable by voice mail, email, and fax. Eventually Felix sent email and told me I would just have to wait for the agreement to arrive in the regular old mail. It arrived in my Austin POB on the 22nd of August, well past the nine days. I felt that agreement was significantly different that that which we had talked about at mediation, and indeed, it contained the names of both Sally Ray, Steve Thorne, and explicitly mentioned Caryl Dalton as having input. The list of people involved only grew as more details came to light. Steve Thorne said he was a data processing type, and he was going to look at everything available from the very beginning including records and the input of other professionals. He asked me to bring documents, "and police records." This was the first time I had heard about "police records" since Brian said H* was slandering me. There are none. This appeared to open Pandora's box of Farely, Ezel, H*'s policeman friend, and a host of others. If this were the case, it made perfect sense as to why the other side had agreed to it. And why wouldn't they bring this stuff up? It had been there makings of their case for years, why would that suddenly change? If this were how it was to unfold, then we would be asking Thorne to overrule at least three other respected professionals, and to make his way through a tangled web of deceitful records. I would have to work very hard to make this turn out well.

My first reaction was to tell Felix to drop the agreement, and go back to the negotiating table. He told me that it was done deal, and if I didn't follow through with the agreement, that I would end up in front of a judge. He told me I had no choice about it. Instead of answering questions, he just issued ultimatums. Then suddenly about a week before it was to be implemented, he called and was real friendly. I welcomed the advance. I call it the *miracle calls*. We finally got to discuss Steve Freitag. He agreed to contact him. He agreed to look into the documents issue for preparing for the Thorne request, which was now only a week away. Strangely, he hung up on me when I brought up how to defend against Ezel's slander. Still, I thought we had turned a page, but the next time I tried to talk with him, we were back with the same ol' Felix. Yes, he had hung up on me, it wasn't real. It was bullshit. Felix later said he recorded the conversation, so I suppose it was a setup.

The agreement Felix made is called a Rule 11 agreement and it is binding on the clients according to Texas Law. Rule 11 agreements are made just between attorney*s and require no input or agreement of the clients.* However, settlement agreements do require the signature of the clients, and this agreement constituted a settlement agreement, and I hadn't signed it.

I called Thorne. I explained to him that I had not signed the agreement, that my attorney was taking an independent course, and that I hadn't even the agreement. I explained that I did not want to throw the baby out with the bathwater in case the agreement had value. I was going to try and make it work if possible. I had two weeks to sort things out, prepare the requested documents, and to figure out what our story was to be. After I saw the agreement, I decided it wasn't workable and called Thorne back to tell him.

I had not called Ray back. The agreement I was holding said she would be the co-parenting coach. I mulled this over. Did I want a co-parenting coach? Somehow, through my attorney, we had agreed to one. It certainly would be nice to have an intermediate person who would say such things as "H* it is not nice to send D* to his fathers in small sized clothes," and such. It seemed possible that a co-parenting coach would just become another tool for H*. It had taken John Campbell two or three months to see through her act – and he was my attorney. H*'s attorney talked about such things as "H* feeling comfortable," and she appeared to be sincere, so she clearly didn't get it either. Furthermore, I didn't see Ray as a straight shooter. I suspected that she would continue to tell me whatever I wanted to hear, while doing whatever she felt was right, independent. That would just extend what I viewed to be the Felix model – and Felix referred to her as a friend, so perhaps it would literally be an extension.

A host of issues came up at the beginning of the school year (Fall of 2006). D* brought his dog, and the dog was lame, and had no tags. We needed information from the vet. Felix told me that Ray would handle that. H* had the doctor give D* shots duplicated from the travel clinic. I was still attempting to save the relationship with my attorney, and he had given me the distinct impression we would be done if I didn't make an appointment with her, so I called the first number Felix had given me for Ray, and got her voice mail. I tried to start out on a good note, and left a nice introductory message that said how much we could use parent co-ordination. Ray's assistant called back and said that I would have to call another number to make an appointment. In the mean time, the list of the miracles that Ray was to perform only grew. I got the impression that Felix had gone AWOL on the legal front. When I pressed this, I had the miracle call where Felix became friendly, and then the next day went back to the old Felix. I wondered why we would have a co-parenting coach during custody evaluation. This 'coach' wouldn't even know who the custodial parent was.

I complained more about the agreement, I told Felix not to sign any more agreements without running them by me first. I got no response, so I put it into an email message. He replied that he would do no such thing.

As I steadfastly refused to use Sally Ray, Felix dictated that I do so. He withdrew over the issue, while citing a "communications" problem.

302

After Felix stopped working I dropped the law suit. Some months later Margo Fox served me the day before Thanksgiving vacation with an emergency request for supervised visitation. Felix was pissed off, and sent incredible emails threatening such things as slander suits if I talked about it. He noted he had sued another client for slander and I could look it up.

H* Tells D* She Doesn't Love Him

On 2006 06 04 we were having dinner and D* started crying in earnest. I didn't know what was wrong. I consoled him. Apparently he was saying that his mother told him she didn't love him. I had my laptop on the table and turned it so the web cam faced him. I knew it would be hard for both of us, but clearly it was something that we had to talk about. Also, I felt this would be very important for us to document. D* was confused and I had to work to hold his attention. I spoke to softly but he was not responding, so I told him directly. He responded to that and sat down. I then asked him to explain what he said:

father	Now what is this about like and love, can you explain this?
D*	She said that you have to love a person if you like a person.
father	She said that?
D*	Yeah.
father	Did you tell her that you liked her? What happened?
D*	We were in the living room and she asked Jay the question, and he didn't say anything.
father	What question?
D*	Why should I love him if you don't love ... why should .. why should ... why should you love me.. I mean .. why should D* love .. I can't say it! .. Just can't.
father	That's ok D*, sit down. Take you time. Take a deep breath.
D*	She said why should I love D* if D* doesn't love me.
D*	And why does she think you don't love her?
father	I told her that.
D*	You did?
father	Yes.
D*	Ah, what were your exact words?
father	I love you but I don't like you.
D*	Ah, so what happened after you told her that?
father	That was a few weeks ago, and I think I told it that week, and
D*	Well how did she react after you told her that?
father	Same question.
D*	What question is that?
father	Why should I love you if you don't love me.

303

D*	But you said you loved her, you just said that you didn't like her.
father	No I meant the opposite.
D*	You like her but you don't love her?
father	Actually the opposite.
D*	You love her but you don't like her.
father	So you told her you loved her, you just didn't like her.
D*	yes.
	and she misunderstan.. what is happening now?
D*	She made it so I like I made me so I say that, I said. She got me to actually say a few weeks after that. .. "I like you."
father	She forced you to say that you liked her?
D*	Something like that. Not exactly force. Made me want to. Like, she like, she kept saying it and saying it. Like you won't get out of this. []She mainly said something like you're going to answer me, and after awhile I answered her. I answered her that I liked her, because she would eventually ask the question again and again.
father	What did she say you weren't going to get out of?
D*	Well that was a mistake I shouldn't have said that.
father	ok
D*	That was not really happen. I actually said that.
father	What didn't really happen?
D*	The thing I said about "you won't get out of something."
father	That's enough D*, lets go watch the movie some, its getting late.

Figure 69: H* Tells D* She Doesn't Love Him

Afterwards we sat on the couch and I held him. I can still feel his pain. Why would a mother say such a thing to a child? The case is that H* often relates to D* at the same age level. She is setting up emotional deals with him so that they are becoming cross coupled with each other, and dependent upon each other for emotional support.

Birthday Party With Crew – Dad Arrested for Public Intoxication

On my birthday in 2006 some of Mystique's crew and I met a private residents and had some drinks on my birthday. Apparently the neighbors didn't approve and a policeman came and awarded the birthday boy a gift of a class C misdemeanor ticket for public intoxication. This was brought up many times in subsequent hearings. At the passport papers hearing I was referred to as a "drunken sailor."

Discussion with D on 2006 09 02*

Stream of conscious speaking is where someone just talks about whatever comes into their head. D* does this once in a while, and I think it is a good thing. It helps him sort things out. The following is such a conversation. D* had started talking about some old memories of his Grandpa, so I grabbed the recorder and took up at the point he was at. The square bracketed words are mine, the plain text is D*. Comments are in angle brackets. Many of this issues he brings up probably do not make sense without the context of the prior parts of this manuscript, the following is quote from D*:

[Have you seen your Korean Grandpa?] When I was 2 ½ my Korean Grandpa and family from the Korean side came. I told them I went to Iowa skiing school. I told the psychologist the trip might have been to Iowa.

[Why has the expression in your class pictures changed so drastically.] My mom told me my pictures were bad as I need to smile. My mom wanted me to be silly. You know about parents and kids and the subconscious mind. All kids like their parents. I wanted to please her, so the last class pictures turned out like that.

I remember when we were in the hammock together. <I had built D* an crib that hung under an A frame. It was large enough for two people. This is a very old memory.>

You know the thing about the eyes? My mom said that your dad might be telling me lies. <D* has difficulty looking at me when I talk.>

[Why were you scratching so much this afternoon?] The one thing is hard to remember .. my mom says war is bad, but I still play it. That is why it has been hard for me to read the book. That is why I was itching.

I have a prediction when about my breathing funny. I'm breathing funny because it is stressful, because thats the 'prediction' (I think its true, but it might not be). It was because my dad might be lying – like when we are in serious discussings and thinks you are lying. .. like about these things. She said I shouldn't know about the divorce decree because every time divorce – go to the bathroom or breath funny. I don't like this, need to find a way out of it.

Caryl Dalton asked "Does father lie?" She also talks to my mom secretly. It is none of her business.

It might not be true: my mom told me that when I'm stressed I should go to the restroom (it might not be my mom). I remember the room it had white tiles may be green walls was CPS room like my old psychologist <Peggy Farely?> In the room there was a chair with wheels on the bottom. At time after time, some plate on of the plates <draws a plate that is sectioned with letters written around the edge.> Mom was there, no you were there, think you were there. Not sure, maybe one of my aunts, parents, grandma, and grandpa. I barely remember a little, and my mom told me it. [Told you what?] The restroom thing. That I have go to the restroom to make room. I remember I had diapers. She said did you know your dad lies a little bit, she said it in a nice way.

And I did see her kick the dog ... I remember her over hyper. Something else, not important, she wears black shoes, a little bit high but not like a boot – No I meant my grandpa, you know, when they were talking at that dinner. He was talking about what happened over here, what happened at mom's house and those things. That was the edge when you guys were going to court. Mom told grandpa about the divorce last time he came in 2004. Mom said we are soon going to divorce, "yes."

My mom told me that my tummy would explode if I didn't do that a little time after you eat. One time I was a lot more overweight than this, she told me if my tummy would explode if I ate more.

You know in the swimming pool? <D* fell in the pool when he was about a year old, and was pulled out right away.> I feel I was leaning, leaned a little too much.

[Did mom ever ask you to eat something gross?] These parts feel heavy, they do. This here hurts around my head. <pointing above his brows.> I remember eating something I that was gross <D* was on the verge of crying, and pointing on a spot on his head.> Candy in a needle bag – candy was gum drops. I was in the car she said I was doing a good job and gave me a candy, a gum drop. We drove and came back. I didn't say anything, there was a needle with thread, I climbed up to get it. Mom caught me, got in trouble, but not much. That is when I saw the needle there was .. she does lie because she was screaming at me for spilling water. She was screaming at me she was making a big fit. I was sitting on a chair watching and feeling bad.

I did think of some gross things like dead bodies with germs growing on them, and coffins like in movies – remind me of the dead bodies I saw one – Great Grandma <crying>. I don't like thinking about that – my Great Grandma, ok? Whenever I think about it I cry <balling>. All the great times I had with her and now she is dead. <going after the box of Kleenex.> Like it better when grandma and grandpa live close by where we were <my folks moved to Sun City>.

[Tell me something fun you remember doing with Great Grandma.] The funniest one I remember best when I shared her a boat I made a boat made of legos, but I couldn't make a mast. When I was younger, too young to go into the army <probably referring to Ian, who lived with Great Grandma at the time>. One time he was not doing a military assignment or something.

The longer I meditate the more I itch. I remember being *embarrassed*, that is the thing I couldn't remember earlier, another person said it was gross, felt bad because I don't like eating gross things. <May refers to an incident age 2 ½ when D* took his lunch to the French school, and another child made fun of his food.>

My mom said, sometimes when you listen to your dad something bad might happen. [When did she say this?] When I was 4 ½ or 5 <Note, D* often does not place things correctly in time.> She asks questions over and over. My mom told me not to listen to you. What I mean is this: my mom said once don't ... the candy bag she had it for a reason. I was young, 2 ½ maybe 3, like doing things like going to the restroom correctly or something. She probably gave me candy every time I went to the restroom. [Don't guess, tell me actual memories]. My mom gave me a candy for some promise about you she was talking about the divorce – and she says she never talks about the divorce – and that is a lie! Mom said she give you candy if you didn't listen to your dad. She said said I'll give you candy to break promise. She said again and again.

Mom tells everything to J sometimes in my brain it makes me think I should tell her everything she needs to know. Kind of feel *embarrassed* if I told about the meditations. Mom said you should not talk about the divorce. Mom said I should be cute. The first psychologist was in the same building, think about it for 10 minutes. Went into this building, went to the floor she was on. When we got there I played with these toys for awhile then she asked me in the middle, "do you like your dad?" She told me to *think* about it for 10 minutes. She talked to my mom and then she gave me a Jolly Rancher and we went. <D* started making a happy baby face>. Some happy thought came into my mind. Remember we had playing room with wood floors and a restroom with a window that I didn't like? I remember we went to the Indian Pow Wow and afterwards had dinner. I just want to think about it, ok? <D* closes his eyes and starts pouting while holding his face in his hands, then lifts up and smiles.> dad I remember when you made the raspberries – when you were cooking. <When D* was three we found wild black berries, and made a dessert with them.>

I remember how you guys argue. Mom said I'm not supposed to be talking. [Does your mom talk about the divorce?] Yes.

She said dad started the divorce and she connected it to the pillow thing.

I remember questions CPS. How did feel? That was the day I asked to live with my dad and she said she give me consequences and I stopped talking.

Saw her face little short coat made of jean fabric there wasn't only once with her in that tall tower. Do whatever your dad said Caryl Dalton asked me why I called dad but not mom.

My mom is blaming you for stuff you didn't do, like the Deepwood shirt. You never got one before today <On this visit D* arrived with a Deepwood shirt.> She says they are over here when they aren't. She is blaming you for the divorce. Dog has been blamed on you twice. She blame me for accidentally crashing into her car. She blamed the other driver stopped about to leave, and blamed the man in there for crashing into her car when it hadn't moved. And a teacher blamed me for hitting her when I didn't. I got a fine for $70 for being kicked out of the science program. I know one more thing – about the pillow. She said you did something bad and covered me up with a blanket. Mom says I have a square head.

ARC Nurse Tells D: "You Don't Look At All Like Your Father"*
2006 09 15

D* had poison ivy. The nurse was very snooty to me. I gather she had some sort of man issues. She couldn't help her self. She even placed her body between us when she talked to him. She didn't look at me. She started in on D*, "You Don't Look At All Like Your father."

Live in Boyfriend Has D Put Message On Machine Saying D* is Not Home, and Has Him Not Answer the Phone and Listen To It When His Father Calls*

H* only answers the phone when her attorney says she has to. That makes it about once every two years. She complains that D* doesn't call her or return her calls, but in truth, she doesn't even answer when he calls. I was recording a failure for D* to get through on H*'s cell phone, when D* just started talking about something else – the outgoing message on the home phone number that is in D*' voice.

H*'s boyfriend at the house, Jay, would hangup the phone or pull the plug when D* was talking to me. Other times he and H* just didn't let D* answer. Jay had D* put the outgoing message on the machine to say that D* wasn't home, but D* had a great deal of guilt about this as is shown below, because he was home. He did not like being forced to lie to his father:

2006 09 16

D*	... and the message is true about the voice thing
father	what message is true?
D*	the voice message
father	uh?
D*	"D* is not home," that voice message.
father	Oh yeah, so you are never home when I call and nobody answers?
D*	No. That's a dumb voice message, why did Jay <mumbling softly> Jay just tricked me.
father	Jay what now?
D*	Jay tricked me.
father	How so?
D*	About doing that voice message, and I can't find the frisbee.
father	Why do you say its a trick?
D*	Because I asked about voice messages and then he told me to do one and he told me to do that one.
father	Why do you think it was bad doing that one.
D*	Because it is not true!

Figure 70: H's Boyfriend Doesn't Let D* Answer Calls From His Dad*

D*: You Should Buy a House 2006 09 17

I find this conversation interesting because it ties in D*' request that I buy a house, which he made at a time he was in a different developmental phase even as a toddler, with his desire to come to the Christmas dinner I hosted last year at the Driskill. (Only adults had been invited.) D* very much wants to do be my business partner, and felt left out.

D*	I think you should buy a really big house that doesn't have any furniture
father	You think I should by a house, huh?
D*	Yeah.

308

father	Why do you think I should buy a house.
D*	Business reasons, thats one. Another reason is you can't have a business dinner on that boat like yours, you know why?
father	No.
D*	You don't have enough room for all the food, *and* the people.
father	So you think I should buy a house just for business meetings?
D*	and for docking your boat.
D*	I don't want you to buy a house in Hawaii for one reason. Some of your islands have active volcanoes. Must have really high houses.
father	So why are you bringing up the subject of houses suddenly? Do you think about houses a lot?
D*	Sometimes. Sometimes the idea pops in my mind. An idea pops in mind about, it was like how your business meetings were, and how fancy it was. Those wouldn't have to pay as much money if you just got a house. Eventually get fancy things, .. big sparkles and those things ..

Figure 71: D* Says Dad Should Buy A House

D*: Mom Wants Payback On You 2006 11 05

D* was trying very hard to articulate a thought and he started talking about his mother throwing something. I grabbed the recorder, he said in a halting voice "I think mom .. wants .. payback and and .. putting her anger on you .."

Surprise Service for 'Emergency' Hearing Served 2006 11 22

After Felix quit I had not done any work on modification matter. The day before Thanksgiving break Margo Fox served me with a motion for an emergency hearing. Margo Fox was Sara Brandon's de facto replacement after the records transfer ordeal, though she was officially co-counsel. The hearing was scheduled to be in the middle of my and D* Christmas break, so we wouldn't be visiting his grandparents after all. I had to scramble to get an attorney. Margo Fox absolutely refused to reschedule because "it was an emergency," though not too much of an emergency to do it right away, but so much so that it couldn't wait until we got back from break. She asked for supervised visitation, i.e. that I not be allowed to see D* except when supervised by a professional. The following is H*'s emergency affidavit.

Dr. Dalton Supports the Emergency Request for Supervised Visitation

Dr. Dalton supported Mrs. Fox's motion for supervised visitation for dad on an emergency basis. She even came to testify on December 19th, though did not get a chance to speak as Judge Jergins granted my new attorney a continuation.

In doing this she violated ethics in psychology for two reasons, firstly, Dr. Dalton's support for the motion meant she was placing herself in the position of a custody evaluator as well as being D* therapist. This is called playing a "dual role." A recognized authority explained that dual role testimony was unethical, Dr. Randall Sellers, and he provided some articles including the following which was given to the court: S. Greenberg, and D. Shuman, "Irreconcilable Conflict Between Therapeutic and Forensic Roles," The American Psychological Association, Professional Psychology: Research and Practice, No 1, pp50-57. Greenberg and Shuman note:

> The Committee on Psychiatry and Law of the Group for the Advancement of Psychiatry (GAP, 1991) concluded in 1991 that "While, in some areas of the country with limited number of mental health practitioners, the therapist may have the role of forensic expert thrust upon him, ordinarily, it is wise to avoid mixing the therapeutic and forensic roles" (p. 44). Similarly, the Ethical Principles of Psychologists and Code of Conduct of the American Psychological Association (APA, 1992) admonishes that "In most circumstances, psychologists avoid performing multiple and potentially conflicting roles in forensic matters" (p. 1610). Finally, the most recent and the most specific of these codes, the American Psychological Association's (1994) guidelines for conducting child custody evaluations, concluded the following:
>
>> Psychologists generally avoid conducting a child custody evaluation in a case in which the psychologist served in a therapeutic role for the child or his or her immediate family or has had other involvement that may compromise the psychologist's objectivity. This should not, however, preclude the psychologist from testifying in the case as a fact witness concerning treatment of the child. In addition, during the course of a child custody evaluation, a psychologist does not accept any of the involved participants in the evaluation as a therapy client. Therapeutic contact with the child or involved participants following a child custody evaluation is undertaken with caution. A psychologist asked to testify regarding a therapy client who is involved in a child custody case is aware of the limitations and possible biases inherent in such a role and the possible impact on the ongoing therapeutic relationship. Although the court may require the psychologist to testify as a fact witness regarding factual information he or she became aware of in a professional relationship with a client, that _psychologist should decline the role of an expert witness who gives a professional opinion regarding custody and visitation issues (see Ethical Standard 7.03) unless so ordered by the court. (p. 678)_

The emphasis here is mine. In layman's terms the purpose of separating the therapist from the forensic role is simple. Therapist testimony on custody betrays the patient. Poor little D* went to Dr. Dalton for help and understood what was said would be in confidence, but instead found her gathering evidence and spinning that evidence into a custody evaluation to be presented in a public courtroom. It would be impossible for her to regain the trust required for therapy after such and action.

The second violation by Mrs. Dalton was that she had never met me. This is issue is covered both in Dr. Dawes book, "House of Cards," and S. Lilenfeld, S. Lynn, M. Lohr, "Science and Pseudoscience in Clinical Psychology." In short, a psychologist are not oracles of truth and knowledge, instead they are practitioners who have access to and the knowledge of how to use a number of diagnostic tools. Without having even met a subject is impossible for a psychologist to apply these tools. Giving testimony with having used rigorous methods is irresponsible and potentially damaging. This exacerbates the dual role ethics violation.

My attorney had the articles from Dr. Sellers, he was aware of the issue, he could have knocked her out, but he didn't.

CAUSE NO. <u>06-1054-F395</u>

IN THE MATTER OF	§	IN THE DISTRICT COURT
THE MARRIAGE OF	§	
	§	
THOMAS WALKER LYNCH	§	
AND	§	395TH JUDICIAL DISTRICT
H	§	
	§	
AND IN THE INTEREST OF	§	
D , A CHILD	§	WILLIAMSON COUNTY, TEXAS

<u>RESPONDENT, H 'S AFFIDAVIT</u>
<u>IN SUPPORT OF MOTION FOR ADDITIONAL TEMPORARY ORDERS</u>

BEFORE ME, the undersigned authority, personally appeared H
, who, by me duly sworn, deposed as follows:

"My name is H . I am the Respondent in this cause.
Petitioner is THOMAS WALKER LYNCH.

"I am requesting the Court grant a Motion for Additional Temporary Orders for the following reasons:

"THOMAS WALKER LYNCH and I signed a Rule 11 Agreement on July 7, 2006 and August 8, 2006 regarding D ' passport, conservatorship, co-parenting therapy, D ' therapist, discovery, and a custody evaluation with Dr. Stephen Thorne. THOMAS WALKER LYNCH has violated these agreements, as well as the terms of the Final Decree of Divorce signed on December 13, 2001 by:

1. failing to adhere to the agreement regarding D ' passport. As of November 8, 2006, THOMAS WALKER LYNCH has kept possession of D ' passport despite two of my requests to follow the terms of the Rule 11 Agreement dated July 7, 2006, by delivering the passport to the Frost Bank safe deposit that requires both parties' signatures. See Exhibit A1 attached;

2. failing to submit to the custody evaluation to be prepared Steven Thorne by August 18, 2006;

3. interfering with D ' therapy with his child therapist, Caryl Dalton, by telling D that he has fired Caryl Dalton and, further, by instructing D not to talk to Caryl Dalton;

4. failing to attend the co-parenting therapy with Sally Ray;

5. failing to respond to Respondent's Requests for Disclosure by the deadline, August 18, 2006. August 18, 2006 was the deadline for the second extension my attorney gave THOMAS WALKER LYNCH. As of November 8, 2006, THOMAS WALKER LYNCH still hasn't provided my attorney with a list of witnesses; he has refused to answer a number of questions regarding specific allegations against me, as

EXHIBIT
A

312

well as a number of questions concerning his own financial history, police record, and psychiatric record. THOMAS WALKER LYNCH provided a copy of the CD that contains the edited video; however he did not provide the original video;

6. failing to adhere to the terms of the Final Decree of Divorce property settlement and permanent injunctions. The Final Decree of Divorce restricts THOMAS WALKER LYNCH from being on my property, except during specific visitation periods. The Final Decree of Divorce clearly states which items belong to THOMAS WALKER LYNCH and awards me all items not specifically stated. Despite these terms, THOMAS WALKER LYNCH went to my home with D   during my absence, and took the dog that had lived with me since the divorce was finalized. THOMAS WALKER LYNCH has subsequently claimed, in response to the Round Rock police inquiry, that the dog belongs to him; although he refused to admit that he had the dog in his possession. He also accused me of not giving the dog its rabies vaccination, yet I was able to show the Round Rock police the dog's vaccination records. THOMAS WALKER LYNCH also accused me of not feeding the dog or giving it water, both of which are false; and

7. failing to adhere to the terms of the Final Decree of Divorce by interfering with my possession and parenting of D   . THOMAS WALKER LYNCH has purposely under minded my authority of D   by doing the following:

a) THOMAS WALKER LYNCH, without notifying me, has attempted to fire D   ' physician, Dr. Gritzka without obtaining written authorization from me to take D   to a new doctor, as required by the Final Decree of Divorce. THOMAS WALKER LYNCH took D   to another doctor to get a Hepatitis A vaccination. Further, he did not subsequently notify me or D   ' physician of the vaccinations. I found out about this only after informing THOMAS WALKER LYNCH that I had taken D   to Dr. Gritzka for his Hepatitis A vaccinations. I requested the name of doctor and the medical record, but Thomas still did not, and until this date, November 8, 2006, has not provided them to me.

b) THOMAS WALKER LYNCH has told D   not to take any medicine I give him without first getting the medication approved by THOMAS WALKER LYNCH. THOMAS WALKER LYNCH has told D   not to take Claritin for his oak pollen allergy, which was recommended by D   ' doctor. As a result, D   refused to take the Claritin.

c) THOMAS WALKER LYNCH has accused Caryl Dalton of hypnotizing D   , and has told D   he has "fired" her. THOMAS WALKER LYNCH also made comments to D   that Caryl Dalton hates him so he instructed D   not to go to see Caryl Dalton. This causes a great conflict between me and D   when it is time to see Caryl Dalton. This also causes great stress for D   when he is forced to decide who to obey when his parents are giving him conflicting instructions. THOMAS WALKER LYNCH has also called the Round Rock police with the complaint that D   was being hypnotized by Caryl Dalton, expressing to the police that D   was in danger. All of these allegations of hypnotizing D   are false.

d) THOMAS WALKER LYNCH has told D   to limit any television viewing while in my care to only Friday night. THOMAS WALKER LYNCH has told D   that the television will make him an idiot. This undermines my authority in my own house and prevents D   from seeing programs which I consider to be part of his

2

education. Contrary to the television restrictions placed on D during my possession of D , THOMAS WALKER LYNCH and D have watched many movies on TV during THOMAS WALKER LYNCH's possession of D , including several television programs I consider inappropriate for an 8 year old child.

e) THOMAS WALKER LYNCH has told D that if I punish him by reducing his allowance, that he will give D the money. This undermines my authority and limits my choices for modifying D ' behavior. I have email records supporting this allegation.

f) THOMAS WALKER LYNCH has repeatedly made serious allegations against me that were all dismissed during the divorce proceedings. THOMAS WALKER LYNCH shows pictures to D of D in bed with me, and tells D that the pictures show that I am trying to smother him with the blanket. THOMAS WALKER LYNCH also tells D that I beat him in the sinuses when he was small, and that is the reason D has allergies. He tells D that I have to poison his dad. This is also documented in a Round Rock police report claim by THOMAS WALKER LYNCH during the divorce. THOMAS WALKER LYNCH tells D that mothers want to kill their children, and shows D internet articles about the Andrea Yates case in Houston, where a woman has killed her children. He asks D questions about whether my leg touches Di when I lay down with him to put him to sleep, insinuating to D that I am sexually abusing him.

g) THOMAS WALKER LYNCH has repeatedly made allegations in front of D that I have abused the dog, Laika, by not giving Laika her rabies vaccinations. I did give the dog her rabies vaccination which I have record of. THOMAS WALKER LYNCH took the dog from my back yard, and immediately took it to a vet with D in attempt to show D that I was not caring for the dog. THOMAS WALKER LYNCH duplicated the rabies shots that the dog already had. When the Round Rock police contacted THOMAS WALKER LYNCH about the dog, THOMAS WALKER LYNCH refused to acknowledge that he had done this, and with D listening, further accused me of not giving the dog its shots and not feeding or watering the dog. All of these accusations are complete lies. In fact, I had been told by the vet in the spring to cut back on the dog's food because it was gaining too much weight, and Laika had since then lost 10 pounds.

h) THOMAS WALKER LYNCH has told D that I have been responsible for ending his hockey and violin lessons, as well as his attendance at a private school run by French administrators, because I hate his dad. The French school program had to end because THOMAS WALKER LYNCH could not pay the tuition payments for the private school, as required of him in the Final Decree of Divorce for any non-public education. The hockey lessons ended because D was preparing to enter the third grade, had more homework, and D was taking swimming, Taekwondo and hockey lessons. D had little time for school work. Because of this I ended the swimming lessons and hockey.

i) THOMAS WALKER LYNCH has made the claim that I am denying dental care for D in his first Responses to Requests for Disclosure. I pay for dental insurance for D . D has been to the dentist two times this year, but THOMAS WALKER LYNCH has not contacted me for the dental records. Instead, he makes unfounded and false claims that I am denying D treatment. This again,

3

314

appears to be intended to impress upon D   that I am not caring for him properly.

8. THOMAS WALKER LYNCH has ignored instructions in the Temporary Restraining Order which prevents the parents from involving the child in parent to parent communications concerning this case. THOMAS WALKER LYNCH prods D   to ask totally inappropriate questions insinuating that I have sexually abused him. THOMAS WALKER LYNCH has asked D   to tell him what beer or other alcohol is in my refrigerator. He also tells D   that the psychiatrist, Caryl Dalton, hates him. These conversations have occurred during the nightly phone conversations that are agreed upon in the Rule 11 Agreement signed on June 14, 2006. THOMAS WALKER LYNCH continues to encourage these topics during the phone conversations. I have informed THOMAS WALKER LYNCH that these topics are not acceptable, yet he continues, and does so increasingly.

"I request that that Court grant my Motion for Additional Temporary Orders.

Further affiant sayeth not.

SIGNED on November 15, 2006.

H'   , Affiant

SUBSCRIBED AND SWORN TO BEFORE ME on November 15, 2006, H'   I.

LENA RENE HIBBARD
Notary Public, State of Texas
My Commission Expires
December 12, 2010

Notary Public, State of Texas

4

Figure 72: H*'s Affidavit For Emergency Hearing During Dad's Christmas Break

This affidavit is a quintessential attack as the best form of defense piece. It raises new allegations that have no basis, and it spins other issues. False allegations made by mom are common in divorces, and perhaps the reason for that is because they are affective. They play into a judges sense of 'looking for the criminal.' One of Margo Fox's styles is to represent things the opposite of what they are. It immediately turns a negative issue for her side into a he says she says debate. All of this stuff fills the landscape full of land mines, because the opposition must address each of these are they remain standing. Margo managed to get a couple of these past the judge.

So in their first point, H* did not lose the passport fight, instead she had one it and I had refused to turn over the passport. The Rule 11 agreement she refers to requires trading at Frost bank, but apparently no one asked them, as they refused to host the exchange. Also recall that this rule 11 agreement they are referring to was part of a settlement that I never signed up to.

The second point was also part of the rule 11 settlement agreement. Also, at this point Steve Thorne had not provided records in accordance with our agreement for an open process.

The third point about Caryl Dalton is related to our divorce decree. H* and I had a joint managing conservatorship for medical. This was uncontested. I had agreed to let her pick doctors while I maintained a veto right. I made this compromise because she had expressed a fear that I would pick doctors who did not like her. However, H* did the exact thing that she said she feared I would do, and picked doctors who would not co-operate with dad. When I tried to fire them, she cried foul. D* did not like Dr. Dalton and complained about her vociferously.

Point four complains that I did not work with Sally Ray, she was in fact the deal killer for the Rule 11 "settlement" agreement as previously explained. So again this is just complaining about the Rule 11 agreement. As the reader will see later when Sally Ray testifies my instincts on this one were right on the mark.

Point five about not responding to disclosure is a low blow, it was never requested from me. I suspect that Margo Fox would say this wasn't a lie because it had been sent to my attorney. This paragraph is then mixed with stuff about the dog. The dog is a sore point for them because D* had written about his mom kicking it, and because he had brought it to me to "save it." Why any of this constitutes an emergency for interrupting D* visit to his Grandma and Grandpa is beyond me.

Point seven is multipart, and it claims to be a list of reasons I had interfered with H*'s parenting. As D* is with me during the Christmas break, what reason could parental interference with H* possible be germane to canceling our vacation?

Point 7a is a serious problem for H* and Margo Fox, as part of the argument for refusing to sign travel papers was that D* did not have travel shots, so I took him to get travel shots and showed them the documentation. It appears to me that after demanding it Margo Fox did not provide the medical information to H*, at least that is an explanation for the accident, as H* took D* to Dr. Gritzka for a second Hepatatis A shot before the end of the boster period. Dr. Gritzka had refused to work with me or to coordinate with another doctor, he had denied sending me records even after a written request. I had tried to fire him for these reasons as I considered it a dangerous situation. Hence, this point vindicates my actions in fire Gritzka, not the other way around.

316

I have to laugh about point 7b as point 7a just got done explaining the problem with trying to coordinate medicine and doctors with H*. I did ask D* to call me and tell me if he was taking anything because of this issue.

Point 7c is inaccurate. Up until compiling this text I was unconvinced that there was any hypnosis going on. The hypnosis accusation was made by Dr. Freitag. Dr. Freitag's opinion did concern me a great deal, and I wanted it investigated further. At the time of H*'s affidavit, no specific hypnotist was named by anyone. H* is either jumping to conclusions here are making a confession. Dalton was guilty of not working with the whole family when she was clearly given the option to step aside in favor of someone who could. She had also initially given me a hard time about providing records, finally sending them to the pediatrician instead. By providing an affidavit and custody opinion Dr. Dalton also violated violated her license by playing a dual role of custody evaluator and therapist. Essentially this means that she sold out D* trust in her by picking a parent. This motion makes this point self-evident, as Dalton's affidavit was with it. This makes this point 7c self contradictory.

Point 7d is another one that made me grin. It is true I am not a fan of daily television viewing especially by a six or seven year old. I discussed this with D* and he did an incredible thing for a child, he decided not to watch as much television. You may recall that H* took D* out of day care after day care as each refused to prevent me from visiting my son. As a last resort she started taking him home from school at 2:45. However, she works full time, so while she telecommuted she put him in front of the television every afternoon. When D* came home from school and complained that he wanted to do something else, she hit the ceiling and started accusing me of parental interference. This was a very old problem by the date of this affidavit, but suddenly now it is an emergency.

Point 7e is of course related to the hundreds in dollars in fines D* had accumulated from his mom as was discussed earlier. He was crying about it at my place, and I calmed his nerves by telling him I would pay his allowance. This is another "black is white" point. Normally a parent would be embarrassed to admit they had docketed so much money from a child's allowance, but now somehow it is my problem.

There is an adage in law, that if you don't have anything convincing to say, say a lot. The very volume of material will make it look serious, so the list continues.

Point 7f is a rewrite of history. The pictures I believe H* is referring to are the ones of her next to D* with his face down in a pillow that were entered into record during the temporary orders hearing. There was an incident at my place where D* was looking through my photo album and started screaming "liar liar liar." It turned out that he had been told what had happened after the Indian Pow Wow as though the temporary order hearing history could be rewritten for D*. Also note, that "pillow" is now called a "blanket." Though, I do regret that D* saw something in my photo album that tipped him off, it is also my opinion that if he had been given a prior explanation he would not have found anything unusual in the pictures.

The next point in 7f turns out to be important as it is also been a subject of spin, and it reappears in yet a different form in her boyfriend's testimony at the final hearing. H* says, "Thomas Walker Lynch tells D* I beat him in the sinuses when he was small." D* had a chronic sore spot on his forehead which he attributed to his mother having hit him. This was highly interesting because of all the accident trips to the hospital due to things such as "running into cabinet doors," and all the testimony at the temporary orders hearing about his mother hitting him. I saw it myself. And despite the existence of all this testimony in the file, D* complaint is now to be blamed on me. Note though, she isn't saying that he actually has the complaint of a pain on his forward, now it is the cause of "allergies." So we are to interrupt our Christmas vacation to the grandfolks because she thinks D* was told by me that H* hitting him caused his allergies when in fact there was already evidence on record that she hit him in the head to cause injuries? So she is mad that it was allergies not injuries D* complained about? This is further testimony that H* is actively working on having me blamed for things she was blamed for at the temporary orders hearing.

The next point in 7f actually speaks to the television point. D* was left free with the remote, and he was watching news shows. They could have picked from among several adult themes that D* was talking about. This one plays into my views about misandrists.

Point 7g is a 'black is white' allegation. D* has been writing essays about his mom kicking the dog, and now H* claims that he is not writing what he saw, but rather that I have been telling him that the dog has been kicked. This is now an example of Dad talking bad about mom and it is bad for dad to do. No one who has listened to D* on this subject has expressed any doubts about the origin of the problem, but D* doesn't get to testify – rather the paid misandrist psychologist is to testify for him. It is also interesting how they spun the dog being lose without tags into a debate about vaccines. I suppose one of the tags is the rabies tag, but the significance of the dog not having tags was that it appeared to have been set out on its own, and if it bit someone, there were be no tags on the dog. This type of sideways allegations is how attorneys like Margo Fox hide the truth of a matter during a hearing within a big mix up of issues. Another example of this same technique of obfuscation found in this document is the changing of the beating on the forehead to an issue on allergies.

Point 7h is a very low tactic to get a judges attention and to blame me again. Of course D* knows his mom refused to take him to practice and lessons on her days. Funny she then goes on to explain why she took him out, thus admitting she did so rather than it being D   choice. This contradicts her other testimony.

Point 7i This is an attack as the best defense to cover the fact that H* did not take D* to the dentist for the first couple of years she was the primary care taker.

Point 7g is more attack as the best defense. D* says that Dalton hates his dad. No one told him to say it. D* did call me once complaining that his mom was drinking and he did not feel safe at the house. This ended up as a police record as he repeated it. As far as the rest of it no evidence of my saying bad things in phone conversations was ever presented to the court.

H Threatens D* if He Doesn't Go See Dr. Dalton 2006 12 21*

Says she will wipe his Penguin World account clean. This is three months of accumulation in virtual world of toys, money, and skill. Both D* and H* understand this. In addition she says he will not get to have an overnight with his friend. Given the lawsuit they filed one can understand her desperation to make D* go.

It is clear that D* doesn't like the therapist, and dad doesn't like her, why does she continue on? Years prior I sent her a letter suggesting we use a different therapist who could work with both parents, but she continued on.

318

H* and the Too Small Clothes

After the divorce we had the usual petty stuff such as the small clothes always coming back to my place. Unlike for most couples, this would never end. Just this last weekend of December 1st 2006 D* arrived with a pair of pants I hadn't seen in two years. They were the dress pants he had worn to Grandma's funeral. He had them on so tight that the steel clasp was bending.

D* got a laptop this year and has been writing essays on it. He also wrote this one about the clothes:

> My mom was keeping all the underware and now she is keeping all the pants. And she is sending me back in jim shorts. I do not like that and so does my dad does to. She is alsoe sending me back in the same close as I came in with out eving washing them. She alsoe did that with the shirts to. And she did that with my boots. to In sept she sendid them back there to small. [D* 2006 09]

H* tends to recirculate shirts and pants that I send back to her in the exact same condition as she receives them. For underwear she typically keeps the boxers, and sends back the jockey shorts. The problem is that D* grows so fast, that after two or four weeks some clothes no longer fit well. However, there is an exception for pants that fit well. D* is overweight and it is very difficult to shop for his pants, as those that fit his waist tend to be too long. Because of this H* took taken up sewing in order to shorten pants. I hemmed some by hand or bought elastic wastes. When I send him back with pants that fit well, he is returned in gym shorts. With all the other stuff going on, I have always just ignored this.

Apparently H* enjoys sewing and enjoys the image it creates of her mothering D*, as she bragged about it. I'm all for clothes that fit. I'm not for needles in the carpet or food.

Apparently for the case of the dress pants, D* said he refused to wear the pants she wanted to send him in because they were dirty, so she reached farther into the stash.

H* also targeted clothes that had any meaning. She disposed of a T-shirt that he got on a trip with his dad on the Silverton Line from Durango. H* kept the suit D* wore to great grandma Maxine's funeral. The boot and hat were returned exactly one year after the funeral, and were too small by then. And as I mentioned above, the pants just now made a return.

Hired Attorney Mark Roles December 2006

The Texas Bar runs an attorney referral service. The bar, being a professional organization for attorneys simply provides the next name on their list. Any attorney in good standing may be on the list. The person who answers the phone has no knowledge the attorneys. The database allows the referral service clerk to search under specialty and location. I called the attorney referral service and requested an attorney who specialized in both legal and medical malpractice. They gave me the name and telephone number of Mark Roles Esq.

I called and Mark answered the phone directly. He confirmed that he did both legal and medical malpractice. I explained a little of what was happening. He said he would address the family matter first.

I was relieved to have found an attorney an attorney who would work on the case at last.

The Emergency Hearing December 19 2006

Mark had all my friends come to the hearing. People were outraged that H* would ask for supervised visitation, and willingly complied. Mike Taborn, Ray Truitt, Annie Truitt, Paul Wood, Mark Scheyer, Penny Gastineau, and Gary Gastineau all sat in the hall and waited. All but three of them had driven up from Galveston where D* and I had been spending the majority of our time, as Mystique was moored there. H* brought two witnesses, Caryl Dalton, and David Baxter. I spoke with David in the hall, and I couldn't figure out why he was there. He is the father of a child that D* plays with.

Mark came out of the courtroom and said that the judge ruled there was no emergency.

I was wiped out. I had been up for days preparing material and organizing witnesses. I needed sleep. We were supposed to have been in Arizona visiting grandma and grandpa, and we were planning to drive. On the 21st I spoke with my folks about driving up. It made little sense. We would be two days in the car, could only stay a day, maybe two at this point, and then would have drive back. And these were just our plans. All of the people who waited in the hall also interrupted their schedules by taking off work to be there.

H*'s attorney, Margo Fox tried twice again to push the supervised visit, and twice again was denied.

Mark Roles: Give the Passport Back, Will/Won't/Will/Won't Subpoena Steve Thorne's Records

Right out the gate Mark Roles created a confrontation by insisted that I follow the settlement agreement Felix Ripply had made when he knew that Felix had just been fired due to it.

Mark insisted that I give H* the passport. I had just got done suing to get the passport renewal papers signed, a judge had to order H* to sign them. H* had used the opportunity not to renew it to ruin my vacation. Why would I now just hand her the passport? I compromised. I told Mark that if H* provided international travel plans, and a promise to return the passport upon return, I would give it to her before the travel. But H* had no travel plans, she just wanted to control the passport. In H*'s mind, she owned or had to own everything. Mark wanted that I put the passport in a Frost Bank safety deposit box where only representatives from Frost Bank myself and H* would be present when the box was opened. Felix had original suggested this. First off, why would I do this? Secondly, it is unworkable. No one else asked Frost Bank. I stopped by the branch where we were to supposed to do this and they said there was no such bank service, and they would not make up such an accommodation for us.

Then Mark insisted on using Sally Ray – exactly the issue that fomented problems with Felix Rippy. Sally then told Mark that she was closing her practice due to having cancer.

Mark insisted that I use Dr. Thorne. Everyone agreed it was to be an open process. "Good," I said, "then show us the papers that Sarah Brandon and Margo Fox sent over there." Well it was an open process, but not open for me. I was assured by Mark that all of the papers would be seen after the report was complete. What is the point of that? One the report was made there would be nothing to debate. Dr. Throne agreed with me that we should not

320

continue until the question of the papers was settled. However, he also stipulated, that he would not provide any of the papers he had unless the other side agreed. There had never been any constraint placed on an 'open process' before. No one said only the parts with permission were open. Margo Fox did not give permission.

I requested that Mark subpoena the records. He said he didn't want to. He didn't give any legal reason. He did not given any reason related to the case, or my son's well being or my well being. It was his personal preference. I hired Bill Jang and Glynn Turquand to provide Mark with an opinion. When we met, they all agreed that the records should be subpoenaed, and Mark agreed to do it.

But there was no subpoena. Mark had changed his mind. I got everyone together on a phone conference. Again we, including Mark agreed to do it. This time Mark sent me an email saying that 'several' of Austin colleagues recommended he not write the subpoena. I asked him who it was that was working on my case besides him. He would not tell me who the several were. I said, 'several' that is six or seven people. He said it wasn't that many.

I again brought Glynn Turquand in to give an opinion. This time Mark simply withdrew rather than write the subpoena. I was really screwed.

I remain of the opinion that the records sent to Dr. Thorne, if indeed he still has them, contain a direct damaging information for my ex wife's case and attorneys involved in this case, or why else would the attorneys fight their discovery so strongly? And this wasn't the end of the fight over not showing the Thorne records. There was to be much more.

Carol Dalton's Long Maniacal Laugh, 2007 02 14

My son begged me to do something about Caryl Dalton. I felt something was happening so I decided to draw her out by taking up her now years old invitation to come visit. I had a recorder in my pocket. One of the more interesting things about this meeting was Caryl Dalton's maniacal cackle, when she was asked if D* had any opinions. It sounded just like the Wicked Witch of the East, no joke. Note also, Dr. Dalton explains that she uses a room that is too small for two adults to be in it at the same time, so no one gets to observe her.

Dalton quit as D* therapist after this, and just about the same day H*'s attorney proposed a new one. This time there was some fight first.

H* would not tell me the time of the appointment, so I came early with my laptop and sat in the waiting room. As I was walking up a woman was coming out with her children. While I was there another woman with her child left. Right after they left, Caryl Dalton picked up the phone. One could hear plainly in the waiting room. She dialed and said, "Hello Sara?" She continued to discuss the prior patient, a door closed, and then I couldn't hear anymore. A little later D* came in.

D*	Dad!?
H*	Use the restroom
father	What's this?
D*	A little drawing board.
H*	You need to get into the restroom.
D*	It is an erasable drawing board.
	[Waiting D in restroom.]
Dalton	Hi! I heard you all come in.
H*	Yes
Dalton	He in the restroom?
H*	Uh um have you met tom lynch
Dalton	No I haven't
father	Actually I think I saw you in ah
Dalton	I've never met you before. So I'm Dr. Caryl Dalton
father	[not shaking hand] Yes I know
Dalton	Ok well
H*	I haven't invited him because I don't know. He was trying to talk to me about when there was a session and what day. And ah, here. He said he found it. That's fine but.. I don't know what. Usually you have an interview separately with the parent and then something like this. I don't know. [H* had declined to provide appointment info to dad.]
Dalton	This is D*'s session right now. If you would like a session I think I've given you plenty of opportunity to set that up.
father	I think I would like to observe D*.
Dalton	I'm sorry but I don't do that with parents. This is the play therapy session with D*. If you would like to come in for that.
father	I would like to know what play therapy is.
Dalton	I'll be glad to set up an appointment with you to discuss that.
father	I would rather watch.
Dalton	That's not an option.
father	D* tells me that you have been asking him to imagine scenarios.
Dalton	Well if you would like to discuss some things with me I would be glad to set a time to do that, but this is a time with D* and I'm not going to put him in the middle by having you ask me to have him to ask those questions. That is not an appropriate thing.
father	I didn't say anything about putting D* in the middle.
	All I said is that I would like to observe.
Dalton	Yes sir, and I am not willing to do that.
father	I would like to ask you again to stop seeing my son.
Dalton	Uhm. I hear that. Uhm. I think that there is an instruction from the judge.
father	That was in 2001 and we have had many years
Dalton	No sir this was recently. There was an instruction that your attorney conveyed to me and the other attorney conveyed to me, and the judge

322

said that his therapy should not be interfered with. Uhm. If I am misunderstanding that I would appreciate some notification from you attorney in that regard. I would be *happy* to set up a time for you and D* to do a family session if that is what you want, but this is a time I setup to be with D* and I don't have parent's observe that. First of all the room is too tiny for two adults and a child, and it would not be his therapy.

[D* enters]

father	Do you want to be here?
D*	No
father	D* tells me he doesn't want to be here. He has told me this a number of times over the years. I would like to know why.
Dalton	D* enjoys being here with me.
Dalton	You are putting him in the middle and this is really bad for him.
father	No. D* doesn't get a voice?
Dalton	He does get a voice but ..
father	D* lets hear your voice.
D*	I don't want to be here.
Dalton	Ok D* when I have asked you that question, you have said you liked being here.
father	How many times did they ask you? [father to D*]
D*	A bunch!
father	He tells me that you guys ask him over and over again.
Dalton	This is really inappropriate to put D* in the middle like this.
father	It is inappropriate that I have to come out here to protect my son from you.
Dalton	D* would you go in the other room please.
father	D* would you stay here please.
D*	Ok
H*	Do you want to talk to me outside? Lets go? Because they have grown up talk.
Dalton	It is grown up talk time.
father	No its time to listen to D*'s side. I came here so that he could speak without feeling threatened.
H*	Common on D* …
Dalton	[in a soft pathetic voice] D* I have ever threatened you? Look at me not your dad when you answer.
D*	[looking directly at Dalton] yes
Dalton	[still in a pathetic voice] how have I threatened you?
D*	Like saying that my mom will ground me and such.
Dalton	No I have never said your mom will ground you.
D*	Yeah you did!
Dalton	No I didn't. That is not a threat to you from me and I have never done that.

D*	Yeah you did.
father	I think I have heard enough about you that I believe him.
Dalton	You know I think this is very inappropriate it is putting your son in the middle and it making him really uncomfortable.
father	No No this is my protecting my son. Do you feel uncomfortable about this D*?
D*	[interpreting this as visiting Dalton in general] Yeah
Dalton	I feel very uncomfortable too. [very kindly] D* what were you and I going to do today?
D*	I don't even *want* to be here.
Dalton	I didn't ask you that.
father	Actually I think that is highly significant that he doesn't want to be here.
Dalton	You know he is saying that to make you happy Mr. Lynch.
D*	No I'm not!
Dalton	Ok, what were you and I going to do today?
father	He is saying this .. [because that is what he thinks, Dalton talks over top.]
Dalton	You asked me to let him answer, I would like for you to let him answer. D* what were and I going to do today.
D*	Playing here. I don't like playing here though! I would rather be at home. It is boring here. You ask me a bunch of questions!
Dalton	Of course I do.
D*	I don't like it.
Dalton	I ask you questions, you ask me why do you ask me that, because I ask all kids, how did you have a good time at Christmas.
father	Look if in five years if you haven't been able to make a better rapport with my son than this.
Dalton	I have a good rapport, but you are interfering with it right now.
father	I'm his father, I'm not the interfering party, but there is someone else who is
Dalton	I'm not going to do this in front of your son, because it is inappropriate [walks over grabs the door]
father	Thank God
Dalton	It is mom's possession time. It is time to be with mom. It's not father's time. So you know, I can step out of the way, but its your mom's time, and your father can not make you go with him.
father	[to D*] She is not a judge it is not her place to dictate laws.
Dalton	It is not about being a _judge_.
father	I thought you said you were leaving?
Dalton	You know I am not going to let you put words in *my mouth*! So ..
H*	We came here for to correct his behavior.
father	I came here to observe ..
H*	The school counselor asked it too.

father	The school counselor?
H*	Yes! Everyone ..
father	The school counselor hasn't said anything to me.
Dalton	Lets not have that discussion in front of D*, that's not gonna be helpful. [The school counselor was asked not to work with D*, but does anyway. Dalton may not want this known.]
H*	[talking to D*] I know you are having more fun playing with the kids. That is for sure. I understand these. But you want to be a responsible right?
D*	I don't want to be here!
H*	I know..
D*	You just ask me questions.
Dalton	That is not true.
H*	You can ask question too!
Dalton	D* that is not true.
D*	Things that you didn't even talk about.
Dalton	[sing song voice] D* that is not true.
father	It appears to me that he is afraid to express his own opinion without my being here.
Dalton	Scoffing D* expresses his opinion *big* time [highly sarcastic, breaking off into a cackle -- no exaggeration ~9:40]
father	Well lets hear his opinion then.
D*	I don't really want to be here.
father	I think you are leaving.
Dalton	[To H*] If you want to go ahead and play it might be useful.
H*	Yeah.
D*	No..
H*	This is ..
D*	Only if my dad gets to be there.
Dalton	[curtly] No. It is not his time. I have told your father he could make a different time. You and your father and I could talk at a different time. This is your time. I've told your father that before too.
D*	My mom told me that my dad should be here. Now he is here and ..
H*	Should be here?
D*	Yeah that is what you said.
H*	No.
D*	Now you say when he came here he shouldn't be here.
H*	Should be here or shouldn't be here, I don't understand. [in a cute voice] I don't talk about this thing at all.
D*	[audible heavy sigh]
father	Hey D* do you think these sessions are useful for you?
D*	_No_
Dalton	I don't think that is a appropriate thing to ask him Mr. Lynch because I'm not sure he will be able to make the determination.

father	How convenient for you.
H*	I think we should show respect, that is what D* has to learn
father	No I would have showed respect years ago but um..
H*	Should respect for the other people, that is what *he has to learn*
father	I think what we need now is for D* to not to be forced to do something he doesn't want to do.
D*	I show respect!
Dalton	You do, you do a nice job of showing respect
D*	What do you mean I don't show respect to other people?
Dalton	She wasn't talking to you
father	She was saying that is what D* needed to learn. I think he interpreted the statement correctly.
D*	Look at lunch I giving people ice creams OK? with my lunch money! That what .. How am I not…
Dalton	No D* she did not say you did not have respect.
D*	Yeah she did, that is why I am in here. AND I DO
H*	You do respect yes
Dalton	Sometimes you do
H*	Not Not always though
Dalton	Sometimes you told me about how you yell at your father, sometimes you tell me how you yell your mom.
D*	I didn't yell, tell that I yell at my father too. I don't yell at my father.
Dalton	Sometimes you told me you had done that..
father	Talk about putting kids in the middle, it is amazing.
Dalton	Ok
father	You know a lot of your colleagues could serve the role of meeting all of us. [Dalton walks out in mid sentence, you can hear the door slam]
H*	This is my time, and this is not appropriate really. You should leave.
father	If D* is staying here I am, unless ..
H*	You don't have any right for that. What What
father	I have a perfect right to be here.
H*	Wow.
father	He is my son too.
H*	I never denied that.
father	D* has told me a lot of things that make me concerned, and you have not been willing to discuss those things with me.
H*	He *waaas* doing very good, ok? We had a good time at school and the Valentine party and everything look.
father	And I ruined that?
H*	Yes. You are.
D*	How? Just because he didn't get donuts, you didn't get donuts.
H*	[laughing] what donut things?
D*	How did he ruin it?
H*	D* don't touch that trim ..

326

D*	How did he ruin it?
	[pause]
father	Anyway I am not here to have the discussion with you right now, I am here because …
H*	This is my possession time you don't have any right to come over here.
father	If you would like to leave with him that is fine.
H*	No you have to leave. She is not going to see him today. You are destructing me.
father	Well if she is not going to see him today, then why are you staying?
H*	You are here so there is no way. You are not supposed to here, that is why. We are not supposed to meet each other.
	[pause]
H*	[childish voice] You want to leave with me?
D*	I want to live with my dad.
H*	[angry] No LEAVE. [soft again] Right now.
D*	I would rather leave with my dad, but I would like to leave .. right now.
H*	No this my time, tomorrow is dad's time, ok? Thursday.
father	I'll pick you up tomorrow
D*	Ok … dad? Can you come to lunch tomorrow.
father	I'll see if I have time, I can't promise.
D*	Ok
H*	Lets go.
D*	Can I hug my dad before I go?
	[after getting home, H* called D* a liar, and grounded him.]

Figure 73: Discussion With D Child Psychologist*

H* to D*: You will Never See Your Best Friend Again If You Tell, 2007 02 20

T> How long did you get grounded for?

D> A day.

T> Just one day?

T> Turn around so I can hear you.

T> what is that?

T> what did you say?

D> I'm not going to see T* if I do it again.

T> If you do what again?

D> Tell about it.

T> Tell about what?

D> Use my voice.

T> Whats that?

D> Use my voice.

T> What do you mean. Tell about what?

D> About her and Caryl Dalton thing.

T> If you talk about it again what is going to happen?

D> I'm going to get it.

T> What?

D> Ground for ah I'm sure I'm not going to get see T*, and get grounded.

T> What do you mean about finding your voice?

D> Talking saying the things, telling

T> So she told you not to tell the truth?

D> No she said I was lying.

T> Yeah, but were you telling the truth?

D> Yes.

Figure 74: D Punished For Saying He Wants to Live With Dad, Threatened If He Says It Again*

dad Investigated By CPS, Brings Recordings and Is Told: "You are not allowed to give evidence."

A friend who was very concerned for D* gave me Lt. Governor Dewhurt's phone number. Lt. Governor Dewhust had run for election on the plank of reforming CPS. Indeed it turned out to be his cell phone number. I did get to talk to him personally, though I never heard back anything.

I was then reported to CPS by someone, if I were to hazard a guess, it was someone at the school as they had the book I gave the principal. I was investigated for giving D* anti-feminist views.

I was initially contacted by Stephanie Mousakowski at 388-6139 on 2007 02 23. I returned her call, and then went to the CPS office and dropped off a CD with the recordings of D* talking about his dog being kicked, being given needles in his candy, being threatened if he "used his voice", among others.

I was then told to come for an interview and that Stephanie was no longer handling the case. Instead her manager had taken over. We went upstairs to a woman's office (Bridge Johnson?) she said she was the manager. She wanted to know if I had read a book called, "War On Boys." She was concerned that I may have an antifeminist view point, and asked me such things as how I would feel if my boss was a woman. I said I wanted to talk about the disk. I was told the disk was not being put in the file because "**you are not allowed to give evidence.**" She explained that evidence could only come from investigators such as herself.

I informed Lt. Governor Dewhurst's office. There was no reply. Later I also informed the CPS investigator Charity Rowlins of the recordings. She said there was nothing she could do. I called Stephanie Mousakowski back this year as they never told me if they closed the investigation. My understanding is that a person is supposed to be both informed of the opening and closing, but I have never received any correspondence from CPS. She did not return any or my calls.

Mark Withdraws of Thorne Records, H* Loses Request for Temporary Orders, Appointment of Attorney Amicus James P. Wallace 2007 03 02

Mark had quit working on the case for some time, but his official withdraw hearing was in the morning of March 02. I couldn't imagine holding him against his will as I figured he would just screw me even worse, as the other had done, so I did not oppose it. He withdrew rather than subpoena the records from Dr. Thorne, but at the withdraw he called it 'a communications problem with his client' It was bizarre, and it made me feel bad in the pit of my stomach. I was screwed. By default I became a pro se' litigant. This is not something I wanted. I was actively searching for another attorney.

That same day Margo Fox, H*'s attorney scheduled a temporary orders hearing, requesting supervised visitation, yet again. She lost, but Judge Jurgin's appointed an attorney Amicus. A Mr. James P. Wallace. Mr. Wallace is the son of a Texas Supreme Court justice, and himself has run for judge in Williamson county.

Interview With Attorney John Izzo

John Izzo has an office in the downstairs of what appears to be a newly built old house. John has added all sorts of additions inside to make the place look like grandma's place. The Texas Bar referral told me that John would charge $25 for an initial consultation. He charged me $450 instead. He has sent me an invoice for an additional $18 every month since then.

John spent a long time telling me about his story. He was divorced in Arizona and, like me, his wife tried to keep his kids from him. He then became a pro se' litigant, like me. This was before he got his law degree. He says he managed to get co-operation between both democrats and republicans to get the laws changed, to then just watch his wife move away. He said that in the end he won, because when his son was 16 he flew himself back to John's place. I begged to differ, missing one's child's complete childhood, and half of his teenage years, is not "winning." John appeared to take insult to this.

John told me that he knew even before he had launched into his story, that he knew he wouldn't take me as a client, because I had had other attorneys before. It is a rule among attorneys, which has now been explained to me by half a dozen attorneys, that attorneys should avoid clients who have had other attorneys before. Those who explain this say it is because the it indicates a problem with the client. I actually agree, the fact that a client complains indicates that he is catching on to the fact that he is getting screwed, and this of course will be a problem for the next guy who tries to screw him, as John did by taking $450 from me so I could hear his life story. What John did is identical to what Larry Schubhut did, and that is he talked about unrelated items to take up time for them, and then charged for it, which had the added benefit of making him appear diligent.

Hearing on April 24ᵗʰ - Jergins Recuses Himself In Favor of Death Penalty Judge Jon Wisser

At two in the morning the night before the hearing, someone knocked on my apartment door loudly and woke me up. I did not answer it.

Still I felt the hearing went well. I caught Margo Fox lying, she said she was not going to call witnesses, but did. Later Margo made a depends on what the word "is" "is" argument and said that she did not 'intend' to call witnesses. No matter I had no warning. James Wallace did not at all come across as a neutral party. At one point the judge had to tell him to sit down. The judge made a remark or two that was not becoming.

The transcript done by Judge Jergins court reporter Paula Jones came back with a couple of the less favorable things taken out, including the part where Jergins told Wallace to sit down. I asked for them to be put back, the next day the judge recused himself. In his place we were assigned the Honorable Judge Jon Wisser. Judge Jon Wisser is best known for doing death penalty cases. He has sent hundreds of to their deaths.

This was unfortunate. Of the many issues put before judge Jurgins, we had not lost one.

When Judge Wisser heard our divorce modification hearing, we were given a court all to ourselves. The judge had no other cases, he was there just for us, so the room was always empty, all except for us. Nor was there anyone waiting outside to be next. When judge Wisser would seat himself, he would walk in very quickly without looking at anyone. He hold his arms up causing his black robe to open below his arms like to large black wings. it would then settle down as he seated himself. At first I considered that because he was a small man he did this so that the robe would not catch on the wood framing around his elevated seat, but I came to see it as a dramatic show. Surely it put the fear of God into the hearts of those waiting to see if they were going to be sentenced to death to see a very image of the angel of death. The alpha was easily enough identified. He was the largest and blackest of them all, and he was perched the highest.

From the start Judge Wisser fell over himself to be friendly with the opposing counsel. He smiled and chatted with them from the bench, it was though he was being apologetic for their having to be there. In contrast when I spoke to him he once called me "irresponsible."

One of of the things he joked about was that doing death penalties was easier than divorces. He did this from the stand also put this in his email's to counsel. After he did this a number of times, asked him to stop talking about death penalties in this context of the divorce, as I thought it was inappropriate for a divorce modification hearing. I asked him to consider how it made us feel. He didn't bring it up again in the open courtroom, but he did tell my nine year old son he did death penalties during the conferral. It was a sort of kick under the table.

James Wallace and the Attorney Fee Shakedown

I made up an information packet for Jim Wallace. It documented my raising D* and our activities together and dropped it by his office on a disk. When I got there I spoke with the receptionist to see if she knew how to read it. I had been burned using digital data with Larry Schubhut Sr. and I didn't want to have it happen again. She invited me around the corner, and I showed her how to put it in the machine and click on it. She thanked me, then I left.

A little later I got a call from James Wallace. I was still in Georgetown. He was pissed. He said he didn't want me 'using his office's computers'.

According to the Texas statute, Mr. Wallace's fees must be set by the court, and they must consider my ability to pay. Mr. Wallace did not subscribe to this point of view, and he demanded payment of $5000, which I just didn't have. In order to get leverage towards his demand, Jim Wallace did not interview a single one of my witnesses. The reasoning appeared to be that only H*'s story would be presented to the court as only she had paid him. If I wanted to have D* experience told to the court, well I would have to pay Jim Wallace. I explained to him that I didn't have enough money to pay that much as his colleagues had already gotten all my money, but would pay him later. He wouldn't cut me any slack, the quid pro quo remained, and my witnesses were ignored. I had $1200 I that was set aside for my boat insurance, and I gave it to him. then he sued me for the rest of his fee.

Judge Wisser repeatedly called Mr. Wallace an ad item. I even gave judge Wisser a copy of judge Lerhman's book on child advocacy in Texas, but he continued. After Mystique sank and there were real damages, and James Wallace resigned as attorney amicus. Upon his parting, Judge Wisser ordered me to pay James Wallace an additional $3000 although he had just resigned and no longer needed the retainer. I was to pay him simply because the attorneys can force a person to do so.

Mike Boulch wrote Jim Wallace and brought up the issues of Caryl Dalton.

From the Desk Of Michael Boulch   March 26, 2007
2693 Lake View Drive
Canyon Lake, TX
830-899-7614

James Wallace
213 A West 8th Street
Georgetown, Texas 78626

RE: In the Interest of D   ,
Mr. Wallace,

I am a forensics specialist and a certified expert witness.   I specialize in interviewing suspects as well as victims of crimes and abuse. I have interviewed hundreds of people, many of them children.   I am an adjunct professor at the University of Houston Downtown CJC.   I have taught forensics since 1979 throughout the US and Canada.

I interviewed D   on March 04, 2007, and again on March 21, 2007, and I must agree with Dr. Freitag.   There are indications that this child has undergone some form of mental conditioning to be apprehensive about his father.

The child has recounted a session, which he attributes to Caryl Dalton, where he was instructed that if he "lived with his father he would never see his mother again."   The child also states that his mother reinforced these images. The child also attributes to the therapist and his mother: that he was told that he would not live with his father because his father does not have a house.

Asking the child about these items, or to talk about what happens during visits with Caryl Dalton in general causes the child a great deal of stress and anxiety. However, when his father returned to the office the child immediately became calm.

In my opinion it would be prudent to further question the motives of the mother, and to keep the child in a positive and safe environment.   If you have any questions, don't hesitate to contact me.

Sincerely,

Michael Boulch

Figure 75: Mike Boulch Confirms Hypnosis Being Used On D*, Informs Jim Wallace of Issues With Caryl Dalton

332

Hired Attorney Tim Whitten 2007 05 09

Tim said he would try the case diligently, he would bring up that Dalton said she was a student of shamanism, and that he would subpoena the Thorne records. I explained that I didn't want a bunch of psychologists involved because I didn't believe they had value and they were too expensive. He agreed to take the case for $20,000 dollar retainer. He said that it could not possibly run out to $45,000 total when we were done. He said he had never seen one go that high. Because I had been burned so many times, I brought an attorney to the corroborate what Tim Whitten said, a Mr. Howard Skaist who owns the Berkeley Law and technology group agreed to this.

I borrowed the $20,000 that Tim Whitten required for a retainer and it was wired to him on Monday morning, 2007 05 14.

The Dalton deposition was set for 05 14. The first hearings were set for 05 18. Margo Fox refused to continue matters. She felt that I had already spent too long looking for an attorney, and she express being pissed off that the 2007 05 08 hearings were delayed while Glynn Turquand looked at the case. (Glynn Turquand could not take the case after he found out that Brian Walters had been involved at an earlier point, as Brian was a a law partner.)

As Steve Thorne would not be a custody evaluator until the records issue was settled, Tim wanted a replacement. Tim also wanted to agree to the a therapist.

Tim spent an inordinate amount of time talking to me about my finances. I told him what I knew, and asked him to ask my accountant. He drilled me over and over again. It was obvious that he thought I was hiding something, but I wasn't.

Othe stand H* and asked if she wanted a custody evaluator she replied by asking, "Isn't that what we are doing here?"   I thought to myself, "yes, isn't that what we could have done at just about every hearing since a year ago?"   I didn't want a custody evaluator, and now I find out that it wasn't H*'s idea either. The lawyers had created it by telling each of us the other insisted. This was yet another data point that suggests that the divorce was a creation of the lawyers. The prior one was when H* and I hired Brian Walters to end divorce and fire the other attorneys - but they kept going. Nor did Brian follow through. Had he brought this before a judge and explained what had happened, it would have ended then.

Mr. Whitten took a pass on the therapist motion and allowed it.

Margo Fox again failed to get her temporary orders request.

The judge ruled that he was not against seeing the child, but not now.

I had prepared an motion to dismiss the attorney amicus. All through this hearing the judge kept calling Jim Wallace the attorney *ad litem*, not *Amicus*. Mr. Wallace explained that he was not an ad litem. The judge ruled that he would keep the Amicus.

Judge Wisser accepted the Motion for Payment of Attorney's Fees from Mr. Wallace. I was given until June 15 to pay $2, 500.00. So much for my boat insurance renewal.

During the interim attorneys fee request hearing the opposing counsel asked me what was the most amount of money I ever made in one month. I answered honestly, $360,000. That was a month I closed on the sail of the intellectual property from my business. I had used it to buy a place to live, the boat. Tim Whitten did not follow up. He left me there with my fanny hanging out in the wind looking like a millionaire, but no cross examination by Tim Whitten. I knew he knew better because if anything he had spent time talking about finances. I was ordered to pay $8000 in H*'s interim attorney fees. My accountant had been there in the morning, but Tim had let him go.

I was living on my boat in Galveston and coming to Austin for hearings and to visit D*. Because of expenses I had to let the apartment in Austin go. During the discussion of my finances Tim suggested that I was probably wrong about my being able to claim the boat as a homestead. This is the second email he sent on the subject. The thing that caught my attention in his saying the "your boat is primarily for pleasure," while I was living on it.

Tom Lynch <

(no subject)

Carla   Tue, Jun 19, 2007 at 5:32 PM
To: Tom Lynch <
Cc: Howard Skaist   , Tim Whitten <   >

Tom, attached are two sections out of the Legal Treatise regarding homestead and exempt personal property. I did a little research about whether or not your boat could be used to satisfy a judgment for attorney's fees. I am not an expert on real estate law and if you really want to dig deeper, it would be a good idea for me to confer with one of my fellow attorneys who is board certified in real estate law. It looks like to me that the boat would not be considered a homestead. Generally, homestead is exempt from seizure for satisfaction of debts or judgments except for limited circumstances as you can see. However, it appears that homesteads are for land, whether they be urban or rural. The personal property exemptions in the second attachment do specifically mention boats, but they require the boats to be used in a trade or profession. I have not done any specific research to try to flesh out what is meant by trade or profession. My understanding is that your boat is primarily for pleasure, but I am not completely sure about the use.

So, without doing more, it looks like to me that you do have some exposure. This is something that we will need to think about when we think about what type of strategy we will have with the case and how we are going to proceed. If you feel like I need to do more research regarding this issue, please let me know and I will talk to another attorney with more experience in this area. Of course, the real estate attorney would want a retainer in order to research this issue, assuming they do not know the answer right off the top of their head. I estimate an attorney could spend 3-5 hours at least researching this issue so it could cost you some money.

We can talk more about this later when we have our conference call.

Cc: Howard Skaist

Tim Whitten

Board Certified – Family Law

Texas Board of Legal Specialization

Confidentiality Notice: This email and any files transmitted with it are confidential and intended solely for the use of the intended addressee. This communication may contain material protected by the attorney-client privilege and is not intended to be disclosed to anyone other than the intended recipient. If for any reason you believe that you are not the intended recipient or the person responsible for delivering the email to the intended recipient, please be advised that any use, dissemination, forwarding, printing, or copying of this email is strictly prohibited. If you have received this email in error, please notify Tim Whitten or his staff immediately by replying to this message or calling us at 512-478-1011. Thank you.

Figure 76: Whitten's Opinion that Mystique Can be Taken

335

Then came the hearing to compel discovery of the Steve Thorne records. I had written the motion. Tim had agreed to argue it. He didn't want to, but I held him to his promise. This is the very issue that I had paid very dearly to have heard. The Honoroble Judge Jon Wiser looked down from the bench and specifically asked Margo Fox, the opposing counsel, what was in the records. *Tim Whitten answered.* When Mrs. Fox hesitated, Tim took the attention of the judge, "I believe I can answer that your honor." It was a little strange. How could he have any idea of what was in the Thorne records? That was our whole point, we needed to discovery them.

Margo Fox argued that Steve Thorne was now her consulting witness. It was a lie (I would later subpoena Thorne, and he would testify that he was not Margo's consultant.), but Steve Thorne was not there. Why wasn't he there? Tim Whitten had let him out of the subpoena.

The After the May 18 Hearing, Tim's First, $29,000 Invoice from Tim Whitten

After the hearing Tim invoiced me for the entire $20,000 retainer, plus another about $9,000. He now explained the new numbers to Howard Skaist, but repeated his promise that he would see the case through.

Tim was not interested in hearing about the history of the case. Like all the others, he couldn't tell me what was on the case disk. His only interest was in settling for as little money as possible and he felt that this could be done through mediation. He harped on my to think about H*. Although he wasn't familiar with the case history, he was convinced we would lose.

Mr. Whitten was way off base about mediation. Mediation had never worked with H*. H* would go into a mediation and ask for everything, and set that as a bottom line. And why wouldn't she, with the exception of the passport issue, H* had never lost. As Felix Rippy put succinctly, H* felt that the American legal system was a Burger King, she would get it as she ordered it. When I explained this to Tim he simply didn't believe me. As it turned out Tim got his way – we did end up mediating. H* walked in, asked for everything, sat for four hours not giving and inch, and left.

When my opinion didn't fit with Tim's world view, it was because I was not being unreasonable, not because Tim's world view was inaccurate.

Tim burned up our time together arguing with me about what he wanted for case strategy, when I steadfastly requested that he follow through as promise, do his homework about the case, and then try the case. Howard Skaist reminded me that he Tim Whitten had an obligation to do what he was hired for, and he called Tim Whitten just to make sure that Tim Whitten understood what I wanted.

---------- Forwarded message ----------
From: "Howard Skaist" <------>

To: "Tom Lynch" <----->

Date: Mon, 16 Jul 2007 20:22:47 -0800

Subject: RE: Lynch

Fyi – told Whitten that you want him to go to trial and try to win, even though you realize the odds are against winning.

He also said that he was only referring to one hour long conversation. I quizzed him a bit about that. I am beginning to agree with you that he may be a bit slippery.

Regards,

Howard Skaist

Founder/Principal Counsel

Berkeley Law & Technology Group, LLP

17933 NW Evergreen Parkway, Suite 250

Beaverton, OR 97006

Figure 77: Howard Skaist Letter On Objectives Given to Mr. Whitten

Tim kept saying he wanted to discuss strategy. Sometimes he became nice again, like the time Felix had, but then we would be back at can't do anything a short time later. The bank and fourths were really nonsensical.

Because I would not relent and wanted the case tried by a professional attorney who had done his homework, Tim Whitten withdrew. Though I gather the fact that Mystique was lost, as described in the next chapter, also contributed to his withdraw as he talked about money incessantly. His parting invoice was $40,000 dollars – making him more expensive than Ted Terry. He noted that he would not be collecting the extra $20,000 beyond the retainer.

At the withdraw hearing, I argued that Tim should continue. I needed an attorney. Tim argued that there was a communication problem. Now isn't that funny? How do you when and argument with someone who says you can't agree? The attorneys must find the 'can't communicate exit' a hoot. I tried to argue that there was not a communication problem, but Judge Jon Wisser interrupted me. He said that he was letting Tim Whitten go. Judge Wisser commented that he thought I was an intelligent person and could handle the case. Screwed by an attorney again, and Pro Se'.

The Leviathan Takes Mystique 2007 07 04

A few miles outside the Texas coast there are a series of barrier islands. It can be difficult for a deep draft vessel, such as mystique, to make it between these islands to make landfall. The army corp of engineers maintains a channel known as the intercoastal water way between the islands and the mainland. They have also made cuts between the islands so that commercial traffic may enter the intercoastal waterway. We were coming up from Mexico and were at the same latitude as the southern end of the King Ranch at a place known as the Port Mansfield cut when some weather came up. We entered through the cut and waited out the storm. On the way out we hit sand in an area marked as part of the channel. Mystique's five ton bulb keel that hung below the boat buried itself in the sand. Because I had been ordered to use the last of my available funds to pay the court appointed attorney amicus, Mystique wasn't insured for replacement, and because she wasn't insured, no one would come to tow her. She partially broke up and eventually was stolen or swept out to sea before I could convince a barge tug to come get her. That probably didn't matter by the time the barge tug who would work with a non-insured boat owner was identified Mystique was already a complete loss due breaking up and salt water damage to the equipment and machinery.

The wreck of Mystique was reported in the Corpus Christie Caller Times article on 07/15/2007 "Shallow Water & Deep Trouble." The following picture comes from that article.

Figure 78: Corpus Caller Times Picture of Mystique On Sand Shoal

At the time of this picture the journalist found Mystique on her side and blown in towards the rock jetties. All the rigging is gone, the radar arch has separated from the deck, the keel has broken off, equipment has been stolen, she has been rummaged through and torn apart inside, and she is full of salt water. I was living on the boat, so all of our belongings were aboard, and were stolen, washed away or ruined.

For a short time after Mystique was lost I was homeless and broke. I stayed at some friends places. Back in Austin I slept in the back of my truck waiting to get paid again. Fortunately, this was during H*'s summer break with D*.

2007 10 19 Hearings – Compel Discovery Dr. Thorne – Motion to Strike the Amicus Report – Motion to Confer With Child – Motion Summary Judgment

I subpoenaed Dr. Thorne and he came. He testified that he was not a consultant for Margo Fox, had never been a consultant, and would not contemplate becoming one.

Q. Are you a consultant for the respondent?

A. I have --

Q. A paid consultant for the respondent.

A. A paid consultant for the respondent? No.

Q. Have you played a role as a consultant for the respondent specifically, a non-neutral role?

A. No, I have not.

Q. Have you represented in any form, shape or manner that you wanted to do such a thing?

A. No. I made it pretty clear to both parties that I -- once my role of the custody evaluator ceased, that ethically I couldn't have any kind of consulting role in terms of providing information to either party.

Figure 79: Dr. Thorne Testifies He is Not Margo Fox's Consultant

Dr. Thorne goes on at some length to explain why he can't be a consultant.

Margo Fox had filed a protective order to prevent Dr. Thorne from testifying. She lost that argument as Dr. Thorne himself said he was there to testify.

Q. Did you request to the respondent that she file a protective order to prevent you from being here today -- from having to testify today? Excuse me.

A. No, I did not.

The Honorable Judge Wisser ruled that he was a consultant and that his records were not discoverable. I filed a Writ of Mandamus with the third district, while noting the deadline for the final hearing and asking for a timely clarification. They denied the writ without reason.

The judge again delayed on conferring with D*. There is surely something very interesting about these records that has the attorneys very concerned.

I argued that the other side had not presented any evidence pertaining to the child. All of their arguments ragged on me. I suggested there were grounds for a no evidence summary judgment. The other side took the motion seriously enough. They argued it. It was denied.

A secondary reason for asking for a summary judgment was to stress the point I needed this over. Gopi Ganapathy now at the MNC Group, a venture capital firm, was doing diligence on my Turing Processor business plan. He had a marketing guy involved, and we had met with other members of the group. I had told them we would be done by last April. Then it was May, then it was October. Now I was having to say December. (It is now April 2008 and nothing became of the project, and I am still in the courts.)

2007 12 06 though 2007 12 10, Final Hearing

The following goes over the high points of the hearing as I see them. Not every point raised, and not every person who testified is discussed here. I have tried to make this is a well balanced portrayal. I am writing this largely from memory as the transcripts are not yet complete. I requested and paid extra to receive Sally Ray's transcript early so I was able to quote from it. Janie Veach was done earlier by deposition, so I have that transcript also.

My good friend Gene McCabe came from Tennessee to help organize the case and acted as an assistant. Gene testified up front as a character witness who has known me since we were kids, and then with the judge's permission stayed to assist. Paul Wood came up from Galveston to help with the case presentation, he did not testify. Annie and Ray Truitt who are also Galveston friends also came to Austin. Annie delayed a doctors appointment to be there. She was having back problems that require surgery but still withstood the car ride so she could be present in person for D*.

Dad flew in from Arizona, and friends from all over Austin came as well. Mike Taborn interrupted his crunch time before the holiday vacation to be there. J Moore rearranged his calendar at the University where he is chairman of the computer science department so that he could speak.

None of our witnesses heard any of the recordings, nor had they been given any of the case material. The only preparation I provided them were general technical pointers about testifying and cross examination. I did not request that anyone say or not say anything specific. Margo Fox touched on this point in her cross examinations asking one of the witnesses if he had heard recordings, and of course he answered that he had not. Our witnesses came for only one reason, and that was because from their own points of view it was the right thing to do.

H* brought local people to testify. She had no family present though most of her family lives abroad. She brought no one who said they were friends of hers and boyfriend, or went out with them. Only one person said their child played with D*, and at this, it was the case the child was dropped at H*'s place apparently to be baby sat.

As for the pretrial motions, we had a courtroom to ourselves. We had our own judge, the death penalty judge, Judge Wisser. We did not have to wait in line for the case before us, nor was there anyone waiting in line after us. There was no one in the room accept the parties and their representation and assistants, the court reporter, and occasionally my dad.

Margo Fox told me that H* spent $80,000 dollars. H* had three attorneys working on the case. Two of them were present during proceedings. I counted a staff of about four. They brought in boxes upon boxes of papers, and filled a row of seats with them. On the second day we discovered that they were not leaving the courtroom at lunch time with everyone else. They had their lunch brought in. I had laid my case across the table, but we had to pack it all up.

As soon as Gene saw the judge talk with the opposition he figured the deck was stacked against us, as he puts it:

General Affidavit

State of: Tennessee
County of: Williamson

PERSONALLY came and appeared before me, the undersigned Notary, the within named Gene J McCabe, who is a resident of Williamson County, State of Tennessee, and makes his statement and General Affidavit upon oath and affirmation of belief and personal knowledge that the following matters, facts and things set forth are true and correct to the best of his knowledge:

I, Gene J McCabe, am a long-time friend of Mr Lynch, was an early witness, and after my testimony acted as a legal aid to him for the remainder of the hearing, staying in the courtroom the majority of the time.

It was clear from the moment Judge Wisser first entered the courtroom that he knew H   's attorneys well. In addition to the initial casual greetings one would expect between acquaintances, Judge Wisser and H   's attorneys used breaks to share numerous accounts, happenings, recent developments and stories of both a personal (pregnancy, trips, etc.) and public (political, professional etc.) nature. On Friday December 7, 2007 shortly after noon when Mr Lynch was outside of the courtroom, Judge Wisser and H   's attorneys had a particularly lively discussion lasting several minutes. I was struck with how comfortable and at ease they were with each other and felt helpless to address. I recall thinking that this one-sided interaction and relationship could not be in the best interest of D   . A person is more likely to help a friend over a stranger when a choice must be made. Judge Wisser and H   's attorneys exercised their rapport so frequently that it didn't stop during the proceeding but rather continued in a more subdued manner due to the requirements of the procedural legal formalities. The many mutual interests and common ground shared by Judge Wisser and H   's attorneys was in sharp contrast to the interaction between Judge Wisser and Mr Lynch which was cordial and typical.

Having witnessed the above first hand, I cannot understand how Judge Wisser could remain adequately unbiased in rendering a decision in this case.

DATED this 14th day of April, 2008.

_____
Signature of Affiant

Figure 80: Gene McCabe Affidavit On Friendliness of the Judge With The Opposition

In the pretrial motions the judge certainly hadn't be been typical with me. At one point he had called me irresponsible, and when I say I pay my bills he scoffed and pointed out the bankruptcy. The bankruptcy was on his mind. The feeling I got early on was that I was being put on trial rather than us discussing what was best for D*.

The final hearing lasted three days, Thursday, Friday, and Monday. My understanding from the conversation on Friday with opposing counsel and the judge was that Monday was just to the testimony of the parties. Gene heard the same thing I did. Gene's and dad's plane flights were set to go out on Saturday, and as it was just H* and I left, they flew back. Paul went back to Galveston. So I went in Monday without any assistants and only preparation for interviewing H* to find they had brought rebuttal witnesses in addition to doing the parties. It was a marathon all day event. I stayed in the courtroom through lunch as I didn't want to disturb the order of all my notes. The bailiff watched the courtroom while I went to my truck where I had some oranges left over from the day before.

During the hearings Judge Wisser leaned back in his chair, slid down in his seat, often with two fingers on the bridge of his nose, with his eyes closed and appeared to be sleeping. Gene and I discussed it, I told Gene that I believed he was listening. It was unfortunate that he slid down so far in his chair, as he did not see Margo Fox signaling witnesses. Also the Fox team orchestrated cat calls and sighs during testimony. When I testified Margo Fox made funny faces, and mocked me moving her mouth with a scrunched up face while I talked. At one point when I called attention to Margo's signaling witnesses, the judge sat up straight and he had a reddish face and it looked to me as though he had just woken up.

Judge Wisser did not rule at the hearing. Rather he waited a few days. Immediately after the hearing I saw Margo Fox in the hall and it appeared to me she was pouting. When we discussed passport issues she told me that I would be managing the passport. My impression was that Margo knew we had won.

The night before the first day the following was left anonymously on my computer screen by one of my assistants:

> tomorrow you will hear the birds cackling, "tom is bad," "tom is bad,"
> but remember ·
> D* the child has found that his relationship with his father is rich
>
> you will hear them cackle tomorrow "tom is bad," "tom is bad,"
> but remember
> you have been charged with no crime,
> you have been a welcome visitor in classrooms ...
>
> so start by describing that rich experience

Highlights of Testimony Dad's Side

Janie Veach, Principal of Deepwood Elementary

Janie Veach was due to be at a family reunion on the hearing dates, so I deposed her on 2007 11 27. We then read her entire testimony into the record during the hearing. We did skip spots where Margo Fox and I argued over her desire to play the video of D* explaining his mom didn't love him – without the sound, as she had done earlier in court.

Janie Veach was the principal of Deepwood elementary when D* was in K-3. She was now retired in during the first few months of D* fourth grade year.

Janie testified that she knew D* well, knew both parents. She said that he had a great relationship with his father, but that mom should still have some influence. In other words she tactfully recommendation that D* should live with his father and visit mom:

> THE WITNESS: My opinion is that D*
>
> needs both parents involved in his life. I would like for
>
> the parents to work together to create an atmosphere that is
>
> healthy for D* to where he has permission -- or where
>
> the expected is to love both parents equally or to -- you
>
> know, I know that he has a great relationship with his
>
> father. And, you know, that needs to continue, but I still
>
> think that a mother -- you know, that he needs his mother's
>
> influence as well.

Figure 81: School Principal Deposition, Great Relation With Father, Influence Needed With Mom

In addition she said that D* seeing his father at the school was the highlight of his day:

> A. It's possible. But then again, that was the
>
> 2 highlight of D*' day, for his father to come have lunch
>
> 3 with him. And, you know, if it happened every day, I would

Figure 82: School Principal Deposition, The Highlight of D's Day is His Father Coming for Lunch*

Annie Truitt, Social Worker and D*'s Friend

We knew Annie since bringing Mystique to Galveston. Ray had a boat done the pier from Mystique. Annie was Ray's wife, and she was often on the pier working on the boat and at our Saturday parties. She was short red head with a fire cracker personality. But what we didn't know until the getting into the hearings was that she was also a PhD social worker with experience working with abused children. PhD social workers have a great advantage over child psychologists in that they see the child functioning in their own environment. Annie had an even bigger advantage in that she was D* friend.

Annie explained to the court that D* was suffering from "learned helplessness." This was a result of repeated failure in his requests to spend more time with or to live with his dad. She said that the best cure was to start listening to him, and she proposed that his wishes be made known to the court, perhaps even by coming and testifying.

Her opinion ran counter the "Child's Bill of Rights" in the county, where apparently it was even against the rules to tell the child there was a divorce hearing at all. The Child's Bill of Rights belittles children when they have an opinion or are the prime movers to the custody question. Accordingly, D* is supposed to be ignored when he gives an opinion about who he wants to live with. Annie pointed out that this was exactly the problem.

344

Annie had filed an affidavit with the court:

CAUSE NO 06-1054-F395

IN THE MATTER OF	§	IN THE DISTRICT COURT
THE MARRIAGE OF	§	
	§	
THOMAS WALKER LYNCH	§	
AND	§	395TH JUDICIAL DISTRICT
H	§	
	§	
AND IN THE INTEREST OF	§	WILLIAMSON COUNTY, TEXAS
D , A CHILD	§	

EXPERT AND FACT WITNESS ANNIE TRUITT's AFFADAVIT

BEFORE ME, the undersigned authority, personally appeared ANNIE TRUITT, who by me duly sworn, deposed as follows:

Please allow me to introduce myself and briefly describe my background, My name is Annie Truitt, I'm 53 years old, and have lived in Galveston,Texas for the past seven years. In 1976, I graduated from Texas Christian University, where I was listed in the *Who's Who of College Students*. I later attended the University of Texas at Arlington School of Social Work and graduated summa cum laude in 1995 with a Master of Science in Social Work (M.S.S.W.), with duel specialization in both child/family/mental health counseling, and biofeedback. (Note: Social workers share many of the same areas of study as psychologist, but this degree is much more extensive than a masters level psychologist, and places more emphasis on the social setting or environment. And the biofeedback training offers skills in hypnosis/relaxation and self control.)

In conjunction with my graduate studies, I completed a one year practicum at the Arlington Community Clinic, primarily counseling children referred by the Arlington I.S.D. for parental abuse issues. I continued on-staff at the clinic after graduation, while I began my coursework in the Ph.D. program. After two years, I left both my practice and the Ph.D. program when diagnosed with *Common Variable Immune Deficiency* and *Systemic Lupus Erythematosus*. I now work with my husband in the company we formed, Truitt-Cole Development, Inc.

I first meet Tom and D   a little over a year and a half ago, and have spent time with them both, primarily at the marina in Galveston. I find them interesting and intelligent individuals, who's company I enjoy. One of my first impressions of Tom, was his affection for and dedication to D   , and Tom's pride in his son. This dominated many of our earliest conversations.

And I have no doubt that D   adores and enjoys his father and they do many activities together. For example, once I was walking by, and heard the sound of hammering and laughter coming from inside their boat. I yelled "what's going on in there?" and Tom pops up from the salon, followed by D   who says

1

345

"Dad's teaching me how to work on cabinets, and we're' remodeling". There was a look of delight on both their faces, and as I walked away, there was a smile on mine. All of my observations indicate that they make very special father son team. I believe they have a positive and healthy relationship, deducted from both casual observation over time, and from many conversations with Tom and Di　　, both together and separately. D　　 is active and pleasant at the marina and interacts well with others at the adult gatherings.

And I believe that D　　 is under a great deal of stress due to current legal visitation proceedings. I also learned that Tom is being accused of responsibility for much D　　' anxiety because he has discussed what is happening with his son.

Trying to protect him by not discussing what's going on, is counter productive in my view. Children typically know much more than adults credit them, and when they are kept in the dark, they usually imagine things are worse than they might really be. It's only logical that children would wonder "why are adults hiding things from me- it must be so bad that..." Adults too fear the unknown- it's often an innate reaction for survival of the species- though it varies due to life experiences, personal temperament, etc. And for kids it's worse. They typically see themselves as powerless in an adult world. Plus they haven't had enough life experiences to show that things can appear to be bad, and still turn out ok.

It's also my view that D　　 is not only able, but would actually benefit from the opportunity to give the court his view and desires relating to the outcome of these visitation proceedings. D　　 is exceptionally bright (understatement). And having his 'say' and knowing the court is listening, in a matter that drastically effects his life, would give him a sense of empowerment.

For example, Tom recently wrote to me the following: *At one point Di　　 asked me* (Tom) *to "do something"* (visitation dispute), *at another point he asked me "why aren't you doing anything". More recently he has become more timid, and even said "if you can't help me, then save my dog".*

To me, D　　 ' statements reflects a form of 'learned helplessness'. In lab rats, when a shock is administered at random times- not for any behavior, or lack thereof, they first do all in their power to avoid what could cause the shock. But the rat soon learns that nothing they do can prevent it and they no longer try- they just passively take it. This can generalize to human behavior and D　　 probably feels helpless, and is transferring his 'pleadings for help' to the next living thing down the ladder. Siblings often to do this- "if you can't help me, please help my little sister".

I'm saddened by what life is teaching D　　 at his young age. His mother, a person that should nurture and protect him, is teaching him to expect the worst. *Mom is divorcing Dad* and his world shakes, but *Dad proves he's still very much a part of his son's life* and Di　　 clings to the knowledge that his dad

2

346

won't leave him. Then he's faced with *Mom is trying to separate me from Dad* and his world trembles again. I beleive D_____ would benifit from a little empowerment. As well as a quick end these legal proceedings, which have been in progress for over a year.

Another point I would like to make, is when discussing sensitive topics with a child, *how* it's discussed, is as critical as *what* is discussed. Children tend to believe that conflict between their parents, is somehow their fault, and conversations with child should address this. And the child should be encouraged to express their honest feelings, which should be respected. Then one can talk with the child in a manner that is constructive and doesn't discount their feelings.

I have seen evidence that D_____ holds-in his feelings. It's as if he's afraid that if he says anything about his what's burdening him, it will make things worse. I discussed this with Tom and he said he's aware that it's often difficult for his son to express his feelings. He said he and D_____ together read a book about Gandhi's life, because it demonstrated constructive ways to be able to express one's feelings. And doing so is *ok*.

I volunteered to be a witness to what I have observed, at the December 19th hearings in Georgetown. (Note: I was not offered money to testify, I have never received any form of financial compensation, and I paid my own expenses to attend the hearings.) It was there that I was able to witness the stress D_____ is experiencing from these proceedings. D_____ wasn't allowed in the building and I wasn't allowed to speak, so we waited outside together. It was a cold day, and we sat together in my van. D_____ appeared agitated and rarely made eye contact with me; very different behavior than I had seen before. He was climbing over the seats and rummaging around in the compartments of the van. I asked him to sit next to me in the front seat and gave him a deck of cards to shuffle. I took the opportunity to tell D_____ that none of the proceeding inside the building were in any way, his fault. I explained that most kids feel it's somehow their fault but that wasn't true. And that his obligation here is pretty simple... tell the truth. If asked by those who are involved... tell them how you really feel. Then I said, "you don't have tell me, but you're my friend and I want to know for sure... what are you thinking right now, about all this legal stuff?" Without a moments hesitation, he went directly to the point saying "I want to live with my Dad." And all of his overt actions, body language, and words... for the year and a half I've known him, have supported that statement. He delights in being in his fathers presence, he smiles and touches his dad with affection. He appears secure and confident around Tom.

I'm also aware that there has been an amicus attorney assigned to this litigation, and I would appreciate the opportunity to discuss my observations with this officer of the court. I was told to expect his call, but it has not happened. When a child's life can be drastically effected by a courts decision, surely the court wants to glean all relevant information, and from both sides of those in dispute.

3

347

04/19/2007 17:34 FAX 4097413741 004/004

In closing, I consider myself a staunch children's advocate. It has always been my personal and professional view that any child's welfare is paramount to all else. This is both the professional and the mother in me, as I have two sons of my own. And I believe that D needs his father. Especially this stage of development, as he's learning about his role in this world. Tom sees D ' role as lofty and limitless, and my observations indicate Tom will help him explore his path in a positive manner. He's dedicated and his son's welfare is his highest purpose.

It's my hope that these proceeding can be brought to speedy and just conclusion, for D ' sake. Thank you for your time and attention.

SIGNED on April 19, 2007

Annie Truitt
Annie Truitt

SUBSCRIBED AND SWORN TO BEFORE ME

JOHANNA M. KOVACEVICH
NOTARY PUBLIC
STATE OF TEXAS
My Comm. Exp.05-10-09

Johanna M. Kovacevich
Notary Public, State of Texas

4

Figure 83: Annie Truitt Affidavit

J Strother Moore

J's first name is actually just the one letter. J has known H*, D*, and I since D* was born. Before that he and his wife knew us as a couple. J is a world recognized researcher and educator - and a caring father. J testified about D*'s science fair project and complemented me on my "Socratic" teaching style. I think J brought out that D* is learning and growing with his father and shares an aptitude for science with him. In my testimony I added the Miss Fortune cookie project. Others talked about sailing.

Second Grade Teacher Barbara Coplin

Mrs. Coplin testified that D* had written an essay in her class saying he wanted to grow up to be an inventor like his dad. She testified that D* new year wish had been to live with his dad. She complemented my coming to read for her class and in giving a math lecture to the class.

Highlights of Testimony Mom's Side

H*

One of the things that struck me was that H* didn't have any friends that she entertained with or who had kids D* played with. There was the one child who was dropped at her place often, but she didn't entertain with them or anything. So I started with this. She said her friends were too busy to come. Many of our friends had driven all the way from Galveston, Annie had not only driven from Galveston but had delayed some out patient surgery to be there, but H*'s friends were too busy to leave work.

```
14    having been previously sworn, testified as follows:

15                    DIRECT EXAMINATION

16    BY MR. LYNCH:

17        Q.   I'd like to start with a simple question.   I don't

18    see in the evidence or even coming to the hearing mothers of

19    any other children prior to October, when the hearing started

20    to become more intense, and certainly from before these

21    proceedings started.

22             Where are your friends?

23        A.   They are my friends.

24             MS. FOX:   Objection, Your Honor, argumentative.

25             THE COURT:   Overrule the objections.   Unless you're
```

106

1   using some document for the witness, you're supposed to remain

2   at your place of bar or counsel table.

3   MR. LYNCH: I was a little concerned after watching

4   Pam and Ms. Fox communicating on the stand yesterday, so I

5   thought I would break their gaze so I didn't see anymore

6   signals.

7   THE COURT: I've found with cases like this it's

8   safer to keep a physical distance between folks. We overruled

9   the objection. If you want to restate the question.

10   BY MR. LYNCH:

11   Q.   Where are your friends?

12   A.   Could you -- my friends?

13   Q.   Yeah. Where are your friends?

14   A.   My friends are at work.

15   Q.   So they didn't have time to come?

16   A.   I didn't want to involve them as much as possible.

17   Q.   Well, who are your friends, then?

18   A.   My friends --

19   Q.   When we're talking about friends, mothers of other

20   kids, et cetera, people you go do things with with D   .

21   A.   Yes.

22   Q.   Who are they?

23   A.   Baxters.

24   Q.   I can't hear you. Speak up, please.

25   A.   The Baxters.

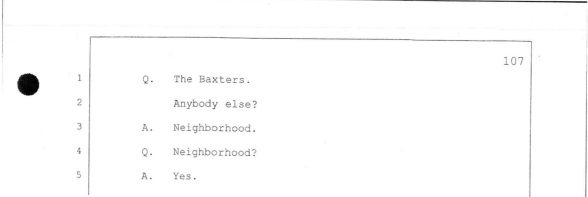

```
                                                        107

  1    Q.    The Baxters.

  2          Anybody else?

  3    A.    Neighborhood.

  4    Q.    Neighborhood?

  5    A.    Yes.
```

Figure 84: H* Can't Think of Any Friends

The only friend she mentions are the Baxters. The Baxters have a little boy named T* who is at H*'s house often. David Baxter had testified that he dropped T* at the house and left, and that D* was not invited their house. I.e. they were not friends of H*s in the sense of socializing together, rather their child played with D*. Their child is the only friend H* allows D* to have, as is made apparent later in the testimony.

Note on page 110 she repeats that I had secretly worked behind her back to divorce her. This is the very thing that John Campbell had believed and stood to him to mean that I was somehow deceptive, but it was H* who tossed me out, and I taped her when she did it, note tape transcript Figure 24. H* had asked for a divorce many times before that, including the time she invited me to leave when announcing she was pregnant.

On page 113 she says she never discussed me with Sally Ray. As you can see later in the Sally Ray testimony, that didn't stop Sally Ray from testifying against me.

On page 117 she contradicts her prior testimony that she had only provided phone information to the Garcias, and now says that she knew the Garcias were angry and that she fed the fire by telling them that I was capable of harming children.

On page 130 she says that D* asked her why she hit him in the head. Her claim is that D* goes around saying this not because it happened, but because I told him it happened. Though that doesn't explain why he had a pain on his forehead in the first place. She expresses no concern for him, and the only explanation remains the one offered by D*.

352

You stated in your affidavit -- your first affidavit

that D blames pain on his head -- well, what is it that he blames the pain on his head for?

A. I think he was -- well, several occasions, especially when you come back from your house, that, "Mom, why you hit my head? I have sinus problem here."

You know, he's accusing me.

Figure 85: H Says D* Blames Her for Hitting Him in the Head*

Page 132 we go back to the incident where she stuck D* head in the pillow after we came back from the Indian Pow-Wow. This had already been litigated seven years prior. She explains D* saw a picture on my laptop that set him off. She goes on and the explanation is now back to he was sleeping rather than he was hiding his face from something that I did that was bad. She uses the same “how could any mother do this” as a defense, and then muses that if this was really happening why would Tom take a picture instead of doing something about it. (The answer to that is I didn't initially understand what was happening.)

On page 138 she beat me on the violin issue, I didn't think to bring out the email. I then lead her through many of the incidents covered in the prior pages of this document. H* explains she never put me down in the school directory at D* school five years in a row because I didn't pay the $5 PTA fee. (Though I don't think other parents with two names and numbers listed paid twice.) H* goes on to try and explain why she didn't include me on any enrollment forms or extracurricular activities going so far to take him out of each one I visited:

22   Q.   Mr. Johnson explained while he was on the stand that

23   you did not put Tom down on the Taekwondo enrollment forms,

24   nor consequently Tom is not on the e-mail list. Consequently,

25   Tom is not informed of tournaments or events. Why did you do

1   this?

2   A.   Because it's after-school program. That's

3   specifically for my possession time and I'm -- I'm always

4   going there. That's no time for you to be there. I'm always

5   thinking --

6   Q.   So this is not my extracurricular activity with

7   D: ; this is your extracurricular activity with D   ?

8   A.   Especially since you don't like Taekwondo. Yes. I

9   don't feel like if I put your name on it, if I invited you to

10   the Taekwondo --

11   Q.   What makes you think I don't like Taekwondo?

12   A.   That's what I heard from D   .

13   Q.   So, basically, according to our divorce decree,

14   there's your time and there's my time?

15   A.   That's correct.

16   Q.   Dr. Lynch, where's D   ' time in that equation?

17   A.   D: ' times are always with us, either with you

18   and either with me.

So according to H* there is H*'s time or my time, but never D*'s time. And according to the pleading she filed, my time was to be limited. On page 139 she later testifies:

354

```
20          A.   -- and I ask D            to choose which one he wants

21   to do most, and D         choose Taekwondo.  And I told him

22   after he get to the black belt, "You can choose anything you

23   want.  If you want to do ice hockey, fine.  If you want to do

24   soccer, that's fine."

25             So it is delayed.
```

As of May 8 D* got his black belt about two months ago. He is excited about playing hockey but his mom won't let him. (Hockey is something that D* and I enjoyed together when he was younger. We could go to the stick and pucks etc, but in order to play games he had to go to practice. Practice occurred bi-weekly, so unless H* took him he missed three quarters of the practices. She took him for a short while, then stopped. I got stuck with all the equipment for both of us.)

On page 137 and 138 she admits that D* did not want to go home with her on several occasions, but claims that I was always there before she arrived.

Later Sally Ray would try to cover for H* not being cooperative with the terms of the divorce decree, but on page 174 H* says she has always been a stickler, going back years. H* is complains I moved a lot. They harped on this as a reason for H* not being flexible, and perhaps to make a point I wasn't stable. Though I found this to be an irrelevant argument as D* hadn't been living with me.

H* went through some of her affidavit material. She blamed me for Dr. Mirrop quiting. This was the doctor that got caught between Dr. El-Youssef of the Mayo Clinic saying there was an issue, and H* saying there wasn't. There was an issue, and Dr. Mirrop quit.

The divorce degree requires binding arbitration for disagreements about education. She says that "my priest" sent a letter saying I couldn't afford the private school. That must be a mistake on the part of the court reporter. I was there but don't recall who she said called, but it is moot, as I did tell her this. After H*'s attorney Sara Brandon destroyed my livelihood I did tell H* I needed her help to pay for the school. H* said she would "not pay a penny." Yet in her earlier testimony she said she would be glad to help with education costs. They then beat me up for not paying for the school.

They go over the money and point out that H* has been paying health care. This is true, but not quite what sounds like, it is part of her work benefits.

She complains that the YMCA got a picture of H* screaming. This picture was in the file with the temporary orders decree from the file box I pulled it from. It did get faxed unintentionally, though it was also public record.

355

H* blames me for her taking D* out of day cares, making the argument it was because I created scenes, rather than because she had left my name off forms, and left directions for people to call security if I showed. She complains about not having access to the passport. I had steadfastly agreed to give it to her if she provided travel plans. She goes through her affidavit stuff. She claims I went into her backyard and stole the dog, twice. (This is not true.)

She talks about the painting D* gave me and says I took it from the school (see Figure 66 305). In K-4 H* this is the only piece of art work that was shared with me.

The discovery material included a number of pictures of H* and D* with groups of smiling kids. There were numerous kids in every picture. This was provided as evidence that D* was allowed to have more than one friend. So I went through the pictures one by one while she was on the stand and asked her to identify the children. The one friend H* was allowed to have, the Baxter kid, and a child she had to fill out a birthday card for were the only kids she could identify. She kept saying "I don't know." "I don't know."

```
21          These are a number of things sent in discovery from

22   Margo and they're photographs.  This actually ties into an

23   earlier subject on kids.

24          Who's in those pictures?

25      A.   D       and T      in Houston, NASA.
```

```
1        Q.   And who's in those pictures?

2        A.   D:        and T     at Korean school.

3        Q.   And who's in these pictures?

4        A.   D:        and Aunty, D         and T

5        Q.   You can limit your responses to just the kids.

6   That's fine.

7             Of course, just the bottom one here, because there's

8   only one -- only D         in the top one?

9        A.   It's T    's birthday.  D         got invited.

10  There's other kids.

11       Q.   There's other kids.  Okay.

12       A.   Uh-huh.

13       Q.   What are their names?

14       A.   I do not know.  T    's friends.

15       Q.   Who's in the top one here?

16       A.   Oh, that is D.        and other kids from San Antonio

17  Sea World.

18       Q.   I see.  So you don't know their names?

19       A.   Yes.

20       Q.   Who's in the bottom photo?

21       A.   This is Korea school, D        and T    .

22       Q.   Who's in this picture?

23       A.   D         and T     's classmates.

24       Q.   And what are their names?

25       A.   They are -- I don't remember the names because they
```

1   changed.

2   Q.   And the bottom picture?

3   A.   This is Korea school. It's very old.

4   Q.   And the top picture here, is D   in that

5   picture?

6   A.   Yes.

7   Q.   Which one?

8   A.   Left one.

9   Q.   I see. The left kid -- okay. He's moving. He's a

10 little blurred there. But the other kid is --

11   A.   They're going to play, plays at --

12   Q.   Do you remember her name?

13   A.   No. It is old picture, 2002. She quit after about

14 four months.

15   Q.   Who's in this top picture?

16   A.   Mrs. Hanson (phonetic) came to D   ' Taekwondo

17 championship, and T   .

18   Q.   And this one?

19   A.   Yes.

20   Q.   T   ?

21   A.   T   .

22   Q.   Okay. Who's in the bottom picture?

23   A.   D.   and T   and other kids from our

24 neighborhood. She -- oh, his name? He moved away after a

25 year later.

1   There's another kid over here. I've invited him.

2   Q.   And what's his name?

3   A.   I forgot.

4   Q.   Who's in the top picture here?

5   A.   D   and A   . That's our neighborhood kids'

6   birthday party, and T   got invited because we are friends

7   through D   .

8   Q.   So A   's family invited you to this one?

9   A.   Yes, and invited T   as well.

10   Q.   And who's in the bottom picture?

11   A.   D   and T   .

12   Q.   And who's in the top picture here?

13   A.   D   and T   . Of course, T   and D

14   are very close friends.

15   Q.   This one in the top?

16   A.   Oh, that's C   and D   . That's

17   classmates.

18   Q.   C   ?

19   A.   Yes, that's C   . She's a classmate. She

20   moved away, but --

21   Q.   And that's another kid in there. Who's that?

22   A.   I do not know. That's C   's family.

23   Q.   Who's in the top one here?

24   A.   D   and T   . There are other kids, but I

25   just took the pictures because they are very close.

```
 1      Q.   Who's in that one?

 2      A.   There's another --

 3      Q.   No.  It's from the same one with C        .

 4      A.   This is C          .

 5      Q.   Okay.  Well, D       and T    , D       and T     ,

 6   D       and T    ?

 7      A.   I could bring more pictures.  There's many other

 8   friends that are coming to visit my house.

 9      Q.   Yeah.  That's a recent development due to my

10   criticisms?

11      A.   Yeah, over one year, yeah.

12      Q.   Yes, it is.
```

Note, the proceeding had started nearly a year ago, so H*'s new efforts were covering bases for the hearing. I had more pictures but Judge Wisser was yawning and looking at me. It appears he didn't get the point, so a little further down in the transcript I asked her outright if D* has more than one friend dating before a year ago, she says yes. I ask what their names are, an she says she can't remember.

Margo Fox tried very hard to bring in the expunged material up though it was a) expunged and b) before the prior order c) unethical for her as an attorney to do so. Margo tried to mix it in with "my arrest," i.e. my birthday citation from Austin.

She claims I call her late at night on the phone. (Untrue, and no phone records were presented to buttress the claim.)

She wants me to pay her more money.

In cross examination she admits she never saw me in her back yard. She admits that she took my office files and didn't return them for nearly a year. She admits to keeping THS assets (listed on income tax depreciation) of book shelves and desks.

H* gives me no credit for my hard earned child support, claiming that I don't pay for anything. This surprisingly comes right after I asked her how often she receives a child support check from me, and she had answered bimonthly:

18   Q.   But you say that I don't pay for anything. How is

19 that?

20   A.   You don't pay for anything?

21   Q.   You're telling me I didn't pay for after-school

22 programs, I'm not paying for medicine, I'm not paying for all

23 sorts of things.

24   A.   After-school program -- which after-school program

25 you have paid? Which medicine you have ever paid?

274

1   Q.   So I don't pay for medicine and I don't pay --

2   A.   Medicine -- why -- on the care you paid it probably,

3 but you never requested it. But that time --

4   Q.   What have I ever paid for that D   has at your

5 place? Anything?

6   A.   What did you pay? I do not remember anything.

7   Q.   Nothing at all, huh?

8   A.   Please help me. I do not remember anything.

I had asked for records from Dr. Gritzka, H* did not help, she testifies that my requests was "harassment." (Put this in juxtaposition with her mistake of giving D* duplicate shots.)

4   Q.   You say you would like a parenting coordinator?

5   A.   Yes. I do have parenting coordinator.

6   Q.   Do you think Sally Ray would make a good parenting

7   coordinator?

8   A.   She was -- she was and she will be. But I think you

9   are saying that she's biased probably, so I do not know. But

0   she's good, she's nice and I learned a lot from her.

1   Q.   Would you be surprised if she thought I was

2   dangerous?

3   A.   You know, many people -- if you get harassed, then

4   yes.

5   Q.   So you think I harass Sally Ray?

6   A.   The way you talk to other people that way, yes.

7   Q.   Do you think I harass Sally Ray?

8   A.   I think so, yes.

I had never met Sally Ray, as Sally Ray testified. The only conversation I had with her was the time after Felix suggested we hire her and I called and interviewed her. The conversation couldn't have been more than 5 minutes and was in the afternoon.

Jay Norwood

Jay is H*'s boyfriend. D* tells me he comes and goes from the house, and he is listed with another address and a woman with the same last name. I asked him a lot of questions about what H* thinks, as she is a party.

```
13    BY MR. LYNCH:

14         Q.   So what makes a good mother?

15         A.   Well, she's trying to raise her child right, that's

16    all.

17         Q.   What's right?

18         A.   Well, the most important things to her right now, I

19    think, are D        ' education and that he's well cared for,

20    you know.
```

H* had testified that the thing she admires my ability to teach D*, so it looks like they must think I'm good at raising him. I would draw this as an analogy to H*'s prior statement that "he is a good father" at the original temporary orders hearing.

```
7          Q.   Well, as you opened the door to this, I guess I'll

8     ask it.  Were you aware that I woke up one night and H

9     was on top of me holding her hand over my mouth and my nose?

10         A.   No.  She exactly said the opposite.

11         Q.   Oh, so she spoke to this matter?

12         A.   She said that you've tried to smother her before.

13         Q.   So H        has described me to you?

14         A.   Of course, yes.

15         Q.   Okay.  How does she describe me?

16         A.   How does she describe you?

17         Q.   Yeah.  Yeah.  What's her description of me?

18         A.   I think she thinks you're evil.
```

So H* claims that I tried to suffocate her instead of the other way around, it is now my fault. At least this documents an event. In further testimony Jay explains that H* told him that I abused her parents. Between this and what she told the Garcias, as she admitted in her testimony, I believe it shows that she is actively recruiting witnesses who have never met me to testify against me. It is the cry that calls the flock, so to speak.

I'd like you to ask my question -- or answer my

25   question. What is evil in this view?

                                                                    99

1   A.   I think in this case, it's telling D   things

2   about his mother that aren't true.

3   Q.   Well, does she think I'm dangerous?

4   A.   I think she knows you're dangerous.

Ok, so Jay reports that H* thinks I am evil, and she knows I am dangerous, but apparently I am trustworthy:

13   A.   I think she trusts you to take care of D   when

14   he's in your care.

15   Q.   If I'm such a dangerous, evil person, how could she

16   possibly trust me to have D   in my care?

17   A.   I think she trusts you to take care of D   .

18   That's all I think.

19   Q.   I'm having a hard time --

Yes, I'm having a hard time understanding that logic. But the reader might come to understand it better that if parental interference is illegal. This is testimony behind the motivation for that. In my opinion, his testimony in fact establishes interference, especially when you consider that considers himself to be a good father for D*:

16   Q.   So what have you done to be a good father for

17   D   ?

18   A.   I do anything H   asks me to do. I travel with

19   him along all their vacations. I don't know what else. He's

20   included in my family.

21   Q.   So you travel on a vacation and stay in a hotel

22   room?

23   A.   Yes. We've gone to Nassau and we've gone to

24   Disneyland.

364

So we also learn from Jay that after H* delayed the passport renewal, and killed our sailing trip to the Caribbean, they got on a plane and took him to Nassau. And he shares their future travel plans:

```
18        Q.    Have you discussed going to Korea?

19        A.    We discussed visiting Korea this Christmas.

20        Q.    Who would you visit in Korea?

21        A.    We'd be visiting her parents and brother, sisters.
```

And Jay is 'invested in the process:'

```
15        Q.    Have you helped pay for this proceeding?  I

16    understand it's $80,000.

17        A.    Yes.

18        Q.    I see.  How much have you paid?

19        A.    Probably 10,000 of it.

20        Q.    How much do you make a year?

21        MS. FOX:  Objection, Your Honor, relevance.
```

Sally Ray

Felix Rippy had wanted Sally Ray as a "parenting coach." Felix said I could trust her because, "she is a friend of mine." As I noted earlier Sally Ray is the husband of Paul Womack, a district judge. Sally is an attorney and a licensed counselor. She often used the word psychotherapy which has no official meaning in Texas, but would lead many of us to believe she is a psychologist, but she is not a psychologist, rather she is a counselor.

Sally starts by explaining she has had cancer and has not yet resumed her psychotherapist practice. In fact, she has been out of commission for over a year, since the time her name was proposed, and had told us that she could not be a parenting coach. But as a parenting coach who never saw the child, and as a person with undergoing chemotherapy, what could she possible have to say about the case? Why was she even here?

Sally was short and rotund. She had no hair due to the chemotherapy. Her eyebrows were painted, and her head was bald. She took the stand and looked over at our table. My friend and assistant Gene was sitting next to me, and behind a couple of rows was my dad, grandpa Tom. Sally didn't know which of the two of us was at the table, she looked us both over long, and then gave Gene a dirty look. I smiled. For once it wasn't my fault. After her testimony my dad shook his head and said, "what a piece of work she is." Perhaps you may agree after reading this.

```
17      A.   I am a family therapist, psychotherapist.

18      Q.   And have you recently ended or stopped your

19 practice for a period of time, or are you resuming your

20 practice now?

21      A.   No, not quite.

22      Q.   Are you recovering from an illness?

23      A.   Yes, from cancer.

24      Q.   Well, thank you for being here today.
```

Ms. Ray expressed that H* was accommodating to me and she had advised her to stop cooperating, she repeated this twice at different points in her testimony. She said that H* followed her advice to not cooperate, and she felt better and D* behaved better now that they weren't cooperating with dad. Note, that Sally Ray is saying this in December of 2007, and she had only met H* the first time the year before, so she was talking about H* stopping the cooperation with dad late 2006 and in 2007. However, by 2005 H* had already terminated every extracurricular activity dad could come to, and she had already taken D* out of day care and was watching him at home so that I couldn't visit him during this times, and she had already refused any sort of co-operations of schedules. H* even testified that she had been a stickler from at least 2003.

20   I also suggested that she be extremely firm

21   with her ex-husband about following the court order to

22   the letter. She apparently had in the past been, tried

23   to accommodate some of his requests, to deviate from

24   that, but that was not going well. So I suggested that

25   she stick with the court order to the letter.

20   I also suggested that she be extremely firm

21   with her ex-husband about following the court order to

22   the letter. She apparently had in the past been, tried

23   to accommodate some of his requests, to deviate from

24   that, but that was not going well. So I suggested that

25   she stick with the court order to the letter.

1   Q.   And do you know if that helped circumstances?

2   A.   Yes. She, within even the next week, she came

3   in and her anxiety was significantly reduced. She was

4   feeling happier, feeling like things were going much

5   better with D   .

Ms. Ray, had phoned Mark Roles in December of 2006 and said she was closing her practice due to her cancer and couldn't work with us. Now Ms. Ray, who had just got done explaining her practice had been closed for the entirety of the time we knew of her tells the court now she has visited with H* ten times:

15   Q.   How many times did you visit with H   ?

16   A.   Ten times.

As another point, she blamed me for not following an agreement to see her. She is referring to the Felix Rippy settlement agreement that I did not sign. H* had not given me any papers or art work form the school, as noted earlier. She even went so far as having D* collect and return a painting he gave me. This is expert Sally Ray's opinion on that:

367

```
 2        Q.   (By Mr. Lynch)  So do you think it would be

 3   proper for a mother not to share in any of the school's

 4   papers, artwork, et cetera, with the ex-husband?

 5        A.   I believe there are cases in which that is

 6   appropriate, yes.
```

Ms. Ray probably doesn't realize it, but this testimony about Rule 11 agreements and her other testimony demonstrates that Margo Fox biased her view of the case. This violates boundaries both for Margo Fox and for Sally Ray, and the damage violating these boundaries is all too clear from what happened as a result of Ray's testimony.

Ms. Ray says that she does not believe in joint managing conservatorships as a way to explain it is ok to leave dad out of decisions. Judge Jon Wisser in his final order protected Mrs. Ray by taking away all of my parenting rights, and then writing at the top "joint managing conservatorship," as a defense for Ms. Ray. He also came to her defense in the same manner during her testimony by providing his own testimony that she was correct:

```
 6        A.   There is not a standard about that.  I find it

 7   changes from case to case, who has the authority to

 8   consent to counseling and what role the other parent

 9   plays.

10        Q.   So what does a joint managing conservatorship

11   mean to you?

12        A.   Not really a whole lot.

20             THE COURT:  I will take judicial notice of

21   the fact that a joint conservatorship appears and can

22   state to be whatever the judge says it is, and it varies

23   from case to case.  And some of them look exactly like a

24   sole conservatorship, but they are called joint.  And in
```

Ms. Ray now testifies that H* should decide when dad gets visitation time, independent of what the court order says. Note, this is the same woman who just got done saying it was important for mom to stick to the letter of the decree:

368

```
 4        Q.   Yeah, would it be unreasonable for H        to

 5   deny Mr. Lynch scheduled visitation that is in the

 6   divorce decree?

 7        A.   It would depend.   If she felt the child were in

 8   danger, then it wouldn't be unreasonable.

 9        Q.   Have you seen anything -- do you have any

10   personal knowledge of events that would point, rise to

11   that level?

12        A.   No.
```

I asked her a series of questions about the state of the case, and she didn't know the answers to any of them. "Did you know that Mr. Lynch had a sole managing conservatorship?" No. She didn't know that I had not signed onto the agreements. Hence, the prep information that Sally Ray received, which she shouldn't have received in the first place, was one sided.

Sally Ray was evasive when I questioned her, often asking me to repeat questions and seeming not to hear well. Gene suggested that she was purposely stalling for time. I stepped closer so she could hear me better, or rather couldn't complain that she couldn't hear me. This lead to an interesting exchange:

```
 6        A.  No, not personally, but I think you might be

 7  dangerous.

 8        Q.  Have we ever met before?

 9        A.  No.

10        Q.  So you have come to this conclusion simply by

11  talking with H     ?

12        A.  I have come to this conclusion primarily

13  watching her affect.

14        Q.  Has H        ever told you that she thought I was

15  dangerous?

16        A.  You mean physically?

17        Q.  In any manner whatsoever.

18        A.  No, not necessarily.  She has told me that she

19  thinks that you are significantly hurting your son

20  emotionally and psychologically especially.
```

So Sally Ray asks me to back up because she thinks I might be dangerous. Her only indication that I might be dangerous to her and need to back away is that her parent coaching client, H*, told her that she though I was psychologically bad for our son, so she claims, but note H*'s testimony from page 113 of vol 5:

```
                                                          113

 1   parenting D.       with conflicting situations.

 2        Q.  So you didn't discuss Mr. Lynch with Sally Ray

 3   whatsoever?

 4        A.  No, no.
```

Figure 86: H Testifies She Never Discussed Mr. Lynch with Sally Ray*
Where did Ray's information come from then? My guess would be Margo Fox.

 Otherwise the contradiction makes little sense. In further questioning she says she thinks I might be dangerous because I had not gone to counseling. Now isn't that a convenient conclusion for a counselor, those who do not go to counseling, or more to the point, don't pay a counselor, are dangerous people. And where did she get that information from?

At the end of the session she admits that she has no evidence, has never seen me before, has never seen me interact with D*, and has never seen me interact with H*. The portion about not having evidence actually runs for a whole page as she is evasive, reinterpreting the question each time it is asked. I asked about a half dozen times.

```
10        Q.  So you have no direct empirical evidence

11   concerning the person for who you are making conclusions

12   about here?

13        A.  If you are asking me if I have ever met you

14   before today, no.

15        Q.  Have you seen me interact with D        ?

16        A.  No.

17        Q.  Have you seen me interact with H        ?

18        A.  No.
```

Figure 87: Sally Ray, No Evidence, Never Seen Dad Interact With Anyone, Never Met Dad

Judge Wisser protected Sally Ray by ordering me to turn over the passport in his proposed order, thus making her backwards testimony appear forward. Judge Jurgins had just got done ordering H* to sign travel papers to renew the passport and give it to me, not the other way around. Ray created an issue where there was none, and Wisser followed her lead and made it one.

In his findings of facts Judge Wisser wrote that Sally Ray was a credible witness. Judge Wisser, how could you???

Testimony of Dr. Caryl Dalton

Dr. Dalton opened her testimony by talking about what a great religion Shamanism is, after that she largely followed her affidavit:

CAUSE NO. 06-1054-F395

IN THE INTEREST OF	§	IN THE DISTRICT COURT
D ,	§	
	§	395TH JUDICIAL DISTRICT
A CHILD	§	
	§	WILLIAMSON COUNTY, TEXAS

DR. CARYL DALTON'S AFFIDAVIT

BEFORE ME, the undersigned authority, personally appeared CARYL DALTON, Ph.D. who, by me duly sworn, deposed as follows:

"My name is Caryl Dalton. I am competent to make this affidavit. The facts stated in this affidavit are within my personal knowledge and are true and correct.

1.   "I am a Texas licensed psychologist. I received a Masters Degree in Special Education from the University of Texas at Austin in 1977, and a Doctorate in Educational Psychology from the University of Texas at Austin in 1987."

2.   I have been treating D   for approximately 5 years after the divorce to help with his adjustment to the divorce and then in the last two years to help with his behavioral issues. I am concerned for D_____' emotional well being. It is my professional opinion that Thomas Lynch (hereinafter "Tom") is causing D immediate and irreparable emotional injury.

3.   I have cause for D   emotional well being based on several incidents of which I am most concerned about Tom's recent conduct in my office on February 14, 2007. On that day, I had a scheduled 4:00 p.m. therapy session with D

4.   H   , D   's mother, brought D   to my office for his session. I came out of my office to greet D   and saw Tom and H   in my waiting room. D   was not in the room at the time. I have never formally met Tom prior to February 14, 2007 although I have been treating his son for several years. H   attempted to introduce me to Tom, but Tom refused to shake my hand saying that he had seen me in court.

5.   Mr. Lynch told me that he wanted to observe the play therapy session because he wanted to know what took place during the sessions. I agreed to discuss the sessions in a private appointment with Tom because it is not my practice to allow parents into the sessions. During this conversation, D   came out of the restroom. H   suggested that she go outside with D   because my conversation with Tom was "grown-up talk." D   refused to go outside with H   . Tom then asked D   if he liked to play with me. Tom also asked D   if he was scared of me. D   said that he preferred to play at home and did not like to play with me. I asked Tom to discontinue his questioning of D   as it was inappropriate. He did not stop.

6.   I then cancelled the play therapy session with D   as a result of my confrontation with Tom. I am concerned that Mr. Lynch has potentially damaged

what has been a strong therapeutic relationship.

7.   I am concerned that Tom Lynch has received copies of my records and has used them to interrogate D   .

8.   I believe that D   is in danger of emotional and psychological harm as a result of his father, Tom Lynch's behavior.

Further affiant sayeth not.

SIGNED on February 21, 2007.

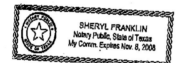

CARYL DALTON, Ph.D, Affiant

SUBSCRIBED AND SWORN TO BEFORE ME on February 20, 2007, CARYL DALTON, Ph.D.

Notary Public, State of Texas

After she refused to step aside many years ago in favor of someone who could work with the whole family though she agreed such a person existed, after my complaint about her using a discredited subjective technique, after she came to hearing as a partisan with concerns other than for therapy with D*, and after refusing to let me observe by explaining the room was too small for two adults (no one gets to observe), and of course in the context of accusations of hypnosis and her claiming to be a student of shamanism – her decision to stop seeing my son is my fault. I don't see the logic here. I don't know, perhaps you do.

She has still never met me in a clinical capacity. She does have access to the court records yet she concludes that I am injurious to D* mentally due to my visit in her office where D* told her he wanted to live with his dad and she cackled like the wicked witch in the movie Wizard of Oz saying, "he has opinions *big time*.. hah hah hah." (see Figure 73 p344), while D* watched. Though she admits that D* said he was scared of her, and he is. I have seen it first hand when the threat of going to see Dr. Dalton is used by H* to motivate him. Also Mike Boulch had commented on it (see Figure 75 p349).

H* is now taking D* to another therapist. This therapist provided me a letter saying he was trained in hypnosis, though he says he doesn't see that as an appropriate technique to use at the time of the writing. The therapist was picked by H*'s attorney. In person the new therapist questioned Dr. Freitag's credentials, but when I introduced them through email so that I could hear an response from Dr. Freitag, the new therapist refused to reply.

Even the Clerk's Office

There is not a single man sitting among the desks at the largish Williamson county district clerk's office run by Lisa Davis. Attorneys may write subpoenas directly, but I, as a pro se' must get the clerk's signature. The clerk's office has a lot of policies, most of them are not written down. They are announced to me as I run across them. "It has always been that way." I am told. Two days before our hearing I needed a subpoena. In the past they had been signed on the spot. This time I was told that it would take "three days." I pleaded with the clerk. Lisa Davis called security and had me lead out of her office. Opposing counsel was informed and brought it up while I was on the stand.

Ms. Davis called security on me a second time when I went to get record copies. The county failed to send records to the state for the appeal, the dead line being the end of last month. It is now May 8 and I got a hold of them today and was told that they have an extension until the end of July to send the papers. I asked for an index of the records, and they sent one that is not legible. They explained they are late because the clerk who was assembling records for the appeal has left the department. None other than Ms. Davis is now doing the work. I'm told that the county charges a dollar a page for files sent to the appeals court. I don't know if this is "policy" or law. There appear to be between 1500 and 2000 pages in the file at this point. Oh, also, they tell me they are converting to a new computer system, and they hope not to lose anything in the transfer.

Testimony of April Perry

I had interviewed with Steve Copenhaver about taking the case. He told me he knew April Perry a former legal assistant of Sarah Brandon's. He said that she had had a reckoning and realized that she had done bad things and felt guilty about it. He said she would like to talk with me. I was very excited about it, as it would crack open the whole of the shenanigans. Mr. Copenhaver did not have a phone number for her. I stopped by her apartment in the early evening and knocked on the door, but she was not home. I came back at 8pm and still she was not there, so I tried in the morning. In the morning she cracked open the door and I explained that Steve suggested I talk with her. She said she didn't want to talk to me, so I left. That was it.

According to another witness, April Perry was out in the hall running her hands through each other like a crazy person. She came in and cried on the stand saying I had looked backwards through the peep hole, that I looked in her windows, and that I had come back very late at night. I did not cross examine her, but refuted her testimony in my own testimony. I was perfectly within my rights as a person putting together a case to go by and talk to potential witnesses, I had done nothing to harass her as she claimed, and when she said she didn't want to talk I left.

Now here is an interesting question as this happened shortly before the hearing, how did she know to link up with my ex wife and her attorney, in a different county even. There was no information exchanged at the door. I asked to talk to her, and she said she didn't want to talk.

Though I suspect this was a setup gratis of Mr. Copenhaver, and an out right performance by April, but suppose I am wrong. That would mean that the very sight of me put the fear of God into April Perry. What has April done to other people that she knows to be so horrible that she lives such fear of meeting a simple computer architect who politely asked if he could talk to her?

According to Texas law one person's fear of another doesn't have anything to do with anything. A threat is a different matter, but April never said that I had threatened her. Judge Wisser put in his findings of fact that she was afraid of me, but not that there was a threat, and wrote a protective order anyway.

April Perry's testimony had nothing to do with the divorce no mention was made of D* or parenting skills. Perhaps April could have filed a matter in another venue, though there is no way she would have succeeded.

The Bailiff gave me a long dirty look as he lead April Perry still crying down from the stand and out the door. He was going to protect her from me.

Judge Wisser listed her as a credible witness, though it is not clear as to a witness as to what.

Kacie Nesby of the YMCA via Deposition

Kacie was the administrator at the YMCA who accepted H*'s enrollment form with no dad listed, and then sought to enforce that form when I came to visit my son at the YMCA program. She testified that I was rude. In my opinion I was not rude, but rather forceful. I was not going to take no for an answer when it came to visiting my son and had a righteous air. It obviously upset Kacie. Kacie also relayed a phone message where I said I would sue if they blocked my visits, and would never drop the issue. I think anyone who has read this book up to this point would have no problem understanding that truth of that. Though Kacie viewed this as a very negative and threatening, I'm convinced it is a positive thing when dad doesn't give up on his son.

Pam Wacholz

At the time of the hearing I did not recognize her, but she claimed to have been a playground monitor for a period when D* was in Kindergarten, i.e. four years prior. She said she saw me when I came to lunch, and that she had made up a nick name for me "psycho dad". She claimed I took D* out of the school often without signing him out. She also tried to discredit the school principal, who did not note any such problem, by saying she was losing her memory.

Gene McCabe and I didn't really know what to do with her. Her mannerisms, attitude, and language were hysterical in nature and thus not very credible. I didn't remember her at all, and by her accounts she hadn't seen D* or I in over four years. In divorce modifications one wouldn't normally find old information very important anyway as the legal predication for a modification hearing is a change of conditions. The opposition might challenge by saying the old conditions haven't change by bringing new material, but there is no legal benefit in establishing the past. Gene pointed out that it was unprofessional for someone to have made up a nick name for a parent and to have circulated it, so I asked her for specifics about the name circulation in cross examination. She then contradicted herself and said that she had only told the nick name to her husband. In addition to being hysterical and having old information she was now caught lying, so she could not possibly have mattered as a witness.

Judge Wisser shook his head after her testimony and commented something to the order of "they get like that when they wait out in the hall too long." This confirmed that judge Wisser had noted her hysterics.

It wasn't until after I showed a draft of this chapter to a neighbor some weeks after the hearing that I found out the story of Pam Wacholz. Five years ago, in 2003, a teenage boy put started racing his large gas engine powered go-kart on the little jogging track at the elementary school while D* and some other five year olds were playing soccer inside the track. It was a very dangerous situation. I stopped the boy and told him he couldn't run on the track. I said it nicely, and noted that when I was a kid we drove out to a go-kart track that was used for racing. He told me he had his mother's permission. Indeed she was standing in the parking lot. She came over and pleaded with me that her son had been tossed from the high school jogging track and there were no go-kart tracks near by. I told her too bad, as the kids were playing soccer and it was their field. She then said she had cleared it with the school principal, Ms. Veach and they were going to run the go-kart anyway. I borrowed a phone and dialed the police and talked to them while she watched. She heard me explain that a crazy woman had given her son permission to race go-karts around the five year olds playing soccer, and while I was talking they packed up and left. Perhaps the reason Ms. Wacholz was confident in speaking for the school principal is because she is the education reporter for the Austin Statesman. She waited five years to 'get even' with me by coming to the our custody hearing and testifying against us. After I found out who she was I wrote the judge and copied the opposing counsel. Margo Fox didn't deny it.

Judge Wisser put in his findings of facts that Pam Wacholz was a credible witness.

First Grade Teacher, Mrs. Hernandez

Of course, Mrs. Hernandez was there, and she was still upset about having been corrected in class after more than three years had passed. She testified that I had not understood a math lesson she was teaching in her class. In cross examination I approached her with a picture of a diamond drawn on a piece of paper and asked her what it was. Judge Wisser told her not to answer. He said it was irrelevant. I found it highly relevant as it would discredit her testimony. He didn't allow the question.

Mrs. Hernandez also testified that I sent her an email that said that H* did not like Americans. True, I had. Though 'thought they were easily manipulated' is what I thought I had wrote, but close enough. I was hoping she would wake up and see that she was being used.

Mrs. Carboneau the School Counselor

Mrs. Carboneau had been subpoenaed by the other side, so I subpoenaed her as well, while asking that she bring a number of materials, including her last four divorce decrees, email, notes and other documents. She claimed that my subpoena had been quashed, but there hadn't even been a hearing on it. Judge Wisser allowed her to testify. Mrs. Carboneau brought out papers from her purse to buttress her statements while she talked.

Judge Wisser did not mention her in the findings of fact.

Can you imagine the liability these two misandrist women are creating for the school system at Deepwood elementary?   There are men in this world, such as David Mack, who are fed up with women taking their hatred out on their relationships with their children and they do not see writing a book as the best the best course for rectifying the situation.

The Garcia's

Mrs. Garcia testified that I had hurt her child in the school cafeteria during one of my lunch visits causing several bruises on his arm. Mrs. Veach countered this allegation in her testimony. It is a preposterous allegation as the school cafeteria is a crowded place with many monitors. Apparently Pam Wacholz was at one them, and if one believes her testimony, I already had a reputation as a person to be watched.

I subpoenaed her husband Mr. Garcia, but he refused to come. The judge told me he would have him arrested if he didn't show, and he came and I relayed this statement to him via cell phone. He testified that his wife had talked with H* on the phone, and what H* said had affected her. Between this and H*'s boyfriend's testimony, it should have been clear to the court how H* inspired her witnesses, and this should have also explained the demeanor of her witnesses.

Summary of Testimony

Witness	Testified to Child Parent Interaction	Last Seen D*	Summary
D*'s School Principal Janie Veach	Yes	7 months prior	D* should be with dad have influence of mother.
D* friend, Social Worker Annie Truitt	Yes	1 month prior	D* has a wonderful relationship with father, stress about mom, due to dog etc.
D*'s 2nd Grade Teacher Barbara Coplin	Yes	Recently	D* loves his dad deeply.
Educator and Friend J Moore	Yes	10 months prior	Tom is a wonderful father. Teaches D*.
Mike Taborn	yes	recently	Tom and D* have a strong father son relationship.
Penny Gastineau	Yes	recently	Tom and D* have a strong father son relationship.
Ray Truitt	yes	recently	Tom and D* have a strong father son relationship.
Tony Garcia	No	Never	H* affected his wife.

Figure 88: Summary of Our Witnesses

Their witnesses:

Witness	Testified to Child Parent Interaction	Last Seen D*	jist
Counselor Sally Ray	No	never	Dad is potentially dangerous.
Pam Wacholz	No	4 years prior	Dad is a "psycho".
Kacie Nesby	No	4 years prior	Dad was rude.
First grade teacher. Carol Hernandez	No	3 years prior	Dad was rude.
Psychologist and Shaman Caryl Dalton	No	More than 1 year	Dad was rude.

School Counselor Betty Carboneau	No	Recently	Dad was rude.
April Perry	No	Recently	She is afraid of Dad.
Mrs. Garcia	No	Never	Dad beat up her son in the school cafeteria.
Mr. Johnston	Yes	Recently	H* gloats over D* (during their 1 hour taekwondo practice) Dad was rude.
David Baxter	Yes	Recently	Corroborated the never see your best friend again incident.
Jay Norwood (boyfriend)	Yes	Recently	H* is a good mom. I am a good father to D*.

Figure 89: Summary of Opposition's Witnesses

The first thing I noticed was that their case was stale and off topic, I had never met or had not seen most of their witnesses for years. The witnesses did not talk about parenting. I would argue that Sally Ray had nothing to do with the case at all, as she only knew what H* had told her and no contact with anyone else or any sort of evidence. Johnson and Baxter had barely ever seen H* and D* together.

There was also an interesting qualitative difference between those who came to testify for D* and I, and those who testified for H*. The demeanor of our witnesses on the stand was friendly and informative. They all talked glowingly about D* and his relationship with his father. Sometimes they did this as a means to contrast the absence of such a relationship with his mother, but not trying to hurt her. My witnesses were kind, mature, well meaning people and I am proud to be associated with them.

The negative testimony we had was targeted at a factual issue with H*'s parenting. The school nurse testified that D* was enrolled without a doctors note for his diary enzymes for grades K through 2, and that she even ignored the Mayo Clinic doctor. Also, we used Mr. Garcia to counter Mrs. Garcia, and to show the court how H* worked. H*'s boyfriend was not our witness, but he did also helped the court understand how H* worked.

On the other hand, with only one exception H*'s witnesses were angry people, especially the women. They scowled on the stand, were excessively anxious to make accusations, and then they delivered these accusations in highly accented intonations. Clearly their intent was to "get dad," and they executed this intent to the exclusion of talking about D* and his relationship to either parent.

H*'s live in boyfriend, Jay, testified that he was a good father to D* and would continue to be. He testified that H* had told him that I tried to kill her. This was amazing testimony, as it demonstrated clear intent to disrespect and interfere with my position as a father, complete with the justification provided by H*. This alone in any unprejudiced courtroom would determine the outcome.

David Baxter is the father of D*'s one allowed friend. David was the one of the witness called by Margo Fox who did not scowl or accuse. He testified to my having called him to discuss H*'s threat to D* that 'he would never see his best friend again if he didn't see doctor Dalton,' and my request that he not send his son to the house the weekend of the threat for a sleep over so that his son could not be used in this manner or worse. In cross examination David acknowledged that it was a reasonable thing to do and simultaneously corroborated the threat incident.

In my opinion the people who testified for H* all had in common that they were insecure and prone to making displays. Ms. Hernandez came back after four years to once and for all correct the criticism that she taught a math lesson to first graders incorrectly. Ms. Carboneau with her four divorces plasters "respect" program posters all over the school. D* said she had one up in every room. I saw she had three just on her office wall. Ms. Garcia after talking to H* was willing to believe that a grown man could beat up her child in the school cafeteria during lunch. April Perry was afraid to the bone of either not playing along, or of a past opposing client coming for her, depending on one's take of her performance. Kacie Nesby waited outside because she was afraid of dad coming to complain about an intake form. Mr. Johnson put up a tough man facade talking in a deep voice and knowing everything. I wonder what he is compensating for. David Baxter talked softly and oh so much couldn't make up his mind up about testifying because he wanted to be neutral, but worked with the other attorney without calling me. He couldn't help himself. Even Jay the boyfriend when he comes with H* to protect her during an exchange stands safely behind her. In my opinion these are gullible people who need propping up, and H* gives them the prop.

In contrast, the women who testified for D* and his relationship to his father had an atypical personality characteristic in that they were self assured critical thinkers. None of them required reassurance from others or the comfort of following popular belief trends to support their opinions, and in fact they did not hesitate to dismiss something that did not make sense independent of its affiliation. These people were the opposite of being gullible.

Which of these two crowds would D* be better off primarily growing up around? Surely the answer is obvious. I hope my son grows up to be a well adjusted critical thinker, not an insecure gullible person with a propensity for making displays.

The Texas legislature has put into family law a presumption of best interest of the child. This is one of the more enlightened laws we have in divorce custody, and it was hard fought for. In the 1960s in America there was a rebellion against the direction attorneys had taken divorce. This resulted in adoption of no fault divorce in most states, including Texas. The divorce industry moved to protect its profitability by creating a nightmare over custody instead of property. The legislature reacted by making "best interest of the child," the presumption. Unfortunately, the lower courts have remained corrupt. The de facto objective of todays divorce courts has nothing to do with any member of the divorcing family or relationship between any of them.

None of the serious accusations against me had merit and fortunately, nor were they shown to. This latter point is not always a given in the divorce courts. Nor was it established that my being rude was related in anyway to parenting. I would submit that I was appropriately rude in order to be able to see my son, as at the YMCA, and to be able to get my subpoena, as at the clerk's office, etc. Indeed, if standing up for one's parental rights is rude, then more dads need to be rude more often. I hope my son grows up to be rude in this manner. The judge

380

seemed to have the attitude in the courtroom that if anyone was rude in any way, that this person was insulting the judge himself, and was somehow a bad parent. There is no such parenting theory in the books, and there certainly wasn't one introduced in our proceedings. I have was warned about this by many attorneys, as it makes it impossible to represent oneself since one inevitably appears to be rude when putting witnesses on the spot during cross examination.

A child custody case is not about the parents. It does not matter which parent would benefit or otherwise, it matters, where the child is better off. Margo Fox ignored this, and employed an attack is the best defense strategy. As is the case in attack is the best defense, the true purpose of the apparent defense was to change the focus from D* to 'father is bad'. Her entire case was a personal attack on me, often times employing people I had never met or did not know.

Judge Wisser's Independent Questioning on Trailers

In my opinion the sinking of Mystique scares the attorneys as it represents significant monetary damages directly stemming from their actions in the attorney amicus fee shakedown. In support of this opinion, while I was on the stand Margo Fox grilled me over the sinking, even suggesting that Mystique didn't sink at all but that we had hauled her away on a trailer. I took great interest in this line of questioning as it was completely irrelevant to the custody case. It was however relative to a plan to seize the boat to pay for "attorney fees," or whatever they were getting at. Seizing assets to pay for divorce attorney's fees is become much too popular in Austin Texas. As another indication in support of my opinion, both Mr. Wallace and Mr. Whitten withdrew from the case immediately after learning that Mystique sank, and Mr. Whitten had sent an email expressing an opinion that the boat could not be considered my homestead even though I was living on it.

Mrs. Fox dropped the "it didn't really sink" argument after I gave her the Coast Guard report number and a link to the Corpus paper article. However, Judge Wisser continued his own investigation of this by personally interviewing my witnesses, he even did this without attorneys being present. He even did this with my son. He would bumping into them and then bring up the topic of sailing. He would say that he was a sailor or that he had friends who were sailors. Somehow the conversation would then lead to trailers.

Ray Truitt is a building architect in Galveston, Texas. He is also a sailor and a buddy of D* and mine. As I mentioned, he came and testified to the vibrancy of D*'s relationship with his father. Since he was a sailor I sent him some email to see if he had been approached by the judge in private and asked about trailers. He had been:

book almost done

ray truitt < >   Mon, Apr 14, 2008 at 11:54 PM
To: Tom Lynch <   >

hey,

good to hear from you.
tell me about d   , he is frequently on my mind.
anytime I hear about quantum computing methods and programming for it, you cross my mind.

yes, I do remember a conversation in the hall with the judge. we bumped into each other in the hall and he
asked about my boat. I told him it is a cheoy lee 44 - perry cutter and he offered "that's a very sea worthy
craft" and I invited him to join us for a sail whenever he may come to galveston, just give me call and we
would get it together. then, curiously enough, he did mention that "that's way to big to fit on a trailer" and I
agreed but it could be put on a truck. however, it would be a lot more fun to sail it some place. never gave
that comment another thought. as a matter of fact boats like Lee-Bre' do get moved by tractor trailer from
time to time. he said that he was also a sailor and was looking forward to a trip to costa rica (?) to go out
sailing with a friend of his next week.

glad you are writing a book, it would be good for d   to read how much he means to us. undoubtedly he
will need to be reminded just how special we all think him to be.

hey, are the visitation schedules still as problematical as they looked like they would be or has she seen the
wisdom of having a real father in her son's life helpful?

when I get Lee fixed up after our last "equipment testing" program let's go sailing. I planned to take lee on a
jump down the coast to port aransas and got caught in a norther that gave us the choice to run down wind for
two days in force 8 winds. lost all three sails and broke much stuff but we got home ok and when Annie gets
over the fact that just because I'm missing at sea for 3 days does not mean that I'm not ok we will all be
restored to our original condition.

yep, lee needs more hand holds, a good drogue, and some other improvements. the sea anchor worked
well. We replaced the staysail roller furling, fixed the faraday cage (handrail), SSB antenna, man overboard
gear (no we didn't lose anyone), force 10 barbeque, add a "SPOT" position reporting device, floor mats
(sucker got pretty slick when the ocean came in), repaired the auto helms (both are working again), working
on the bimini (lost the old one - it was really time to replace it anyway), added a back up fresh water pump
and lee cloths for the salon, repaired the refrigeration system - again-dang will it ever stop, fixed the hatch -
the sucker just flew off, and I am moving the life raft and the dingy.

The dingy just washed out of its restraints--just amazing! gonna hafta beef up the emergency steering gear -
we bent the sucker! however, the stars were magnificent, the waves were beautiful, and the glowing plankton
was a visual treat. yep, 27 foot seas....what a ride. there is nothing else in my experience like surfing down a
20 foot sea on a 44 foot surf board. not since the 60s have a had a fire hose full in the face....still just as cold
and just as special, now as then.

I've attached a story my brother wrote about the trip for your amusement.

later, my friend.

Ray

Figure 90: Ray Truitt's Email on Independent Examination by Judge Wisser

Paul Wood my assistant was also stopped by the judge and questioned:

CAUSE NO <u>06-1054-F395</u>

IN THE MATTER OF THE MARRIAGE OF	§ IN THE DISTRICT COURT § §
THOMAS WALKER LYNCH AND H	§ § § 395TH JUDICIAL DISTRICT § §
AND IN THE INTEREST OF D A CHILD	§ WILLIAMSON COUNTY, TEXAS §

Paul Wood'S AFFADAVIT OF FACT

BEFORE ME, the undersigned authority, personally appeared Paul Wood, who by me duly sworn, deposed as follows:

My name is Paul Wood and I live in Galveston, Texas.

After the hearing ended on Friday, October 19, 2007, in the 395th Judicial Court, William County, Texas, Judge Jon Wisser made some comments to the people in the courtroom. He looked in my direction and started talking about boats. He mentioned something about people that have boats seem to enjoy the time they spend on them (or something like that). I replied that I like working with boats. The judge's conversation about boats was pretty much one sided. He talked quite a bit, and I only made the one reply. He went on to mention his friend's boat that was transported on a trailer.

SIGNED on _26 MAR, 2008_

Paul Wood
Paul Wood

SUBSCRIBED AND SWORN TO BEFORE ME on _March 26_, 2008

Sheryl L. Caldwell

> SHERYL L. CALDWELL
> MY COMMISSION EXPIRES
> July 9, 2009

Notary Public, State of Texas

Figure 91: Paul Wood Affidavit On Independent Examination By Judge Wisser

D*, Paul and I were together when I first asked Paul if he thought the judge had an unusual interest in Trailers. D* then volunteered he too had a conversation about trailers with the judge. He said he had been reading about them in Sail magazine. Paul talked to D* further and discovered that D* had a great knowledge of trailers, so much so that he says it could not have come from Sail magazine. This is a bit of a mystery as D* and I have never owned or used a trailer.

Judge Wisser's Conferral With D*

Felix Rippy had originally suggested that D* should talk to the judge. We felt that D* had a lot to talk about that a judge would find more than interesting. I suppose it was for this same reason that H* did not want D* to talk to the judge, though I suspect she would say that it had more to do with the Child's Bill of Rights. According to these local rules a child is not supposed to be exposed to the divorce. What the Child's Bill of Rights authors hadn't considered, or perhaps they did, was that this shuts up the child. It isn't always the case that a divorce is only about the attorneys. Sometimes the child is the prime mover.

Judge Wisser agreed to see D*, though the date of that meeting kept getting delayed. It didn't happen until the end of the second day of the hearings. After the conferral Paul, Gene, Grandpa, D*, and I went out for dinner. D* was bouncing off the walls just as he was the weekend that he came over after his mother had told him she couldn't love him if he didn't like her. He couldn't look me in the eye. He couldn't sit still. All he said that Judge Wisser told him about all the people he sent to jail and that he gave death penalties. Later that evening he told me he had said that he wanted to live with his dad, but had explained his mom was OK. He didn't want his mom to get hurt. As mentioned in the previous section he also said he had discussed boat trailers with the judge.

Gmail by Google BETA

Tom Lynch <   >

Friday Evening December 7, 2007

Paul Wood ·
To: Tom Lynch

Mon, Dec 24, 2007 at 10:02 AM

Tom,

After the second day in court (Friday, December 7, 2007), from the time we left the courthouse and through our dinner, D   seemed to be upset and secretive about his meeting with Judge Wisser. He would only talk about the large number of criminal cases that the judge heard in his career including death penalty cases. I don't recall the number of cases, but D   was quoting a number. D   would not talk about what was bothering him in the car or at dinner while you, your dad, Gene and I were present. When asked about what he said to the judge, D   would not say anything and he would look away and fidget.

Paul

Figure 92: Paul Wood on D* Talking About The Judge Doing Death Penalties

384

Judge Wisser talking about death penalties with my son in conferral is quite a slap in the face since I asked him in court to stop bringing the topic up as I felt it was inappropriate, asking him how he thought it made us feel.

Judge Wisser's Ruling

Judge Wisser removed all of my parenting rights related to medical or educational decisions, and he put at the top "joint managing conservatorship." This is a definite message to me sent via Sally Ray's testimony.

Judge Wisser fined me "attorneys fees" that now exceed $50,000 including fines from the pretrial motions and the $10,000 I'm ordered to outright give Margo Fox if I file an appeal. He nearly doubled my child support. I think my prior child support amount was a little high, but about right for a year ago. It is difficult to calculate exactly because I am not salaried. However this year has not been as productive due to the time I have been spending on the divorce case. It has been time consuming learning about law, drafting motions, and planning cases. Also contributing to less income is the fact that the patent purchase rate has slowed. They have been very slow coming out of the law firm, and in cases turning around from point of purchase to payment. As an additional factor I have a great deal of damage loss this year do to the loss of my home and possessions. As a result the new child support is over 8 times what I calculate from the formula. Judge Wisser also moved the payment schedule back. My child support was paid on December 15 through January 15, he then ordered me to make my next payment for the new double amount on January 1, so I had the privilege of paying child support twice in January. The judge may have averaged my gross *business* income going back four years and then added more for "medical" to derive the support number, or perhaps he just got it from Margo Fox.

Instead of picking D* up at school on Thursday and dropping him off at school on Monday morning, my odd weekend visits have been cut back to exactly 48 hours from Friday afternoon to Sunday evening. Also there is no off week visit as is standard. This appears to be due to Pam Wocholz's incredible testimony that I took D* out from school without signing him out -- some four years ago. Janie Veach the school principal had no such complaint. Apparently Judge Wisser finds more credible the testimony of an apparently erstwhile playground monitor who worked four years ago on issues of signing children out, over those of the school principal.

Judge Wisser reduced my greater than 100 mile summer visitation to 30 days instead of 42 days. This is following the attorney amicus's description of his parting letter.

Amazingly, in his proposed final order he condoned the use of hypnosis on D* by H*:

IT IS ORDERED that H*   shall have the exclusive right to hire and fire any medical, dental, psychological, and psychiatric professionals (including but not limited to professionals in the field of hypnosis) of the child. If THOMAS LYNCH takes the child to see or consult with any medical, dental, psychological, or psychiatric professional (including but not limited to professionals in the field of hypnosis) other than in an emergency involving the physical health of the child or involving a serious physical illness of the child, he will have violated the terms of this order.

Figure 93: Judge Wisser Condones Usage of Hypnosis On D*

I sent the proposed order to a news organization, and I believe they called the judge to ask about this. Judge Wisser took the parenthetical out, but his intention remains clear.

Judge Wisser also enjoined me from going near April Perry or *any* of Margo Fox's staff or Sara Brandon's staff. April Perry had put on a performance, but the law says there has to be a threat in place to justify such language. There were no threats, nor did the judge find that there were. Also,Margo Fox or her staff had not made any complaints at all. Perhaps the worst part is I don't even know who these people are and I certainly don't recognize them. We are talking about a couple dozen people and a dynamically changing list. I could go to jail for standing next to someone I don't know. This order literally makes me a second class citizen who must make way for the the superior lawyers and their staffs, and a person who can be manipulated at their will. I was in a restaurant the other day, and I thought I saw Margo Fox, and when this happens, whether I have a date or whatever, I'm supposed to clear out. I remained in fatherly defiance.

386

2008, After the Hearing and The Appeal

Judge Wisser Comments on Memory in Old Age

Barbara Coplin D* 2nd grade teacher and one of our witnesses told me that she knew Judge Wisser. She said their kids played together. Barbara Coplin was not a legal sort so I didn't fault her for not mentioning it earlier, but I thought that Judge Wisser should have disclosed it, so I wrote him to ask why he didn't. Mrs. Coplin had talked like it was recent, but then after I copied her on the email she pointed out that it had been 25 years prior. However, Judge Wisser's reply turned out to be more generally interesting the the original question:

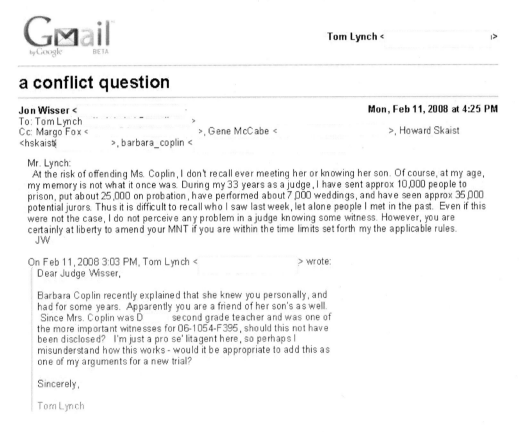

Gmail by Google BETA

Tom Lynch <   >

a conflict question

Jon Wisser <   · >   **Mon, Feb 11, 2008 at 4:25 PM**
To: Tom Lynch   >
Cc: Margo Fox <   >, Gene McCabe <   >, Howard Skaist
<hskaist(>, barbara_coplin <   >

Mr. Lynch:
   At the risk of offending Ms. Coplin, I don't recall ever meeting her or knowing her son. Of course, at my age, my memory is not what it once was. During my 33 years as a judge, I have sent approx 10,000 people to prison, put about 25,000 on probation, have performed about 7,000 weddings, and have seen approx 35,000 potential jurors. Thus it is difficult to recall who I saw last week, let alone people I met in the past. Even if this were not the case, I do not perceive any problem in a judge knowing some witness. However, you are certainly at liberty to amend your MNT if you are within the time limits set forth my the applicable rules.
   JW

On Feb 11, 2008 3:03 PM, Tom Lynch <   > wrote:
   Dear Judge Wisser,

   Barbara Coplin recently explained that she knew you personally, and had for some years. Apparently you are a friend of her son's as well. Since Mrs. Coplin was D   second grade teacher and was one of the more important witnesses for 06-1054-F395, should this not have been disclosed? I'm just a pro se' litagent here, so perhaps I misunderstand how this works - would it be appropriate to add this as one of my arguments for a new trial?

   Sincerely,

   Tom Lynch

Figure 94: Judge Wisser Email on Conflict

Though he didn't do it for the child conferral, here the judge was respectful of my request not to bring up death penalties in the context of a divorce modification and didn't put these in. For discussion sake lets not consider these for now, they are probably only in the hundreds relative to the thousands of jail sentences. Now lets do the math. There are 52 weeks in the year. Four weeks are for holidays. The judge also gets vacation, personal time for sick leave, conferences, continuing education, running for election, and other obligations. Lets suppose another five weeks during the year for these things. I suppose that judges are typically on the bench 7 hours a day, so:

33 years * (52 wks/yr – 9 wks not on bench) * 5 days/wk * 7 hours/day = 49,665 hrs

Wow, that is almost 50 thousand hours sitting on the bench. Doing weddings and selecting jurors could be quicker than hearing crimes. Suppose these averaged 30 minutes each, then hours left over with the judge on the bench hearing criminals is:

49,665 - (½ hour) * (35,000 + 7000) = 28,665 hours hearing crimes

Now we can divide this by the number of crimes the judge has heard to get the time he spends on average on a case. We don't know the total number of crimes, as he didn't tell us how many people he found innocent. He only reports the ones he sent to jail or put on probation. I think this fact by omission is interesting by itself. This plus his comments in court about doing death penalties, and his explicit pointing only his death penalty hearings in his email when talking about schedules, leads me to think the judge is rather proud of having found so many people guilty. On the topic of the scheduling email, it is possible that all that he had on his calendar were death penalties. Suppose he found %30 of the criminals not guilty relative to the ones he found guilty, then we can can calculate an hours spent per criminal case by:

28,665 hrs / (10,000 + 25,000) * 1.3 = .63 hrs per criminal case

.63 hours is 37.8 minutes. That is less than 40 minutes per case. Some criminal hearings would last for days, so that pushes the others down even further in order to keep the average.

I suspect there is a two part explanation for Judge Wisser's efficiency. Firstly, as the Judge brags about his record perhaps his 'golf score' is missing a few strokes. One of my assistants suggested a second reason. Judge Wisser may be using a heuristic to determine outcomes rather than deriving the outcome from testimony and evidence. We hypothesize that his heuristic is to look at the stability of employment of the parties. Supporting this hypothesis is the fact he mentioned 'stability of employment' in his findings of facts against me. We hypothesize that Judge Wisser saw my irregular income due to sales of my patents and the wire payments from an overseas broker, didn't understand, and concluded that I made money illicitly. Perhaps I'm more cynical than my assistant, I bet that many of these greedy people actually think I have a large offshore account that I pull money from when I want and if they make me uncomfortable enough he money will come pouring out.

I'm not very happy to hear the Judge Wisser is having difficulty remember people he saw last week, as we presented a lengthy case and there was more than two weeks lapse between the final hearing and his ruling. I wonder how he could notice and then remember important testimony. Fueling this concern is the fact he completely left out some important witnesses, including the school principal, from his findings of fact. I would imagine the folks sitting on death row as a result of the death penalty hearings we were working around to schedule our custody modification would be even less happy to hear Judge Wisser explain he is having difficulties remembering people.

Findings of Fact of Facts and Conclusions of Law

Judge Wisser provided his ruling without any explanation as to how he derived it. As a first step towards an appeal I filed a request for an explanation. This is known as a request for findings of facts and conclusions of law, or FOF for short. He replied to Margo Fox and me asking us to provide proposed FOF. I was surprised, as I thought that a judge had to derive

388

his or her ruling from the findings, and that it would only be a question of text formating to provide the FOF. Instead, it was to be a laborious process to draft FOF derived from the ruling instead of the other way around. Not surprisingly Margo Fox's proposed FOF read like her case, what else could be expected? The ruling did not follow at all from my proposed FOF, and it only stood as a guide of what *not* to write. The findings arrived nearly on the last day available for the FOF schedule.

The first thing Judge Wisser put in the FOF is the list of attorneys that Margo Fox claims I have had. Attorneys must officially place their names on record to be part of the case. There are three attorneys of record for my case, each occurring in succession. Felix Rippy, Mark Roles, and Tim Whitten. The judge lists two more attorneys, Steve Copenhaver and Glynn Turquand, who had considered taking the case but had not. The reason this is important to the judge as a long list of attorneys helps him justify his large attorney fee amount. He needs the extra attorneys because H* had three attorneys of record also, and there were at least six people listed in her correspondence, so there wouldn't be an imbalance without the extras. In addition the judge did not list H*'s attorneys, so the reader would assume there was a ratio of 5 to 1, rather than a ratio of 1 to 1.

Judge Wisser notes that H* has exclusive right to determine the geographic location of residence of the child with no restrictions.

He finds that my pleadings were amended on December 15, 2006 to ask for supervised visitation, but he has it backwards. H* amended *her* pleadings and asked for supervised visitation in an emergency hearing that occurred during D* and my vacation to visit Grandma and Grandpa. We had to say in Georgetown wondering if we would ever have a vacation again, yet Wisser puts the blames this on me. Judge Wisser may have mislead the court here by error, or he may have done it on purpose. It is considered very bad form for an attorney to declare an emergency hearing for immediate supervised visitation, lose the hearing, and then later have Judge Wisser award her attorney's fees. FYI, my pleadings were amended in 2007 requesting a shared parenting arrangement.

He writes:

> A. Both the child's therapist, Caryl Dalton, and the child's pediatrician, Samuel Mirrop, who were treating the child at the time of the Final Decree of Divorce in 2001, have since discontinued their services to the child due to the actions of Thomas Lynch.

I find it particularly insulting that I am being blamed for Dr. Mirrop's quitting. Dr. Mirrop himself has refused all phone calls and contact, even go so far as to hire a law firm to protect himself. When grandma wrote him a letter, he sent the law firm, and had them reply and provide a copy to the judge. I gather he has become defensive so that his mis-diagnosis and refusal to even allow a nurse to check won't cause him a lawsuit. In my opinion, it is unfortunate that he is more concerned about this inconvenience than about his patient. Anyway, there was nothing I could do to contact him and have home come explain. Caryl Dalton was in deep with a dual role ethics violation playing both custody evaluator, mom advocate, and therapist. Yet, it is my fault for her quitting.

Here is an interesting FOF point for you home schoolers. I never said in my testimony that I wanted to home school D*. This issue was raised by the other side and then pushed. My plan was to have D* tested and to figure out what the best next course would be and I said as much. I had not ruled out homeschooling is all that I said, and I took issue when they said home schooling was asocial as some places, like Austin, have communities. Here is Judge Wisser's FOF on this point:

> N.   Tom Lynch expressed an interest in home schooling D* Lynch in opposition to testimony of expert witnesses who claimed that D* Lynch needed social interaction with peers and authority figures other than Tom Lynch.

So you home schoolers should note that having the opposing attorney say you "expressed an interest" in home schooling is now a justification for taking away a father's parental rights if an anonymous "expert" thinks a child needs social interaction.

However, the most repugnant part of Judge Wisser's point "N" here is his authority figure comment. I'll have to go back over testimony, but I don't recall anyone saying this. But who is an authority figure in a child's life?   It is his father. I have long been saying that one of the reasons that judges are willing to rule against fathers is that they are threatened by the father as an authority figure. The judge wants to be the only authority figure. Here it is in black and white. D* is to have other fathers than Tom Lynch.

The FOF is in general a damnation of dad that is only loosely based on the case. Everything that did not fit the ruling was thrown out, including testimony. Here is Judge Wissers comments on the witnesses, this is the entire list:

> 5.   The Court makes the following findings of fact regarding witnesses:
>
>> A.   Caryl Dalton was a credible witness.
>>
>> B.   Sally Rae was a credible witness.
>>
>> C.   Pam Wacholz was a credible witness.
>>
>> D.   April Perry was a credible witness.
>>
>> E.   Margo Fox was a credible witness as to attorneys fees.
>>
>> F.   The testimony of Annie Truitt was of limited value.

The first thing to notice is that Jannie Veach the school principal who suggested that D* should be with dad and have mom's influence, and who said that seeing D* dad was the highlight of D*'s day, is not listed at all. Nor is D*'s second grade teacher, Barbara Coplin, who said that D* aspired to be like his dad listed. Annie Truitt the only expert who talked on topic, and talked about how much D* loved his dad and needed to be listened to is "of limited value."   Why? Her degree is just as credible as the other experts. The only logical reason any of us can figure is that it is because her conclusions did not fit those the judge's ruling.

In contrast, the woman who steadfastly refused to work with the whole family, who D* said hated his dad, who violated dual role ethics, who is the most likely candidate of using hypnosis (which Judge Wisser condoned), who had never formally spoken with dad, and who did not comment on child parent relationships, is listed as a credible witness. Sally Rae who violated regulations of the APA in giving testimony on someone she had never met and had no evidence against, who admitted that she had her facts wrong, and who didn't talk about the parent child relationship is a "credible witness."   Pam Wacholz who's hysterical testimony even raised a comment form the judge, and who backed off of her testimony in cross examination, who did not talk at all about parent child relationships, is a "credible witness." April Perry who is a biased party due to being a legal assistant for the opposition, who's sole meeting of either party was to say she didn't want to talk spoken through a cracked open door, who said nothing of parent child relationships is in Judge Wisser's view a "credible witness."

Post Judgment Hearing

The new order, and the child rights, say that phone calls are to be allowed, and that mom is not to interfere with them. She hadn't allowed phone calls since 2003. I listed unanswered calls since the order in the Motion For New trial (which was denied). She still didn't answer calls. So I filed a Motion for Sanctions with my subpoenaed telephone bill. The opposition answered the motion complete with documentation that they were running all of D* calls through a computer. She started allowing calls just before and after the hearing. The quality is horrible. It appears that her boyfriend who has a hobby of audio mixing has arranged a Skype line to go through the computer where apparently he records, and listens to the call in real time as we are cut off if I say something they don't like. For example, tonight I asked D* if he was still watching TV everyday. He said he was. I asked him if it was a problem, cut, no more talking. There are also drop outs where the line just goes silent. This happens about 30 minutes into a call. The opposition counter sued saying I hadn't paid child support, though I was late, I had paid it. I had a third motion which I had provided to the opposition saying I was preparing to file it, but had not filed it yet.

I came out of Kinkos on the way to the hearing to discover my keys were locked in my truck. Someone at Kinkos offered me a ride, and I was running about 20 minutes late. I called the court house, but the judges office didn't answer as they were at a hearing. Glynda had not forwarded her phone to a receptionist. The clerks office initially said there was nothing they could do, but called back and told me that they had all left.

Judge Wisser ruled that I had purposely blown them off. Even though there were 30 missed calls, and the answer to my motion was complete with pictures of the computer system and an explanation, and I wasn't there yet, he ruled against my motion for sanctions. He was OK with the idea that the opposition would violate the order and the Child's Bill of Rights, and in fact he ruled that it was frivolous that I would even complain about it, and awarded the other side attorneys fees of a total of three thousand dollars for the twenty minutes.

Birthday Surprise

The weekend before I had not noticed the school schedule had D* out on Thursday instead of Friday, and I was late to pick him up. I called her on the phone and apologized. D* and I went to the Starbucks for the drop off on Sunday April 6th on schedule, but mom was not there. So this was going to be her tit for tat thing. I didn't mind, I can spend a long time with D*. We waited about half hour, and H* came in and told D* to come and she went back to the car. I stepped out the door with D*. H* was sitting in the drivers seat while D* was getting in the back. It was unusual that her boyfriend was not lurking around behind her somewhere. While H* was sitting there in the drivers seat she looked at me and grinned big, as I hadn't seen since the temporary orders after she got off the stand. I wasn't the least bit upset, and for a split second I was glad to see her smiling, but I was curious.

April 10th was D* birthday. H* was to drop him at 6:00 at the Starbucks, and I was to return him at 8:00. I checked my bank account to see where things were at, and found that it had been frozen. H* had filed a "write of garnishment" for attorney's fees in the amount of $36,000 against the account, but here was $3000 dollars in the account, but it is frozen. I spent most of the day trying to figure out what that was and how serious it was. I was told by the attorney who did my bankruptcy in 2002 that this can be done in Texas, and that there is nothing I can do about it. All the money in my account will be given to H*.

As D*'s account has me as a co-signer, and they were able to file the writ against it also. The remaining $100 profit from D* fortune cookie business will go to pay Margo Fox. This will become the basis of a lesson to D* on how poor think kills initiative.

I went over to the consignment store where I had put D* and my hockey gear. The gear had been over there since before we went sailing and they hadn't sent anything. Most of it had sold, and they gave me a check for $140. This is the same amount as it costs to put gas in my suburban. I had the suburban because I used it to haul stuff for the boat and as an onshore sail locker. Now I'm just stuck with it. There was still a quarter tank of gas, and that lasts a couple of days. I went to the sporting goods company's bank, Bank of America, to cash the check. Bank of America said they required a $5 fee to honor checks presented to their bank. I refused to pay it, and they waived the fee. I bought D* a book for a gift.

At the Starbucks we met, and I told D* about a good Mexican restaurant I had found, and we went and had dinner. We returned to the Starbucks at 8:00.

Fortunately I have a patent sale pending, though as of April 21 it hasn't paid. I am now late on child support, and the apartment rent bounced. Last week they gave me ten days notice to leave or pay. Today the management was knocking on the door, or perhaps that is service from H*. I was indisposed at the time of the knock, and when I got there they were gone. It probably wasn't service as there was an envelope with a letter from the manager left at the door. Last time the child support was late H* sued me over it and got another $3000. I'm back on a forced diet of one meal a day, mainly beans and rice. For some reason the knowledge that I can not afford to eat whatever and whenever makes me all that much more hungry, though on the other hand I am accustomed to long passages.

I managed to feed D* well this last weekend. We splurged and added hamburger and organic spinach. We even had a drink at Starbucks after the soccer game and did a math lesson. H* arrived ten minutes early this time, and interrupted. She had done this once before. We were eating at the restaurant down the mall when she came in early insisting he leave early. We were doing a math lesson that time also. That time she told him that it was

392

important to go right away because she was grocery shopping next door. I guess it was an emergency grocery shopping trip. I suggested she come back after shopping, but she said she couldn't. This time her reasoning for him leaving a little early was that I should be flexible. After all she had been flexible two exchanges prior when I was late. I really don't mind about ten minutes here or there, but what I do mind it being by design. The first time she could have gone shopping and come back, or this time gotten in line and gotten a drink, indeed that is what her boyfriend was doing. H* and D* sat in the car waiting while he got his drink.

Court Reporters

What is actually said in a courtroom does not matter afterwards as much as what the official court reporter says was said. Court reporters work for judges or they are independent contractors who work for themselves, though they may be assigned work through a firm. Reporters depend upon attorneys and judges to give them work, and especially so in small communities. They typically set their rates and their bill collection policies. I have now met a dozen court reporters, and all have all been women. Court reporters work with the same group of people day in and day out. As we saw for Judge Wisser, over a career this amounts of tens of thousands of hours spent with the same people. Surely at some point relationships develop. When something goes wrong chances are that the court reporter will have allegiance to those who find her work.

Court reporters in Texas take dictation to paper tape, so we must depend on the court reporter to correctly transfer obscure dictation from a paper tape. Everyone involved admits this is a difficult and error prone process. But who will the errors facilitate? A reporter may optionally make an electronic recording. It has been my experience that if someone requests to have the electronic recording reviewed, the reporter will tell the person that she has recycled the tape for another hearing. She has no obligation to keep the electronic recordings.

At the April 24th hearing I noticed some errors in the transcript. The main one was that the Judge telling Jim Wallace to sit down was not transcribed. I gave the recorder Paula Jones an errata sheet, and she said she "did not have time" to fix the errors. After I pestered her she fixed only one and said she didn't have time do do any more. Her tone was as though I was being greedy as though I didn't appreciate the one errata repair. After all how many could I want? Typically I spoke with her, but after I asked for the statement for Jim Wallace to be fixed in email, she blocked her email address to me.

In my own deposition there was a point where Margo Fox was trying to make me look bad over doctors, and I pointed out the game saying that she had really got me going. My comment was not in the final transcript. I complained about this. The deposition has not been mentioned since.

The first thing Margo Fox did after the Janie Veach deposition was to offer the court reporter a job. I thought the message there was clear enough.

393

An individual who wishes to appeal is obligated by law to pay the reporter to transcribe the paper tape dictation for the appeals court and to do so in a timely manner. All the reporters who worked for me requested money up front against an estimate of the cost of transcribing. They all exceeded their estimate, some significantly, except Paula Stone. The two reporters who did the final hearing made it clear that nothing would be filed with the court until they were paid in full.

Here is an email from Joan Wilson, who did the first two days of the final hearing, a transcript which is mandatory for the appeal:

G**M**ail
by Google   BETA

Tom Lynch < |>

Appellate Record: re: D   Lynch

JWilsonCSR@aol.com ·   Thu, Apr 10, 2008 at 10:19 AM

Mr. Lynch,

Please find attached Invoice for Appellate Reporter's Record, dated 4/10/08, In the Interest of D Lynch, TC# 06-1054-F395, Court of Appeals # 03-08-00184-CV, ordered by you 3/14/08 with a deposit amount of $3,260.

As previously emailed to you, the Balance due and owing on this record is $548.

I will be out-of-state after April 14th, so I will need payment before that time to process and file the original and copy of this order. Therefore, payment must be in the form of certified funds, Cashier's Check or Money Order, for this amount, $548.

Please send payment immediately so that I can get this to you and meet filing deadlines. The address to send payment is: Joan Wilson,

Joan Wilson
Certified Shorthand Reporter
State of Texas

Planning your summer road trip? Check out AOL Travel Guides.

📄 **Lynch Invoice.doc**
   221K

Figure 95: Court Reporter Ultimatum

Our appellate deadline for filing transcripts is the 24th of April. Joan had prior told me that she would not file the transcripts until the $548 was paid, and I had taken note of that. She had originally notified me on April 2 that there would be a $548 fee for the index, which I had asked her to do. This is not a cost overrun, but an index required by the court and it is work she needs to be paid for. However, now on the Thursday she tells me she needs payment by Monday, not the 24th, because she will "be out-of-state", and she provides no contingencies. She tells me I will miss my appellate deadline for the transcripts if I don't pay her by Monday.

My bank account had been frozen by H* and I knew this timing not to be possible. I told Joan it would be next week until I could get her the money, and requested she send the material to Affiliated reporting to have it filed when it was paid for, to make corrections, and to verify the work. She refused . As of the time of this writing Joan has made no indications that she will file the transcripts, nor has she arranged to get them to me. I spoke with another reporter who knows her. She says Joan left for family reasons and thinks she thinks Joan has arranged for someone else to file the transcripts with the court while she is gone. If this is the case, then the court will get the transcripts before I can see them or have them verified.

Joan Wilson already has the $3200 some dollars I paid her up front. Another reporter charged $1800. Another asked for around $500, and then came back for $550 more. The Janie Veach deposition was expensive as well. I will probably have a couple thousand more due to another pretrial hearing and the recent post trail hearing. All of this had to be paid as part of the appeal.

Appeal Brief

I am currently drafting the appeal brief. I'm told that an appeal process may take two years. I think I have a fairly strong grounds for appeal, but the most that can be hoped for is that the prior order is struck and we get a new trial and get to go through it again. I take no joy in learning law and trials. I law find it sad and taxing. When I walk down the hall of the courtroom and see all the people waiting to be judged, perhaps because they did mean things, and perhaps they will go to jail, I feel like Dante walking the 7 levels. It doesn't seem like a very good place for divorces.

In The Words of Others

Grandma and D* are now exchanging email, he is the tail end of a thread on houses:

   D   >

(no subject)

sandralynch   **Thu, May 1, 2008 at 11:35 AM**
To: D

Hello D
 I was thinking today about you and also about your concern that your dad does not have a house. Let me tell
you what the difference between a house and a home.
A house is a building with bedrooms, bathrooms, kitchen and so on. That is it. You will see houses on the
street that have no one living in them, You will see houses with people in them. Some are happy and some
are not. It is just a house. What about people?
A home is where you have love, unity, and security. It is where you feel the love all around you. So your dad
does not have a house for you, but he has something more important. Your dad makes a home for you. It is
full of love.
 I have lived in many houses growing up, but it was my family that lived in these houses that was my home. I
hope you will understand what grandma is telling you. You have a home with your dad, it just not in a house.
I love you very much and take care Love Grandma Sandy L

A1

CAUSE NO 06-1054-F395

IN THE MATTER OF THE MARRIAGE OF THOMAS WALKER LYNCH AND H AND IN THE INTEREST OF D l, A CHILD	§ IN THE DISTRICT COURT § § § § 395TH JUDICIAL DISTRICT § § § § WILLIAMSON COUNTY, TEXAS §

WITNESS J Strother Moore's AFFADAVIT

BEFORE ME, the undersigned authority, personally appeared J Strother Moore, who by me duly sworn, deposed as follows:

My name is J Strother Moore. I am a full professor in the Department of Computer Sciences at the University of Texas at Austin and chair of Department. I hold the Admiral B. R. Inman Centennial Chair of Computing Theory and a member of the National Academy of Engineering. I met Tom Lynch in May, 1995, when I was hired as a consultant to AMD to verify the floating-point division microcode for the AMD K5 processor, which was then about to be fabricated. Tom Lynch was the lead designer on the floating point team and I worked closely with him and another colleague to prove, mathematically, that the design was correct.

I have known D   since he was born. My wife and I have interacted socially with Tom and D   several times a year since then.

The Attorney Amicus, Mr. James P. Wallace, has not attempted to contact me, which is unfortunate as I feel that have important information to contribute.

I find Tom Lynch to be an exceptionally dedicated father, especially when it comes to D   understanding of nature, science, and mathematics. In virtually every encounter I have had with them, Tom has taken pains to peak D curiosity, to listen to his explanations of how and why things behave the way they do, to encourage research and discovery, and, when necessary, to explain.

A good example of this is Tom's encouragement of a science project to discover the basic principles of flotation. D   constructed a variety of "boats" out of aluminum foil, loaded them in different ways, and observed how they floated. He ultimately discovered his young and not entirely precise version of Archimedes' principle, that a floating object displaces an amount of water equal to its weight. These experiments were conducted over several weeks and I witness the construction by D   of many boats. His craftsmanship was not equal to his

A2

intellect so the experiments were rather messy and the project was ultimately not very impressive from the perspective of school science fair presentations. But I would wager that D＿＿ learned more about science with his project than the winners of that year's fair!

I have seen Tom present D＿＿ with all manner of puzzles and challenges – in a friendly and encouraging way. While D＿ no doubt has inherited a lot of intelligence and curiosity from both parents, I think his way of approaching the world and his open-minded search for answers is in large part due to Tom's attitude toward the world.

SIGNED on April 16, 2007

J Strother Moore

SUBSCRIBED AND SWORN TO BEFORE ME on April 17, 2007

LORRAINE SANCHEZ
Notary Public, State of Texas
My Commission Expires
NOVEMBER 08, 2008
Notary without Bond

Lorraine d. Sanchez

Notary Public, State of Texas

A3

IN THE MATTER OF	§ **IN THE DISTRICT COURT**
THE MARRIAGE OF	§
	§
THOMAS WALKER LYNCH	§
AND	§ **395TH JUDICIAL DISTRICT**
H	§
	§
AND IN THE INTEREST OF	§ **WILLIAMSON COUNTY, TEXAS**
D	§

WITNESSES <u>GARY AND PENNY GASTINEAU'S AFFADAVIT OF FACT</u>

BEFORE ME, the undersigned authorities, personally appeared Gary and Penny Gastineau, who by me duly sworn, deposed as follows:

Our names are Gary and Penny Gastineau. We live in Round Rock, Texas. We have 4 adult children and 3 grandsons and have many years of experience nurturing children. We are both business owners and are raising one of our grandsons who is eight-years-old. We have known Tom Lynch and D since September of 2004. They have a wonderful father son relationship.

We were on the witness list for the hearing on December 19, 2006 and spoke to Attorney Mark Roles. We could not sit by and let the court eliminate Tom from D ' life. Their time together is too short as it is. We arranged our schedules to be in Georgetown to be witnesses and waited in the hallway but did not get to testify that day or at the two other hearings that were scheduled (March 23rd) and rescheduled (March 26th). The court appointed an Amicus Attorney, James P. Wallace, who has not contacted us in any way or left messages for us to return a call. We continue to be ready to testify. The following is our testimony by affidavit since there has been no other way to speak for them.

We have spent time with Tom and D on several occasions at our home, at their home, at our lakehouse, and just recently in Galveston on their boat. D respects his father, is very comfortable at home just being D , and is well behaved when he is with Tom on our observation.

When we are at their house in Austin, D tries to teach our grandson how to play GO, a complex strategy game, not many of their peers know how to play. Tom and D built a telegraph and D has learned Morse Code. Tom is an excellent cook and is sensitive to D allergies to some foods.

Tom Lynch is a good father and role model. Their relationship is essential to D overall development and it would be irresponsible for us to let the court do anything but make more time for them to be together.

SIGNED on April 16, 2007.

Gary Gastineau

Penny Gastineau

SUBSCRIBED AND SWORN TO BEFORE ME on April16, 2007.

Notary Public, State of Texas

A5

CAUSE NO <u>06-1054-F395</u>

IN THE MATTER OF THE MARRIAGE OF	§ IN THE DISTRICT COURT
	§
	§
THOMAS WALKER LYNCH	§
AND	§ 395TH JUDICIAL DISTRICT
H'	§
	§
AND IN THE INTEREST OF	§
D|	§ WILLIAMSON COUNTY, TEXAS
	§

<u>WITNESS RAYMOND DIXON TRUITT'S AFFADAVIT OF FACT</u>

BEFORE ME, the undersigned authority, personally appeared Mr. Raymond Dixon Truitt, who by me duly sworn, deposed as follows:

My name is Raymond Dixon Truitt. I live in Galveston, Texas where I have a Cheoy Lee 44 – Perry that has provided me an opportunity to participate in the father son team of Tom and D   . I am 63 years old and an experienced father of three adult sons and three grand daughters. I am a professional Architect who is registered in the state of Texas. I have been uniquely blessed to know Tom Lynch and D since December of 2005. I wish to tell you that Tom and D   have an extraordinary father son relationship.

I was on the witness list for the hearing on December 19. I was so concerned that someone would suggest that D   s' time with Tom should be limited that I interrupted my holiday and drove from Galveston to Georgetown to be a witness.   I stood in the hallway waiting, but did not get to testify. Since the first hearing I have been informed of two more hearings and rearranged my schedule accordingly, just to find out again that I would not get to reflect my observations. Since late February I have been waiting for a call from the Amicus Attorney assigned to the case, a Mr. James P. Wallace. He has not contacted me in any manner, nor left any messages. Waiting for such an important phone call is burdensome on my practice, as is planning for and/or making trips to Georgetown.   Surely there is no plan to quash my testimony.

Also, in June of 2006 I arranged my summer vacation to join Tom and D   on a sailing trip, just to learn they had been held up in Georgetown in hearings over D ID renewal, without compensating time. I had also hoped to see Tom and D   the week of spring break starting on the 9th of March, just to be disappointed again. These are good guys with whom I enjoy sharing my time.

Now let me explain about the testimony I will make.   D   is more than just well behaved when I see him with Tom Lynch. D   trusts his father implicitly, looks up to his father, and is in intrigued by him. Tom Lynch is clearly D   role model.   If you were to take D   from his father it would be a crime, nothing less. Such an event would be detrimental no only to them but to us all. Treasures such as D   are to be both enjoyed and nurtured.

A6

Let me tell you about a time I saw Tom Lynch and D   together working on the boat. Tom would carefully measure scribe and cut a piece of flooring hand it back to D   who would take it, place it, and then sand it so that it fit perfectly. Not all the time were the pieces perfect. When improvements were needed they would just look at each other, look at the work, and with out saying a word reserve the piece for the next opportunity and begin again. Men work together differently than women and that makes all the difference.

I have witnessed Tom Lynch teach D   how to handle tools, give him life lessons, and protect him from harm. Tom has only to place his hands to his shoulders to remind D   that life jackets are required. D   spontaneously reacts to care for his dog, Lyka, when she needs to get on or off of the boat or is "missing" (as only dogs can do). D   ' self-confidence springs from the pride and support he receives from his father. I need to tell you that when D   arrives it takes him several days to calm down and make meaningful actions. For example, a few weeks ago D   came bounding down the quay strapping on his life jacket as he flew and banged into my arms where he allowed me to hug him and kiss his head. My foot recovered nicely from the experience and we talked and walked back to where his dad was unloading the car. D   did not have to be asked to help, nor directed in his actions, he stacked the stuff into the cart efficiently while talking and dancing as if his mind was on fire with ideas – it was. The next time I saw D   he was tying up his fishing rod talking with his dad about the relative merits of fishing. Yep, it's called fishing not "catching"; we must eat but be respectful of the life we must take.

D   clearly needs more time with his dad not less. Their projects together go in fits and starts. It seems that "just the time they get together they have to say, so long". D   has toys, kits and tools given to him by Tom that he has not even had time to open. My belief is that D   just counts the hours between the times he can be with his dad. D   really likes telling me about his fish maze and how the fish learn. Reminds me of my friend Dr. Wood, the Cephalopod guru at Bermuda. D   is not an ordinary young man.

My observation with my children is that when they were young they needed their mother, but then they reached that age where they needed their father. And then, when they became fathers, they need both their mothers and their fathers; and their friends. Let's work together to enrich this delightful person's life.

SIGNED on April 18, 2007

Raymond D. Truitt

SUBSCRIBED AND SWORN TO BEFORE ME

SILVIA FERRARA
NOTARY PUBLIC
STATE OF TEXAS
My Comm. Exp. 07-01-08

Notary Public, State of Texas

A7

CAUSE NO 06-1054-F395

IN THE MATTER OF	§ IN THE DISTRICT COURT
THE MARRIAGE OF	§
	§
THOMAS WALKER LYNCH	§
AND	§ 395TH JUDICIAL DISTRICT
H	§
	§
AND IN THE INTEREST OF	§ WILLIAMSON COUNTY, TEXAS
D A CHILD	§

WITNESS B   'S AFFADAVIT

BEFORE ME, the undersigned authority, personally appeared B   who by me duly sworn, deposed as follows:

My name is B   . I am 44 years old and am the mother of a beautiful 12-year-old daughter, S   We reside at   TX. I have been aware of Tom Lynch, only through his son Di   , being our neighbor for nearly 3 years now, as the apartment is where he has visits with his son. I would also like it noted that we are not romantically involved, nor have been nor intend to be. I really only know Tom Lynch as Di   ' father.

D   and S   play together as often as possible when he visits his father. Di   and S: look forward to playing together as both are only children, and more importantly they have a great time together. They: play outside, make forts, rafts, climb the tree. create tree house inventions, ride bikes, have gone for walks with me, attended S   's birthday, play with D   :' dog, and enjoy just being children. I, too, enjoy D   . He is a very sweet, intelligent, polite, wonderful child.

From what I have observed, D   enjoys and looks forward to being with his father. On a couple of occasions, D   has commented about not being able to see him more often and how it feels like 'forever' between visits.

Tom is a good, able, caring, and attentive father. He respects D   and allows D   to make choices for himself in regards to things that they could do together. Di   is always rested, healthy, well groomed, and in good spirits when we see him.

Due to Tom's respectful, caring behavior with his son, I have felt confident in allowing my daughter S   to go bike riding with them at Town Lake, to go shopping and out to eat with them without my presence.

A8

I had been awaiting a call from the Attorney Amicus; I know how important this is to D   and his father, especially since I, too, am a single parent and have been for 7+ years. The Attorney Amicus has not contacted me, so in lieu of contact, here is my affidavit.

Thank you.

SIGNED on *April 17, 2007*   By: _____

SUBSCRIBED AND SWORN TO BEFORE ME on April 17, 2007

A9

CAUSE NO 06-1054-F395

IN THE MATTER OF THE MARRIAGE OF	§ IN THE DISTRICT COURT
	§
THOMAS WALKER LYNCH	§
AND	§ 395TH JUDICIAL DISTRICT
H	§
	§
AND IN THE INTEREST OF	§ WILLIAMSON COUNTY, TEXAS
D , A CHILD	§

PAUL WOOD'S AFFADAVIT OF FACT

BEFORE ME, the undersigned authority, personally appeared Paul Wood, who by me duly sworn, deposed as follows:

My name is Paul Wood. I live on my 65-foot MacGregor sailboat in Galveston, Texas. I am 61 years old. I am a retired naval architect. I have been involved in boating for over 55 years and sailing for about 50 years. I have designed motor yachts, sailboats, a research vessel, and I was a member of the design team for the largest (and last) containerships built in the United States. I have a passion for sailing--both cruising and racing. While in high school, I was the skipper of a small sailboat with a crew of two other students on a month long cruise that took us from San Diego to Los Angeles to Catalina Island back to LA (for a few days of racing) back to Catalina and finally home to San Diego. In 1973, I won the national championship in the Victory sailboat class. In 1975, I was a crewmember and helmsman on a 37-foot boat in the TRANSPAC ocean race from Los Angeles to Honolulu. I was a watch captain for the return of the boat to San Francisco. I have sailed more than 15,000 miles on offshore voyages and races. I have known Tom Lynch and D   since January of 2006. I did not meet Tom and D   when they arrived in Galveston in December 2005 because I was on a little cruise on my own boat at the time. Since I met them, I see that they have an extraordinary father son relationship.

I was on the witness list for the hearing on December 19. I was concerned that someone would attempt to limit the time that D   spends with Tom. I was concerned enough to take a couple of days to travel to Georgetown to be a witness. I stood in the hallway of the courthouse waiting, but I did not get to testify. Since the first hearing I have been informed of two more hearings. Each time, I was ready to travel to Georgetown, but the hearings were cancelled or postponed. I understand that Mr. James P. Wallace is an Amicus Attorney assigned to the case. I expected a telephone call from the Amicus Attorney since late in February. I have not received a call or any type of message or communication from him. If this is a tactic to discourage witnesses, it is not

A10

working. However, it is disappointing to be reminded of how inefficient our legal system is with respect to peoples' time.

At the beginning of summer of 2006, I was ready to join Tom and D   on a sailing trip into the Caribbean. We were unable to make that trip because of delays and court hearings in Georgetown in order to get D   's passport renewed. By the time the passport issue was settled, D   did not have enough time left with Tom to make the whole trip.

More recently, we expected to see Tom and D   sailing out of Galveston the week of spring break which started on March 9. That did not happen.

I offer the following testimony.

I think most experts agree that a boy needs a male role model and the boys father is usually best. I am not a trained expert in this, but I know from my own experience that this was true. My father was an engineer before I was born. Early in my education, I intended to go to college to study science or engineering. That clearly came from my father. My mother also went to college, but her studies were in accounting—not my field. When I was about five, my father and grandfather took me and my sister (she was three) out in a row boat to fish. My mother did not go in the boat. My father taught me how to row. I remember that first time in a small boat, and learning to make the boat move and to steer with the oars. Some years later, my family moved to California, and my dad taught me, and my sister, how to sail. That early experience in row boats started my interest in boats, the sailing got me interested in the sciences related to boats and ships, and that lead to my career. I see D   enjoying similar experiences with his father.

D   is interested in boats and sailing. Tom noticed this, and was able to buy a boat that the two of them could sail together, to learn new things together, and if sufficient time is available, they can go adventuring together. Tom has also arranged his career to allow him to work from a cruising sailboat. D   has a fantastic opportunity to learn from his father.

Tom is a good role model for D   . D   clearly looks up to his dad. Like his dad, D   wants to invent things. I see that D   has a strong interest science and math. I see them often when they are both on their boat in Galveston, and Tom is usually teaching his son a math concept or something related to science or engineering, but they also take time for D   to be a kid. Father and son things like taking the dog to the beach.

Tom and D   are both learning new things on the boat. Both of them are learning boat carpentry. Things like how to make a level cabin sole (floor to a shore based carpenter) when everything in the boat is built at different angles and the wind makes the boat heel so a level can't be relied on to read level.

A11

Tom teaches D   to handle tools and to always wear safety goggles when the chips might be flying.

Tom has been a crewmember on Galveston's tall ship, the _Elissa_. I am sure that he will pass some of the knowledge he gained while working on that ship onto his son.

D   has learned to steer the boat into the wind as his father hoists the mainsail, and on a mostly steady course while sailing. There are lots of things to learn and they are just getting started.

D   clearly needs more time with his dad not less.

SIGNED on ___17 APR. 2007___

Paul Wood
Paul Wood

SUBSCRIBED AND SWORN TO BEFORE ME on April 17, 2007,

_B. Ro_

Notary Public, State of Texas

> BETTY M. ROGERS
> Notary Public, State of Texas
> My Commission Expires
> November 03, 2010

A12

CAUSE NO <u>06-1054-F395</u>

IN THE MATTER OF THE MARRIAGE OF	§ § §	IN THE DISTRICT COURT
THOMAS WALKER LYNCH AND H	§ § §	395TH JUDICIAL DISTRICT
AND IN THE INTEREST OF D A CHILD	§ § §	WILLIAMSON COUNTY, TEXAS

Dr. Robyn Dawes AFFADAVIT

BEFORE ME, the undersigned authority, personally appeared, Dr. Robyn Dawes, who by me duly sworn, deposed as follows:

My name is Robyn M. Dawes Ph.D. I am of sound mind, capable of making this affidavit, and I have been a professor in the Social and Decision Sciences department at Carnegie Mellon University since 1985 (now a University Professor), belong to the Center for Behavioral Decision Research and Risk Perception, am a fellow of the American Statistical Association (and many other professional groups), and am author of many apropos papers and a book which explores the basis for the practice of psychology. In short, I appear to be a nationally recognized expert on the efficacy of methods used in psychology, and I am willing to offer my services to this court to help it distinguish between real science and what is loosely termed "junk" science.

I feel strongly enough about the endemic misuse of psychology in family law cases that I have accepted Mr. Lynch's request to comment on the procedures proposed in this family law case, without payment; however, my administrative staff and I are becoming frustrated with the short notices before hearings, and the dearth of information that has been provided.

I remain available for a reasonably scheduled telephone deposition, and to speak with the Attorney Amicus.

SIGNED on *April 24, 2007*

Dr. Robyn Dawes

A13

Epilogue

The original explanation about the needles in the candy was delivered through a wall of tears. Two years later D* had a new explanation, that the candy was being saved with the sewing kit stored in a safe place, but he had used a chair to get into it by himself when no one was watching. He said it was an accident, and it was all his fault. The fact he wanted to talk about the subject, the level of detail after so much time past, especially when considering his age, and his knowledgeable attribution of fault to himself made it clear to me someone had been working with him. Recently there is yet another incarnation, D* says that there was once a bag used for candy, but it was later used for needles, and he was disappointed by this change in usage of the bag and that is why he was upset and crying when he originally explained it to me. This appears to be the version he had ready for the court. I asked him why he changed the explanation. Being ten years old he didn't catch on that this was a loaded question. He just answered it. Here are some excerpts. He was pinching himself while talking.

"She keeps asking me these questions. I was tired on the couch. It happened on different couches, and once in the car."

"She kept doing that." "She kept doing a whole bunch of times over and over." "It changed last year."

He went on to explain that the needle candy memory had "four parts", and "I can't remember two of them." The two parts he remembers were candy in the bag, and then later needles in the bag. *In apology for changing the recounting of the event with the needles in the candy D* volunteered that he had refused to change his memory of his mom kicking the dog though he had been repeatedly asked to.*

Caryl Dalton quit as the psychologist. She didn't say it was because there were implications that she was using coercive techniques, nor because she had definitely used discredited techniques, nor that she had left out dad, nor because she had violated dual role ethics rules, rather she said it was because 'the presence of dad in her waiting room had disrupted the psychologist patient relationship.' According to her it was all my fault. H* immediately sued for a replacement and requested Dr. Gary Yorke as her first choice. I countered that D* needed a father not another psychologist. Judge Wisser ordered us to use Dr. Yorke.

Initially I told Dr. Yorke that I didn't want him to work with my son. I was curious to know if my input was going to matter, or if we had another Caryl Dalton on our hands. He said he didn't care if I wanted him or not, that he would just push the court order. As he started to work with D* I emailed Dr. Yorke a great deal of information and confirmed with him that he had received it. As examples, I gave him transcripts and recordings of H* putting D* on the phone to ask for the only painting back, of D* talking about candies in the needle bag where he said, "she doesn't to it anymore," of H* telling him that D* won't see his best friend again if he talks, the dog stuff being being dumped on my head while D* cited the ABCs, H* telling D* not to like his dad, D*'s explanation of H* telling him she didn't love him, and D*'s explanation that his mother wanted the dog to torture it. I explained to Dr. Yorke the incident where toddler D* was playing in a water puddle with a 220VAC line. Texas requires a professional to report child abuse to CPS. Months have passed and there is no CPS report.

E1

Dr. Yorke explained he was trained in hypnosis and gave me a letter that said this, though he added that he did not consider it to be an appropriate mode of therapy for D*. He did not say he wasn't using it, nor did he say his opinion about appropriate modes would not change later. Dr. Yorke said Dr. Freitag was not credible and that he had not heard of the organizations listed on his affidavit. Dr. Yorke had not contacted Dr. Freitag, so he had no records from him and had not discussed anything with him. I sought to remedy this by introducing Dr. Yorke to Dr. Freitag through a mutual email. Dr. York did not reply to the email and informed me that he would not be talking with Dr. Freitag.

Frost Bank sent another letter. Previously they had deducted a $50 dollar account seizure fee. That isn't something you see every day. Now they were deducting another $500 as 'an attorney retainer.' The letter explained that the bank felt it was necessary to hire an attorney to protect the bank's interests against my ex wife's attorney, and that according to the account rules I had to pay for this. Like the seizure fee it was deducted from the account after they had received notice to turn over funds but before they had complied.

Due to my accounts being seized, the rent, child support, and summer vacation money was all gone. The money taken was business income that had not yet been processed. Professional fees and taxes had not been taken out. Legal fees, court ordered fines, and child maintenance payments are not tax deductible, so though I have no money, I must pay large taxes. Ironically, while I am paying taxes on money given to my ex, she is receiving thousands of dollars in tax deductions due to being a single parent. I was on a month to month lease and could not pay it, so I gave notice. D* was due to arrive for his summer vacation.

According to the decree D* would be with dad for just 30 days in the summer as Wisser had reduced our time. D* was delivered at Starbucks. I borrowed some money from my parents and from a colleague. It damages my reputation to advertise such a situation with my colleagues especially as the nature of my business requires building investor confidence for projects and legal fees. Of course I am embarrassed and very concerned, but I am more determined yet that D* has access to his father in what appears to be as normal a situation as possible during the short time I see him.

This was not the first time I was homeless due to the privilege of being a father in the context of a broken legal system. On a prior summer break when a new employer rescinded their offer letter apparently after learning of the issues, but my obligations continued, I took D* to a state park on the beach. We camped for two weeks and had a great time. On another occasion over spring break we camped in the woods at a state park. It was great fun. However this case is of a different nature as the numbers are much larger, my business has slowed, and they are taking the bank accounts directly. Should I be imprisoned for getting too far behind payments are still required so the debt will continue to accrue.

In 2006 H* violated our decree by refusing to allow me to renew D*'s passport. I spent $5,000 on an attorney to pursue this so we could have ID for him while sailing on Mystique in case we were stopped on the water or coming into port. This tiff also caused D* and me to lose weeks of vacation and the judge did not replace these. The current divorce decree still says I can have the passport for ID, though now I can't put any visa stamps in it. H* again did not comply this summer. Frankly, she has no reason to comply as there have never been repercussions and there is no indications there will be a change in that trend. Of course this time I don't have $5000, nor do I care to spend weeks of my vacation in court anyway. We just left without picture ID.

E2

D* and I had a great vacation camping and sailing, but all too soon it came to an end. By the end of the trip we had landed in the U.S. Virgin Islands. Shortly before D* was to fly back I sent email and asked for the passport again. The passport could easily become an issue at small airports in the islands. H* replied with vim and vitriol citing the decree and citing policy saying it wasn't needed. And sure enough the airline refused to accept D* without some picture ID. We went to another island with a bigger airport, and Delta took him based a copy of the birth certificate. However, H* said she would pick him up at Starbucks, not the airport. Indeed the decree says he is to be delivered to Starbucks. I simply could not afford two full fare tickets and a rental car. I canceled his flight explaining I would send him when she could pick D* up at the airport. H* agreed and gave the excuse she didn't know he was flying alone.

We re-booked for July 3rd making us two days late. I got email from H* accusing me of violating the decree and telling me everything was my problem. We went to the airport, and at the ticket booth D* said he did not want to go back. The two young girls were sympathetic and listened to D*'s explanation that he thought his mom was mean sometimes. They then said they wouldn't accept him on the flight because he didn't want to go. This created a dilemma, as the court order is clear. H* was the boss, and if she said he had to go back, then by God, he had to go back. I rescheduled for the next flight on July 5th.

On July 4th D* reached his mom on the phone. We were in a hotel room and I was on my computer. The computer badly needed a charge so I was tethered to the outlet. D* pushed the speaker phone button on the cell phone in order to make it louder, and I overheard the conversation between him and his mom. It started out with her talking about the divorce decree, but then it became sinister, so I took notes during the call. I had expected she convince him to return by talking about how much fun they would have. She is planning to take him to Korea to visit in August. Instead she punished and tore him down with insults. D* barely had a chance to talk. These are my notes from the conversation. The statements are from H* directed at D*:

> the way you are talking is weird
> you are mental
> you like a robot just processes
> you not normal not normal kid
> you hiding something from me
> you are obsessive
> you need to see a psychologist
> your dad says all bad things about me
> you are acting more weird when you are with your dad
> you not normal, no respect to mom
> so sad for you
> you are not thinking correctly clearly
> becoming a completely different person when you go there
> he is changing you
> she told him he killed his dog [D* started crying and saying:] liar liar
> interrogated [she wanted specific information about the trip]
> [got real paranoid] "is it going through the computer?" [referring to the call]
> college fund [started talking about this]
> told him he won't go to MIT [note D* is ten]
> your friend John is better
> kept saying that he didn't love her because he wanted more time with his dad
> try to say how bad your mom is is that what is going on

[tried to prove she loved him listing things, D* had never denied this]
[said he was just trying to make dad happy]
am I not caring about you at all

D* hung up on her. His face was long, red and in tears. My stomach felt sick, and now some days later it still does. If I didn't send him back I would probably go to jail, especially given all that is happening with the fines and maintenance fees. Though we are in the Virgin islands, judge Wisser still has jurisdiction. Divorce is like no other legal proceeding in that all of the states have agreed to give other states jurisdiction over people living in their territories if the original divorce was in the other jurisdiction, independent of how long it has been or what has transpired. Ironically this is the misguided legislatures' response to the 'move way mom' phenomena. It does not just apply between states. It applies over most of the world through the Hague convention treaty on child abduction. There is no second opinion or update in the another jurisdiction to be had. Can you imagine, for example, people in New York city giving jurisdiction to a judge in Round Rock Texas for a person who happened to divorce in Texas? Or even more amazing yet, the French giving judges in Texas jurisdiction over people in France who divorced in the Texas? As incredible as it may seem, this is exactly what all the states and most of the nations have done.

A couple of women in the Virgin Islands randomly complemented me on being a good father. This sort of thing had never happened before. Once we were at a beach, another time at a restaurant. I was very surprised and pleased. One of the women had a story about how she had seldom seen her father when growing up and had missed him. The other had a child and wished to see the father more often. Also, the people at the ticket desk seemed primarily interested in D*'s well being rather than some rules or ideology. They spoke to him directly rather than turning to me as other professionals have done. I thought perhaps this would be a good place to find D* a counselor. We would ask the counselor to resolve the issue of D* getting on the plane, then D* would explain how his mom treated him, and then for once someone would actually be concerned more about him than the professional development of their own practice.

D* had a 4:40 flight, and around noon we showed up at a public clinic. It had taken me a day to identify such a place. At the clinic we did not meet a local person, rather we met Bonnie from Boston. She was smiling and pleasant and invited D* and I into a conference room. She asked D* why he didn't wanted to go back to mom, he said it was because his mom was mean and insulted him saying he killed his dog. She asked me the same question and I answered sincerely what D* opinion appeared to follow from the facts, and in addition H* had threatened he would have to got to a psychologist for telling her that he wanted to live with his dad. Bonnie then asked D* to leave the room. After the door closed she accused me of putting D* in the middle for what I just said. I pointed out that she had invited us into the room and asked me questions, and I had simply answered what she requested. She argued, "but you both said similar things." Apparently she was implying that we had coordinated, i.e. that I had trained him to say things. It was a pernicious question that betrayed a strong bias. I explained that the reason our answers matched was because we were both telling the truth. She apologized and we agreed she shouldn't have asked such questions while D* was in the room. Though she then accused me of waging a war against his mom and making D* a victim. I suggested that she should learn some facts before jumping to conclusions. The next time I saw her I gave her a copy of the book.

E4

That night D* talked to grandma on the phone. She was upset with him and told him he was hurting his dad by not going back. I was very unhappy that she said this to him. I told him not to worry about me as I was a grown adult, but he wasn't convinced. He decided to go.

On the way to the airport we stopped by to say goodbye to Bonnie, as she had requested. Bonnie was trying hard to get D* to comply with the divorce decree, as she said this had to be done. D* wasn't of primary concern, rather judge Wisser was of primary concern. Bonnie observed that D* had changed his mind. She may feel some credit for this, but the real reason is that he sacrificed what he felt was right in order to keep his dad safe. D* would do the same for his mom if put in the situation to do so, as when judge Wisser told him he did cases that sent people to their deaths. D* is a kind child who does not wish ill for anyone. I may as well have taken D* to the airport in a basket. The realization that he was "sold out by dad again" was causing his whole world to unravel. He was pale and lethargic with a long face and large teary eyes.

After the plane departed Bonnie called and told me I needed to disengage. She told me again that the war was destroying me and D*. I explained that 'giving up' meant 'giving up on my son.' She said it didn't mean that. I asked her to explain how I could disengage the divorce struggle while still having enough time to be my son's father. She had no answer. Tonight Bonnie called again and asked me a few times, "what are you going to do next?" She had not looked at the book. I suggested she read it if she wanted to continue working on this problem.

H* told me she would have D* call when he arrived. He arrived at 1am last night (2am my time). H* sent email saying D* was too concerned about waking me to call. It is now 8:30pm my time the next day, still no call. I have called a number of times and left messages. It looks like she is not going to let me talk with him. It seems likely he is being punished for saying he wanted his dad, or perhaps he is just nice to her and tells her it was all an act. He is ten years old, and I wouldn't blame him. It seems a sensible enough approach.

It is now 11:07 my time. I called the Round Rock police thirty minutes ago and asked for a 'wellness check.' It is kind of the police to do this service. They don't like doing it and usually grumble, but they go. H* will put D* on the phone for them. They went by the house and checked on him, and said he appeared fine.

Last night D* left, I sent Dr. Yorke the notes from the July 4th call.

As I write this, D* left two weeks ago. I did not get a reply from Dr. Yorke about the July 4th phone call. A few days ago I sent him email explaining that his mom would not let him buy the software he needed, and that she had kept the computer I bought him until I called the police to go get it back, so sharing was out of the question. The email was intended as another data point. For the first time Dr. Yorke replied to my email. Though it was a very limited and polite reply specifically addressing the concept of a computer connection service. Dr. York didn't react to the information that D* was being manipulated, threatened, and demeaned, but he wanted him to have access to computer files. There is a reality disconnect here and I decided to call him on it. Here is the email exchange:

RE: the situation with the telephone, the program and computer

Gary Yorke, Ph.D. <   Thu, Jul 17, 2008 at 1:19 PM
To:

I'm happy to discuss with D⬚ and him mother how to make the telephone calls and communication smoother and more positive. Do you and D⬚ have cameras on your computers by any chance? Also, I might suggest to D⬚ if it's Ok with you, that you be allowed to remote into his computer to help him with his programming. I believe that logmein.com has a free option for one computer. That program also allows you to move files from one computer to the next just by clicking and dragging, so D⬚ could access stuff he created at your house.

Regards

Gary Yorke

E6

RE: the situation with the telephone, the program and computer

Tom Lynch   Sat, Jul 19, 2008 at 2:42 PM
To: "Gary Yorke, Ph.D."

Dr. Yorke,

D[____] needs access to his father, not his computer. The problems with the computer are symptomatic and representative of the problems we had with D[____] learning French, learning violin, learning mathematics, of his advanced education at a private school, of his playing soccer, of his playing hockey, of his having a dog, of his having more than one friend, of his working on models and other projects with his dad – all things that were ended by H[____] - including our summer vacation this year (hindered by the money being taken from the bank), blocked Christmas vacation this year (court date set by her during our time), of summer being blocked last year (court order to pay an 'amicus' – an ability to pay position – with the total in my bank account), of Christmas vacation blocked last year ("emergency" hearing called a month in advance for December 19 in the middle of the time we were to be out of state at Grandmas), of Summer blocked 2006 with court dates as H[____] refused to render passport papers for our planned trip to the Carribean (the court order said she would, she agreed to but didn't, then delayed from Feburary til late June and got a court date, was ordered to sign, but our vacation was gone, and we were not compenstated). H[____] has spent in excess of a hundred thousand dollars with the express purpose of reducing D[____]'s time with his dad consistantly over a period of seven years, has acted directly to limit our time, and punishes and insults D[____] for saying postive things about his dad. They even argue on the phone in front of me over items said as she listens in.

You don't suppose there is a pattern here do you?

Wouldn't a better solution, one that would cover all of these problems, be to send D[____] over to his dad rather than sending a few bits of data over there?

There are also some technical problems with your proposal because I am in the Virgin Islands where I get Internet through my cell phone. I can use one or the other perhaps I could borrow a phone, but still remote graphics would be tedious at best, it doesn't help to move data for licensed software to a machine that doesn't have the software, and licensed software itself can not be moved. And I can't go to Texas. I can't use a bank, and my intellectual property clients are still pissed over H[____]'s attorney calling to say they had my files (gee how would your clients feel if your ex wife's attorney called and said she was reading their case files?) I am trying for a teaching position here at the university that starts in the fall. D[____] is certainly welcome to come here where he will have many friends, a beautiful beach, he will not be called mental or unnormal, and he will be the star of my attention.

Really, who are you working to benefit, H[____] or D[____]?

Tom Lynch
[Quoted text hidden]

E7

RE: the situation with the telephone, the program and computer

Gary Yorke, Ph.D.
To: Tom Lynch

Sat, Jul 19, 2008 at 6:00 PM

Sorry, I was trying to work with the situation as it is, not as you'd like it to be.

Like you, I have no ability to control or change any of your ex wife's choices.

I really don't understand the purpose or point of your last statement.

Perhaps it's best that you don't correspond with me.

My goal is to support D[____] emotionally, as best I can, with the situation as it really is, not how any of us would like it to be.

Regards

Gary Yorke

E8

RE: the situation with the telephone, the program and computer

Tom Lynch   **Sat, Jul 19, 2008 at 9:46 PM**
To: "Gary Yorke, Ph.D." <
Cc: Robyn Dawes <   >, Annie Truitt

Dr. Yorke,

>Perhaps it's best that you don't correspond with me.

Dr. Yorke you are always free to decide we shouldn't correspond simply
by not replying and by ignoring my input. Of course I would be
disappointing to find my input as D   father not respected, but
it certainly wouldn't be the first time.

> Sorry, I was trying to work with the situation as it is, not as you'd like it to be.

No reason to apologize. I was simply trying to work the situation also.

Though I don't get what you are trying to communicate here. If you
were trying to 'work' the situation, then you were trying to change
it, if you were trying to change it then there was a goal. This means
"what you'd like it to be" is a *key* question, not the other way
around.

> Like you, I have no ability to control or change any of your ex wife's choices.

Everyone who participates in a social network affects other people's
decisions. We talk to others for advice, we exchange email, we go to
court and get rulings, etc. As a result of such interactions people
change their decisions all the time, sometimes in a minor way,
sometimes in a major ways. Sometimes it is just a matter of affect
when the decisions are not facilitated or otherwise lead to no action.

Just two emails ago you were invoking this very principal relative to
getting a virtual computing connection going. I was trying to point
out that 'what we would like it to be' is not a virtual connection,
rather a meaningful interaction. Do you disagree? As D
therapist you have a central 'node' in this social network and your
words carry a great deal of weight, more than any of the others in the
network. I believe you to be capable of causing a better 'what you
would like it to be' if you wanted to.

> My goal is to support D   emotionally, as best I can, with the situation as it really is, not how any of us
would like it to be.

At the time you were hired we had just come from a psychologist who,
in my opinion, had worked very hard to make D   happy in the
absence of a father. She really didn't care what D   wanted from
his father or what I wanted for my son. By default it was all about
mom. (This was the source of my "last statement" you said you didn't
get in the prior, as further developed here.) I wondered if you were

E9

another person of the same ilk. There was an easy test. I simply asked you not to take the case. H_____ and I were ordered to find someone and there was a list of names - but you had no such directive, no such order, and no such obligation. Had you said "no" the only event would have been the next name on the list. (Though actually had you said "no," I would have withdrawn my objection.)

If I read my ethics correctly the ethical response to my request for you to not work with D_____ would have been: 1) to say sorry can't take the case because to do this right we need both parents to participate, so go find someone both parents like, 2) to try and convince dad that you would do a good job and thus remove the dilemma 3) go back to the court and point out that dad would hinder your work and ask the judge to resolve the issue.

I think number 2) would be at the least a person who respects a child's parents would do. You did none of these. You did the opposite thing, that which suppressed dad in support of mom's decision, 'As mom's pick I'm taking the case and I don't care what dad thinks about that and he can't do anything because there is a court order mom can leverage – I'll cry for the lack of the child's father participating all the way to the bank with my fees.' Mom is left with the reinforced belief that cooperation with dad is unimportant and dad is left with the impression that his aspirations for his son does not matter. All parties lose, mom, dad and child -- all parties are losing right now. (I hope you don't mind, I'm going to copy Robyn Dawes (CMU), and others, to see if they don't correct my reading of ethics here. I've been studying this question for a long time, enough to suggest a reading, and I have published an item, but I'm always eager to learn something new.)

Now you say that your goal is D_____ emotional well being only, and the implication is that you can address that issue in a vacuum and it is best done without taking any action other than talking with him and mom in your office. You are saying you are sort of like the military psychologist who just wants to keep the pilots in the air no matter what it takes, and whatever, be sure to get the client to re-up. Is this what you are saying? If so, compare this to the philosophy of the social workers who say the exact opposite, that interaction with the environment is what is key to a child's well being. (here I'll copy Annie Truitt also, she was a PhD social worker familiar with this case. Her affidavit to the court makes good reading. Have you looked at the court file? Shall I send you more information?)

The fact is you have the ability to affect this situation and make it more conducive for D_____ growth as a person. You can not only talk sense to me and mom, but you have access to many others involved. Judge Wisser has an email _____ and he has been very considerate and willing to talk with everyone one and the experts. You know how to contact CPS etc.

As you said you are doing your best, so am I. In my position and with my concerns for D_____ it is the socially intelligent thing to use this network connection. I'm not a psychologist, but nor am I an idiot - and nor am I alone. I seek advice from highly qualified people. It is obvious to me that mom should not be telling D_____ he is weird, not normal, or "mental," She should not have put toddler in a puddle with electrical lines, or the host of other things you have been

E10

informed of. It is out of the norm for mom to be imaging that dad is
out to get her or that dad is tyring to turn her son against her to
the point it is nearly impossible to even schedule and air flight. It
is wrong to punish D⬚ for saying something positive about his
dad. In point of fact, some of these things are criminal. Should you
be incredulous, something you have not expressed, it would not take
much digging to verify these things, and many others.

Are you really going to just try and teach D⬚ to just be happy
living with this situation? If he gets the equivalient of needles in
his candy again, are you going to take a cognitive psychology approach
and teach him to reinterpret that memory so he can go on and have it
happen yet again still in another form? Do you think this is the best
approach? If so, I have to humble disagree, and can't we get a
professional who is perhaps a bit more concerned about D⬚ well
being as a whole instead of narrowing the issue of one of him coping
and continuing as is for mom's benefit (my last question again)? ..
someone who can not only teach D⬚ to cope, but who can also help
him reach his goals in life and become a happy and effective person
who does not need a therapist? .. or does none of this matter in your
view except that he is coping? Don't D⬚ wishes for a
relationship with is father, and dad's hopes for his son just matter?
Or is it just fine with you that mom has been able to rough ride dad
out of town .. as long as D⬚ copes .. for mom's benefit?

I do not want you to get the idea I am framing this as a mom versus
dad thing. That is not my thinking about this, and you would know that
if we had a chance to talk about it. However, this is mom's thinking
and that is the situation we are 'working'. To know this all you have
to do is look at the facts and transcripts. Mom thinks I am "evil"
according to her husband in fact. Then there is all the stuff on the
phone call I sent you notes for - directed at a ten year old no less!
It is my opinion that if you can not diffuse the hatred directed at
D⬚, such as in the phone call last week that I sent you notes
from, and just help him cope, you are failing us. This is my opinion
as a father, does that matter to you?

Most Sincerely Yours,

Tom

If I don't miss my guess, Dr. Yorke will not absorb any information about what has been happening to D* from this exchange, but he very well could use it to show that I am too engaged in the problem, as Bonnie did when we asked for her help. Divorce industry professionals are clingy sticky people.

D* is now 10 years old. The divorce professionals have been clinging to him for 7 of those 10 years, and there is no end in sight.

There have been 6 judges (lawyers themselves), 15 other lawyers, 12 psych professionals, 2 doctors, 7 school teachers or administrators, 15 other witnesses, about 45 legal assistants, and 9 court reporters directly involved. Some had fancy titles such as 'attorney amicus' or 'ad litem.' That is 111 people not counting H*, D* or myself. There are probably another hundred or so people who touched this case as part of their jobs.

Hundreds of thousands have been spent by the parties with easily some millions in damages all told. Yet more was spent by tax payers to pay government worker's salaries, keeping of records, and the facilitating of proceedings.

Divorce industry professionals take interest in a child for the feeding. The correct usage is, "ITIO a Child - come get it before it is all gone!"

E11